PUBLIC TRANSPORTATION AND LAND USE POLICY

A REGIONAL PLAN ASSOCIATION BOOK

_____

Public Transportation and Land Use Policy

BORIS S. PUSHKAREV

JEFFREY M. ZUPAN

 INDIANA UNIVERSITY PRESS / *Bloomington & London*

Published in Canada by Fitzhenry & Whiteside Limited, Don Mills, Ontario

Manufactured in the United States of America

Library of Congress Cataloging in Publication Data
Pushkarev, Boris.
    Public transportation and land use policy.
    "A Regional Plan Association book."
    1. Urban transportation policy.   2. Choice of
transportation.   3. Urban land use.   I. Zupan,
Jeffrey M., joint author.   II. Title.
HE305.P87   1977   388.4   76-29299
ISBN 0-253-34682-7   1 2 3 4 5 81 80 79 78 77

No claim of copyright is entered for those portions of this book which
are taken verbatim from preceding reports prepared with U.S. Department of
Transportation funds under contract TS 7131, project numbers IT 090023 and
IT 090031. The findings are those of the authors and Regional Plan
Association and do not necessarily reflect the views or policy of the
U.S. Department of Transportation. This publication does not constitute
a standard, specification, or regulation.

[Americans have been made] acutely aware of the need to build mass transit systems that offer effective and attractive alternatives to the private automobile, and of the need to encourage the more compact patterns of physical growth and development that are essential if those systems are to have a fighting chance of success.

—Russell E. Train,
Highway User Quarterly

America's basic transit problem is not technology but arranging activities so people can ride together.

—John P. Keith, President,
Regional Plan Association

Contents

4. Transit Supply:
Operating Conditions

5. Matching Supply and Demand
at Different Densities

6. Summary and Interpretation

APPENDIX. Procedures for Estimating Transit Demand

ACKNOWLEDGMENTS

This book is based on the study, "Urban Densities for Public Transportation," prepared at Regional Plan Association under contract with the Tri-State Regional Planning Commission, and funded by a grant from the U.S. Department of Transportation, Urban Mass Transportation Administration, with matching funds from The Ford Foundation and The Rockefeller Foundation. A summary of the study was published in *Regional Plan News* No. 99 (August, 1976) under the title "Where Transit Works."

On the Tri-State Regional Planning Commission staff, J. Douglas Carroll, Jr., Executive Director, provided valuable direction and comment; Charles Henry, author of a predecessor study on the subject, provided continuing liaison and advice; Joycelyn Bishop helped with computer programming, and Efrain Lozada with data acquisition. On the Regional Plan Association staff, the authors were assisted by John H. McKenna; editorial assistance on portions of the manuscript was provided by William B. Shore; part-time research assistance by Kenneth Sevitsky, Daniel Marcik, Sylvia Khatcherian, and Paul Menaker. The graphics were prepared by Jerome Pilchman. Unless otherwise indicated, photographs are by Louis B. Schlivek. Typing of the tables was by Miguel Almunia, and of the final manuscript, by Marina Tichter.

Advice on portions of the study was provided by Dick Netzer, Dean, New York University Graduate School of Public Administration. At various stages, portions of the manuscript were reviewed by numerous individuals. Most helpful among them were Jonathan Boyer, Metropolitan Transportation Authority; Thomas B. Deen, Alan M. Voorhees Associates; Ralph Gakenheimer, Massachusetts Institute of Technology; Louis J. Gambaccini, Port Authority Trans-Hudson Corporation; Herbert S. Levinson, Wilbur Smith and Associates; Eugene Lessieu, Port Authority of New York and New Jersey; Arthur E. Palmer, Jr., Regional Plan Association Board of Directors; Paul W. Schuldiner, University of Massachusetts; Ralph W. Richardson, Jr., The Rockefeller Foundation; Edward Weiner, U.S. Department of Transportation.

Regional Plan Association, Inc., is a private, nonprofit organization engaged in urban research and policy formation. It was founded in 1922 as the Committee on Regional Plan of New York and Its Environs, and is located at 235 E 45th Street, New York, N.Y. 10017.

PUBLIC TRANSPORTATION AND LAND USE POLICY

Introduction

The density of urban development in the United States today averages about one tenth of that historically prevalent in the Western world. This low density is both the consequence and the cause of the nation's dependence on the automobile. Public transit, measured in passenger miles, now accounts for only about 4 percent of all mechanized urban travel in the nation. Close to half of this transit travel is confined to the tri-state New York Region.

There are three major arguments against this degree of dependence on the auto. First, it restricts the mobility of those who for reasons of health, age, or income cannot use an auto: even in the United States, half the population is not licensed to drive, and one in five households does not own an auto. Second, it causes inordinate energy consumption and is environmentally destructive: movement in groups, rather than individually, is on the whole more conservative of energy and materials and of the by-products which their use emits into the environment. Third, the downtowns of the nation's larger cities simply lack the space to accommodate all travel by auto at an acceptable cost, and so do inner city residential areas.

These social, environmental, and economic arguments have gained wide acceptance. A variety of efforts have been launched to make public transit more appealing—with lower fares, more frequent and faster service, better amenities, and new technology. Such improvements do indeed attract new riders, both those who previously did not make the trips, and those who previously travelled by auto. Yet improved service has rarely succeeded in increasing transit ridership by more than 50 to 100 percent. Thus, even if a 50 percent increase in public transit use were to be attained nationwide, it would reduce total automobile use in urban areas barely more than 1 percent. Of course, localized impact in the areas served could be much greater.

Generally, transit incentives are appropriate if the policy objective is to improve mobility by transit; but if reducing auto use is the policy objective, transit improvements are not enough; direct restraints on the auto will be necessary. Such restraints do also increase

1

transit use, but the effect is limited because most auto trips suppressed by areawide auto restraints are simply not made. For example, gasoline rationing in World War II reduced urban auto travel as much as 25 percent; but only one third of the foregone auto travel showed up on public transportation, raising use about 55 percent. On a much smaller scale, the 1974 fuel shortage had a similar effect, raising nationwide transit use by a few percent. Again, the localized impact of auto restraints can be greater, such as when parking is reduced in downtown areas.

The effect of higher density of urban development is both to restrain auto use and to encourage the use of public transportation. For example, data from urban areas with large downtowns suggest that, keeping income characteristics the same, neighborhoods with 15 dwellings per acre produce about 30 percent fewer auto trips per person than those with 5 dwellings per acre. Simultaneously, public transit use is more than 100 percent greater. More than half the foregone auto trips show up on public transportation, meaning that mobility is sacrificed less than with auto restraints alone. And, aside from reducing discretionary auto travel, higher density also increases opportunities for walking.

To illustrate, about 5 dwellings per acre appeared to be the average density of urban areas in the United States around 1970; 15 dwellings per acre is typified by attached one-family houses on 30×100-foot lots—still only one thirteenth the residential density of Manhattan. This relatively moderate difference in density has a greater effect on the balance between auto and transit than did the rather drastic curtailment of auto travel in World War II.

Obviously, even lesser changes in the density of the nation's urban settlement are hampered by present land development practices, by diminished urban growth, by the continued concentration of poverty and crime in older cities, and by the fact that attractive alternatives to suburban life styles have only rarely been created in North America. Yet, with smaller households, for whom low density is not always an asset, with more white-collar and service jobs suited to city environments, with rising concern for the preservation of agricultural and open land, a potential to reinforce higher density areas does exist. It could lead to richer choice with less travel, and a more urbane way of life.

This potential will have to be realized if the nation confronts the need to reduce its consumption of energy and other physical resources on a scale beyond present conservation goals. The long-term viability of an auto-dominated urban pattern is uncertain, and higher densities save resources not only by reducing transportation, but also by reducing household consumption of energy and materials and by preserving land.

Aside from long-term environmental and energy considerations, there are more immediate considerations of efficiency which are the main focus of this book. In contrast to the auto, public transportation must be operated by someone other than the user, entailing a claim on another's time and effort. These are not cheap in the American labor market. Furthermore, both labor and other resource costs of public transportation depend on the level of its use; to keep these costs within reason, there must be substantial passenger demand which, in turn, depends on the density of settlement. High-quality transit service in areas of low density and low demand can easily exceed the costs of the automobile not only in dollar terms, but also in energy and materials consumption.

With public transportation increasingly dependent on public subsidy, and in the absence of cost constraints imposed by the market, two types of planning questions arise:

1. Public transit systems are being extended, and new ones are being introduced. It is necessary to judge at what densities they can be most effectively deployed. What kind of transit service can be supported where, at what cost?

2. Incremental residential and nonresidential construction continues. How will its location and density affect both transit use and auto use? If land use controls perpetuate settlement suitable only for the auto, expenditures on public transportation may be wasted.

This book is designed to shed light on these two questions. The intent is also to give the reader sufficient quantitative background to pursue further analysis on his own.

THE STRUCTURE OF THE STUDY

Conceptually, the relationship between the supply of transit service, the demand for it, and urban density can be summarized as follows:

1. Demand for public transportation depends on its service and its price, but even more on the availability, convenience, and price of the competing mode—the automobile.

2. As urban density increases, the density of demand (number of passengers boarding per unit of area) also increases. This is because there are more people present to make trips, and each person makes fewer trips by auto. Auto costs rise and convenience declines with rising density mostly because of the auto's huge space requirements. (During peak periods, an auto occupant on a street needs about 20 times, and on a freeway, 10 times more space than a transit rider at comparable speed and reasonable comfort level.)

3. A level of transit service requires a certain level of expenditures; transit expenditures per unit of area divided by passengers boarding per unit of area equal cost per passenger.

4. At any given cost per passenger, more service per unit of area is provided at higher density because demand is higher; this increase in service in turn attracts a large number of additional passengers.

5. At any given service level, the cost per passenger is lowered with rising density. If translated into a lower fare, this likewise attracts still more additional passengers.

In this light the book is structured as follows. After some introductory historical material, the first chapter deals with how demand for public transportation responds to various aspects of its "price": the fare, the service frequency and travel time, the access time, and the comfort. Some aspects of the substitution of transit trips for auto trips are also touched upon.

The second chapter details the relationships between urban density and transit demand. What proportion of travellers use transit at various densities is first discussed in aggregate terms, and then is analyzed for specific characteristics of the traveller, his trip, and the available transit service. The key role of auto ownership, and how it in turn is influenced by both transit availability and density, is emphasized. Density is measured in two different dimensions—the floorspace density of nonresidential concentrations, and the density of dwellings in residential areas. At the end, a simplified procedure is given for estimating total travel between these two. It is to this total travel that the proportion of transit users must be applied in order to determine the density of transit travel demand.

The third chapter proceeds to deal with the supply of public transportation. It first defines the eight transit modes treated in this book: the taxicab, dial-a-bus, local bus, express bus, light rail, light guideway transit, rapid transit, and commuter rail. Then, the operating and maintenance costs of each of these are treated in detail, followed by a discussion of capital costs for rolling stock and for guideways. A brief discussion of comparative costs, not in terms of money but in terms of physical quantities of resources, is also included.

The costs of supplying public transportation are affected by certain operating conditions, which in turn are related to density and location. Foremost among them are operating speed, the tributary area over which both demand density and service density must be measured (a function of the access distance), and the peaking pattern. These are discussed in the fourth chapter.

The findings of these chapters are of interest in their own right. However, their main purpose is to provide the necessary background for the fifth chapter, which matches the service density of different modes to the prospective density of demand in order to show the cost of providing different services at different densities of urban development.

It should be emphasized that the number of variables which affect the answer to the question "What density of transit service can be supported by what density of urban development?" is very large.

On the demand side, these variables include: density, size, and type of the dominant nonresidential cluster; density of the residential area; the distance between them; the presence of other nonresidential clusters nearby; the density configuration of neighboring residential areas; the household size, income, and labor force participation rate of the resident population; and, last but not least, the fare, service frequency, and proximity to a transit line.

On the supply side, route spacing, service frequency, service span, and operating speed define the density of service in terms of vehicle hours per unit of area; peak-hour demand at the maximum load point and the length of a route further affect the vehicle hours that must be provided to attain a given service level. Cost per vehicle hour for each mode falls within a fairly well defined range, but it does vary within it depending on wage rates and work rules. Further variables affect particular modes, such as acceptable waiting time and the pattern of origins and destinations (whether clustered or dispersed) for demand-responsive systems, and train length and, very importantly, the construction cost of guideways for systems that operate on fixed guideways.

With varying degrees of rigor, the analysis presented in the fifth chapter responds to these variables. However, to make generalizations, it is necessary to assume some arbitrary (though, it is hoped, representative) values for most of the variables in question, and deal only with a few of the more important ones at a time. It is largely to the detailed discussion of such examples that the chapter is devoted. However, comparisons with empirical situations are frequently made to validate the analysis.

The sixth chapter summarizes the findings of the preceding five and provides some policy interpretation.

Lastly, the Appendix deals first with definitions of urban density and with relationships among different measures of density. Next, it presents a "cookbook" which, with the help of nomographs, allows the reader to calculate transit demand following the procedures derived in Chapter 2.

HISTORICAL BACKGROUND

Transportation has always been closely related to the density of settlement and the use of land. Pre-industrial patterns reflected the difficulty of travel: settlements and their market areas were small and compact, confining most activities within walking distance. Mechanical power enabled a huge expansion of the scope of travel and the size of cities. Yet, as long as mechanically powered transportation was basically public transportation, requiring access on foot, settlement remained compact, clustered along transportation channels.

The automobile changed all that. It more than tripled the speed of intraurban travel, from, say, 7 miles per hour in the public transit era (little more than twice the speed of walking) to some 21 miles per hour or more, meaning that the area accessible within an hour expanded at least ninefold. The auto also made access virtually ubiquitous. As a result, opportunities for travel—houses and nonresidential buildings—could be spread about the landscape with at least one ninth the former density and still remain as accessible as they were before.

In this auto-dominated environment, most forms of public transportation cannot exercise their traditional development-shaping role, because of their inherently lower speeds, and because they account for such a small fraction of total access. Rather, if densities supportive of public transportation are desired, they have to be encouraged deliberately through land use and design controls.

To give the reader a sense of scale, a brief look at the range of settlement densities encountered over time is given in Exhibit 0.1. The densities are shown on a comparable basis—urban residents per square mile of built-up land, meaning land covered by buildings, their lots and yards, by streets, squares, and other circulation facilities. Parks, reservations, agricultural, horticultural, and vacant land are excluded.

Though the size of cities has grown dramatically over time—most ancient and medieval cities were a fraction of one square mile in area—the density of the built-up area of most cities for which reasonable documentary or archeological evidence exists appears to have remained quite stable. Apart from relatively short-term declines in the Middle Ages due to plagues and wars, or nineteenth-century urban congestion on the heels of the Industrial Revolution, typical densities of urban built-up land seem to have remained in the 20,000 to 40,000 persons per square mile range from Roman times until the early nineteenth century. The present average built-up density of four Core counties of the New York Region (Brooklyn, Bronx, Queens, Hudson) is in the middle of that range.

The highest urban densities in each period shown fall in the range of 60,000 to 95,000 per square mile of built-up land. This compares to Manhattan's density of 86,000 in 1970 and its peak of about 130,000 around 1910. Historically, people had much less indoor housing space than Manhattanites have today; thus average population densities similar to those of Manhattan could easily exist, even though the density of *structures* was much lower. One should also recall that in the late nineteenth century the most crowded wards of places such as Prague, Paris, and Manhattan reached the equivalent of 280,000 to 520,000 persons per square mile of built-up land in walk-up tenements. It was this kind of densities that early urban reformers fought against, and that the advent of electric streetcars and rapid transit helped to dissipate.

By contrast, a predominantly auto-oriented settlement such as Dallas-Fort Worth or Eastern Connecticut has 3,800 to 4,600 persons per square mile of built-up land. The density of those counties of the New York Region which are outside the Region's Core is similar and includes some pre-automobile settlement. Both Rhode Island and Eastern Connecticut contain early industrial cities, and both Dallas and Fort Worth were given their initial skeleton by electric streetcars. The city-shaping influence of transit was even more pronounced in Los Angeles; it had 1,100 miles of electric railway track as recently as 1946 and did not completely dispense with the system until 1961. Purely auto-created densities fall below 3,000 persons per square mile of built-up land in some of the New York Region's outer counties. Thus the range of auto-oriented densities of settlement generally tends to be *one tenth* of the densities that were historically prevalent. This is what one would expect, given the speed advantage of the automobile.

One should further observe that, compared to the density of built-up land, shown in the box in Exhibit 0.1, gross density varies erratically from city to city. This is so because political boundaries within which gross density is measured contain widely varying amounts of open land. Unfortunately, because gross density measures are readily available, they are often used to make comparisons which in fact are highly misleading: thus, Prague would appear to have about one fifth the density of Manhattan—a seemingly plausible relationship. In reality, the residential densities of their built-up areas are virtually identical and, contrary to what gross density measures would suggest, the densities of most American cities are indeed much lower than those of European ones. This has a strong effect on transit use on the two continents.

EXHIBIT 0.1

Urban Densities and Prevailing Transportation Technology

	Date	Population density per sq. mile of built-up land (residential and non-residential building lots, streets and other transportation uses)	Gross population density per sq. mile of area within political boundaries	Total population
Cities for Pedestrians: Ancient Rome				
Rome	86BC	**95,000**	--	463,000
Pompeii	63	**41,500**	--	10,600
Dura-Europos	100	**32,400**	--	6,600
Cities for Pedestrians: Medieval Europe				
Venice	1363	**62,100**	--	77,700
Siena	1385	**42,700**	--	16,700
Strasbourg	1340	**40,900**	--	30,000
Paris	1292	**40,700**	--	59,200
Cologne	1340	**40,600**	--	50,000
Hamburg	1340	**37,000**	--	30,000
Pisa	1228	**29,500**	--	13,000
Prague	1375	**29,000**	--	50,000
London	1086	**28,000**	--	17,850
London	1377	**31,000**	--	34,971
Florence	1381	**27,700**	--	54,747
Nordlingen	1459	**27,400**	--	10,590
Cities for Pedestrians and Transit: Modern Europe				
Prague	1938	**86,802**	14,482	962,200
Vienna	1938	**86,438**	17,100	1,835,900
Hamburg	1938	**48,466**	20,906	1,094,700
Berlin	1938	**36,572**	12,601	4,299,200
Munich	1938	**35,371**	10,092	760,000
Leipzig	1938	**33,273**	12,738	698,600
Cologne	1938	**28,099**	7,896	765,500
Frankfurt/Main	1938	**27,192**	7,338	551,400
Essen	1938	**26,063**	9,218	670,800
Dresden	1938	**24,223**	13,869	638,300
Dortmund	1938	**19,359**	5,210	546,100
Moscow	1956	**51,699**	37,983	4,839,000

EXHIBIT 0.1 continued

Urban areas for Transit and Auto

Paris agglomeration	1962	**33,387**	13,219	6,457,000
Greater London	1971	**18,959**	12,288	7,418,000
Chicago area	1956	**11,543**	4,181*	5,170,000
Philadelphia area	1960	**8,793**	3,410*	4,007,000
Los Angeles area	1960	**8,387**	840*	7,579,000

Urban areas for auto

Rhode Island	1960	**4,605**	844	859,000
Dallas-Ft. Worth area	1964	**4,265**	2,817*	1,844,000
Eastern Connecticut**	1963	**3,780**	348	1,197,100

New York Region: three density environments in one Region

Total, 31 counties	1970	**6,980**	1,545	19,754,800
Manhattan	1970	**85,989**	69,333	1,539,200
Brooklyn, Bronx, Queens, Hudson	1970	**33,128**	24,571	6,668,700
Remaining 26 counties	1970	**4,423**	924	11,546,900

Metric conversion: 1 square mile = 259 hectares.

Sources: Ancient and medieval, principally: J.C. Russell, "Late Ancient and Medieval Population", *Transactions of the American Philosophical Society*, New Series Vol. 48, Pt. 3, Philadelphia, 1958.

Central European--Otto Lehovec, *Prag: eine Stadtgeographie und Heimatkunde*, Prague, 1944.

Moscow--*Moskva: planirovka i zastroika goroda*, 1958.

Paris--*Schema Directeur d'Aménagement et d'Urbanisme de la Région de Paris*, 1965.

London--*Annual Abstract of Greater London Statistics*, 1971.

Chicago, Philadelphia, Los Angeles, Dallas--respective *Area Transportation Studies*.

New York Region--Tri-State Regional Planning Commission and Regional Plan Association.

Rhode Island and Connecticut--respective state planning agencies.

*Cordon areas of area transportation studies; density within county boundary definition much lower.

**Outside New York Region as defined by TSRPC; includes Hartford

Lastly, the New York Region stands out in Exhibit 0.1 as containing the full range of densities encountered over time. In Manhattan, there is a population of 1.5 million living at a density in the highest urban range. In the surrounding four counties, there is a population equal to that of the Paris urbanized area, living at the same density as Parisians do. In the outer 26 counties, there is a population one and one half times larger than that of metropolitan Los Angeles, living at *half* the density Angelenos do. Embedded in this outlying fabric is a variety of urban forms, ranging from old industrial cities to new amorphous patches of office and commercial development. The nonresidential concentrations, as well as the residential densities, represent the full array of those encountered in the nation. Thus the New York Region represents an excellent laboratory in which the impact of urban density on urban travel behavior can be studied under contemporary technological and economic conditions.

TRANSPORTATION TRENDS

If historical land use and density statistics are spotty, consistent measures of travel over time for individual urban areas are even more difficult to obtain. Still, it is quite clear

EXHIBIT 0.2

Computation of Estimated Domestic
Passenger Miles of Travel by
Mechanized Modes in the United
States, 1900 to 1974

(figures in billions, unless otherwise indicated; assumed figures in parentheses)

	1900	1910	1922	1929	1940	1944	1950	1960	1970	1973	1974
1. Domestic air, total PMT	--	--	--	0.040	1.052	2.178	10.072	33.958	118.608	143.100	146.400
2. Railroads, total PMT	16.038	32.338	35.811	31.165	23.816	95.663	31.760	21.258	10.740	9.308	10.336
3. including commuter PMT	(2.000)	(5.000)	6.132	6.898	3.997	5.344	4.958	4.197	4.592	4.245	4.692
4. Intercity bus PMT	--	--	(1.000)	6.800	11.613	26.920	26.436	19.372	25.300	26.400	27.600
5. Inland waterways PMT	(2.500)	(2.500)	(2.500)	3.300	1.317	2.187	1.190	2.688	4.000	4.000	4.000
6. Electric interurban PMT	(1.000)	(2.400)	3.200	2.800	0.950	2.041	0.721	0.316	0.160	--	--
7. Rapid transit passengers	(0.550)	(0.858)	1.942	2.571	2.382	2.621	2.264	1.850	1.881	1.714	1.726
8. X trip length, miles	(5.50)	(5.75)	(6.00)	(6.20)	(6.40)	(6.50)	(6.60)	(6.80)	(7.00)	(7.00)	(7.00)
9. Rapid transit PMT	3.025	4.933	11.652	15.940	15.245	17.037	14.942	12.580	13.167	11.998	12.082
10. Trolley passengers	(5.000)	(11.000)	13.389	11.787	5.943	9.516	3.904	0.463	0.235	0.207	0.150
11. X trip length, miles	(2.10)	(2.30)	(2.50)	(2.50)	(2.50)	(2.50)	(2.70)	(3.00)	(3.00)	(3.00)	(3.00)
12. Trolley PMT	10.500	25.300	33.473	29.468	14.858	23.790	10.540	1.389	0.705	0.621	0.450
13. Urban bus passengers (including trolley bus)	--	(0.050)	0.404	2.627	4.773	10.880	11.078	7.082	5.216	4.739	5.059
14. X trip length, miles	(2.50)	(2.50)	(2.50)	(2.50)	(2.50)	(2.50)	(2.70)	(3.00)	(3.00)	(3.00)	(3.00)
15. Urban bus PMT	--	0.125	1.010	6.568	11.932	27.200	27.695	21.246	15.648	14.217	15.177
16. Number of taxis (thousands)	--	(5)	(40)	(65)	90	75	125	130	170	182	185
17. X 40,000 = taxi VMT	--	0.200	1.600	2.600	3.600	3.000	5.000	5.200	6.800	7.280	7.400
18. X 0.7 = taxi PMT	--	0.140	1.120	1.820	2.520	2.100	3.500	3.640	4.760	5.096	5.180
19. Subtotal Non-Auto (lines 1, 2, 4, 5, 6, 9, 12, 15, 18)	33.063	67.736	89.766	97.901	83.303	199.116	126.856	116.447	193.088	214.740	221.225

EXHIBIT 0.2 continued

Line											
20. Subtotal Urban Transit (lines 3, 9, 12, 15, 18) (excludes urban water transit)	15.525	35.498	53.387	60.694	48.552	75.471	61.635	43.052	38.872	36.177	37.581
21. Auto VMT urban	(0.020)	(1.353)	(31.648)	(91.298)	130.269	93.679	184.476	284.800	494.543	592.200	589.757
22. – taxi VMT (line 17)	--	1.153	30.048	88.698	126.669	90.679	179.476	279.600	487.743	587.104	582.357
23. X auto occupancy (persons)		(2.4)	(2.4)	(2.2)	(2.3)	(2.4)	(2.1)	(1.9)	(1.7)	(1.64)	(1.62)
24. Auto PMT urban	0.048	2.767	72.115	195.136	291.339	217.630	376.900	531.240	829.931	962.850	943.418
25. Auto VMT rural	(0.020)	(1.067)	(24.980)	(74.055)	121.988	77.264	183.218	303.283	406.449	444.300	428.134
26. X auto occupancy (persons)		(2.5)	(2.5)	(2.5)	(2.4)	(2.5)	(2.2)	(2.0)	(1.8)	(1.74)	(1.72)
27. Auto PMT rural	0.050	2.668	62.450	177.732	292.771	193.160	403.080	606.566	731.608	773.082	736.390
28. Total Urban PMT (lines 20, 24)	15.573	38.265	125.502	255.830	339.891	293.101	438.535	574.292	868.803	999.027	980.999
29. Percent transit (urban) (line 20: 28)	99.70%	92.80%	42.53%	23.72%	14.28%	34.67%	14.05%	7.49%	4.47%	3.62%	3.83%
30. Total Domestic PMT (excludes truck and school bus) (lines 19, 24, 27)	33.161	73.171	224.331	470.769	667.413	609.906	906.836	1,254.253	1,754.627	1,950.672	1,901.033
31. Urban PMT Per Capita of urban population (miles)	500	900	2,300	3,700	4,300	3,600	4,500	4,600	5,800	6,450	6,300
32. Total PMT Per Capita of total population (miles)	436	792	2,038	3,866	5,039	4,554	5,971	6,969	8,609	9,285	8,986

Sources: Lines 1-6 – *Interstate Commerce Commission;* Lines 7, 10, 13, "total" passengers tables, – *American Public Transit Association;* Line 16 – *Motor Vehicle Manufacturers Association;* Lines 21, 25 – *Federal Highway Administration;* Lines 8, 11, 14 – Exhibits 3.1 and 3.2 later; also Area Transportation Study data, and *Regional Survey of New York and its Environs* (for 1924 "length of haul" estimates); Lines 17, 18 – Exhibit 3.2 and *International Taxicab Association;* Lines 23, 26: For background on auto occupancy see: Federal Highway Administration: *Estimating Auto Occupancy* (1972); Federal Highway Administration, *Automobile Occupancy Report Nº 1* (April 1972); Motor Vehicle Manufacturers Association, *1976 Motor Vehicle Facts and Figures* (p.51); Port Authority of New York and New Jersey – unpublished historical data on trans-Hudson passenger car occupancy as follows: 1925-2.50; 1929-2.32; 1940-2.40; 1944-2.47; 1950-2.18; 1960-2.04; 1970-1.88; 1972-1.83; includes weekend travel; weekday only occupancy for 1972-1.64; this is similar to Area Transportation Study data which, for a shorter average trip, tend to be about 1.5; data in table adjusted to match MVMA source.

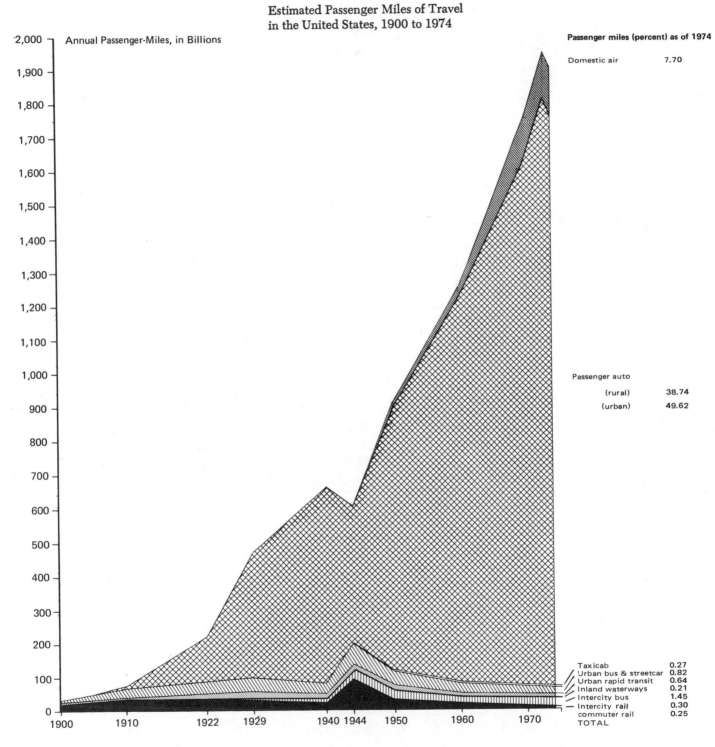

EXHIBIT 0.3

Estimated Passenger Miles of Travel
in the United States, 1900 to 1974

Annual Passenger-Miles, in Billions

Passenger miles (percent) as of 1974

Domestic air   7.70

Passenger auto

(rural)   38.74

(urban)   49.62

Taxicab	0.27
Urban bus & streetcar	0.82
Urban rapid transit	0.64
Inland waterways	0.21
Intercity bus	1.45
Intercity rail	0.30
commuter rail	0.25
TOTAL	

Source: Exhibit 0.2

that late into the nineteenth century walking remained the dominant travel mode even in industrialized Western cities. Carriages were only for the very rich, and riding on horseback was primarily for rural areas. The first public mass transit—the horse-drawn omnibus—appeared in Paris in 1819 and quickly spread to other cities, but it served only a limited travel market because of its slow speed, poor comfort, and high cost. Steam power—so successful on intercity railroads since 1825—did not find widespread intraurban application. It was used on rapid transit in the largest cities, such as London and New York, beginning with the 1860s, and somewhat more broadly to propel cable cars since the 1870s. Horses and mules remained more compatible with the urban environment than the steam engine; street railways equipped with horse cars appeared in New York in 1832 and became an important form of urban travel after 1860. The first major revolution in intraurban transport came only in 1888 with the perfection of a commercially successful electric streetcar. In the following decade, street railway mileage in the United States nearly tripled, and the age of mechanical travel began in earnest.

Beginning with the start of the twentieth century, fairly reliable figures are readily available to estimate the growth in travel demand by various mechanized modes both within urban areas as a whole and for all of the United States. These are presented in Exhibit 0.2,* and shown graphically in Exhibit 0.3. Mechanical travel per capita averaged only about 440 miles annually for the United States as a whole in 1900, and perhaps 500 miles within urban areas, virtually all of it by public transportation. One can surmise this was about double the amount of travel people did on foot.

Travel demand by urban public transit grew to over 900 miles per capita of the urban population per year by 1922, and thereafter began to decline, dropping to little over 200 miles in the early 1970s. The automobile in the United States began to appear in large numbers (more than a million new cars annually) in 1916, about two decades after it was invented, and before 1922 the amount of urban travel by auto appears already to have surpassed the amount of travel by public transportation. The travel diverted by the automobile from public transportation over the next half century is dwarfed by the amount of *new travel* which the automobile created. By 1973, urban travel per capita expanded to some 6,500 miles annually, over 10 times what it was in 1900. And total domestic travel per person in the United States exceeded 9,000 miles annually, 20 times what it was in 1900.

Almost 90 percent of this huge amount of travel is by automobile, about 7 percent by air, about 1.7 percent by intercity rail and bus, and about 2 percent by urban public transportation. For travel within urban areas only, the five modes of public transportation listed in Exhibit 0.2 account for close to 4 percent. The detail of Exhibit 0.2 also shows the fluctuations in automobile versus public transit usage that occurred in World War II and during the gasoline shortage of 1974, referred to earlier in this Introduction.

---

* After Exhibit 0.2 was prepared, the *1974 National Transportation Report Urban Data Supplement* (U.S. Department of Transportation, Washington, D.C., May 1976) was published. It presents, for the first time, a systematic tabulation of both trips and passenger miles by urban transit modes for 241 urbanized areas in the U.S. Because of differences in sources and in definitions, the data do not exactly match those of Exhibit 0.2, but are generally similar. Thus, the combined average trip length of rapid transit and trolley trips in the *Urban Data Supplement* is shown to be 6.7 miles, compared to 6.6 miles according to Exhibit 0.2. The average urban bus trip is shown to be 3.8 miles, compared to 3.0 miles assumed in Exhibit 0.2; thus bus travel may be somewhat underestimated. The only serious discrepancy is with regard to taxi travel, which would appear to total only 2.3 billion PMT according to the *Urban Data Supplement*, compared to 5.1 in Exhibit 0.2.

One should note that the figures shown in Exhibits 0.2 and 0.3 are, in large part, estimates. In particular, the average auto occupancy is not very reliably measured, and authoritative sources listed in the notes to Exhibit 0.2 suggest widely different values. Nevertheless, these and other data uncertainties (such as average trip length by different urban transit modes) do not change the overall shape of the travel trends portrayed. The advent of each basically new form of travel expanded total demand for travel a great deal; the shift of some travel away from previously existing modes was only a secondary effect. The need for each basically new form of travel arose within a given settlement pattern; but once in use, it altered the pattern of settlement far beyond original intentions.

Demand for Transit:

1 The Role of Service Improvements

DEMAND FOR TRAVEL AND THE PRICE OF TRAVEL

In choosing a particular mode of travel—and in deciding whether to make a trip at all—the traveller compares the price of available alternatives. This price has several major components:

- price in money
- price in travel time
- price in access time and effort
- price in discomfort and disamenity.

A high price of travel—measured by the sum of these components—will tend to suppress travel demand. Reducing the price of travel by any particular mode—such as reducing travel time by offering higher speed—will have a threefold effect: it will induce new travel, which would not have been considered worthwhile at the previous high price to the user; it will divert some travel from competing modes, whose comparative position will no longer be as attractive as it was before; and it will tend in the long run to relocate travel destinations (residences and nonresidential facilities) in accordance with the new pattern of easier access, thus further reinforcing the demand for the preferred mode.

Historical trends presented in the preceding discussion support these simple propositions. Railroads and streetcars reduced the price of travel in terms of time, money, and inconvenience. While they did divert some trips that were made on foot or by animal power, their major effect was to open a huge new market for travel. They also created the skeleton of modern cities which, initially, were tightly attached to streetcar lines and railroad stations.

An even more dramatic change occurred with the advent of the automobile. While its price in money per mile travelled was initially higher than that of public transportation, it dramatically reduced the price of travel in terms of travel time, discomfort, and particularly access time, since it required neither waiting nor walking to stations. And it spun its own web of spread-out, low density urban settlement that reinforces its ascendancy.

If in the face of heavy odds more riders are to be attracted to public transportation, one must start with the question of how demand for transit travel responds to changes in the different components of the "price" of travel perceived by the rider. What kinds of reductions in fare, travel time, access time, and discomfort does it take to attract how many riders under what conditions? Initially, we shall not worry about whether the riders attracted represent new travel or diversion from other modes. Later, the issue of diversion from the auto will be explicitly introduced.

THE FARE ELASTICITY OF TRANSIT TRAVEL

The percent change in the number of trips that occur in response to a one percent change in any one of the "prices" of travel (if all others are kept constant) is called demand elasticity. This can be measured either by comparing different situations at the same point in time (cross-sectional data), or changes in the same situation over time (time-series data). In proper statistical terms, elasticity is not simply the ratio by which ridership shrinks in response to a one-time increase in fare or travel time, but rather the instantaneous rate of change along the demand curve. For comparability, only data of this nature are presented in Exhibit 1.1. The elasticity ratio is not independent of the absolute values near which it was measured, and the calculation of elasticities is beset with many other difficulties.[1] Nevertheless, the figures calculated by different researchers do tend to show a broadly consistent pattern.

To begin with, the fare elasticity of New York subway riding is found to be −0.147, meaning that, apart from other variables that have influenced ridership, each 10 percent change in the fare (measured in constant dollars) has been statistically associated with a 1.47 percent reverse change in ridership over the 25-year period investigated.[2] Because the subway trips are predominantly to and from work, it is not surprising that work trips in Boston have a very similar elasticity, and so do transit trips in Montreal.

New York City bus trips, less work-oriented than subway trips, are twice as sensitive to the fare. Again, the figure for Boston non-work trips is very similar. A fare elasticity of around −0.3 has been widely used as an average by the transit industry in the United States,[3] but it seems to be representative of the larger cities.

Exhibit 1.2 shows the fare elasticity of bus travel in urban areas with less than one million inhabitants to be in excess of −0.5. And, in small cities in Iowa with low levels of service, it is even higher.

This range of statistical elasticities, roughly from −0.15 to −0.85 depending on city size, seems to be supported by the experience of fare reductions. Atlanta, with a transit service area of over one million inhabitants, increased its ridership by 30.2 percent in the wake of its 1972 fare reduction from 40¢ (plus a 5¢ transfer) to a flat 15¢ fare. How much of the increase can be attributed to the fare reduction, to improved service that followed it, and to other factors is somewhat unclear, but it appears that "fare was the primary single reason for increased ridership."[4] An analysis of a free-fare experiment in Wilkes-Barre, a city of less than one hundred thousand, concluded that ridership could be expected "to increase 50 percent with the institution of a free fare."[5]

EXHIBIT 1.1

Illustrative Demand Elasticities of
Transit Travel

Type of trip	Price in money	Price in travel time		Schedule frequency
		In-vehicle	Access	
1. New York City subway trips (1950-1974 with fare in constant $$)	-0.147	n.a.	n.a.	+0.240
2. Montreal transit trips (1956-1971)	-0.150	-0.270	-0.540 (waiting only)	
3. Boston transit work trips (1964 cross-sectional data)	-0.170	-0.390	-0.709	n.a.
4. New York City bus trips (1950-1974 with fare in constant $$)	-0.305	n.a.	n.a.	+0.634
5. Boston transit non-work trips (1964 cross-sectional data)	-0.323	-0.593		n.a.
6. Bus trips in 17 urban areas 75,000 to 950,000 in population (1960-1970)	-0.533	n.a.	n.a.	+0.765
7. Bus trips in 13 Iowa cities 20,000 to 200,000 in population (1955-1965)	-0.850 (average)		n.a.	n.a.
8. Boston auto work trips (1964)	-0.565	-0.820	-1.437	n.a.
9. Boston auto non-work trips (1964)	-2.528	-1.020	-1.440	n.a.

n.a. — not available or not applicable.

Sources: Lines 1 and 4: Regional Plan Association (see note below).

Line 2: Gaudry, M. *An Aggregate Time-Series Analysis of Urban Transit Demand: The Montreal Case.* Montreal, Centre de Recherche sur les Transports, 1974.

Lines 3, 5, 8, 9: Charles River Associates, *Free Transit.* Lexington, Mass., Heath Lexington Books, 1970. pp. 17-23.

Line 6: Boyd, J.H., Nelson, G.R. *Demand for Urban Bus Transit; Two Studies of Fare and Service Elasticities.* Arlington, Va., Institute for Defense Analyses, 1973, p.7.

Line 7: Carstens, R.L., Csanyi, L.H. "A Model for Estimating Transit Usage in Cities in Iowa". *Highway Research Record* No. 213, 1968.

Note: Lines 1 and 4 were derived by a method analogous to line 6, with the exception that in addition to the fare and service variables (the service variable for subways was daily trains crossing the CBD cordon, and the bus service variable was bus-miles, as in line 6), Manhattan employment was added to the subway equation and auto availability to the bus equation. This raised the explanatory power of the equations (r^2 0.71 versus 0.56 in the first case, and 0.88 versus 0.82 in the second case) without materially affecting the elasticity coefficients of fares and service. The elasticity of subway riding with respect to estimated Manhattan employment is +0.775, and that of Transit Authority bus ridership with respect to auto availability is -1.046. Both are intuitively plausible since 80 percent of the subway trips are to or from the Manhattan CBD, and since TA buses serve predominantly Brooklyn, Queens and Staten Island, where the substitutability of auto for bus travel is high.

The pattern suggests that the smaller the city, the greater the responsiveness to changes in fares. Transit use in the larger and denser cities is governed more by decisions which are independent of the fare; there is no close substitute for it, hence the low elasticity. On the other hand, where there are more options and where the need to travel by transit is less compelling, demand elasticity will be higher. Such is the case in the smaller cities, where trips are shorter, the proportion of work trips is lower (the fare elasticity of the more optional trips is higher), and the auto is more widely available. The Atlanta experience indictates that auto-owning middle income households contributed overwhelmingly to the ridership increase resulting from the lower fare.

However, in developing policies for transit subsidy, the absolute number of transit passengers in large and dense urban areas must not be overlooked. According to the American Public Transit Association, urbanized areas of fewer than half a million residents accounted for only 11 percent of the revenue passengers in 1974. Even if their responsiveness to fare subsidies were three times as high as that in the larger cities, and if per-rider subsidies were equal, the number of riders generated by the subsidy in the larger cities would be still three times as great as in the smaller ones.

The data presented define the relatively narrow limits within which ridership can be increased through fare reductions. Because the elasticities are all less than one, any such gain in ridership will be accompanied by a loss in revenue, which is of course the reason why in the days when fare revenue was of prime importance it could always be obtained with a fare increase, despite the loss in passengers associated with it.

THE TIME ELASTICITY OF TRANSIT TRAVEL

As has been often stated, ridership is more responsive to travel time reductions than to fare reductions. In both Boston and Montreal, Exhibit 1.1 shows the elasticity with respect to in-vehicle travel time to be about twice as high as the fare elasticity. In the latter case, the elasticity with respect to waiting time is twice as high again. In the former, the elasticity with respect to access time, which includes walking and waiting, is higher still. Where measures of waiting time were not available, elasticities with respect to various measures of service frequency are shown; service frequency is inversely related to waiting time. In two cases, which refer to bus systems, a 10 percent change in bus miles operated per capita is associated with a 6 to 7 percent change in ridership. In the New York subway example the figure is only 2.4 percent, probably because, service cutbacks notwithstanding, trains still run frequently during the hours when most travel takes place. Consistent with the others, the subway service elasticity is higher than the fare elasticity.

The distinctions between in-vehicle time, waiting time and walking time are plausible: in-vehicle time is generally less onerous than waiting time, and a significant majority find waiting less onerous than walking. This gradation is corroborated by extensive analyses of travel behavior in Chicago, Toronto, Philadelphia, and Washington; the "price" of access time tends to be weighed 2 to 3 times more heavily than in-vehicle time.[6]

Though the implicit monetary value which people place on the various aspects of travel time varies over a wide range, it can be said in general that the "price" of time represents by far the largest component of the total "price" which the user has to pay for public transportation. An example will illustrate this point. In the New York Region, travel time on an average transit trip consists of 53 percent in-vehicle time, 30 percent access time, and 17 percent waiting time. Suppose now that the average trip is 6 miles long and takes 36 minutes, which is close to reality. Suppose further that in-vehicle time is valued at 5 cents a minute and waiting and walking time at 10 cents a minute. These values are in scale with past research findings concerning the value of time, with some allowance for inflation.[7] On this basis, the implicit price in time the traveller pays for the average transit trip could be equivalent to $2.65, whereas the out-of-pocket average fare he paid in 1974 was only 45 cents.

This suggests why the sensitivity to travel time is so much greater than the sensitivity to the fare and explains the attractiveness of the auto trip, which eliminates the cost of waiting and minimizes walking.

The opportunities for attracting transit ridership by providing faster and more frequent service should not be exaggerated. There is much less leeway in cutting travel time than there is in cutting the fare. The fare can be cut 100 percent. Cutting in-vehicle time by 50 percent means *doubling* the speed, which is rarely possible. Following the Boston and Montreal experience in Exhibit 1.1, ridership would only increase about 17 percent. Cutting waiting time by 50 percent means doubling the service frequency which, if speed remains the same, also means doubling the operating cost. Following the New York subway and the Montreal experience, this may increase ridership about 25 percent; following the experience of buses, perhaps 70 percent. Using the 1974 New York Region operating cost of 70¢ per passenger (45¢ of which was paid from the fare) for illustration, we can estimate that spending $100 on greater frequency for 1,000 existing riders would add 40 riders in the first case and 149 riders in the second case. Spending the same amount of money on fare subsidy would add 38 riders with a fare elasticity of 0.15, and 95 riders with an elasticity of 0.30. One can visualize situations when a given subsidy would be better spent on reducing fares than on increasing service.

Clustering development around transit stops at four times the existing average density would cut access time on foot in half and thereby increase ridership very substantially at no added operating cost. Obviously though, such a dramatic rearrangement of land use is only possible where new development takes place.

RESPONSE TO COMFORT AND AMENITY

Comfort and amenity in transit include many factors, such as the amount of space per passenger, the availability of a seat, climate control, quietness, smoothness of the ride, cleanliness, and the general sensory and spatial quality of the station spaces,[8] including weather protection, information, and ease of orientation. The degree to which these features, as well as social attitudes involving prestige or fear, attract or repel riders is not sufficiently understood. One can mostly point to indirect evidence. It lacks the numerical precision of the elasticity coefficients, but it does suggest that the less tangible comfort and amenity features have the power to attract ridership on their own.

For example, a pilot investigation of the Bryant Park underpass—a new pedestrian link between two previously disconnected subway lines in Midtown Manhattan—revealed a variety of motives for using this architecturally distinctive transit environment. About 52 percent of the users whose previous travel patterns could be ascertained gained obvious savings in money or travel time. About 36 percent preferred to use the underpass rather than the surface sidewalk even though no gains or losses of time were involved. Most interestingly, some 7 percent chose the "cleaner, nicer" environment even though it involved a time loss. In some instances, the time loss was subjectively rationalized as a significant time saving. Lastly, some 5 percent previously used modes other than the subway, and may have been diverted to it because of the new convenience.[9]

Another instance of gaining amenity at the expense of money and travel time could be observed on express buses in New York City. In the early 1970s, a segment of the City's transit riders, with incomes 30 percent above the average for their area of residence, spent 60 percent more money and 2 percent more time for an express bus ride compared to the mode previously used, which in more than half the cases was the subway. The major gains were an *assured seat* and air conditioning, though a minority also had fewer transfers and a shorter walk.[10] Because express buses in New York City were introduced specifically to serve areas poorly served by rail transit, we have here a case where the bus offered comfort and amenity superior to rail.

The more usual evidence is that rail has greater attractive power than the bus, particularly for diverting auto users, if travel time and fare are similar. Thus, in 1960 the number of journeys to work by public transportation was on the average 30.5 percent higher between parts of the New York Region which were connected by subway or rail compared to those that were not, if development density as well as travel time and the cost differences were kept constant.[11] Similarly in 1964, the number of trips for all purposes made during the peak three hours by public transportation across the Hudson River was 27.9 percent higher between zones that had rail service. This higher use was entirely due to greater diversion from the auto, which cannot be explained by differences in development density, travel time, or travel cost in corridors with rail service.[12] The next chapter will show that the presence of a commuter rail, and particularly a rapid transit line, does suppress auto ownership in its immediate vicinity, compared to the surrounding area which is in varying degrees served by bus. In the case of commuter rail, the greater passenger attractiveness can also be attributed to the more liberal space standards and the superior ride quality. One can speculate that less tangible factors, such as a permanent physical identity and system connectivity, also favor rail over bus.

Nationwide trends in transit ridership are sometimes cited in support of the greater attractiveness of rail: between 1955 and 1970 bus ridership per round-trip route mile in the United States declined by 39 percent, while rapid transit ridership per track mile declined only 8 percent, and ridership per surface track mile actually increased by 27 percent.[13] This evidence unfortunately is weak, because there is no way of separating the relative differences in travel cost and travel time, as well as other extraneous factors, and thereby isolating the attractiveness of rail as such. Thus rapid transit inherently offers greater time savings than the average bus, and also serves high density Central Business Districts where the auto is least competitive. Moreover, after 1972, following 25 years of continuous decline, nationwide bus ridership picked up because of extensive subsidy and service improvement programs, while rapid transit continued to drop, largely because of precipitous employment losses in New York City, where over 70 percent of the nation's rapid transit ridership is concentrated. As for light rail, the increase merely shows that streetcar trackage was abandoned at a faster pace than passengers declined. Clearly, if lightly used lines are abandoned the average ridership per mile will increase.

RESPONSE TO NEW FACILITIES

Exhibit 1.2 presents some evidence of ridership increase which new transit facilities were able to achieve, along with indications of how much of the new ridership represented induced traffic and how much was diverted from the auto. The experience of the three new rail lines illustrated—the Skokie Swift of the Chicago Transit Authority (CTA), the Lindenwold line of the Delaware River Port Authority Transit Corporation (PATCO) in Philadelphia, and the Trans-Bay tube of the Bay Area Rapid Transit District (BART) in San Francisco—is quite consistent. Within one to three years after opening, each attained more than a 50 percent increase in public transit ridership in its corridor. More than half of the new traffic was diverted from the automobile. The remaining share—rather large in each case—was induced.

The reasons for the traffic increase in all three cases include savings in money (mostly parking charges), savings in travel time, and gains in comfort and amenity. An effort to quantify the latter was made on the least glamorous of the three lines—the Skokie Swift. The study concluded that while time savings to the rider were worth about 4.3 cents per minute in mid-1960s prices, the added comfort of the rail line had an implicit value of $1.00 per one-way ride, or was equivalent to a 23-minute time saving.[14] This tends to confirm the New York Region findings that rail transit has an attractive power which cannot be explained by time savings or money savings alone.

Exhibit 1.2 also displays three exclusive busways. These are the Interstate 495 exclusive lane on approaches to the Lincoln Tunnel in New Jersey, the Blue Streak express bus route in Seattle, which uses reversible freeway lanes and an exclusive ramp into the downtown area, and the Shirley busway on approaches to Washington in Virginia. It is evident that within one to two years after opening, each of these likewise attained an increase in public transit ridership in its corridor. The percent increase in ridership varies widely. It is 6 percent on the New Jersey bus lane, 33 percent on the Seattle route, and 104 percent on the Washington route. The New Jersey bus lane provides roughly a 20 percent saving of in-vehicle time, so that with an elasticity of 0.3, one would expect it to attract about 6 percent additional traffic. The Seattle Blue Streak operation provides an in-vehicle time saving of around 60 percent compared to previous operation on local streets, so that its 33 percent patronage increase is not out of line, if one assumes a somewhat higher in-vehicle time elasticity, and if the additional effect of parking charge savings is considered.

The Shirley busway doubled the bus ridership in its corridor, even if diversion from parallel bus routes is not counted, as is the case in Exhibit 1.2. It offers 17 to 38 percent in-vehicle time savings, which might explain about a 10 percent ridership increase. More importantly, the project has been accompanied by extensive service improvements and more than a doubling of bus frequency.[15] Referring to the fourth column in Exhibit 1.1, the latter could be associated with more than a 70 percent increase in ridership. Also, there appears to have been considerable residential relocation into the area, otherwise the large proportion of trips that were not made before (induced traffic) is hard to explain on a facility whose patronage consists of over 90 percent work trips. High parking charges in downtown Washington have likewise been credited with contributing to the success of the busway. In short, the experience with express bus lanes portrayed in Exhibit 1.2 does not seem to be out of scale with the demand elasticities of travel time and service frequency discussed earlier.

As for the ridership-attracting factors involving comfort and amenity, they were clearly minor on the New Jersey bus lane, since it only cut running time and did not alter the passengers' environment, except for eliminating the unpleasantness of stop-and-go traffic. No efforts were made to investigate these factors on the other bus facilities.

Not shown in Exhibit 1.2 because of not fully comparable data is the San Bernardino exclusive busway on Interstate 10 from Los Angeles to El Monte. Between 1973 and 1975

EXHIBIT 1.2

The Effect of Opening New Transit
Lines on Travel Demand

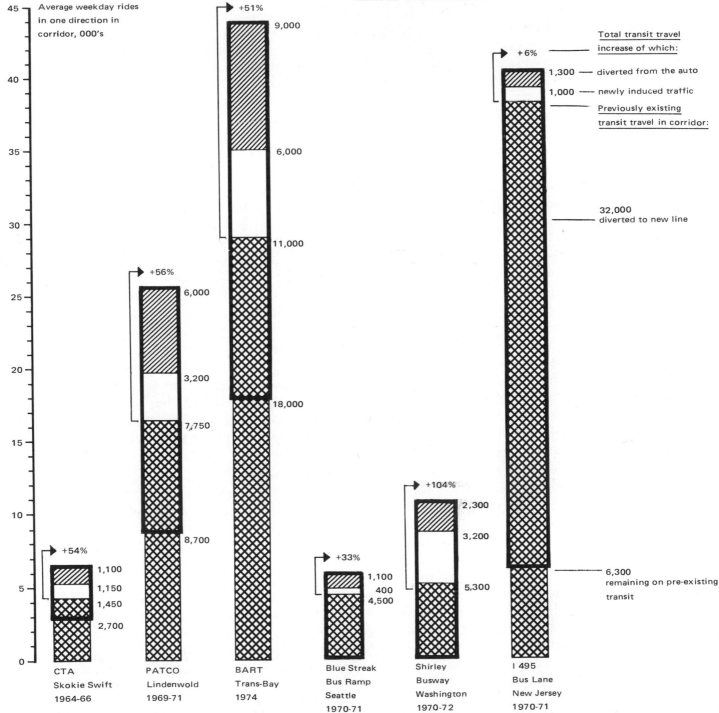

45 — Average weekday rides
in one direction in
corridor, 000's

+51%
9,000
6,000
11,000

**Total transit travel
increase of which:**
+6%
1,300 — diverted from the auto
1,000 — newly induced traffic
**Previously existing
transit travel in corridor:**

32,000
diverted to new line

+56%
6,000
3,200
7,750

+54%
1,100
1,150
1,450
2,700

8,700
18,000

+104%
2,300
3,200
5,300

+33%
1,100
400
4,500

6,300
remaining on pre-existing
transit

CTA	PATCO	BART	Blue Streak	Shirley	I 495
Skokie Swift	Lindenwold	Trans-Bay	Bus Ramp	Busway	Bus Lane
1964-66	1969-71	1974	Seattle	Washington	New Jersey
			1970-71	1970-72	1970-71

Sources: Skokie Swift, adapted from Chicago Area Transportation Study data: Chicago Transit Authority, *Skokie Swift Mass Transportation Demonstration Project Final Report*, May 1968 p. 61.

Lindenwold Line, RPA estimate developed from various published articles and unpublished bus ridership data from Transport of New Jersey. Includes former PRSL rail riders.

BART from California Department of Transportation unpublished tabulation, Fall 1974.

The three exclusive bus facilities from: Herbert S. Levinson, et al. *Bus Use of Highways, State of the Art.* National Cooperative Highway Research Program Report No. 143. Washington, D.C., Highway Research Board, 1973; also: Tri-State Regional Planning Commission, *Interstate 495 Exclusive Bus Lane Final Report.* New York, July 1972.

Note: Figures for the I-495 bus lane refer only to the hours during which it is in operation.

it increased bus patronage in its corridor from 1,000 to 7,750 riders in one direction, or 675 percent. With a 532 percent increase in bus service, this is a traffic growth far above any of the other new transit systems. About 63 percent of its peak hour riders come from households with two or more cars, and over 85 percent previously commuted by automobile.[16] This shows that relationships calculated in areas which have an acceptable transit service in existence may not be applicable in areas which are grossly underserved, and where a large latent demand for transit exists.

DIVERSION OF AUTO TRAVEL TO TRANSIT

We have seen that reducing the price of public transit travel in terms of money, time, and discomfort does attract ridership. Yet, the elasticities are generally less than one: a large effort is needed to increase ridership by a moderate amount, except where existing service is very poor. By contrast, the elasticities of auto travel tend to be much more volatile. According to the last line in Exhibit 1.1, cutting auto travel time for non-work trips by 50 percent will increase auto travel by about 50 percent. This is in agreement with a generalized estimate that freeways have roughly doubled auto speeds, and that about one third of the traffic they carry was newly induced by them. The greater responsiveness of auto travel to reductions in the price of travel is a major reason for its phenomenal growth.

Because of the generally low elasticity of demand for transit travel, there are rather close limits to how much ridership can be increased by service improvements and fare reductions alone. And, because the auto now accounts for such an overwhelming share of total travel, the dent that they can make in auto use is very small. As has been shown, anywhere from 40 to 85 percent of the new traffic attracted by the various rail and bus facilities did come from the automobile. This may sound impressive from the viewpoint of public transit, but from the viewpoint of reducing auto travel the shift was minimal. Thus, while the 6,000 auto users who are shown to have switched to the BART Trans-Bay tube in its early months of operation account for 40 percent of the new transit traffic, they represented only 5 percent of the old auto traffic on the San Francisco-Oakland Bay Bridge. As for the I-495 exclusive bus lane, it actually increased peak-hour auto traffic on the freeway by 39 percent, because the space vacated by buses was promptly filled with automobiles; the total daily auto volume has remained essentially unchanged.[17]

While improving the *attractiveness of public transit* can only have a very minimal effect on auto use, *restraining auto use* does have a rather perceptible impact on public transit. Their different demand elasticities aside, this is true simply because the magnitudes of the two are so unequal. This was pointed out in the Introduction, on the basis of the 1940-1944 and 1973-1974 data in Exhibit 0.2.

That only a few of the auto trips not made show up on urban public transportation during nationwide restraints on auto use is to be expected. The trips that are foregone first are optional long trips for social and recreational purposes, made to widely dispersed destinations, for which there simply is no transit substitute. Many of them occur outside urban areas. One would presume that more localized restraints on auto use, such as have been proposed to implement clean air standards, would have a larger impact on increasing transit ridership.[18] Whether or not such deliberate restraints in local areas will come to pass, a spontaneous reduction in auto use per person on a local scale does occur with rising density of urban development.

EXHIBIT 1.3

Diversion of Downtown Trips by Auto Owners to Public Transit in Relation to the Difference in Travel Time

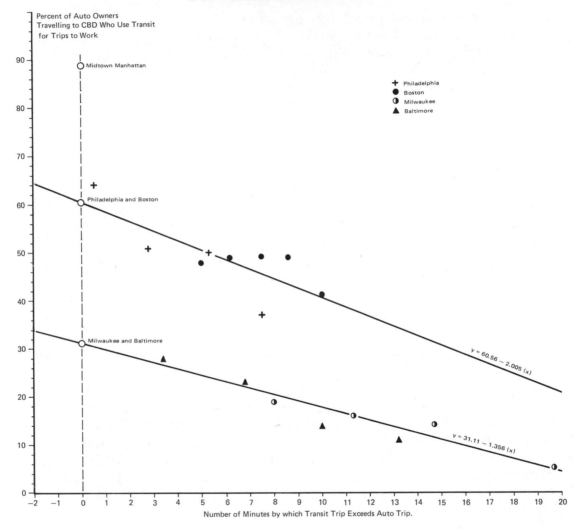

Percent of Auto Owners Travelling to CBD Who Use Transit for Trips to Work

+ Philadelphia
● Boston
◑ Milwaukee
▲ Baltimore

Midtown Manhattan

Philadelphia and Boston

Milwaukee and Baltimore

$y = 60.56 - 2.005 (x)$

$y = 31.11 - 1.356 (x)$

Number of Minutes by which Transit Trip Exceeds Auto Trip.

Source: Calculated from: Wilbur Smith and Associates, *Patterns of Car Ownership, Trip Generation and Trip Sharing in Urban Areas*, New Haven, Conn., 1968. pp. 23-24 and Appendix A.

The next chapter will show that a major reason for increased transit use and reduced auto use at higher densities is not the residential density per se, but rather the greater orientation of trips at higher densities toward larger and denser nonresidential concentrations of activity. Because of data limitations, that analysis will not deal with how the relative speed advantage of auto versus transit affects the choice of mode for travel to downtown areas, so the subject can be usefully brought up here.

The larger and denser the downtown concentration, the fewer of those travellers who do have an auto available choose to use it for the downtown trip. This has to do most directly with the cost of parking which, following the market for land, increases steeply with rising density, and more generally, with the limited capacity of high density areas to accept the auto. Exhibit 1.3 shows that about 90 percent of auto owners travelling to work in Midtown Manhattan use public transportation, if the travel time by auto and by transit is the same. In Philadelphia and Boston, 60 percent use transit under the same conditions, and in Milwaukee and Baltimore, just over 30 percent. Comparative travel times were not available for Midtown Manhattan, but are plotted for the other four downtowns, based on some fairly coarse-grain data.

The curves show that for each additional minute by which transit is slower than auto, transit use by the voluntary riders declines from 1.35 to 2.00 percent. The former figure seems to hold true for the two smaller, the latter for the two larger cities. If the total number of choice transit users and auto travellers to work in a downtown area is known (as it is from journey-to-work census data) a relationship of the type shown in Exhibit 1.3 will help estimate how many additional auto users can be diverted to public transportation by what kind of an improvement in travel time.[19]

The relationship suggests that in the larger downtowns, the door-to-door transit trip would have to be 15 minutes faster than the auto before 90 percent of the auto users switch to transit, as they do in Manhattan. In the two smaller downtowns, it would have to be about 22 minutes faster before 60 percent switch as they do in Philadelphia and Boston. Such travel time reductions are generally impossible when the average trip by auto is under 36 minutes to begin with, as it is in these four cases. Yet commensurate increases in transit use by auto owners are achieved by increasing downtown size and density. So in dealing with ways of increasing transit usage it is necessary to look at the relationship between development density and transit use in greater detail.

Demand for Transit:

2 The Role of the Density of Development

DENSITY OF URBAN AREAS AND THE USE OF TRANSIT

The broadest scale at which the relationship between public transit use and urban density can be viewed is that of an entire urbanized area. Urbanized area boundaries defined by the U.S. Census delineate fairly closely the extent of built-up land. The decennial Census also lists the mode used by workers travelling to work in urbanized areas. Of course, trips to and from work account for only 30 to 40 percent of all trips, and the use of public transit for non-work trips is much lower than for work trips. Therefore, the percentage of transit use for all trips tends to be roughly half of what it is for journeys to work. Nevertheless, the Census statistics for the journey to work do provide an index of public transit usage that is consistent over time. Total ridership figures for urbanized areas were, until very recently, difficult to come by.

In Exhibit 2.1, the percent workers using transit (rail, rapid transit, trolley, and bus) for the journey to work is plotted against average density for 105 urbanized areas in the U.S. in 1960 and 1970. The urbanized areas are those with populations over 200,000 in 1970. To relate the scale of transit use shown in the two graphs to nationwide figures, 12.1 percent of all workers in the U.S. reported using public transit in 1960; by 1970 this figure dropped to 8.5 percent. The percentage of auto users increased from 64.0 to 77.7 percent, and those who walked to work comprised 9.9 and 7.4 percent respectively for the two dates. The remainder either used other means, or worked at home, or did not report the means of travel; of all these categories, only the reported transit users are dealt with here.

In general, transit use can be seen to rise with urbanized area density. If one compares the two plots, a decline in the level of transit use between 1960 and 1970 is also evident. Further, a decline in the density of urbanized areas over time is apparent—most data points are shifted to the left in the lower graph. The line of averages in the lower graph has a

24

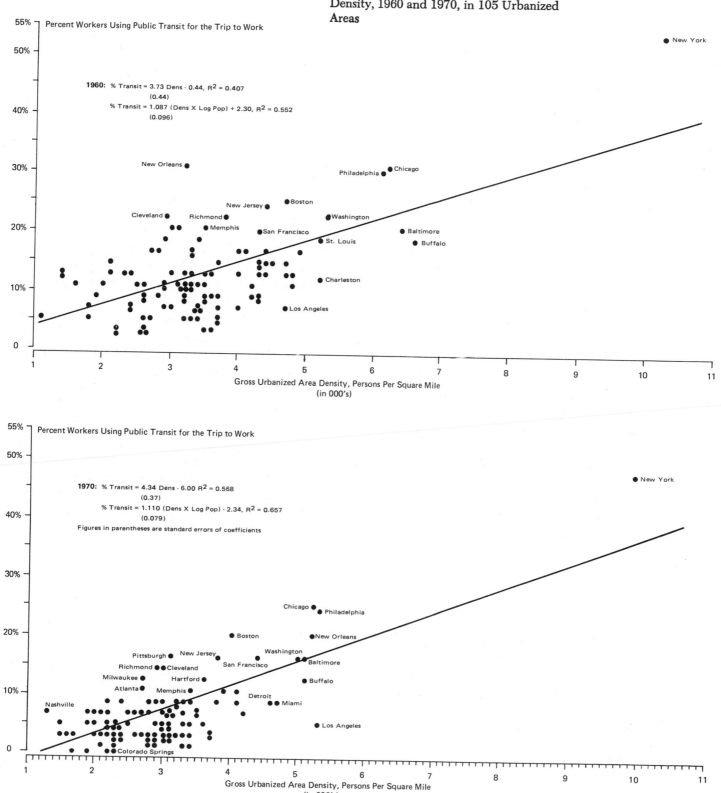

EXHIBIT 2.1

Public Transit Use for the Trip to
Work Related to Urbanized Area
Density, 1960 and 1970, in 105 Urbanized
Areas

Percent Workers Using Public Transit for the Trip to Work

1960: % Transit = 3.73 Dens - 0.44, R² = 0.407
(0.44)
% Transit = 1.087 (Dens X Log Pop) + 2.30, R² = 0.552
(0.096)

New York

New Orleans

Philadelphia ● Chicago

New Jersey ● Boston
Cleveland ● Richmond ●
Memphis ● ● Washington
San Francisco
St. Louis ● Baltimore
● Buffalo

● Charleston

Los Angeles

Gross Urbanized Area Density, Persons Per Square Mile
(in 000's)

Percent Workers Using Public Transit for the Trip to Work

1970: % Transit = 4.34 Dens - 6.00 R² = 0.568
(0.37)
% Transit = 1.110 (Dens X Log Pop) - 2.34, R² = 0.657
(0.079)
Figures in parentheses are standard errors of coefficients

New York

Chicago ● Philadelphia

Boston ● New Orleans
Pittsburgh ● New Jersey
Richmond ● ● Cleveland Washington
Milwaukee ● San Francisco Baltimore
Atlanta ● Hartford ● Buffalo
Memphis ●
Nashville Detroit ● Miami

Los Angeles

Colorado Springs

Gross Urbanized Area Density, Persons Per Square Mile
(in 000's)

Source: U.S. Census

steeper slope, meaning that the higher density areas have held transit ridership better than the lower density ones, many of which have dropped to less than half their former level. This supports our finding about the greater sensitivity of ridership to fare increases and service cutbacks in smaller and less dense urban areas.

Yet the scatter of points around the lines of averages for both years is substantial. For example, at a density of 1,900 persons per square mile in 1970 one can find San Bernardino, where only 1.0 percent of all workers went to work by transit, and Dallas, where 7.2 percent did. Similarly, at a density of 5,300 persons per square mile one can find Los Angeles, where 4.8 percent went to work by transit, and Philadelphia, where 24.6 percent did. Obviously, average areawide density does not tell us much about transit use.

Statistically, urbanized area density alone explains only 40.7 percent of the variation in transit use among different areas in 1960, and 56.8 percent in 1970. The improved 1970 relationship may be the result of a more consistent urbanized area definition. The estimation of transit use becomes somewhat more accurate if population size is also taken into account. Though size alone has an even weaker relationship with transit use than areawide density, a product of density and size explains 55.2 to 65.7 percent of the variation for the two dates, as the lower of the two equations in each of the graphs shows.

In looking for more basic reasons why transit use varies between areas of similar size and density, it becomes clear that those with strong Central Business Districts have above average transit use. So do the areas with at least some rail transit service on exclusive right-of-way. A useful measure of Central Business District size is the square feet of office floorspace, a figure more often available than total nonresidential floorspace.

In Exhibit 2.2, the percent workers using transit is plotted against office floorspace in the main downtowns of 27 urban areas with populations of one million or more in 1970. The heavy dots identify the relationship as of 1970, while the thin lines trace the change from 1960 to 1970. Unlike areawide average density, downtown office floorspace did increase over the period in each case, as seen in the shift of the observations to the right. That the proportion of transit use declined nevertheless is due to the fact that downtown concentration was only a minor part of areawide growth; on occasion, total downtown employment declined despite an increase in office floorspace. However, some of the areas which had above average gains in downtown floorspace—notably San Francisco and Los Angeles—also registered below-average losses in public transit. The smallest loss in transit use—by only one percentage point—occurred in Pittsburgh, which combined close to 50 percent increase in downtown office floorspace with virtually no population growth and hence little suburbanization.

The second equation for each of the two dates in Exhibit 2.2 combines the three factors of areawide density, downtown floorspace, and the presence or absence of rail transit. Taken together, these three explain 67.6 percent of the variation in transit use for 1960, and 78.8 percent for 1970. *Taking the size of the downtown and the quality of the transit service, even in a rough way, into account gives a much better explanation of transit use than areawide average density alone could provide.*

The dependence of transit use on the downtown concentration becomes even more striking if one looks only at ridership on the rail modes—rapid transit and commuter rail. Unfortunately, total ridership figures for different urban areas are weak even for the rail systems alone. Thus transfer passengers from buses are sometimes not included in rapid transit counts and have to be estimated. They account for a large share of rapid transit trips in Chicago, Philadelphia, and Boston. The accounting of commuter rail trips is confused by the fact that purchasers of multiple-ride "commuter" tickets do not make all the trips they

EXHIBIT 2.2

Public Transit Use for the Trip to Work Related to Downtown Office Floorspace, 1960 and 1970, in 27 Urbanized Areas

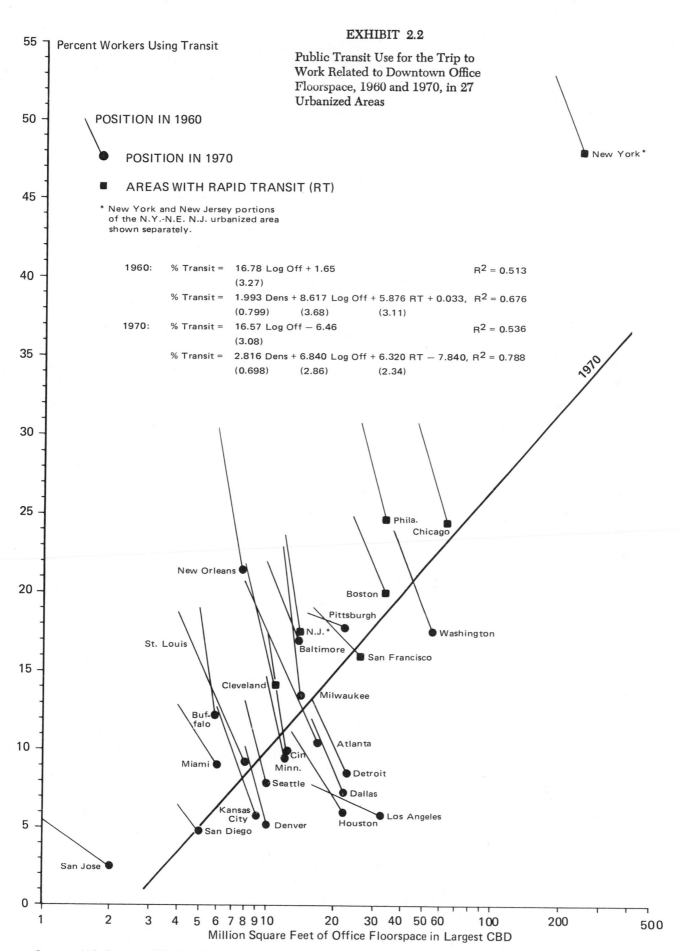

Sources: U.S. Census and Regional Plan Association

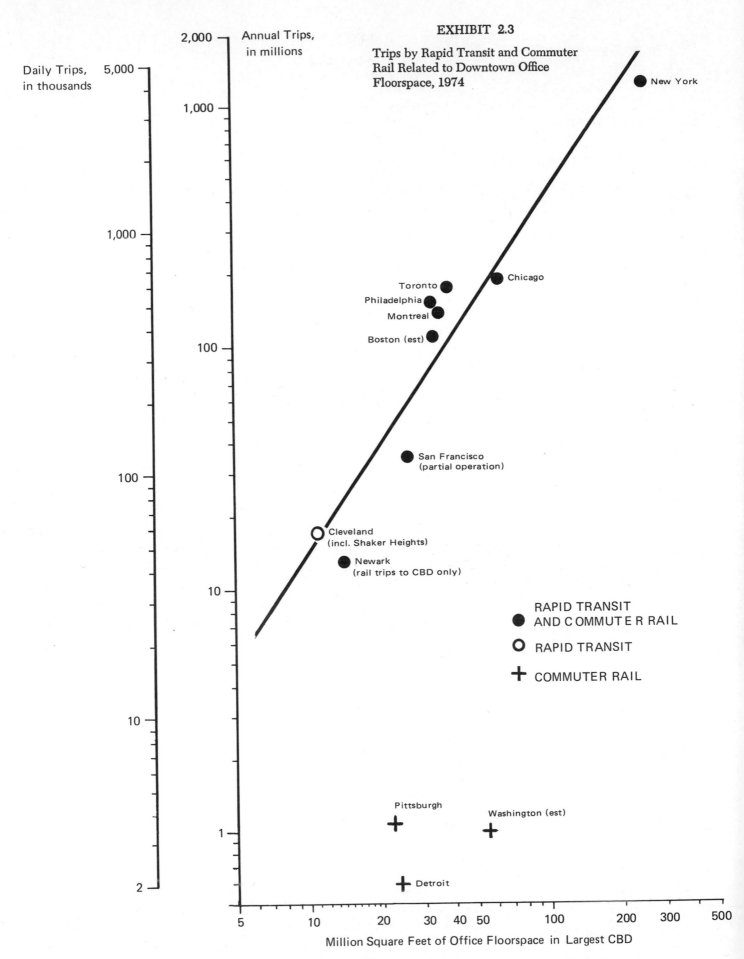

EXHIBIT 2.3

Trips by Rapid Transit and Commuter
Rail Related to Downtown Office
Floorspace, 1974

Daily Trips,
in thousands

Annual Trips,
in millions

New York

Chicago

Toronto

Philadelphia

Montreal

Boston (est)

San Francisco
(partial operation)

Cleveland
(incl. Shaker Heights)

Newark
(rail trips to CBD only)

● RAPID TRANSIT
AND COMMUTER RAIL

○ RAPID TRANSIT

+ COMMUTER RAIL

Pittsburgh

Washington (est)

Detroit

Million Square Feet of Office Floorspace in Largest CBD

Source: Regional Plan Association

pay for (which are reported as having been made), while other passengers assignable to suburban service are often reported as intercity. These data deficiencies, however, do not change the broad orders of magnitude shown in Exhibit 2.3, which relates the combined rapid transit and commuter rail ridership in urban areas to the square feet of office space in their major downtown. The office space scale is the same as in the preceding exhibit.

On a logarithmic scale, ridership by rail and rapid transit is shown to be closely related to the amount of downtown office floorspace in Cleveland, Boston, Philadelphia, Chicago, and New York. The two urban areas which fall substantially below the line of averages are San Francisco, where BART was only in partial operation during the year shown, and Newark, for which only trips to the downtown area are listed. Toronto and Montreal show above average rail transit use. On the basis of the relationship shown one can estimate that most U.S. cities building or contemplating new rapid transit systems—cities that have 10 to 30 million square feet of downtown office floorspace—can expect a rapid transit ridership on the order of 15 to 70 million annually under current conditions of auto ownership and use. Only the Washington system can, upon completion, expect to come close to Chicago with some 150 million annual trips, about one eighth of the New York Region's trips.

Ridership by commuter rail has held up quite well over the past decade and a half, and has experienced a significant increase in Philadelphia. Rapid transit ridership has fallen somewhat, with the greatest percentage drop occurring on the smallest system, in Cleveland. In Chicago, ridership losses were offset in part by gains resulting from major system extensions, and the opening of the Lindenwold line in the Philadelphia area more than offset areawide rapid transit losses over the preceding decade. Thus the position of the line of averages in Exhibit 2.3 is subject to change through long-term secular trends, and also depends on the extent of the individual systems.

Returning now to the analysis of Census Journey to Work data, and looking for reasons why the average density of urbanized areas does not say much about transit use, we may note that apart from the different degrees of downtown concentration, and the presence or absence of rail services on exclusive rights of way, there is a third reason. Except for the extremes of the New York portion of the New York-Northeastern New Jersey Urbanized Area and the overbounded urbanized area of Nashville, 103 of the 105 larger urbanized areas investigated fall into the density range of between 1,500 and 5,300 persons per square mile. Referring to the fourth curve in Exhibit 7.1 in the Appendix, we can estimate that this is equivalent to an average areawide residential density of 2.5 to 6.5 dwellings per net acre, certainly not a very wide range. The suburban spread of the last three decades has homogenized American urban areas a great deal, and conceals internal differences in density such as those between Philadelphia and Los Angeles. Had we followed the Census in treating the two parts of the New York-Northeastern New Jersey Urbanized Area as one (which for other purposes they are), the average density of this agglomeration would not have been much above the others—some 6,700 persons per square mile. To find a wider range of densities which can be related to transit use, we must look inside urban areas.

DENSITY WITHIN URBAN AREAS AND THE USE OF TRANSIT

The Area Transportation Studies undertaken in the U.S. mostly in the early 'sixties provide a wealth of data on travel behavior within urban areas. Unfortunately, the rich experience of these studies has not been sufficiently summarized on a national basis, nor are its lessons widely appreciated. Selected data—condensed for readability—from one of the few studies synthesizing this experience[1] are presented in Exhibit 2.4, along with data based on the Home Interview Survey conducted by the Tri-State Regional Planning Commission in 1963 in the New York Region.

In the exhibit, both total weekday trips per person by all vehicular modes and weekday trips per person by public transportation are plotted against the density of the residential area in which the person making the trips lives. In contrast to the small variation in density presented earlier, the variation here is very large—from 0.8 dwellings per acre all the way to 200 dwellings per acre. The differences in travel demand are, accordingly, also very dramatic.

The average individual living on a 1-acre lot in one of the six urban areas shown—ranging in size from Springfield, Mass. (population 531,000), to the New York Region (population 16,300,000 within the survey area)—made anywhere from 2.0 to 2.6 trips by all vehicular modes on an average weekday. His or her propensity for making trips did not change much if the density increased to 3 dwellings per acre. However, as the density increased from 3 to 30 dwellings per acre, the number of trips per person was reduced anywhere from 50 percent in Springfield and Milwaukee to 16 percent in Seattle, with the New York Region about in the middle with a 30 percent reduction in total trips, very similar to Boston. This reduction in total travel demand was due to a reduction of trips by auto. Transit trips, by contrast, increased even more dramatically with rising density.

At a density of around 1 dwelling per acre, the transit demand in any one of the six urban agglomerations was minimal—anywhere from 0.01 to 0.14 trips by public transportation per person per day. This demand did not increase much up to a density of 7 dwellings per acre, where it amounted to 0.03 to 0.22 trips by public transportation per day. However, with a density increase from 7 to 30 dwellings per acre, transit demand roughly tripled in the New York Region, in Philadelphia, and in Boston, to around 0.6 trips per person per day. In the three smaller urban areas, the absolute number of trips per person by public transportation at a density of 30 dwellings per acre was not as high, but the relative increase compared to the lower density was even greater.

Densities above 30 dwellings per acre are not frequent in American cities; in the three larger urban areas shown, transit trips per person continue to increase in this high density range, but at a declining rate. At a density of roughly 50 dwellings per acre, transit trips become more numerous than auto trips in the New York Region and Philadelphia; at a density of 85 dwellings per acre or more in New York, reductions in total travel demand by mechanical means appear to cease, even though transit travel continues to increase.

Summarizing, we find that *densities in the 2 to 7 dwellings per acre range produced only marginal use of public transportation* within major urban areas of the United States in the early 'sixties. We have seen that the average areawide densities of virtually all urbanized areas in the nation fall into this density range. *Densities of 7 to 30 dwellings per acre were necessary to sustain significant transit use—in the range of 5 to 40 percent of all trips.* Moreover, an increase in density from about 7 to 30 dwellings per acre produced not only a very dramatic increase in transit use, but also a sharp reduction in auto travel.

The general consistency of these patterns notwithstanding, there is still a fair amount

EXHIBIT 2.4 continued

Note: Densities listed represent midpoints of class intervals for which data were available

Source: Wilbur Smith and Associates. *Patterns of Car Ownership, Trip Generation and Trip Sharing in Urbanized Areas.* Prepared for the Bureau of Public Roads, New Haven, Conn., June 1968, p. 107-110, and Tri-State Regional Planning Commission.

* Considering multi-mode trips as one trip by the dominant mode.

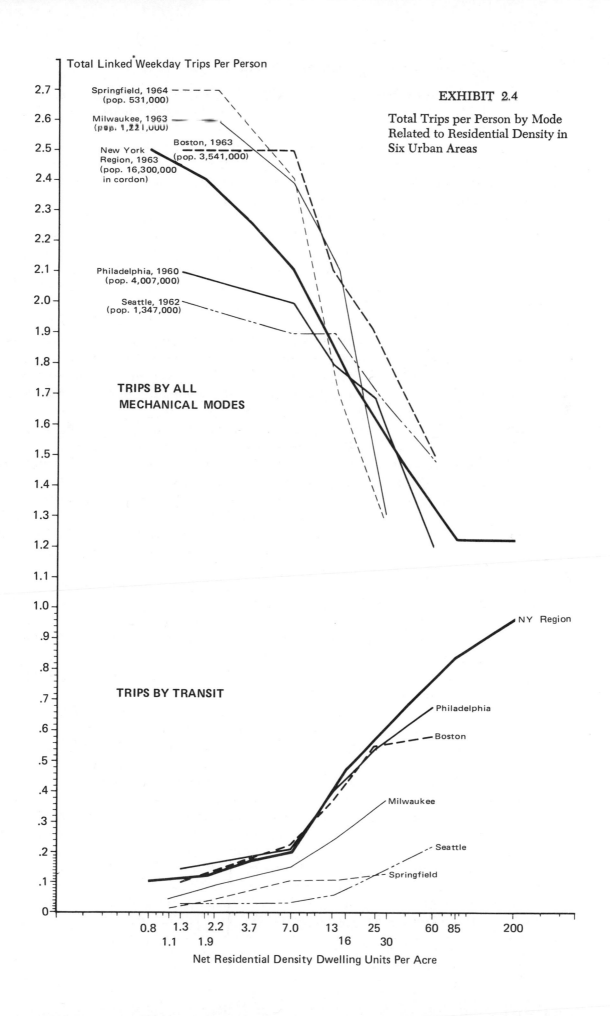

Total Linked Weekday Trips Per Person

Springfield, 1964
(pop. 531,000)

Milwaukee, 1963
(pop. 1,221,000)

New York
Region, 1963
(pop. 16,300,000
in cordon)

Boston, 1963
(pop. 3,541,000)

Philadelphia, 1960
(pop. 4,007,000)

Seattle, 1962
(pop. 1,347,000)

EXHIBIT 2.4

Total Trips per Person by Mode
Related to Residential Density in
Six Urban Areas

**TRIPS BY ALL
MECHANICAL MODES**

TRIPS BY TRANSIT

NY Region

Philadelphia

Boston

Milwaukee

Seattle

Springfield

Net Residential Density Dwelling Units Per Acre

of variation in transit use between the larger and the smaller urban areas. To explain this, a look at Exhibit 2.5 is instructive. In it, the New York Region's home-based trips (i.e. trips to and from home, which amount to somewhat over 80 percent of all trips and over 90 percent of all transit trips) are classified according to where their other end is located. Transit trips to or from the three major Central Business Districts of the Region (Manhattan, Brooklyn and Newark) are distinguished from other transit trips, which are called "local"; the latter do include transit trips to smaller centers.

It can be seen that at a density around 1 dwelling per acre, virtually the only trips that are made by transit are those to and from the main downtowns. These trips are also the dominant component of transit travel in the 2 to 5 dwellings per acre range. "Local" transit trips in that range are minimal. Thus, greater transit use at low densities in large urban areas compared to small ones is due to the pull of their major downtowns. Auto travel to these centers is infrequent (about 0.01 to 0.03 trips per capita throughout the range of densities in the New York Region); such trips as are made are predominantly by transit.

In the middle range of densities, above 7 dwellings per acre, the "local" transit trips increase sharply, in many cases outnumbering the CBD-bound trips. At any level of density, transit use in New York City is higher than in the region outside the City; but if one subtracts the influence of the major centers, transit travel outside the City is no different from that in smaller urban areas throughout the nation.

The reduction in auto use with increasing density is also clearly visible in Exhibit 2.5. Again, this reduction is greater within New York City than it is outside. One can also see that the high per capita travel demand in low density areas is further magnified by school bus trips, which become important at densities of 7 dwellings per acre and less.

It is reasonable to ask the question: To what extent are the lower total travel demand per capita and the greater use of public transportation in higher density areas simply due to differences in income? Exhibit 2.6 addresses that issue, using the same data for the New York Region as the previous exhibit. For each density group, the home-based trips are stratified by these income levels, as explained at the top of the chart.

For the middle income group, the pattern of declining auto use and increasing transit use is virtually identical with that shown earlier for the population as a whole. As density increases from 0.8 to 85 dwellings per acre, total trips per capita by the middle income group are cut nearly 50 percent, auto trips are cut 80 percent, and transit trips increase nearly 18 times. As density increases to 200 dwellings per acre auto trips are cut further, but trips by transit and taxi rise to make up the difference, so that total trips per capita at this highest range remain the same as at the second highest.

The impact of rising density on the upper income group is somewhat less dramatic. At low density, high income people tend to be virtually the only users of transit, because they can afford long trips to the major Central Business Districts. Their use of transit remains higher than that of the middle income group in nearly all the higher density ranges as well: they use railroads and subways more often. In addition, at very high densities they use taxicabs in large numbers. Generally, the upper income group can afford to buy more travel by both auto and public transportation at each density level. Still, its total trips per capita are cut about 40 percent across the range of densities shown. Its auto trips are cut by 70 percent, if one classifies taxis in high density areas as a form of auto use.

The low income group makes few trips to begin with, so that rising density does not have much effect on its total travel; it is cut about 25 percent across the range of densities shown. However, higher density does enable the low income group to substitute transit trips for auto trips to a much greater degree. Its bus use at each density level is about the same as

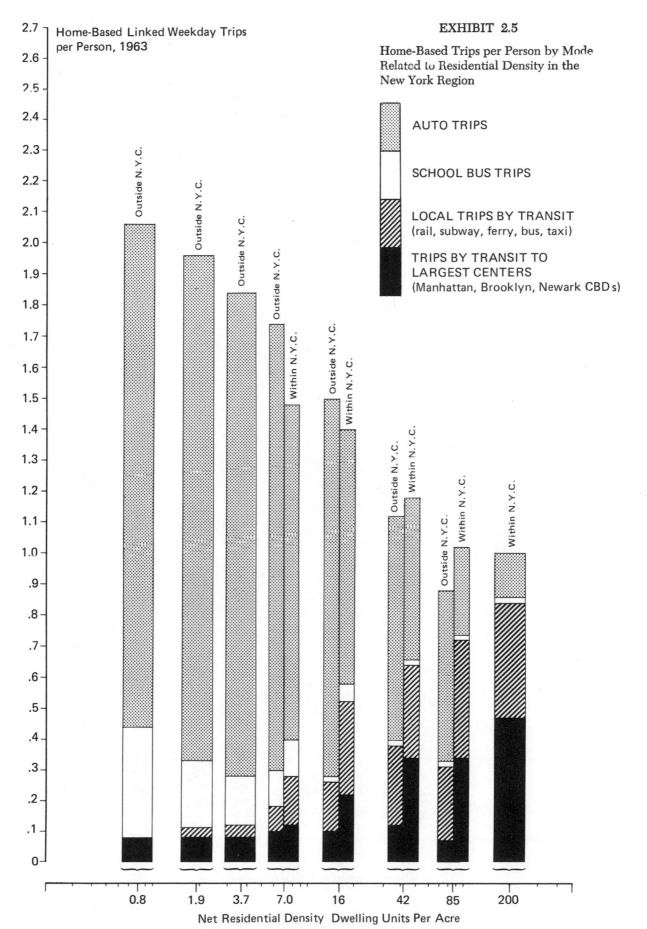

EXHIBIT 2.5

Home-Based Trips per Person by Mode Related to Residential Density in the New York Region

Home-Based Linked Weekday Trips per Person, 1963

AUTO TRIPS

SCHOOL BUS TRIPS

LOCAL TRIPS BY TRANSIT
(rail, subway, ferry, bus, taxi)

TRIPS BY TRANSIT TO LARGEST CENTERS
(Manhattan, Brooklyn, Newark CBDs)

Outside N.Y.C.
Within N.Y.C.

Net Residential Density Dwelling Units Per Acre

0.8 1.9 3.7 7.0 16 42 85 200

Source: Tri-State Regional Planning Commission *Transit Supporting Densities.* ITR 4195-4451, July 1970.

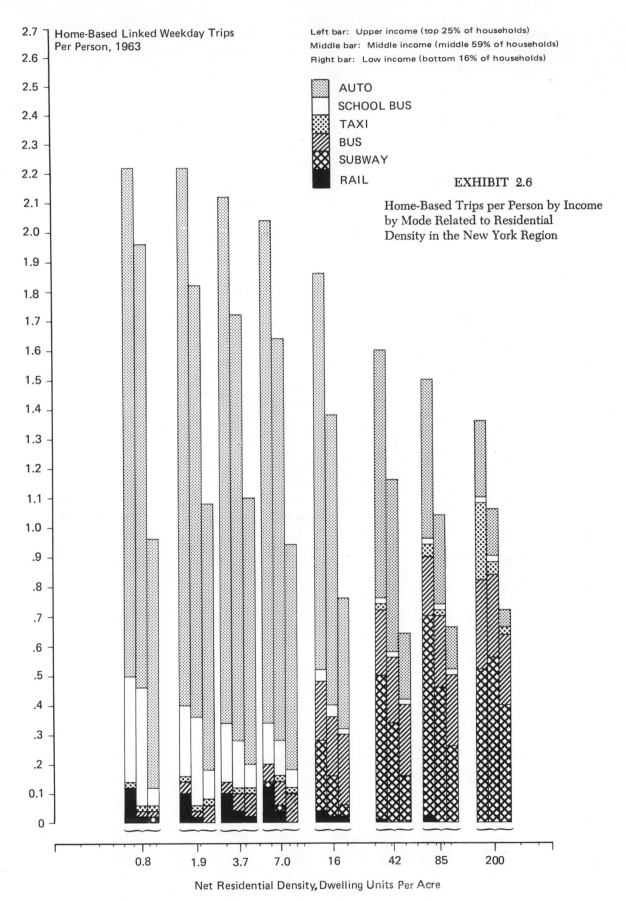

Home-Based Linked Weekday Trips
Per Person, 1963

Left bar: Upper income (top 25% of households)
Middle bar: Middle income (middle 59% of households)
Right bar: Low income (bottom 16% of households)

AUTO
SCHOOL BUS
TAXI
BUS
SUBWAY
RAIL

EXHIBIT 2.6

Home-Based Trips per Person by Income
by Mode Related to Residential
Density in the New York Region

Net Residential Density, Dwelling Units Per Acre

Source: *Transit Supporting Densities*, op.cit.

that by the middle and upper income groups. Subway use is less frequent, and the use of commuter rail negligible. At very low densities, the low income group does register some use of taxicabs—a consequence of its low auto ownership and of sparse transit service in the areas. Generally, travel by the low income group appears to be curtailed both at low suburban densities and at intermediate urban densities. It increases in the two highest density ranges, presumably because of the greater availability and convenience of public transit. Thus, high urban densities cut discretionary travel by the middle and upper income groups, but they have some tendency to increase mobility for the lowest income group.[2]

TRIP END DENSITY AND THE USE OF TRANSIT

So far, we have dealt with percentages of people using transit and with transit trips per capita at different densities. However, what matters from the viewpoint of providing transit service is not just trips per person, but the fact that at higher densities there are more persons around to make the trips. The density of people in an area multiplied by trips per person yields the density of trips. This is charted in Exhibit 2.7 for the residential density categories previously used. The definition of trips, though, is different: instead of assigning both trip origins and trip ends to the residence, only trip ends are shown, regardless of origin. Thus, nonresidential trips that happen to occur at the various residential densities are included.[3] The trip end density is measured per gross square mile, as defined by the fourth curve in Exhibit 7.1 in the Appendix.

The compounding effects of greater density of people and of more trips per person are dramatically evident in the Exhibit. For example, in the New York Region in 1963, trips per square mile by the two rail modes (commuter rail and subway) increase from 12 at a residential density of 0.8 dwellings per acre to an average of 61,452 at a residential density of 200 dwellings per acre. On the log-log graph, the relationship is virtually a straight line. Bus trips per square mile are less numerous than rail trips at both high and low densities, but they bulge out above rail in the middle range of densities. In the New York Region, these areas of predominant bus use are in the 7 to 16 dwellings per acre range, a density typical of outer Queens and much of Bergen and Passaic counties, which are poorly served by the rail modes.

For comparison, analogous rail and bus use curves are also shown for the Chicago area, based on 1956 data.[4] Both rail and bus curves in the two regions parallel each other closely, though bus use in Chicago is higher and rail use lower than in the New York Region. Total transit trips per square mile in both regions were very similar at densities between 10 and 40 dwellings per acre. For the New York Region, the density of taxi trips is also shown in Exhibit 2.8. It reflects a fairly even per capita trip rate throughout the range of densities, though taxi use is disproportionately high in the highest density range, where it serves the upper income group as a substitute for regular transit.

It can be seen from Exhibit 2.7 that in what one might call the usual range of transit supporting densities—between, say, 7 and 40 dwellings per acre—transit trip ends per square mile range from around 500 to about 10,000, given the service levels of New York and Chicago. Transit trip end density approaches 100,000 per square mile only at residential densities in excess of 200 dwellings per acre in New York City. All these figures represent *averages* calculated over areas that contain more than ten, and in some cases several hundred, square miles. Trip end densities in *particular* square miles with heavy concentrations

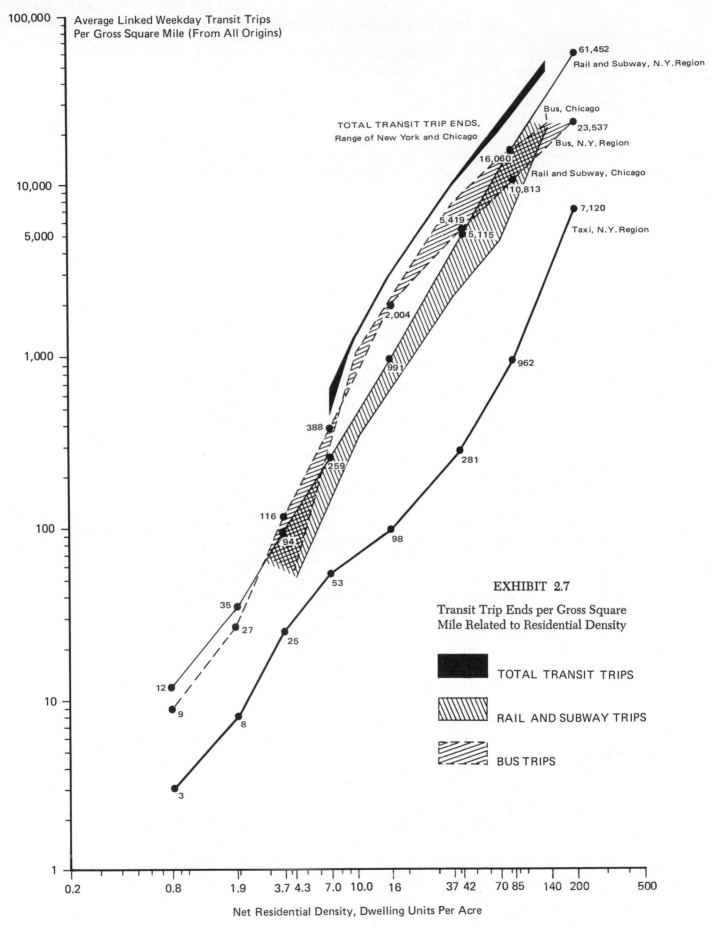

Average Linked Weekday Transit Trips
Per Gross Square Mile (From All Origins)

61,452
Rail and Subway, N.Y. Region

TOTAL TRANSIT TRIP ENDS,
Range of New York and Chicago

Bus, Chicago

23,537
Bus, N.Y. Region

16,060

Rail and Subway, Chicago
10,813

5,419
5,115

7,120
Taxi, N.Y. Region

2,004

991

962

388

281

259

116

98

94

53

35

27

25

12

9

8

3

EXHIBIT 2.7

Transit Trip Ends per Gross Square
Mile Related to Residential Density

■ TOTAL TRANSIT TRIPS

▨ RAIL AND SUBWAY TRIPS

▨ BUS TRIPS

0.2   0.8   1.9   3.7 4.3   7.0 10.0   16   37 42   70 85   140   200   500

Net Residential Density, Dwelling Units Per Acre

Sources: Tri-State Regional Planning Commission, *Transit Supporting Densities*, op.cit., *Chicago Area Transportation Study*, Vol I, pp 108-112

of nonresidential activity, notably in Central Business Districts, are of a higher order of magnitude.

Exhibit 2.8 displays 16 square miles in 15 downtowns of selected cities for which data were readily available; they are ranked in order of their reported trip end density for the late 'fifties and early 'sixties. Trip ends by public transit exceed 100,000 per square mile in the downtowns of Brooklyn, Detroit, Los Angeles, and Pittsburgh, and go over 200,000 in the downtowns of Boston, Philadelphia, and Chicago. They exceed 600,000 in the central square mile of Midtown Manhattan.

Trip ends by auto are shown below the transit trip ends for comparison; they include the trip destinations of auto drivers, auto passengers, and taxi passengers. It can be seen that the differences in auto travel to these central square miles are much smaller than the differences in transit travel. Generally, auto trip ends do not exceed roughly 160,000 per square mile. Only in Midtown Manhattan does this figure approach 200,000, a result of the saturation of the area with short taxi trips (shown separately), and also a result of heavy street use during other than the usual peak hours.

There appears to be a limit to how many trips by auto a square mile can absorb. This limit is dictated by the character and extent of the pavement available for auto movement and by the extent of the space available for parking. Thus, the peak accumulation of vehicles in a square mile was found not to exceed 23,000 to 27,000 in cities with more than half a million people;[5] Midtown Manhattan's peak accumulation is no different—about 24,000 vehicles per square mile.[6] The number of people arriving in a square mile by auto in a 24-hour period may vary over a wider range than the peak-period accumulation of vehicles, because of such factors as different vehicle occupancy, different length of stay, different patterns of off-peak use, different composition of vehicles. Because of the complexity of these factors, the exact "capacity" of a square mile to absorb trips by auto may be difficult to pinpoint on pure transportation grounds. Nevertheless, a limitation of auto access into very high density areas does empirically exist, even short of deliberate restraints on environmental grounds. As total destinations per square mile exceed those which can be taken care of by auto, the surplus is handled by public transit. Largely because of this phenomenon, the higher the density of a downtown area, the greater the proportion of trips made by transit. Exhibit 2.8 demonstrates this in terms of the actual numbers of trips ending in a particular square mile.

It also explains why in small centers—whose density does not exceed their "capacity" to accept trips by auto—few auto owners use transit, and transit riders are predominantly "captive." Only as auto access becomes difficult do riders by choice begin to switch to transit. Of course, the relative attractiveness of transit in terms of all the attributes of speed and comfort enumerated in the previous chapter has a lot to do with exactly how many of them exercise that option.

AUTO OWNERSHIP RELATED TO DENSITY AND TRANSIT SERVICE

In looking at the relationship between transit use and the intensity of urban development from various vantage points, it becomes clear that auto ownership, income, the size or density of the major nonresidential destination, and the level of service which transit provides all influence the choice of auto versus public transit. It is time to account for these influences in a systematic fashion.

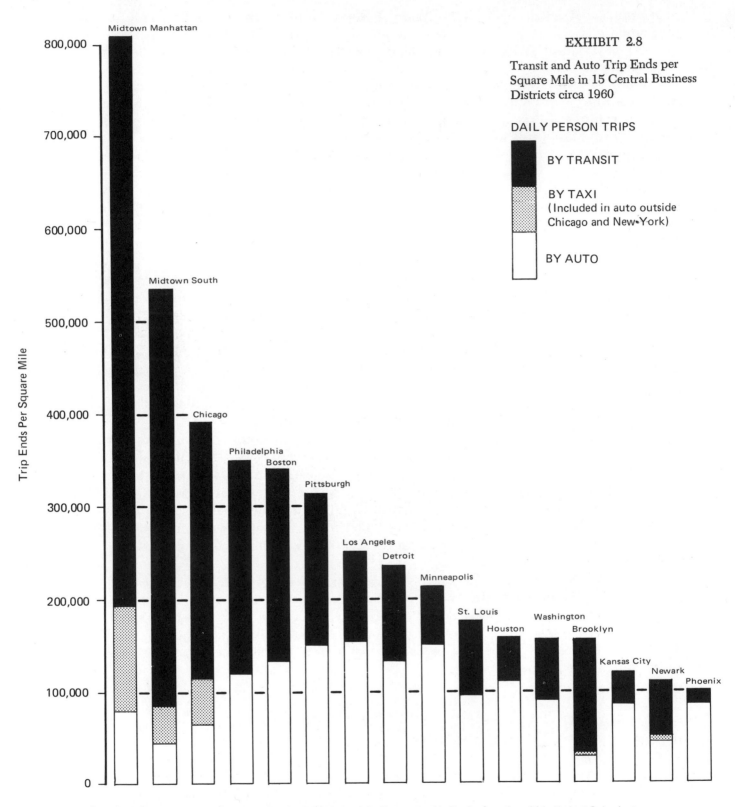

EXHIBIT 2.8

Transit and Auto Trip Ends per Square Mile in 15 Central Business Districts circa 1960

DAILY PERSON TRIPS

BY TRANSIT

BY TAXI
(Included in auto outside Chicago and New York)

BY AUTO

Trip Ends Per Square Mile

800,000

700,000

600,000

500,000

400,000

300,000

200,000

100,000

0

Midtown Manhattan
Midtown South
Chicago
Philadelphia
Boston
Pittsburgh
Los Angeles
Detroit
Minneapolis
St. Louis
Houston
Washington
Brooklyn
Kansas City
Newark
Phoenix

Sources: Tri-State Regional Planning Commission, Chicago Area Transportation Study; for other cities, Herbert S. Levinson, *Modal Choice and Public Policy*. ASCE Conference paper, Milwaukee, Wis., July 1972.

Note: Midtown Manhattan - square mile north of 40th Street;
Midtown South - square mile south of 40th Street.

We shall begin with auto ownership, since the number of autos available to a household obviously has much to do with the traveller's sensitivity to the other variables. Research on auto ownership is extensive, and it is widely agreed that the size of the household (or, more precisely, the number of persons of driving age, or the number of licensed drivers, or the number of workers in the household), the income of the household, and the residential density of the area in which it lives all influence the number of autos a household will have. Less attention is paid to the question whether good transit service starts attracting ridership by suppressing auto ownership in the vicinity to begin with.

The relationships presented here are based on an analysis of some 4,200 census tracts in the New York Region in 1970. To address the question of transit influence on auto ownership, the census tracts are classified into three groups. Those with at least half their residential area within 2,000 feet of a rapid transit station are considered to be in subway territory; those with at least one fifth of their residential area within 2,000 feet of a commuter rail station are considered in rail territory; all others are considered to have no rail service. For each territory, a statistical equation is derived showing how the number of autos per household varies with residential density, income, and household size. The income is median family income in an entire census tract—not the actual income of a particular household. The household size is the mean number of persons per household 16 or more years old—a figure approximating persons of driving age. The equations are shown in Exhibit 2.9.

The curves in the Exhibit display the relationship between residential density and autos per household for nine combinations of transit service and income level. The 1969 income levels are selected to represent the upper fifth of all census tracts with the highest incomes, the middle three fifths with middle incomes, and the lowest fifth with the lowest incomes. To demonstrate the influence of these variables in a pure way, the household size throughout is kept constant at the median value of 1.9 persons aged 16 or over. In real life, this size varies from 1.0 to 2.7 in the census tracts studied. As the equations indicate, for each additional person over 16, the number of autos per household increase by 0.266 to 0.369, keeping all other factors constant. Thus, for above or below-average household sizes, the curves shown in the Exhibit will accordingly move up or down.

The salient relationship in Exhibit 2.9 is the decline in auto ownership with increasing residential density. In the territory with no rail service, a tenfold increase in residential density reduces the number of autos per household in a census tract by about 0.43. This applies to any income group; the poorest fifth of all census tracts simply has about 0.32 fewer cars per household than the richest fifth, at any density. Analogous calculations based on 1963 data, not shown here, also indicate a reduction of 0.4 autos per household with each tenfold increase in residential density in the territory not served by any rail modes. For this territory, the three factors of residential density, income, and household size explain 83 percent of the variation in auto ownership among census tracts; residential density is the most important factor, followed by income and then by household size.

The set of curves for the commuter rail territory has a slightly flatter slope and falls mostly below the set of no-rail-service curves. The key observation here is that *at suburban densities of less than 10 dwellings per acre, the presence of commuter rail reduces the number of autos per household anywhere from 4 to 6 percent in the upper income census tracts.* In the middle income tracts, the reduction in auto ownership at comparable densities is smaller, which is plausible because few middle income residents use commuter rail regularly. In low income areas with commuter rail stations there is no reduction in auto ownership. At higher densities the relationship actually seems to be the reverse; since neither routing nor pricing of commuter rail is designed to encourage use from higher density

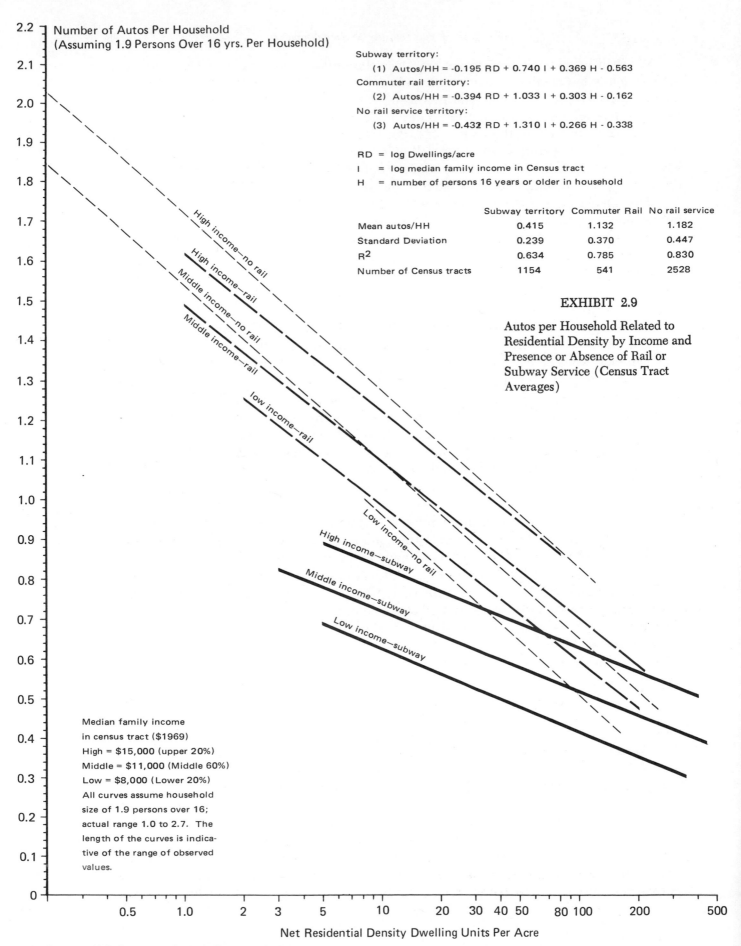

Number of Autos Per Household
(Assuming 1.9 Persons Over 16 yrs. Per Household)

Subway territory:
   (1) Autos/HH = -0.195 RD + 0.740 I + 0.369 H - 0.563
Commuter rail territory:
   (2) Autos/HH = -0.394 RD + 1.033 I + 0.303 H - 0.162
No rail service territory:
   (3) Autos/HH = -0.432 RD + 1.310 I + 0.266 H - 0.338

RD = log Dwellings/acre
I   = log median family income in Census tract
H = number of persons 16 years or older in household

	Subway territory	Commuter Rail	No rail service
Mean autos/HH	0.415	1.132	1.182
Standard Deviation	0.239	0.370	0.447
R^2	0.634	0.785	0.830
Number of Census tracts	1154	541	2528

EXHIBIT 2.9

Autos per Household Related to
Residential Density by Income and
Presence or Absence of Rail or
Subway Service (Census Tract
Averages)

High income—no rail

High income—rail

Middle income—no rail

Middle income—rail

low income—rail

Low income—no rail

High income—subway

Middle income—subway

Low income—subway

Median family income
in census tract ($1969)
High = $15,000 (upper 20%)
Middle = $11,000 (Middle 60%)
Low = $8,000 (Lower 20%)
All curves assume household
size of 1.9 persons over 16;
actual range 1.0 to 2.7. The
length of the curves is indicative of the range of observed
values.

Net Residential Density Dwelling Units Per Acre

Sources: U.S. Census and Regional Plan Association

residential areas, the three rail curves do not have much meaning at densities above 10 dwellings per acre.

Much more important is the impact of rapid transit* on auto ownership at each income or density level. At a suburban density of 5 dwellings per acre, rapid transit reduces autos per household in census tracts near stations by anywhere from 36 percent for the high income group to 38 percent for the low income group. At urban densities around 50 dwellings per acre, the reduction for both is about 30 percent. In absolute terms, the reduction amounts to between 0.4 and 0.5 autos per household at suburban densities and around 0.2 to 0.3 at high urban densities. Thus *the effect of a rapid transit station on auto ownership in adjoining census tracts can be equivalent to that of more than a tenfold increase in residential density.*

Also, the effect of rapid transit service is to reduce differences in auto ownership by density, as evident from the flatter slope of the three auto ownership curves in subway territory. Rather than being primarily a function of density, auto ownership in this territory becomes primarily a function of household size—predominantly, families with several adults have autos when rapid transit service is available—and secondarily, and nearly as important, one of income.

Apart from the immediate purpose for which these relationships are presented here—which is estimating the choice of mode—they are also important for the accounting of benefits that accrue from rapid transit. Whether measured in terms of money costs for the households involved, or in terms of environmental costs, the savings implied here are very substantial. Of course, they only pertain to an area roughly half of which lies within 2,000 feet of transit stations, but in the New York Region, over one quarter of all the census tracts investigated fit that description.

For purposes of explaining the choice of auto versus transit, the average autos per household figure determined for a census tract by the equations in Exhibit 2.9 is but a first step. Individual households in that census tract will own different numbers of autos depending on the kinds of trips they make. If they usually travel to high density places where public transit is convenient and auto access is difficult, they will tend to have fewer autos. Thus the nonresidential density of a habitual destination also affects the number of autos owned by a household at the place of residence.

The different levels of auto ownership sort themselves out in different origin-destination streams. In a stream of people travelling from a low density area to a high density downtown, the auto ownership will be lower than the average in the neighborhood which they come from. In a stream of people who are reverse-commuting from a high density residential area to a low density industrial area in the suburbs, the auto ownership will be much higher than the average for their neighborhood. An illustration of the adjustments necessary to translate auto ownership at the place of residence into auto ownership in an origin-destination stream is presented in Exhibit 2.10 for work trips to downtowns and to spread clusters.

On the vertical scale, the Exhibit shows factors by which the average auto ownership per household at the place of residence must be multiplied to obtain the ownership in an origin-destination stream going from any residential density listed on the horizontal scale to selected nonresidential densities characterized by the different curves.

---

* Defined here to include, along with New York City Transit Authority routes, those of Port Authority Trans-Hudson, Staten Island Rapid Transit, and Newark light rail.

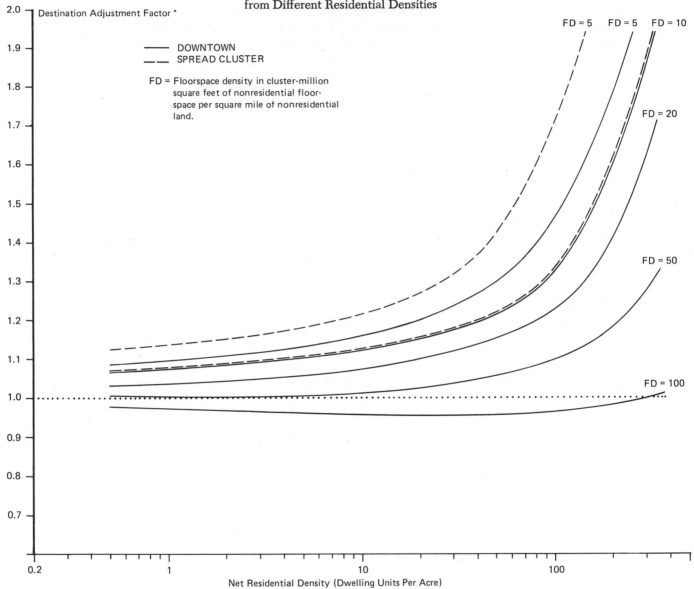

EXHIBIT 2.10

The Influence of Nonresidential
Density at the Destination on Auto
Ownership in Travel Streams to Work
from Different Residential Densities

Destination Adjustment Factor *

———— DOWNTOWN
— — — SPREAD CLUSTER

FD = Floorspace density in cluster-million
square feet of nonresidential floorspace per square mile of nonresidential
land.

FD = 5   FD = 5   FD = 10

FD = 20

FD = 50

FD = 100

Net Residential Density (Dwelling Units Per Acre)

*Number by which average ownership per household as shown in Exhibit 2.9 at the place of residence must be multiplied to obtain auto
ownership in a stream destined for a nonresidential cluster of given density.

Source: Regional Plan Association

It can be seen that the adjustments at low residential densities are quite small. They do, however, become important in the case of reverse commuting from high residential densities. Generally, *travel to the highest density downtowns has a mildly depressing effect on the auto ownership of those who make the trips, while travel to low density nonresidential destinations requires substantially above-average auto ownership,* given the average levels portrayed earlier in Exhibit 2.9.

However, these fractional averages are not easily related to the choice of mode. In reality households will own either no cars, or one car, or two or more cars, and the choice of mode of those who own no cars will be quite different from those who do. Fortunately, the relationship between average number of cars per household in an area and the distribution of zero-car, one-car, and two-or-more-car households is highly predictable. The average figure explains anywhere from 86 to 99 percent of the variation in the proportions of the three household classes, as Exhibit 2.11 shows. The curves in that Exhibit indicate what percent of the households will own what number of autos at what average level of ownership. They are derived from 1970 data in over 4,200 census tracts in the New York Region. The hatching around the curves indicates the range of observations by previous researchers, based on data from the early 1960s in the New York Region, as well as in San Francisco, Baltimore, and southeast Connecticut.

An average ownership level of 0.5 autos per household means that roughly 55 percent of the households have no cars, about 40 percent have one car, and some 5 percent have two or more. Similarly, an average ownership level of 1.5 autos per household indicates that only about 5 percent are without cars, while the remaining 95 percent are split about evenly among one-car owners and two-or-more-car owners.

CHOICE OF TRANSIT RELATED TO AUTO OWNERSHIP, DENSITY, AND TRANSIT SERVICE

With a grasp of what proportion of travellers in any travel stream originating in a residential area of known density, income, household size, and transit service come from zero-car, one-car, and two-or-more-car households, we can focus on the choice of auto versus public transit by these three different groups in relation to the density of *nonresidential* development at the destination end. The analysis will be broken down into two parts: work trips, and trips for non-work purposes. It will differ in the amount of detail available for these two categories of trips. For work trips, the dominant component of the public transit market, sufficient detail could be developed to show the impact of both transit coverage (i.e., proximity to a transit stop) and service frequency. For non-work trips, this kind of detail was unavailable and the analysis deals only with residential and nonresidential density at the two ends of the trip. For both kinds of trips a distinction is made between nonresidential destinations that are downtown-oriented and those which represent spread clusters of nonresidential activity.

Work trips are analyzed on the basis of unpublished special tabulations from the 1970 Census worker file, augmented with development densities from Regional Plan Association's data bank and service coverage and frequency data specially assembled. The basic units of observation are origin-destination streams between residential areas of varying size (groups of census tracts) and 56 nonresidential clusters portrayed in Exhibits 7.3 and 7.5. Approximately 1,500 such origin-destination streams, which include over 2 million trips, are analyzed. The trips do not represent the universe of all work trips to the nonresiden-

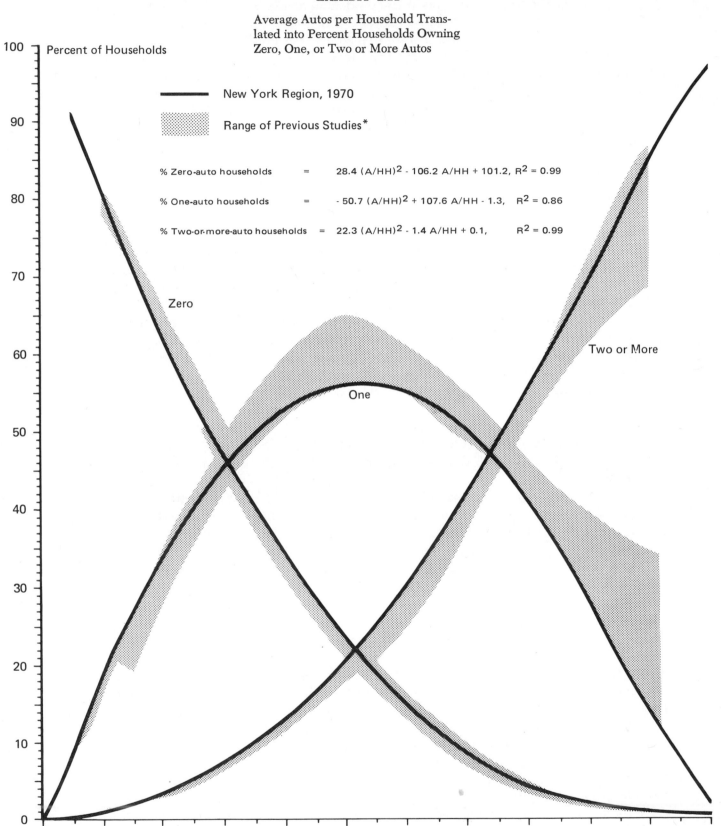

EXHIBIT 2.11

Average Autos per Household Translated into Percent Households Owning Zero, One, or Two or More Autos

100 ── Percent of Households

New York Region, 1970

Range of Previous Studies*

% Zero-auto households $= 28.4 (A/HH)^2 - 106.2\ A/HH + 101.2,\ R^2 = 0.99$

% One-auto households $= -50.7 (A/HH)^2 + 107.6\ A/HH - 1.3,\ R^2 = 0.86$

% Two-or-more-auto households $= 22.3 (A/HH)^2 - 1.4\ A/HH + 0.1,\ R^2 = 0.99$

Zero

Two or More

One

Average Autos Per Household

Source: U.S. Census

tial clusters in question. The coding of many trips was not fine-grained enough to assign them to the quite narrowly delineated nonresidential clusters. The "percent transit use" calculated applies to the sum of all trips by auto and public transit, the latter defined as including bus, subway, commuter rail, taxi (except in Manhattan, where taxi trips were classified as auto trips), and "other" trips, a large part of which represents trips by ferry. Walk and work-at-home trips are not included in the calculation.

A summary of the trips by different modes by auto ownership group included in the origin-destination streams is given at the top of Exhibit 2.12. This is followed by six equations which relate percent transit use to nonresidential density and to three measures of transit service for two types of development—downtowns versus spread clusters—and for three groups of auto ownership. Selected statistical measures of these equations are listed to the right, as well as in parentheses under the coefficients.

The first thing that should be noted is the mean value of percent using transit in each of the three auto ownership groups. For trips to downtowns, it is 76.8 percent for zero-car households, 28.9 percent for one-car households, and 16.2 percent for two-or-more-car households. For trips to spread clusters, the respective percentages of transit use are 71.1, 20.3, and 8.5. It is obvious that auto ownership makes by far the biggest difference in the choice of mode. We should recall that the auto ownership considered here has already been influenced by nonresidential density at the destination and by rail or subway service at the origin, variables which we are dealing with once more.

In view of the huge difference in transit use *between* different auto ownership groups, the variation *within* each group, which the equations in Exhibit 2.12 deal with, is not too great. Nonresidential density and transit service explain anywhere from 13.4 to 31.8 percent of the variation in transit use within each auto ownership group. The dominant influence is that of nonresidential density at the destination end. The three service variables are less important. They are defined as subway coverage (percent of residential area within 2,000 feet of a rapid transit station), bus frequency (average number of buses per hour during the two morning peak hours on routes serving the origin-destination stream studied), and rail service (the presence or absence of commuter rail as an option for the origin-destination stream in question). One might add that in developing the equations, several other measures of public transit service were examined, such as bus coverage (percent of residential area within 1,000 feet of bus lines serving the origin-destination stream), bus-to-subway coverage (same for a bus line connecting to a subway line), and rail coverage (percent of residential area within 2,000 feet of a commuter rail station). None of these measures proved to be statistically significant. In fact, of the service measures used, only subway coverage shows up consistently in all six equations.

To visualize the impact of nonresidential density and of the three service variables on the choice of public transportation for trips to work by each auto ownership group, Exhibits 2.13 through 2.16 portray the relationships graphically. Exhibit 2.13 shows the base condition, with no measures of service included. For zero-car households and downtown-oriented work trips, the transit use increases from about 60 to 90 percent as nonresidential density at the destination increases from about 10 million square feet per square mile to 100 million per square mile. The former represents small downtowns with about 5 million square feet of nonresidential floorspace, the latter represents the largest clusters, such as Lower or Midtown Manhattan. For one-car households, the comparable increase in percent transit is from about 12 to 45 percent, and for two-or-more-car households, from 2 to about 25 percent. Transit use to spread clusters falls off much more steeply than to downtowns in the case of zero-car households. This is so because these households are sensitive to the

EXHIBIT 2.12

Analysis of Choice of Public Transportation for Trips to Work in 56 Nonresidential Clusters in the New York Region in 1970 by Auto Ownership, Density and Transit Service

	Total trips to work with known destinations in 56 nonresidential clusters							Trips not studied	
	By Auto	By Bus	By Subway	By Rail	By Taxi	Other	Subtotal Studied	Walk	Work at home
From 0-car households	23,733	126,547	446,908	9,303	12,585	3,407	622,483	66,289	7,549
	3.8%	20.3%	71.8%	1.5%	2.0%	0.5%	100%		
From 1-car households	311,177	118,151	382,399	89,281	6,558	10,151	917,717	35,911	5,436
	33.9%	12.9%	41.7%	9.7%	0.7%	1.1%	100%		
From 2 or more car households	343,734	40,633	70,350	88,279	1,397	4,724	549,117	9,445	2,697
	62.6%	7.4%	12.8%	16.1%	0.3%	0.9%	100%		
Total by mode	678,644	285,331	899,657	186,863	20,540	18,282	2,089,317	111,645	15,682
	32.5%	13.7%	43.1%	8.9%	1.0%	1.9%	100%		

Equations relating percent transit use for work trips to nonresidential floorspace density and transit service

	Statistical measures of equations			
	R^2	Sd	$\overline{y}$	N

(1) Trips to downtowns from 0-car households

$$\% \text{ transit} = 30.73 \log \text{NFD} + 0.246 \text{ SC} + 11.92 \log \text{BF} \ldots \ldots +28.03$$
$$(35) \qquad (23) \qquad (19)$$

$R^2 = 0.134$, Sd $= 31.61$, $\overline{y} = 76.75$, N $= 797$

(2) Trips to downtowns from 1-car households

$$\% \text{ transit} = 32.32 \log \text{NFD} + 0.264 \text{ SC} + 5.97 \log \text{BF} + 7.62 \text{ RS} - 20.01$$
$$(99) \qquad (49) \qquad (11) \qquad (26)$$

$R^2 = 0.201$, Sd $= 25.09$, $\overline{y} = 28.85$, N $= 1{,}001$

(3) Trips to downtowns from 2-or-more-car households

$$\% \text{ transit} = 23.00 \log \text{NFD} + 0.176 \text{ SC} + 9.07 \log \text{BF} + 7.11 \text{ RS} - 21.16$$
$$(62) \qquad (19) \qquad (28) \qquad (27)$$

$R^2 = 0.174$, Sd $= 22.16$, $\overline{y} = 16.17$, N $= 942$

(4) Trips to spread clusters from 0-car households

$$\% \text{ transit} = 63.82 \log \text{NFD} + 0.407 \text{ SC} + 1.169 \text{ BF} - 11.05$$
$$(31) \qquad (38) \qquad (9.4)$$

$R^2 = 0.318$, Sd $= 36.44$, $\overline{y} = 71.09$, N $= 369$

(5) Trips to spread clusters from 1-car households

$$\% \text{ transit} = 33.10 \log \text{NFD} + 0.300 \text{ SC} \ldots \ldots -19.37$$
$$(32) \qquad (64)$$

$R^2 = 0.289$, Sd $= 22.63$, $\overline{y} = 20.27$, N $= 486$

(6) Trips to spread clusters from 2-or-more-car households

$$\% \text{ transit} = 25.70 \log \text{NFD} + 0.188 \text{ SC} + 0.663 \text{ BF} - 22.45$$
$$(31) \qquad (25) \qquad (12)$$

$R^2 = 0.263$, Sd $= 16.58$, $\overline{y} = 8.51$, N $= 414$

NFD = Nonresidential Floorspace Density, in millions of square feet per nonresidential sq.mi. (incl. adjacent streets)

SC = Subway Coverage, % of residential area within 2,000 feet of rapid transit station

BF = Bus frequency, average number of buses per hour during 2-hour morning peak period on routes serving particular origin-destination stream

RS = Rail Service, noted as 1 if commuter rail is reasonable alternative for a particular origin-destination stream, otherwise noted as 0

Figures in parentheses ( ) are F-values of the individual coefficients; coefficients with F-values less than 4 were not used as not statistically reliable

R^2 = correlation coefficient squared (proportion of variation in transit use explained)

Sd = Standard deviation (measure of dispersion around the mean value)

$\overline{y}$ = mean value of percent transit use in each category

N = number of observations (origin-destination streams) in each category

Source: Regional Plan Association

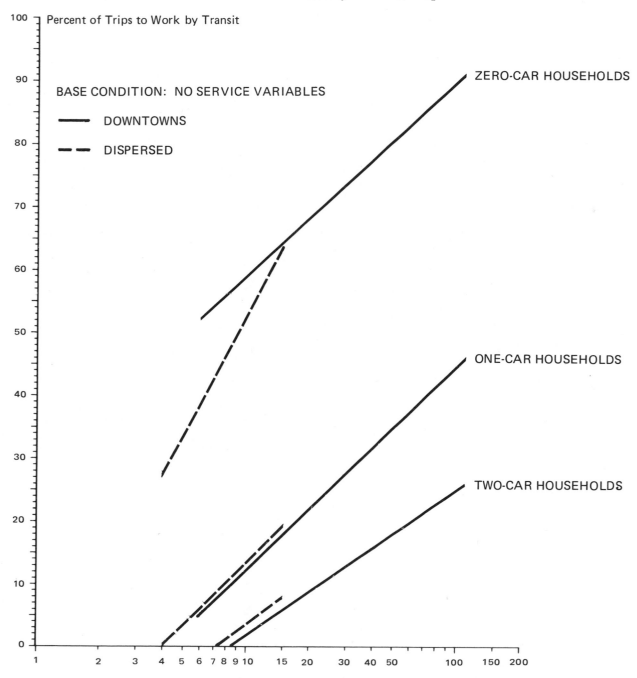

EXHIBIT 2.13

Percent Transit Use for Work Trips
Related to Nonresidential Density;
Trips to Downtowns versus Dispersed
Clusters by Auto Ownership

Nonresidential Floorspace Density (Million Square Feet Per Nonresidential Square Mile)

Source: Exhibit 2.12

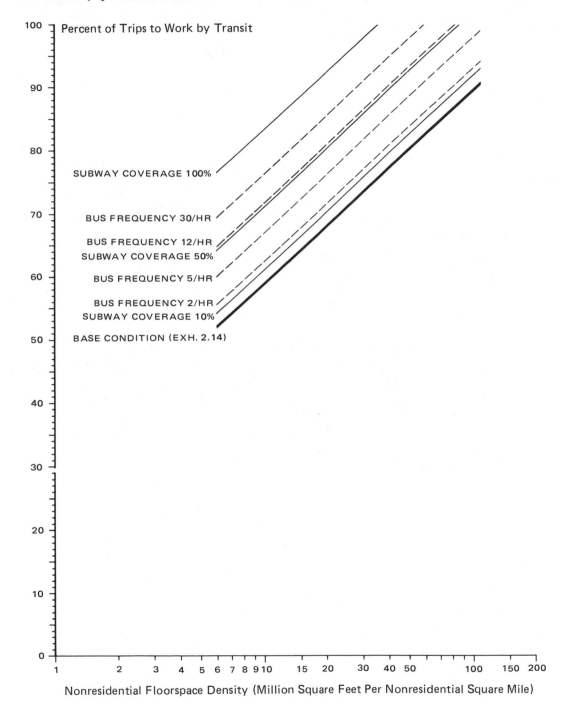

EXHIBIT 2.14

Percent Transit Use for Work Trips
Related to Nonresidential Density;
Trips to Downtowns by Zero-Car
Households, by Transit Service

Percent of Trips to Work by Transit

SUBWAY COVERAGE 100%

BUS FREQUENCY 30/HR

BUS FREQUENCY 12/HR
SUBWAY COVERAGE 50%

BUS FREQUENCY 5/HR

BUS FREQUENCY 2/HR
SUBWAY COVERAGE 10%

BASE CONDITION (EXH. 2.14)

Nonresidential Floorspace Density (Million Square Feet Per Nonresidential Square Mile)

* Proportion of area within 2,000 feet of subway station

Source: Exhibit 2.12

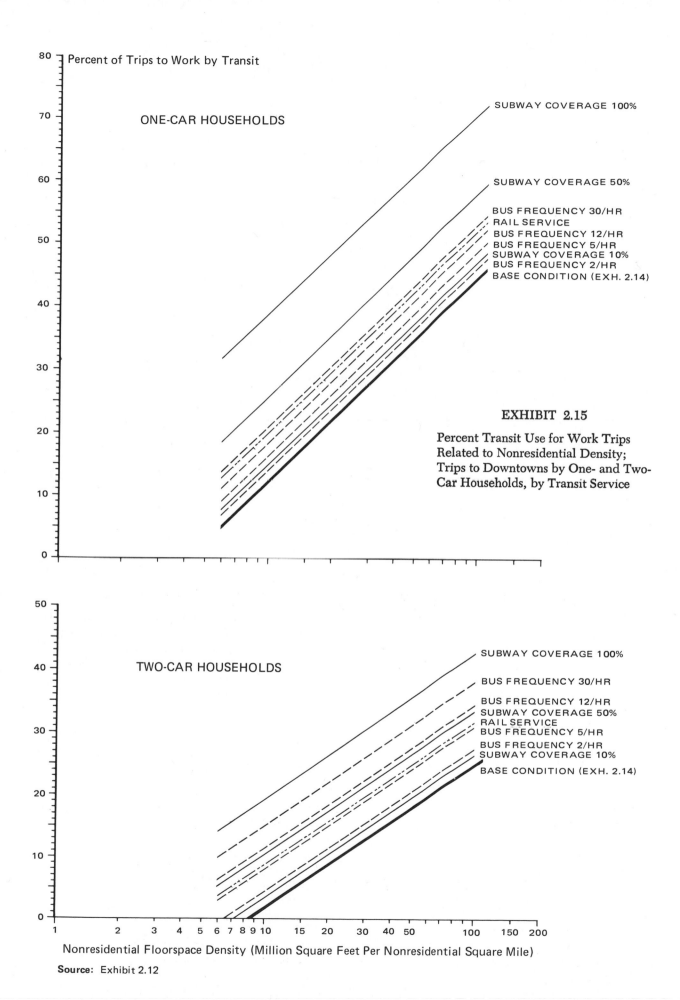

Percent of Trips to Work by Transit

ONE-CAR HOUSEHOLDS

SUBWAY COVERAGE 100%

SUBWAY COVERAGE 50%

BUS FREQUENCY 30/HR
RAIL SERVICE
BUS FREQUENCY 12/HR
BUS FREQUENCY 5/HR
SUBWAY COVERAGE 10%
BUS FREQUENCY 2/HR
BASE CONDITION (EXH. 2.14)

EXHIBIT 2.15

Percent Transit Use for Work Trips
Related to Nonresidential Density;
Trips to Downtowns by One- and Two-
Car Households, by Transit Service

TWO-CAR HOUSEHOLDS

SUBWAY COVERAGE 100%

BUS FREQUENCY 30/HR

BUS FREQUENCY 12/HR
SUBWAY COVERAGE 50%
RAIL SERVICE
BUS FREQUENCY 5/HR
BUS FREQUENCY 2/HR
SUBWAY COVERAGE 10%
BASE CONDITION (EXH. 2.14)

Nonresidential Floorspace Density (Million Square Feet Per Nonresidential Square Mile)

Source: Exhibit 2.12

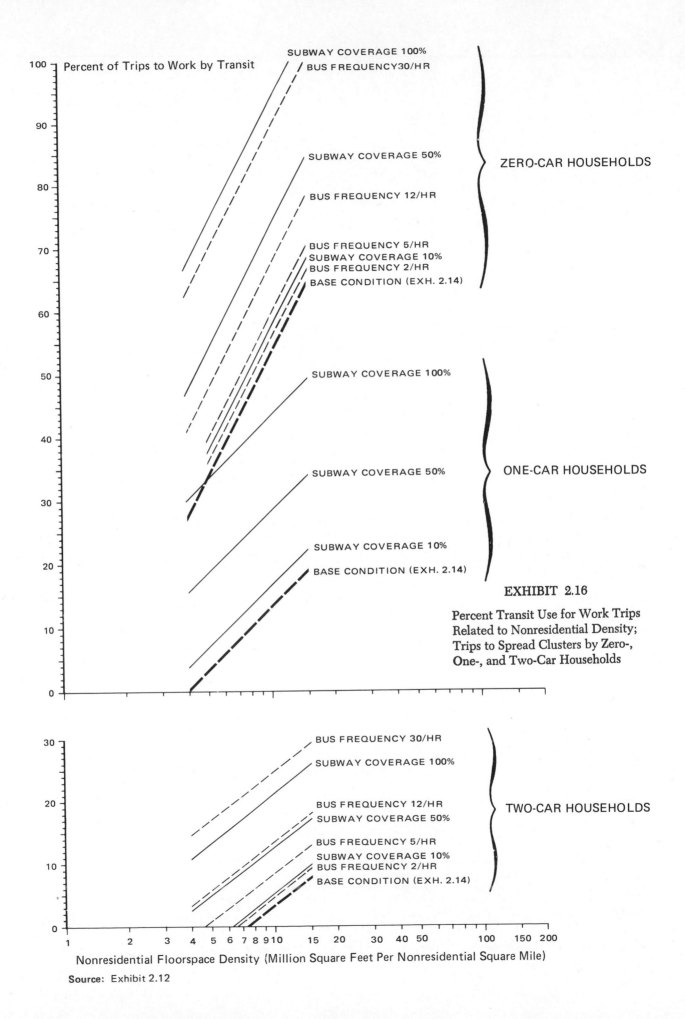

Percent of Trips to Work by Transit

SUBWAY COVERAGE 100%
BUS FREQUENCY 30/HR

SUBWAY COVERAGE 50%

BUS FREQUENCY 12/HR

BUS FREQUENCY 5/HR
SUBWAY COVERAGE 10%
BUS FREQUENCY 2/HR
BASE CONDITION (EXH. 2.14)

} ZERO-CAR HOUSEHOLDS

SUBWAY COVERAGE 100%

SUBWAY COVERAGE 50%

SUBWAY COVERAGE 10%
BASE CONDITION (EXH. 2.14)

} ONE-CAR HOUSEHOLDS

EXHIBIT 2.16

Percent Transit Use for Work Trips
Related to Nonresidential Density;
Trips to Spread Clusters by Zero-,
One-, and Two-Car Households

BUS FREQUENCY 30/HR

SUBWAY COVERAGE 100%

BUS FREQUENCY 12/HR
SUBWAY COVERAGE 50%

BUS FREQUENCY 5/HR
SUBWAY COVERAGE 10%
BUS FREQUENCY 2/HR
BASE CONDITION (EXH. 2.14)

} TWO-CAR HOUSEHOLDS

Nonresidential Floorspace Density (Million Square Feet Per Nonresidential Square Mile)

Source: Exhibit 2.12

poorer transit service in low density areas. For car-owning households, there is basically no difference in transit use to dispersed clusters, as opposed to downtowns, if their density is the same.

Exhibits 2.14 and 2.15 add different levels of subway coverage and bus frequency to the base relationship shown in Exhibit 2.13 for downtowns. Roughly speaking, at each non-residential density, each 10 percent increase in subway coverage adds 2.5 points to the percentage of workers using transit, and each doubling of bus frequency adds about 4 percentage points in the case of zero-car households. The impact on attracting public transit ridership from zero-car households is about the same if 50 percent of a residential area is within 2,000 feet of a rapid transit station (say, an 8-minute average walk), or if the bus frequency is 12 buses during the peak hour (one bus every 5 minutes).

For one-car households, proximity of rapid transit has about the same effect, but the effect of bus frequency is about half of what it was before. For two-car households, the effect of rapid transit is weaker. The generalized presence of rail service (within an area averaging perhaps 50 square miles or so) appears equivalent to a bus frequency of anywhere from 6 to 20 during the peak hour for the car-owning groups. Bus frequencies much in excess of 6 per peak hour being rare on suburban bus routes, this relationship corroborates the findings concerning the attractive power of commuter rail. Of course, detailed relationship by ownership group shown here may be conditioned by the geographic distribution of the different auto-owning groups in different transit service areas of the New York Region, and should not be taken too literally. It is the overall pattern that counts.

Exhibit 2.16 portrays the effect of subway coverage and bus frequency on trips by all three auto ownership groups to spread clusters. The notable point here is the strong effect of the service variables on transit travel by zero-car households. If a spread cluster happens to have good bus service (which may be there due to the proximity of a large downtown), the percent transit use by workers from zero-car households can increase from, say, 35 to 70. If the service is poor, more of these workers, presumably, will be seeking out car pools. The effect of service to spread clusters on car-owning households is not in any major way different from the effect of service to downtowns of comparable density.

Non-work trips are analyzed on the basis of data obtained by the 1963 Tri-State Home Interview Survey in the New York Region. This covers 53 out of the 56 nonresidential clusters used in the preceding journey-to-work analysis. However, the nature of the data—which represent a 1-percent sample in contrast to the 20-percent sample of the Census—prevents using the same procedures for investigating the choice of mode. Specifically, the influence of the service variables in small residential areas of origin cannot be reliably measured. Therefore, net residential density at the place of origin is viewed as a proxy for the quality of transit service. Moreover, the residential areas of origin are not treated individually, but are rather aggregated into some 100 ranges of residential density. The basic units of observation are origin-destination streams which emanate from these geographically diffuse areas and go to the 53 nonresidential clusters. To improve statistical reliability, origin-destination streams representing less than 3 sampled trips are omitted. The "percent transit use" calculated applies to the sum of all trips by auto and public transportation, as earlier; school bus trips are not included.

Exhibit 2.17 presents six equations which relate percent transit use for non-work trips to nonresidential density at the destination and to residential density at the origin for downtowns and spread clusters and for three groups of auto ownership. One might note that the density measures used in this case also differ from those in the journey-to-work analysis.

EXHIBIT 2.17

Analysis of Choice of Public Transportation for Non-Work Trips to 53 Nonresidential Clusters in the New York Region in 1963 by Auto Ownership and Density

Equations relating percent transit use for non-work trips to nonresidential floorspace density at the destination and residential density at the origin

			Statistical measures of the equation			
			R^2	Sd	$\overline{y}$	N
(1)	Trips to downtowns from 0-car households		0.140	23.15	83.67	214
	% transit = 19.48 log GNFD . . . . +57.56					
	(35)					
(2)	Trips to downtowns from 1-car households		0.470	31.81	37.62	417
	% transit = 36.59 log GNFD + 12.45 log RD - 23.87					
	(199) (27)					
(3)	Trips to downtowns from 2-or-more-car households		0.372	23.28	15.44	288
	% transit = 27.51 log GNFD + 6.02 log RD - 19.91					
	(127) (6.6)					
(4)	Trips to spread clusters from 0-car households		0.748	24.81	84.16	31
	% transit = ... 52.39 log RD - 26.29					
	(74)					
(5)	Trips to spread clusters from 1-car households		0.261	22.08	12.76	169
	% transit = 33.71 log GNFD . . . . + 3.43					
	(59)					
(6)	Trips to spread clusters from 2-or-more-car households		0.210	9.87	3.16	141
	% transit = 10.76 log GNFD + 5.50 log RD - 4.78					
	(13) (6.3)					

GNFD = Gross Nonresidential Floorspace Density (millions of square feet per sq.mi. of total area)

RD = Residential density (population per square mile of area in net residential use

Figures in parentheses ( ) are F-values of the individual coefficients; coefficients with F-values less than 4 were not used as not statistically reliable

R^2 = correlation coefficient squared (proportion of variation in transit use explained)

Sd = Standard deviation (measure of dispersion around the mean value)

$\overline{y}$ = mean value of percent transit use in each category

N = number of observations (origin-destination streams) in each category

Source: Regional Plan Association

They are converted into units used generally throughout this book in the two graphic Exhibits that follow.

As in the case of the trips to work, the first feature to be noted is the mean value of percent using transit in each of the three auto ownership groups. For trips to downtowns, it is 83.7 percent for zero-car households, 36.7 percent for one-car households and 15.4 percent for two-or-more-car households. For trips to spread clusters, the respective percentages of transit use by auto ownership are 84.2, 12.8, and 3.2. These 1963 proportions of transit use for non-work trips are similar to the ones determined earlier for 1970 trips to work. Because of the huge difference in transit use between different auto ownership groups, the variation within each group is again a subdued one.

The relationships described by the equations in Exhibit 2.17 are displayed in Exhibit 2.18, which deals with trips to downtowns, and Exhibit 2.19, which deals with trips to spread clusters. In both cases, the density of the nonresidential cluster has the greatest impact on the choice of mode by one-car households. These are the households that have to do most of the choosing. The choice of mode by zero-car households and two-or-more-car households is more predetermined, and varies less with density at the destination end.

Thus, for trips to downtowns, an increase in nonresidential floorspace density from 10 to 100 million square feet per square mile adds 24 percentage points to the percent using transit in the case of zero-car households, 42 percentage points in the case of one-car households, and 32 percentage points in the case of two-or-more-car households. By contrast, a tenfold increase in residential density at the origin has no effect at all on the choice of mode by carless households, and adds only 13 and 6 percentage points, respectively, to the percent transit use by one-car households and two-car households.

For trips to spread clusters, nonresidential floorspace density has no effect on transit use among zero-car households, a very strong effect on travellers from one-car households, and a mild one on those from two-or-more-car households. By contrast, within the framework shown, residential density is the sole determinant of the proportion of transit users among zero-car households for travel to spread clusters. Residential density has no effect at all on that proportion among one-car households, and a small one in the case of two-car households.

Though the contrast among the three auto ownership groups is sharper, the relationships are in essence similar to those portrayed earlier for work trips, if residential density is viewed as a proxy for transit service. For example, for work trips to spread clusters, transit service had a disproportionately strong influence on the choice of mode by zero-car households. We now find that for nonwork trips to spread clusters, residential density is the only significant factor influencing the choice of mode by zero-car households. These trips are sensitive to even small increases in residential density—read transit service—because the alternative is some cumbersome shared ride arrangement. Analogously, transit service to spread clusters had a weak effect on work trips by one-car households, so much so that bus frequency failed to be statistically significant. We now find non-work trips to spread clusters by one-car households to be unrelated to residential density, and only related to the nonresidential density of the cluster. The latter is a measure of the cost and difficulty of parking which restrain auto use as long as some transit service is present. The generally more affluent two-car households are less restrained by high nonresidential density but do display some sensitivity to the quality of service (or to residential density) on work trips or non-work trips. Generalizing, one can say that *people with autos available will choose to drive, unless restrained by an obstacle such as high nonresidential density; the positive features of good transit service have relatively little effect on them.*

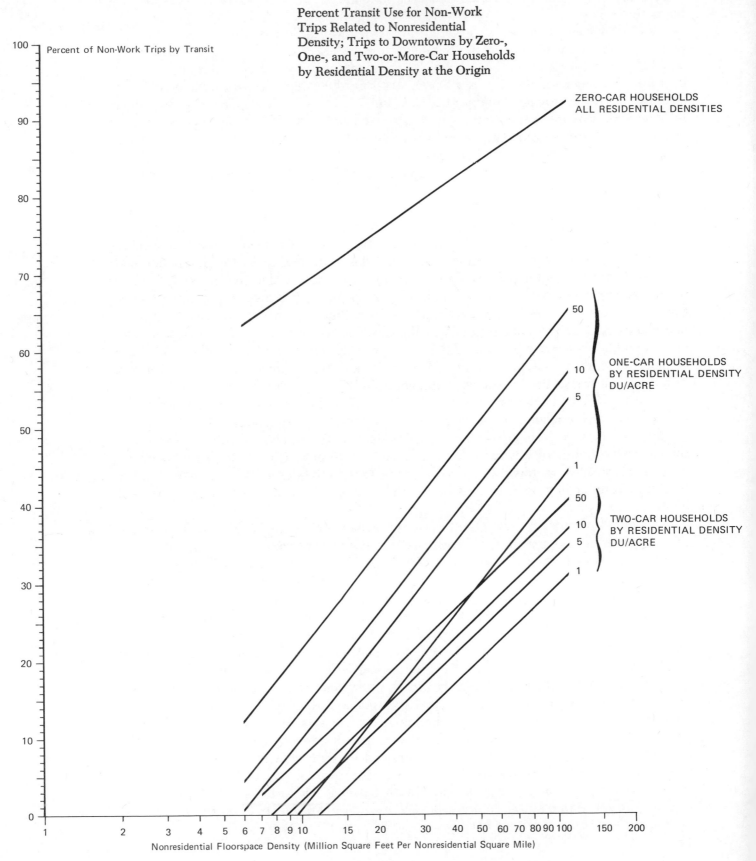

EXHIBIT 2.18

Percent Transit Use for Non-Work
Trips Related to Nonresidential
Density; Trips to Downtowns by Zero-,
One-, and Two-or-More-Car Households
by Residential Density at the Origin

Percent of Non-Work Trips by Transit

ZERO-CAR HOUSEHOLDS
ALL RESIDENTIAL DENSITIES

50
10
5
1

ONE-CAR HOUSEHOLDS
BY RESIDENTIAL DENSITY
DU/ACRE

50
10
5
1

TWO-CAR HOUSEHOLDS
BY RESIDENTIAL DENSITY
DU/ACRE

Nonresidential Floorspace Density (Million Square Feet Per Nonresidential Square Mile)

Source: Exhibit 2.17

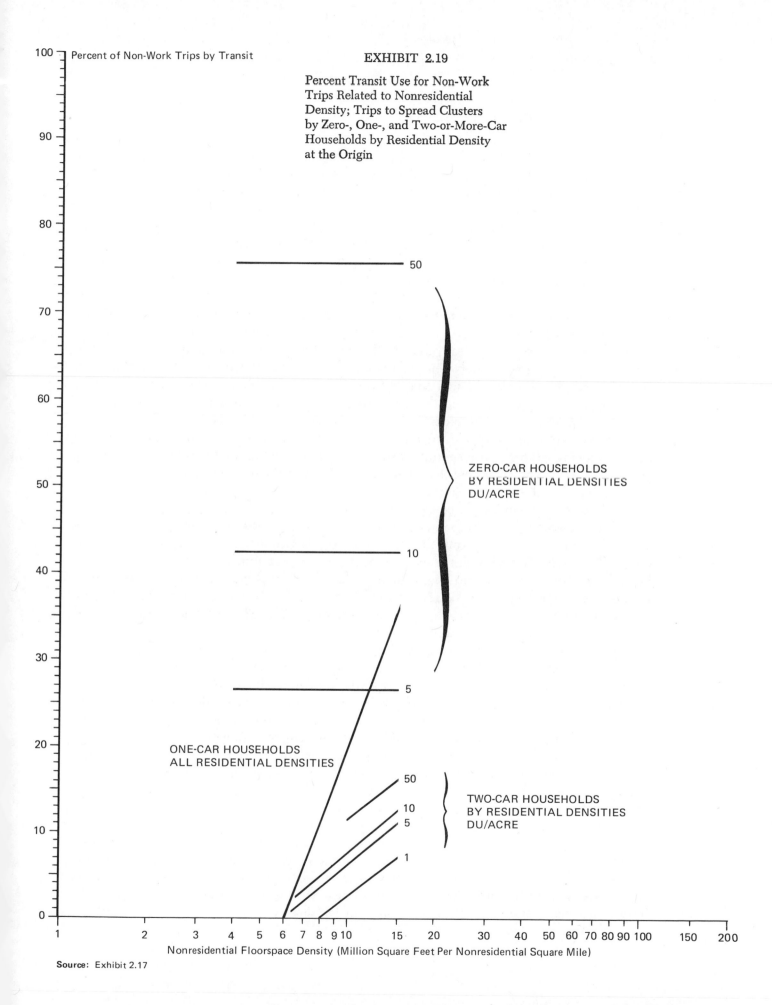

Percent of Non-Work Trips by Transit

EXHIBIT 2.19

Percent Transit Use for Non-Work
Trips Related to Nonresidential
Density; Trips to Spread Clusters
by Zero-, One-, and Two-or-More-Car
Households by Residential Density
at the Origin

50

ZERO-CAR HOUSEHOLDS
BY RESIDENTIAL DENSITIES
DU/ACRE

10

5

ONE-CAR HOUSEHOLDS
ALL RESIDENTIAL DENSITIES

50

10

5

TWO-CAR HOUSEHOLDS
BY RESIDENTIAL DENSITIES
DU/ACRE

1

Nonresidential Floorspace Density (Million Square Feet Per Nonresidential Square Mile)

Source: Exhibit 2.17

TRIPS TO NONRESIDENTIAL AREAS
AS A TRANSIT MARKET

Having determined how each of the three auto ownership groups will choose public transit or the auto depending on the density of development at the destination and on the level of public transit service (or its proxy, residential density at the residence end), we can estimate what percent of total travel between any residential area and any nonresidential destination is likely to occur by public transit. The only remaining question is what total number of trips this percentage should be applied to. Obviously, this is a key question, for the viability of different transit modes depends not so much on their share of the market as on the absolute number of passengers carried.

Estimating the total number of trips between two places has been one of the central issues of travel analysis for more than half a century. The different analytic procedures developed—ranging from the traditional gravity model to subsequent opportunity models to more refined techniques such as direct traffic estimation or econometric demand analysis—generally agree that travel between two places depends on a) the amount of activity at each of the places, b) the cost of travelling between them, c) people's propensity to incur that cost, and d) the degree to which other competing places may capture some of the trips. The main difference between the older and the newer models is that while the former generally viewed the total number of trips to be distributed as fixed, the newer ones build the travel-inducing effects of transportation supply (as in the case of direct traffic estimation) or even of the social and economic characteristics of the travellers (as in econometric models) into the trip distribution procedure.

All of these techniques require very large amounts of data; most of them also require an idealized transportation network, along which the trips are distributed. Resources at hand frequently do not permit this scale of effort, particularly if one only aims for a generalized estimate. To attain that, a short-cut method of ascertaining the total number of trips between a residential area and a nonresidential cluster is used here. It relies on the empirical distribution of trips as it exists in a large and heterogeneous area, the New York Region, and is based on the Tri-State Home Interview Survey of 1963. The limitations of the method should be spelled out in advance.

First, it is not aimed at estimating all urban trips, but only those by mechanized modes from residential to nonresidential areas. Together with the return trips, this category includes roughly 75 percent of all urban trips, the remainder being trips from residences to other residences, and from one nonresidential area to another. The residence to nonresidence trips are viewed here as the primary market for public transportation.

Second, of all the nonresidential land use in the New York Region, only the 53 nonresidential clusters discussed earlier are investigated. Because they reflect pretty much the full range of nonresidential densities and cluster sizes, one may assume that the relationships hold true for much of the other nonresidential use as well; however, trips to nonresidential areas outside the specified clusters are not dealt with explicitly.

Third, straight line distance between a residential area and a nonresidential cluster is used as a measure of travel "cost" between two places, even though it is recognized that travel time is by far the dominant component of the perceived cost of travel. However, the time needed to traverse a unit of distance varies in a complex manner depending on mode, type of facility, surrounding density of development, trip length, and time of day; given the resources at hand, it was not possible to account for these complexities at the stage of estimating total trips. Rather, a distribution of these variables as it existed in the New York Region in 1963 is subsumed in trip attenuation rates over simple geographic distance.

Fourth, the attenuation also subsumes the declining propensity to incur the cost of travel as the cost of travel, or distance from the nonresidential cluster in this case, increases.

Fifth, the trip rates are "fixed," not responsive to differences in the supply of travel facilities or to changes in income or other characteristics of the travellers. These, such as they existed in the New York Region in 1963, are likewise built into the distribution. This fixed character of total travel demand is not a major problem for trips to work—the dominant component of the transit market—since their number is pretty much fixed by the number of workers. For non-work trips, most of the travel demand induced by rising transportation supply and by rising income has been for social and recreational trips to widely dispersed destinations, and as such is in the domain of the auto. However, the evidence presented in Chapter 1 does indicate that new transit facilities also attract a substantial component of newly induced traffic. To the extent that the method shown only allows an estimate of the *diversion* of existing travel to transit, the *induced* component has to be estimated exogenously.

With these caveats, the method of estimating total trips to nonresidential concentrations is as follows. Total nonresidential floorspace in a cluster is used as a measure of trip attraction. To account for differences in trip attraction by different types of floorspace, the nonresidential clusters are classified into three groups: downtown-oriented clusters, spread clusters of mixed use, and retail-oriented spread clusters (those which include major shopping centers). To conform to the analysis of the choice of mode, trips to nonresidential clusters are separated into work trips and non-work trips. The rates of trip production in residential areas are calculated per worker in the former case, and per resident in the latter. These rates of work trips per worker and non-work trips per resident to nonresidential clusters of different size and composition are calculated for each concentric ring of geographic distance.

Four empirical distributions of work trips per worker destined to a nonresidential cluster from concentric rings around it are plotted in Exhibit 2.20. The two heavy lines illustrate the effect of even a moderate increase in cluster size: New Brunswick, N.J., four times the size of Ridgewood, attracts more trips per worker at every distance, and from longer distances. The sharp attenuation of trips with increasing distance is also instructive: at a distance of 5 miles from each center about one tenth the number of trips per worker are destined to it as at a distance of 1 mile, and at a distance of 10 miles, about one hundredth.

The two lighter lines illustrate a different phenomenon: they compare Maspeth and Hicksville, two nonresidential clusters of similar size but widely different trip attenuation patterns. Hicksville attracts trips at a higher rate over longer distances primarily because it is less influenced by the proximity of Manhattan, only 4 miles from Maspeth but 25 miles from Hicksville. Clearly, the accounting of competing destinations cannot be left out of even a short-cut trip estimating method; in the New York Region, the Manhattan Central Business District is the overriding competitor for trips that might otherwise be destined to another nonresidential concentration. However, with distance to Manhattan taken into account, the trip attenuation rates of the different nonresidential cluster groups (downtown-oriented, spread with mixed use, and spread retail-oriented) display broadly parallel patterns which can be summarized statistically.

This is done in the six equations represented in Exhibit 2.21. The rather unusual form of the equations was arrived at as best approximating the types of empirical curves illustrated in Exhibit 2.20. It can be seen that the three variables of total nonresidential floorspace in a cluster, the straight-line distance to the cluster, and straight-line distance to Man-

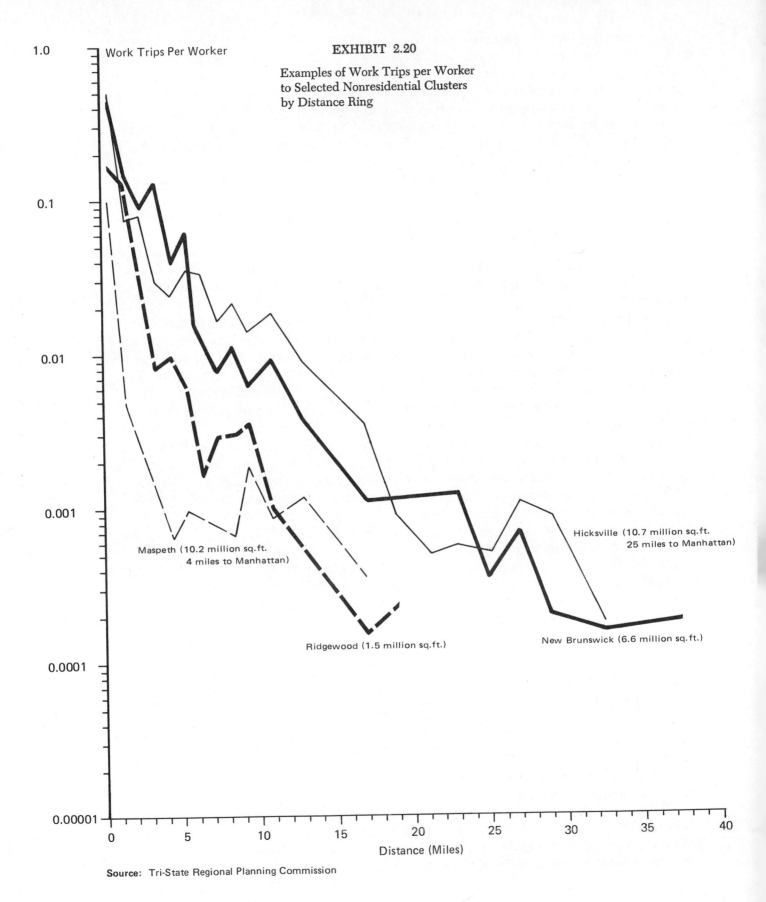

EXHIBIT 2.20

Examples of Work Trips per Worker
to Selected Nonresidential Clusters
by Distance Ring

Work Trips Per Worker

Maspeth (10.2 million sq.ft.
4 miles to Manhattan)

Ridgewood (1.5 million sq.ft.)

Hicksville (10.7 million sq.ft.
25 miles to Manhattan)

New Brunswick (6.6 million sq.ft.)

Distance (Miles)

Source: Tri-State Regional Planning Commission

EXHIBIT 2.21

Per-Worker and per-Capita Trip Attraction Rates to Nonresidential Clusters Related to Cluster Size, Distance from the Cluster and Distance from Manhattan, for Three Cluster Types, Work Trips and Nonwork Trips

Equation form: $Y = 10^{-10^{-K}(logF^{-b_1} \times D^{-b_2} \times M^{-b_3})}$

where $Y =$ trips per worker for work trips or trips per capita for non-work trips
$F =$ non-residential floorspace, in thousands of square feet,
$D =$ distance from origin to NRC in miles,
$M =$ distance from NRC to Columbus Circle in miles,
$b_1, b_2, b_3 =$ coefficients of regression,
$K =$ constant of regression,
$R^2 =$ coefficient of determination
$N =$ number of data observations

Work Trips

Dependent variable

Work trips per Worker from Residential Areas

Nonresidential Cluster Type	Downtown Oriented	Spread with Mixed use	Retail oriented spread
b_1	2.775(284)	1.650(97)	1.101(21)
b_2	-0.488(883)	-0.391(564)	-0.420(428)
b_3	0.119(28)	0.170(39)	0.161(17)
K	-1.656	-1.162	-0.829
R^2	0.713	0.655	0.723
N	438	325	171

Non-work Trips per capita from residential area

	Downtown Oriented	Spread with Mixed use	Retail oriented spread
b_1	1.562(110)	1.305(55)	1.197(7)
b_2	-0.538(1308)	-0.476(757)	-0.641(291)
b_3	0.122(30)	0.192(46)	0.175(6)
K	-0.933	-0.999	-0.647
R^2	0.758	0.711	0.636
N	438	325	171

Note: F—levels in parentheses

Source: Regional Plan Association

hattan explain anywhere from 64 to 76 percent of the variation in trips per worker or trips per capita destined to a given nonresidential cluster. This is quite a respectable degree of correlation, even for more refined and complex models. To facilitate the use of the unwieldy equations, six nomographs have been constructed which are presented in the Appendix.

If both sides of each of the equations are multiplied by the number of workers living in an area (or by the residential population, in the case of non-work trips), then trips from a residential area to a nonresidential cluster are a function of the number of workers in a residential area (or its population, in the case of non-work trips), the nonresidential floor-space at the destination, the distance between them, and the competition from Manhattan. In essence we have here, in a short-cut way, all the elements of a traditional trip distribution model.

In the last two exhibits, the influence of the various variables on trip rates is illustrated. Exhibit 2.22 shows how distance to a nonresidential cluster and cluster size influence trips to work and non-work trips to downtown-oriented clusters which are independent of Manhattan. The influence of Manhattan can be considered to become negligible at a distance of 60 miles; this distance can be used when applying the equations outside the New York Region. It can be seen once more that trip rates decline precipitously with increasing distance from a downtown. Thus, even for a medium-sized downtown of 25 million square feet, trips per person at a distance of 7 miles are one tenth of what they are at a distance of 1 mile, and drop to one hundredth of that value at a distance of 18 miles. The ability of the larger downtowns to pull in trips from longer distances is also clearly seen.

In Exhibit 2.23 the influence of the distance from Manhattan and of the different land use compositions of the nonresidential clusters on trip rates is illustrated. The influence of Manhattan is illustrated with respect to spread clusters of mixed use, which mostly represent highway-oriented development including industrial, commercial, and some office use. As distance from Manhattan increases, so do trips per capita from any nonresidential area to these clusters. For example, at a distance of 35 miles from any cluster, the trips per resident worker destined to that cluster are roughly 40 times greater if the residential area in question is 60 miles from Manhattan, compared to one that is only 5 miles from Manhattan.

The differences in trip attraction rates depending on cluster type are portrayed in the lower part of Exhibit 2.23; the cluster size is assumed to be 5 million square feet, and the distance to Manhattan 60 miles. It can be seen that the trip rate per capita is plausibly higher for the retail-oriented clusters, but that the contrast between them and either downtowns or spread clusters of mixed use diminishes with increasing distance, an indication of the relatively short length of the shopping trips. By contrast, the trip rate to the clusters of mixed use attenuates more slowly than that of the others at distances of over 25 miles, reflecting some of the very long trips that the spread industrial and office patterns generate. At a distance of 40 miles from a nonresidential concentration, twice as many trips per capita will be destined to it if it is a spread cluster than if it is a downtown. Conversely, at a distance of 2 miles, the trip rate will be 1.4 times greater in the case of a downtown.

The potential for public transportation, of course, is created not by trip rates per capita, but rather by the absolute densities of trips in an area. The density of trips is a product of the trip rate and the residential density (or resident worker density, in the case of work trips). What the steep attenuation of trip rates demonstrated here suggests is that *the public transportation payoff from increased residential densities will be the greatest in the immediate vicinity of a downtown or another nonresidential cluster.* For example, two miles away from a downtown of 25 million square feet, a sixfold increase in residential density—

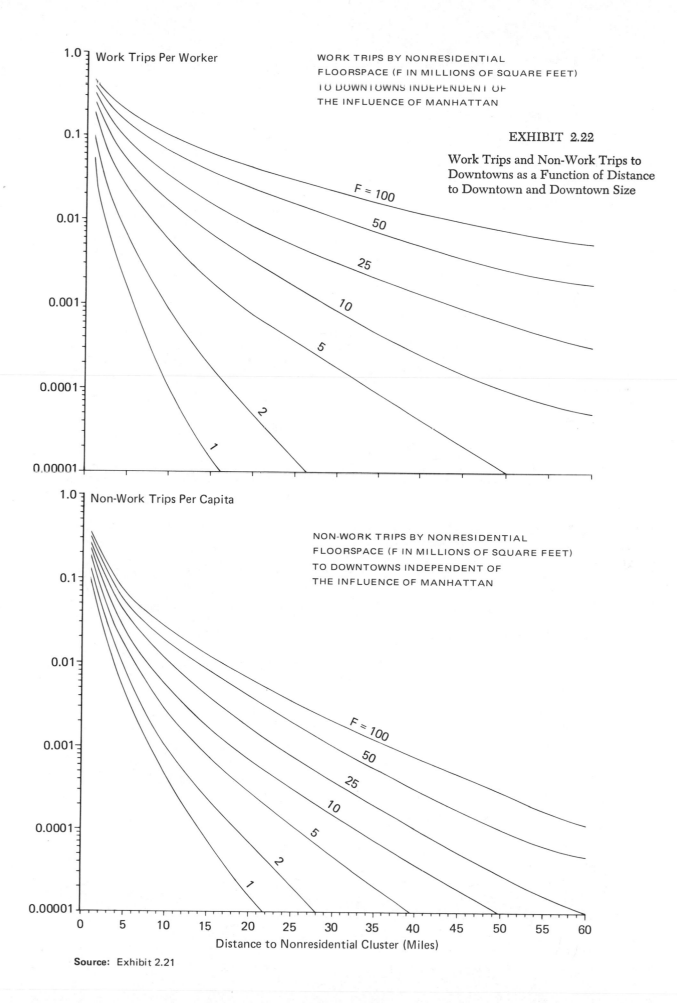

Work Trips Per Worker

WORK TRIPS BY NONRESIDENTIAL
FLOORSPACE (F IN MILLIONS OF SQUARE FEET)
TO DOWNTOWNS INDEPENDENT OF
THE INFLUENCE OF MANHATTAN

EXHIBIT 2.22

Work Trips and Non-Work Trips to
Downtowns as a Function of Distance
to Downtown and Downtown Size

F = 100
50
25
10
5
2
1

Non-Work Trips Per Capita

NON-WORK TRIPS BY NONRESIDENTIAL
FLOORSPACE (F IN MILLIONS OF SQUARE FEET)
TO DOWNTOWNS INDEPENDENT OF
THE INFLUENCE OF MANHATTAN

F = 100
50
25
10
5
2
1

Distance to Nonresidential Cluster (Miles)

Source: Exhibit 2.21

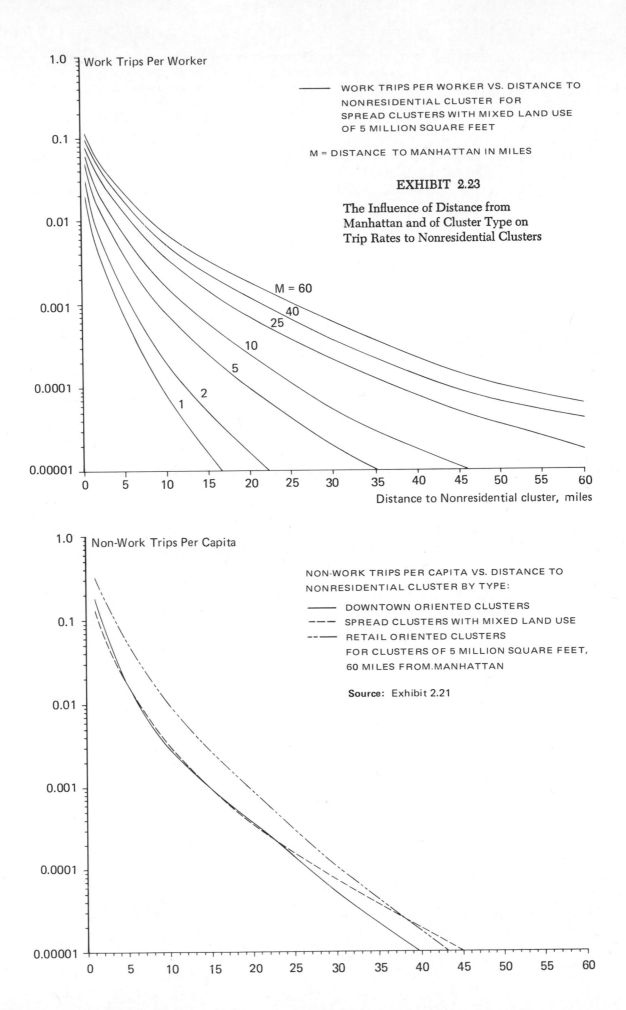

EXHIBIT 2.23

The Influence of Distance from
Manhattan and of Cluster Type on
Trip Rates to Nonresidential Clusters

WORK TRIPS PER WORKER VS. DISTANCE TO
NONRESIDENTIAL CLUSTER FOR
SPREAD CLUSTERS WITH MIXED LAND USE
OF 5 MILLION SQUARE FEET

M = DISTANCE TO MANHATTAN IN MILES

NON-WORK TRIPS PER CAPITA VS. DISTANCE TO
NONRESIDENTIAL CLUSTER BY TYPE:

— DOWNTOWN ORIENTED CLUSTERS
– – – SPREAD CLUSTERS WITH MIXED LAND USE
– – – RETAIL ORIENTED CLUSTERS
FOR CLUSTERS OF 5 MILLION SQUARE FEET,
60 MILES FROM MANHATTAN

Source: Exhibit 2.21

say from 5 to 30 dwellings per acre—will increase the *density* of non-work *trips* destined to that downtown from 2.25 to 13.5 per acre; however, at a distance of 10 miles from the downtown a sixfold increase in residential density will only mean an increase in trip density from 0.5 to 0.9 per acre. In a systematic way, these relationships will be explored in Chapter 5.

To summarize Chapter 2 briefly, it provides, in the first three sections, a general overview of the relationships between development density and the use of public transit. In the next two sections, it gives us a formal tool for estimating the *percent* of total trips that are likely to occur by public transportation depending on the residential density at the origin, the nonresidential density at the destination, and the type of transit service; auto ownership is shown as a key variable influencing these relationships. Finally, the last section gives us a formal tool for estimating *total trips* between any residential area and any nonresidential concentration located at a stated distance from it; it is to these total trips that the percent transit must be applied to determine potential transit travel demand.

The effects of fares, of differences in travel time between auto and transit, of differences in service for non-work trips, and of the phenomenon of induced travel are not incorporated into the formal procedures; they can be explored informally based on the evidence presented in Chapter 1. With this material on travel *demand* by public transportation in hand, we can now proceed to look at the costs of *supplying* public transportation.

3 Operating and Capital Costs

EIGHT MODES OF PUBLIC TRANSPORTATION DEFINED

Different modes of public transportation are distinguished most visibly by the hardware they use, but more importantly by the type of service they provide and by the manner in which they operate. Eight modes of public transportation are examined here: the *taxicab, dial-a-bus, local bus, express bus, light rail, light guideway transit, standard rapid transit,* and *commuter rail.*

Rental cars and limousines, various forms of high-occupancy automobile use, such as car pools and van pools, charter and subscription services, all of which are sometimes classified as forms of "para-transit," remain outside our purview, as do air and water modes of public transportation. Because of the need to establish empirical cost figures, only systems for which there is at least some current operating experience are considered. Technological differences within individual modes—such as trolleybuses or battery-powered buses versus internal combustion buses, or rubber-tired versus steel-wheeled rapid transit vehicles, are not examined. The environmental cost of different public transit modes is only touched upon. A comprehensive comparison can only be made *after* the symbiotic relationship between different modes of transit and different intensities of urban development is established.

Following a definition of the eight modes, their operating and capital costs are examined in this chapter, for it is these costs that largely determine the suitability of the different modes to different density configurations of urban development.

The Taxicab is the form of public transportation that most closely resembles the private automobile. The vehicle it uses is essentially an auto, sometimes modified for conditions of intensive public use. Its routes are completely flexible, and it shares the roadway with other vehicles. Thus its service area is nearly as ubiquitous as that of the auto, but it is also subject to the same congestion delays. It operates on demand, rather than on a schedule, either by being hailed or summoned by telephone, and it provides door-to-door service, usually exclusively for the party which is paying for the trip, though shared riding is sometimes permitted or tolerated.

The relationship of the taxicab to other modes of public transportation is ambivalent: it is often *competitive* in high density areas, where the taxi diverts from other public transportation mostly high income riders who can afford to pay a premium fare for a premium service; it is *complementary* in low density areas, where the taxi often serves as a feeder to other public transit, or where it is the only form of public transportation available.

Of all public transportation modes the taxicab tends to be the most expensive because of the high ratio of drivers and vehicles to passengers. Due to empty travel to pick up patrons, the taxicab is occupied by less than one passenger on the average. This ratio is not significantly higher where shared riding is permitted.

Dial-a-bus represents an effort to lower the high per-passenger cost of a taxicab by encouraging group riding, while preserving the advantages of a flexible, on-demand, door-to-door service. The vehicle is typically a van or a mini-bus, which shares the streets with other traffic just like the taxicab. However, the dispatching—whether manual or by computer—is aimed at placing several passengers with similar origins and destinations in the same vehicle. The passenger pays in three ways: first, he no longer has the privacy of a vehicle that is exclusively his for the duration of the trip; second, his route is typically longer than necessary, as the vehicle makes detours to pick up and deliver other passengers; third, his waiting time is typically longer than for a taxicab, since the vehicle, making other pick-ups and deliveries, cannot respond to his request for service immediately. In return for these inconveniences the rider does, in theory, get a ride at a lower cost than the taxicab. In practice, the difference is often negated by the higher wage rates of the more professional drivers. Furthermore, the potential for dial-a-bus only exists where the *population density* is sufficiently high to be able constantly to assemble groups of passengers with similar origins and destinations. As density declines, either waiting times and detours must increase to a point where the service is no longer attractive, or vehicle occupancy shrinks to a point where it is no different from that of a taxicab.

Another method of increasing taxi occupancy that is frequently mentioned but will not be treated here is *jitney* service. The vehicle generally follows a relatively fixed route along which there is known high demand, and is hailed by passengers who wait for it in the street. This service approximates that of a local bus, with the exception that neither stops nor schedules are fixed. To keep outdoor waiting time—in the absence of a known schedule—within reasonable limits, and still provide a fairly high occupancy per vehicle, the density of demand in the area must be quite high, higher than that for a scheduled bus. Jitneys therefore compete with conventional transit and dilute its patronage. For this reason, and because of erratic passenger service, regulations to curtail them were passed in the U.S. early in this century. Surviving services are in areas of very high density—San Francisco, Atlantic City, Pittsburgh—often geared to the special needs of ghetto areas.[1] In less industrialized countries, jitneys compensate more often for inadequate regular transit, but the population densities they serve—whether those of Caracas, Manila, Istanbul, Teheran, or Mexico City—are also very high.

Local Bus represents the dominant form of public transportation in the United States today. Single vehicles, with the capacity to carry 35 to 50 seated passengers plus additional standees during periods of heavy demand, operate along fixed routes, sharing the roadway

Dial-a-bus was intended to provide low-cost door-to-door service where densities are insufficient to support regular buses. In fact, cost per passenger frequently turned out to be higher than that of taxicabs. One of a relatively few successful operations is shown here in Batavia, N.Y.

Photo RGRTA

Though not as labor-intensive as taxis or dial-a-buses, regular buses never-theless incur relatively high labor costs. On heavily travelled routes, labor productivity can be increased by making the vehicle larger, as in the case of double-deck buses shown here in Manhattan. With their 14.5-foot height, however, the double-deckers require clearances that are not always available. *Photo MTA*

with other traffic. In areas which can only support infrequent service, the operation is usually according to a schedule, which is meant to be publicly available. More frequent service is on a headway basis—one vehicle every so many minutes—without published schedules. Just as the route is fixed, so are the stops, though stops with no passengers are skipped. The service, as a rule, is not door-to-door; groups of riders are assembled by waiting for the schedule or headway and by walking to the bus stop. If the development density is sufficiently high for the bus to be able to assemble reasonably large groups of riders from the tributary area of its route—actually, as few as 7 persons occupying a vehicle on an average daily basis—it offers them transportation at about one-fifth of the per-mile cost of a taxicab ride, despite much higher operator's wages. Though the vehicles run fairly empty most of the day, the large size is needed to carry peak hour loads without adding too many additional drivers; the capital cost of the vehicle itself represents only about one tenth of the cost of running a bus or a taxi.

The rider pays in several ways for the lower cost of a ride in a larger group: he lacks privacy; he must fit his schedule to the bus schedule and wait outdoors, rather than in his home; he must walk to the bus stop; he may have to change buses if the route does not go near his destination; and, in addition to the general traffic delays, he is delayed by the bus stopping for other passengers. Thus, while relatively cheap, local bus travel is also very slow.

Express Bus represents an effort to get around this handicap by serving only selected origins and destinations with a non-stop run. The non-stop run may be on local streets, on a freeway in mixed traffic, or on a reserved bus lane. Clearly, the probability of there being a large enough group to travel together from one neighborhood to a single destination depends on the size of that destination, typically a downtown. At the residential end, the area over which passengers are collected can be expanded with a park-and-ride arrangement if the express run is sufficiently more attractive than the parallel auto trip. That, again, is more likely to be the case in the vicinity of a downtown. To justify, in addition, a reserved bus lane, the number of express buses travelling in a corridor must be substantial. Otherwise, the road capacity may be more efficiently used by private autos.

The major limitation of express buses is that they are highly selective: they operate predominantly during peak periods, and they do not represent an interconnected network, but only isolated runs.

Light Rail Transit is a new name for an old mode of public transportation—the streetcar or tramway which, before 1920, covered the urban areas of the United States with a network of nearly 50,000 miles of track. Less than 2 percent of that trackage remains in existence in 10 cities in North America. In the world there are over 300 cities with light rail systems, about a third of them in the Soviet Union, and over half in the rest of Europe.

Vehicles operating singly or in short trains run on tracks in a variety of rights-of-way: with mixed traffic in streets, in reserved lanes with grade crossings, or on fully grade-separated facilities. The tracks fix the route much more permanently than the route of a bus, and stations, which often have low-level platforms, are also more substantial. Service is usually on a headway.

While streetcar operation in mixed traffic is no longer found acceptable, there is renewed interest in service over reserved rights-of-way, which provides independence from street congestion similar to reserved bus lanes. The larger vehicle size with an option for operation in trains can offer labor-cost economies compared to the bus. These are expected to be realized with the new U.S. Standard Light Rail Vehicle. Its capacity at the same speed is equivalent to about two buses, and is 40 percent greater than that of its predecessor PCC (Presidents' Conference Committee) car. However, a doubling of vehicle size on a route

The Standard Light Rail Vehicle—the new streetcar produced to Urban Mass Transportation Administration specifications. Larger capacity and higher speed are intended to attain operating economies compared to its predecessor PCC (Presidents' Conference Committee) car, manufactured in the United States in 1936-1952. *Photo Boeing*

A reserved streetcar right-of-way on Canal Street in New Orleans as it looked in 1946—a rather spartan prototype for more richly designed downtown transit malls in the future. *Photo Schneider—Headlights*

also means doubling the headway and doubling the average waiting time. Without jeopardizing ridership, this is feasible only on routes where service is already very frequent.

Also, the fixed costs of track and power construction and maintenance presuppose a substantial traffic volume for justification. These costs may be partially offset by design and environmental benefits. Thus, electric traction permits underground operation without costly ventilation facilities, and ride quality and amenity of a tracked vehicle are generally superior to those of a bus. There is also the less tangible aspect of identity, of a permanent physical presence, which seems to play a role in attracting ridership.

Light Guideway Transit is a designation for a large variety of new transit systems that have been under development since the early 1960s and are known under a multitude of acronyms and trade names such as AGT (Automatic Guideway Transit), ACT (Automatically Controlled Transportation), ICT (Intermediate Capacity Transit), Skybus, Airtrans, and so on. Sometimes, the designation PRT (Personal Rapid Transit) is loosely applied to them. Strictly speaking, none of the systems presently in operation (mostly at airports and other activity centers such as the university campus in Morgantown, W. Va.) are true PRTs.*

Light guideway transit represents a response to three basic shortcomings of traditional systems of public transportation: the inability to provide very frequent all-day service without incurring huge labor costs; the need to delay all passengers by stopping for others; and the high cost of building fully grade-separated guideways to achieve high speed with large conventional transit vehicles. Thus the key to most of these systems is fairly small vehicle size (20 to 25 passengers) and automatic operation, with no attendants on board. This makes it possible to run the vehicles frequently all day. Also, the small vehicle size reduces the probability that every one will need to pick up and discharge passengers at every single station, and therefore stations are typically located off-line, enabling vehicles to bypass them. Some of the systems provide the option of demand-activated service during hours of sparse use, and fixed headway service during hours of heavy use. Some can operate in short trains to increase capacity during the hours of heavy use.

While the conceptual advantages of light guideway transit are obvious, difficulties have been encountered with implementing the systems in practice. One major difficulty has to do with the mechanical and electronic complexity of the small automated vehicles. Their reliability has been spotty and their maintenance needs are great. In varying degrees, the costs of supervision, maintenance, and central control offset the savings from having no operators on board. The other difficulty is that the cost of building light guideways did not turn out to be much lower than the cost of conventional transit structures. Many arguments in favor of light guideway transit were made on the assumption that moderately scaled-down elevated structures would be acceptable to the public even in downtown centers; community response suggests otherwise.[2] If downtown distribution is to occur underground, the smaller cross-section of existing light guideway vehicles allows a reduction in tunnel cross-section (and, approximately, in tunnel cost) only on the order of 25 percent compared to standard rapid transit. The high cost and bulky appearance of even "light" elevated structures led to a proposal for a greatly scaled-down "two-in-one" guideway.[3] Its simple steel-wheel technology, however, requires vehicles quite different from the present generation of rubber-tired light guideway transit.

---

* Strictly defined, PRT differs from the present generation of Light Guideway Transit in that the vehicles are much smaller (4-6 passengers), operate only on demand (the vehicles wait for people rather than vice versa) and only non-stop between origin and destination.

The automated Light Guideway Transit system in Morgantown, West Virginia. While theoretically attractive because of their demand-responsive features, systems of this type have experienced practical difficulties both with automatic operation and with the high cost of guideway construction. The bulky guideway will not fit easily into an established urban fabric.

Photo UMTA

ON ELEVATED STRUCTURE:

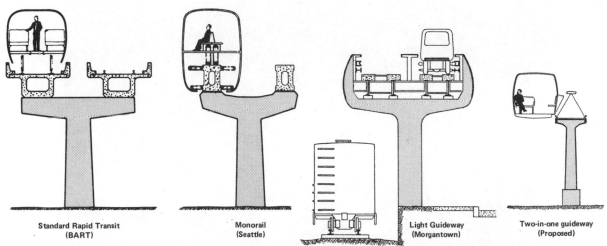

Standard Rapid Transit
(BART)

Monorail
(Seattle)

Light Guideway
(Morgantown)

Two-in-one guideway
(Proposed)

Standard rapid transit requires a rather bulky and costly structure whether above or below ground. To reduce obstruction to light and air on elevated structures, the monorail was invented; as evident from this comparison, the reduction is marginal, while mechanical complexity is much greater. Nor did the first generation of light guideway transit reduce guideway requirements a great deal: the cross-section of the Morgantown system is similar in size to the BART cross-section. An ingenious proposal for a dramatic reduction in guideway dimensions and cost is also shown here. Patented as Project 21, the single, open-web triangular beam that is only 5.5 feet wide carries two-way traffic in 20-seat vehicles which are manually operated in trains of up to 4 cars. In an underground application, the clear area of the needed tunnel is only about 215 sq. ft., compared to 400 sq. ft. for a conventional subway. The system offers grade-separated guideway transit to smaller cities which could not afford it otherwise.

Photo Lawrence K. Edwards

Standard Rapid Transit represents an intraurban train service on tracks using an exclusive, fully grade-separated right-of-way which is either in a subway, or elevated, or open near the ground level, and which is for the most part separate from that of intercity railroads. The concept dates back to 1863 in London and 1867 in New York when the first rapid transit lines opened. These were initially steam-propelled. The introduction of electric traction before the turn of the century gave a strong impetus to the expansion of rapid transit, so that by 1940 some 930 miles of route were in operation in 18 major cities of the world. Construction slowed down in the following two decades, but resumed with great vigor after 1960; by 1975, 51 world cities had rapid transit systems totalling 1,890 route miles as shown later in Exhibits 5.15 and 5.16.

The key feature of standard rapid transit is its ability to carry very large numbers of people—up to 40,000 per track per hour at a comfortable space standard—at moderate to high speed, independent of surface traffic. This continues to keep modern versions of an old system popular even in an auto-dominated environment. All the design features of the system are directed toward the goal of carrying large numbers of passengers. The cars are large, designed for 90 to 150 people at a comfortable space standard, and able to carry perhaps twice that number under jammed conditions. The trains are long, consisting of up to eight large cars, or up to eleven smaller ones. Fare collection is at stations, not on board the vehicle, and stations have high-level platforms, flush with the vehicle floor, to expedite loading and unloading. The latter two features have been adopted by light guideway transit, but are absent on most other systems.

Inevitably, the capital costs of rapid transit are also high. Yet, if enough passengers are present, the operating and maintenance cost can be lower than that of buses.

The large passenger-carrying capacity of standard rapid transit also establishes its limitations. The necessary passenger volumes occur only in large cities, and are generated primarily by their Central Business Districts. At any but very high residential densities, rapid transit must collect its patrons from a relatively wide tributary area, which makes it dependent on auxiliary feeder modes such as buses or autos. It tends to attract long trips—about twice as long as those served by local bus or streetcar. This can provide significant relief in selected traffic corridors, but in the general picture the select trips which rapid transit serves make up only a small proportion of total urban travel in an auto-dominated environment.

Two versions of rapid transit that will not be treated here are the *monorail* and *gravity-vacuum transit*. The former represents an effort to reduce the cross-sectional area of elevated structures by making the trains ride either straddling or suspended from one beam. On installations built thus far, this requires a very complicated suspension system and cumbersome switches. The reduction in visual intrusion has not been sufficient for the concept to gain wide acceptance. However, the "two-in-one" guideway proposal mentioned earlier does address the issues of simplified suspension, switching, and reduced bulk, while accepting the moderate speed which systems of this type are limited to. By contrast, gravity-vacuum transit was conceived to achieve extremely high line-haul speeds at low energy consumption by accelerating trains through both gravity and air pressure in partially evacuated deep-level tunnels. The high prospective capital costs, combined with the fact that the market is limited to the largest cities where conventional rapid transit exists, have so far prevented development work that would make this proposal operational.

Commuter rail represents a train service between downtown terminals and the suburban territory of major cities, operating over intercity railroad facilities which it usually shares with other railroad traffic. The trains run much less frequently than those of urban rapid tran-

The Metro in Washington, D.C. which in 1976 became the ninth urban area in the United States and Canada to operate a standard rapid transit system. Because of the concentration of 90 million square feet of nonresidential floorspace in downtown Washington, and because of a large latent demand for intracity travel, the system promises to be successful when fully developed. Remaining opportunities for full-scale rapid transit in other North American cities appear to be more modest. *Photo WMATA*

Commuter rail has been evolving in the direction of greater similarity with rapid transit. The latest step in this direction is the gas turbine electric car, shown here on Long Island, designed to bring rapid transit car performance into non-electrified territory and to obviate the need for changing equipment. Where there is no third rail, the car makes its own electricity with the help of a jet engine. *Photo MTA*

sit and follow published schedules rather than headways. To reduce delay to the predominantly downtown-bound passengers, not all trains make all stops, and patterns of express and local service are often developed. Compared to intercity railroad service, passenger density is high and stops are frequent. This requires specialized seating and door arrangements and high acceleration and deceleration which distinguish commuter equipment and tend to make it, in some ways, similar to the equipment of rapid transit. Where the density of traffic warrants it, commuter rail lines are electrified and the self-propelled cars have automatic doors, served from high-level platforms. Where high capacity is not required and slower speed is acceptable, locomotive-hauled trains and traditional low-level platforms are used. The labor-intensive collection of tickets still occurs on board the trains, although some applications of zoned fare collection and automation are being introduced. Trips by commuter rail are by far the longest of all urban trips by public transportation; they average between 15 and 26 miles in different American cities, which is about three times the distance of rapid transit trips. Accordingly, there is much more attention to passenger comfort—all passengers have seats and there is one and a half to two times more space per passenger than on a bus.

OPERATING AND MAINTENANCE COSTS

Recent trends. In recent years there has been an unprecedented increase in the operating and maintenance costs of public transportation in the United States. Nationwide, the operating cost per passenger rose 85 percent in *constant dollars* between 1965 and 1975. The reasons have more to do with broad social trends than with the transit systems themselves. Rising auto ownership and declining central city population caused transit revenue passengers to drop 17 percent over the decade. However, to prevent still greater passenger declines, transit service was not cut proportionately; it was allowed to drop only 1 percent on a nationwide basis. In fact, considerable expansion of service in many areas between 1972 and 1975 helped to arrest the decline in riders. But the result was a sharp drop in productivity—fewer passengers carried per vehicle or per employee. Even if the cost of providing the service had remained the same, the cost per passenger would have risen about 20 percent, as fewer passengers remained to share it.

In fact, the cost of providing a unit of service has also risen steeply. The sharp increase in energy costs between 1973 and 1975 has contributed to this, but by far the largest cause was the dramatic increase in real wages and benefits per employee. Nationwide, transit workers' wages alone increased 26 percent in constant dollars over the period, substantially more than in the economy as a whole. National data on fringe benefits are not available, but in New York City, where transit wages and salaries alone also rose by 26 percent, wages plus fringe benefits increased nearly 40 percent in constant dollars during the 10-year period.[4]

Lastly, while public transit nationwide has generally become less labor intensive over the period from 1946 to 1970, the subsequent five years saw a reversal of this trend and an increase in the number of employees per vehicle. This further contributed to a higher cost per passenger. To what extent this represented improved service, and to what extent reduced productivity, is not clear. There is no question that some aspects of public transit service have improved over the years—for example, rush hour overcrowding has been significantly relieved by the decline in passengers. Rising expectations have masked this real improvement.

In an effort to stem declining ridership, fares, on a nationwide average basis, have remained stable in constant dollars between 1965 and 1975. This average does mask significant local differences: New York City subway fares were raised 90 percent in constant dollars over the 10-year period, while in numerous other cities across the nation they were significantly reduced. The result has been a rapidly widening gap between expenditures and revenues. The New York City transit system became a permanent deficit operation in 1962, and public transit nationwide crossed the deficit threshold in 1968. Of the total annual nationwide operating expense of $3.7 billion for buses, trolleycars, and rapid transit in 1975, only $2 billion or less than 55 percent was covered by fares and other operating revenues; the rest was public subsidy. One might note that roughly half that subsidy essentially covered an income transfer from the population at large to transit workers, whose income was substantially above the national average.

Because of the historically unusual nature of the 1965-1975 trend, any projection of public transit costs is highly conjectural. Thus, as a part of its fiscal retrenchment, New York City succeeded in freezing transit workers' wages for a two-year period in 1976, and similar if less dramatic measures have been taken elsewhere. However, an allocation of the costs and comparisons among transit modes can be studied at one point in time, in this case 1974. The purpose is to understand the reasons why costs vary among different transit modes; these reasons are largely independent of the actual level of costs in any given year.

A summary of transit passengers, passenger miles (PMT), service (vehicle miles of travel or VMT), expenses, and revenues in 1974 is presented in Exhibit 3.1 for the Tri-State New York Region, which accounts for about 45 percent of the passenger miles of transit travel in the nation.

The basic output that any form of passenger transportation offers is passenger miles of travel—the number of passengers multiplied by the average length of their trips. Exhibit 3.1 shows in the ninth column the costs of providing one passenger mile in the New York Region in 1973-74 by various modes of public transportation. These range from a high of 23.5 cents per passenger mile on some local buses to a low of 7.3 cents on one of the commuter railroads. Rapid transit fits in the middle of that range, averaging about 10 cents per passenger mile. Commuter bus operations show a slightly lower cost. The cost of all public transit travel in the New York Region in 1973-74, excluding taxicabs, averaged about 11.5 cents per passenger mile, of which 4.3 cents was public subsidy.

For comparison, the average intercity bus fare in 1974 was 5.2 cents per passenger mile, the average airline fare close to 7 cents, and the average cost per passenger on Amtrak intercity trains about 11 cents, of which about 5 cents was public subsidy. The average cost of operating an automobile, according to Federal Highway Administration estimates, was 15.9 cents per vehicle mile. The average cost of transit travel thus equalled that of travel by auto if the auto was occupied by 1.4 people, based on nationwide averages. In dense urban areas, auto costs can be twice as high due to parking charges, tolls, and higher insurance costs. Thus, in urban areas transit can still maintain a significant advantage over the auto in purely economic terms, especially if the huge public expenditures that would be needed to replace transit with private auto travel are considered.

Major Components of Transit Operating Costs. The economics of public transportation are complex, and their comprehensive presentation is beyond the scope of this book. Instead, a simplified and illustrative approach will be taken, aimed at singling out the major cost components and explaining which variables affect them most, so that differences in providing service by different modes of public transportation can be understood.

EXHIBIT 3.1

Performance and Costs of Public Transit Systems in the New York Region, Annual for 1973-74

	Passengers (000's)	PMT (000's)	VMT (000's)	$ Revenues (000's)	$ Expenses (000's)	Revenue$ / pass.	Expenses$ / pass.	Revenue covers:	Expenses$ / PMT	Expenses$ / VMT	PMT/VMT	PMT/pass
Bus NYCTA	388,774	777,548	68,485	142,866	182,554	.367	.470	78.2%	.235	2.665	11.4	2.0
MABSTOA	331,511	663,022	42,847	117,862	131,109	.355	.395	89.9%	.198	3.060	15.5	2.0
NYC Private	89,853	238,027	26,114	47,263	47,023	.526	.523	100.6%	.198	1.801	9.1	2.7
NYC Bus	810,138	1,678,597	137,446	307,991	360,686			85.4%	.215	2.624	12.2	2.1
MSBA	17,701	79,654	9,024	8,972	11,664	.507	.659	76.9%	.146	1.293	8.8	4.5
LI other	2,215	8,552	1,852	599	1,332	.270	.601	44.9%	.156	0.719	4.6	3.9
Westchester	20,862	52,155	8,081	9,152	9,532	.439	.457	96.1%	.183	1.180	6.5	2.5
NYSN other	1,337	4,011	778	456	611	.341	.457	74.6%	.152	0.785	5.2	3.0
NYS Bus out of NYC	42,115	144,372	19,735	19,179	23,139			82.9%	.160	1.172	7.3	3.4
Conn bus	12,531	42,977	6,821	5,867	8,242	.468	.658	71.1%	.192	1.208	6.3	3.4
NJ Commuter	46,260	648,554	51,643	49,836	52,903	1.077	1.144	94.1%	.082	1.024	12.6	14.0
TNJ	96,315	481,575	47,484	50,833	61,126	.528	.635	83.1%	.126	1.287	10.1	5.0
NJ other	50,897	108,092	15,533	16,804	19,315	.330	.379	87.1%	.179	1.243	7.0	2.1
Bus NJ	193,472	1,238,221	114,660	117,473	133,344			88.1%	.108	1.163	10.8	6.4
Total Bus	1,058,256	3,104,167	278,662	450,510	525,411			85.7%	.169	1.885	11.1	2.9
RT NYCTA	1,096,007	7,891,250	317,754	391,294	779,612*	.357	.711	50.2%	.099	2.453	24.8	7.2
SIRTOA	3,950	27,255	1,432	1,416	5,000	.358	1.266	28.3%	.183	3.492	19.0	6.9
PATH	37,774	147,319	10,507	12,189	44,509	.323	1.178	27.4%	.302	4.236	14.0	3.9
Nwk	2,355	5,888	576	884	898	.375	.381	98.4%	.153	1.559	10.2	2.5
Total RT	1,140,086	8,071,712	330,269	405,783	830,019			48.9%	.103	2.513	24.4	7.1
LIRR	57,000	1,541,298	48,474	83,206	145,090	1.460	2.545	57.4%	.094	2.993	31.8	27.0
NYSN RR	28,742	791,660	24,555	60,487	85,678	2.104	2.981	70.6%	.108	3.489	32.2	27.5
Conn RR	8,156	256,940	7,932	14,458	18,742	1.773	2.298	77.2%	.073	2.363	32.4	31.5
NJ RR	34,528	732,288	26,905	33,949	56,696	.983	1.642	59.9%	.077	2.107	27.2	21.2
Total Rail	128,426	3,221,009	107,866	192,100	306,206			62.7%	.095	2.839	30.8	25.9
Ferry	19,732	108,526	224	987	13,000**	.050	.659	7.6%	.120	58.035	484.5	5.5
TOTAL TRANSIT	2,346,500	14,606,591		1,049,380	1,674,636	.447	.714	62.7%	.115			6.2

Metric conversion: 1 vehicle mile of travel (VMT) or 1 passenger mile (PMT) = 1.609 vehicle kilometers or passenger kilometers

Sources: Tri-State Regional Planning Commission *Technical Manual 1017-3305* (February 1975); NYCTA *Transit Record* (August 1974)

*Incl. $167,538 transit debt service paid by NYC
  Excludes cost of Transit Police - $89,518

**Estimated

PMT=passenger miles of travel; VMT=vehicle miles of travel; PMT/VMT=average vehicle occupancy; PMT/pass.=average trip length (miles)

To begin with, a note of caution is in order regarding Exhibit 3.1. The data, though the best available at the time, are not always internally consistent. Not all figures refer to the same year within the 1973-74 period and, more importantly, accounting practices vary widely between different transit properties. For example, the seemingly high cost of the Port Authority Trans Hudson (PATH) rapid transit is largely a matter of bookkeeping. Capital costs contained in the figure include, aside from capital charges on a fleet of rather new cars, the cost of building the World Trade Center terminal, and operating costs include a proportionate share of the Port Authority's general overhead expense, which includes many services usually carried out by general-purpose government. Comparing pure operating costs, PATH and the New York City transit system turn out to be quite similar.

Since the major accounting differences are in the reporting of capital costs, such as depreciation and interest, these are excluded from Exhibit 3.2, the purpose of which is to illustrate *pure operating expenses* for a range of public transit modes under different operating conditions. Due to data availability, only selected systems are listed, but their range is expanded to include, among others, taxicabs, dial-a-bus, and the automated PATCO Lindenwold rapid transit line. An effort is also made to present data more consistently for 1974, even if some estimates were required to do this.

Economists typically distinguish between fixed costs and variable costs. The most important fixed costs are capital costs, but some operating costs are also fixed. Fixed costs depend only on the size of the operation and are independent of the amount of service provided. Typical examples are garage costs for a private auto or a bus, or station and track supervision costs for a rail system. Variable costs, in turn, can be subdivided into those which depend on vehicle miles operated and those which relate to the amount of time the vehicles are in operation. Maintenance of way, maintenance of equipment, energy costs, and insurance costs largely depend on vehicle miles travelled. Labor costs incurred in vehicle operation, on the other hand, depend primarily on the amount of time the vehicles are running, since labor is basically paid by the hour.

A review of recent operating statistics of U.S. transit systems suggests that vehicle hour-related costs generally account for more than half the total transit operating costs. Vehicle mile-related costs amount to roughly one third, and the small remainder is assignable to fixed costs, if depreciation and other capital charges are excluded, as they are for the moment. The vehicle hour and vehicle mile variables are closely related to each other, so that the former can, if need be, serve as a substitute for the latter. Thus, a statistical analysis of U.S. bus systems has shown that 96.8 percent of the variation in their transportation expense could be explained by vehicle hours of operation alone.[5] This relationship is weaker for rail systems, with their large fixed plant and greater site-specific differences, but it still warrants emphasizing vehicle hours of operation as a measure of transit output that relates to costs in a rather consistent manner.

For a summary discussion such as the one presented here, we will not try to allocate *portions* of operating costs to vehicle hours, vehicle miles, and vehicles, as is usually done. Instead, we shall take *operating costs as a whole* and relate them step by step to employees, vehicles, vehicle miles, and vehicle hours,[6] and then look at how many passengers it takes to support a given number of vehicle hours at what cost. The procedure outlined is presented in Exhibit 3.2.

One should also add that the *average hourly cost*—a ratio widely used in subsequent analysis—does not necessarily equal the cost for a *particular* hour; the latter is likely to be different depending on labor agreements allowing split shifts as against continuous shifts, depending on overtime pay, night-time differentials, and so on. Just as five feet of lumber

	Annual Operating Cost (excluding interest & depreciation)						Labor intensity	Annual vehicle use	Operating speed	Use by passengers:				Employee productivity: PMT VMT CUMT* per employee per day (average of 365 days)		
										Passengers boarding		Trip	Veh. occupancy			
	$/Employee	$/Vehicle	$/VMT	$/Veh-hr	$/Pass.	$/PMT	Empl/veh	VMT/veh	VMT/veh-hr	per/VMT	per/veh-hr	length mi.	PMT/VMT			
	(1)	(2)	(3)	(4)	(5)	(6)	(7)	(8)	(9)	(10)	(11)	(12)	(13)	(14)	(15)	(16)
Taxicab**																
New York City fleets	12,000	42,000	0.56	6.44	1.74	0.757	3.5	75,000	11.5	0.32	9.7	2.3	0.74	48	59	390
Suburban Long Island	8,000	16,200	0.41	5.93	2.12	0.707	2.0	39,633	14.7	0.19	2.8	3.0	0.57	31	54	360
Dial-A-Bus***																
Average of eight systems	14,890	34,240	1.06	13.50	1.82	0.91	2.3	32,300	12.7	0.57	7.4	2.0	1.16	42	36	580
Bus****																
NYCTA Manhattan			3.57	20.50	0.390	0.260			5.74	9.13	52.5	1.5	13.70			
NYCTA Brooklyn	21,553	76,255	2.89	21.27	0.455	0.239	3.53	28,600	7.36	6.35	46.8	1.9	12.10	250	22	1,170
NYCTA Queens			2.45	20.98	0.452	0.215			8.55	5.43	46.5	2.1	11.40			
NYCTA Staten Island			1.86	21.82	0.743	0.232			11.74	2.50	29.4	3.2	8.00			
MSBA Nassau County	15,783	40,082	1.29	17.97	0.659	0.146	2.54	31,010	13.90	1.96	27.3	4.5	8.83	291	33	1,920
TNJ statewide	20,712	44,340	1.46	20.20	0.713	0.143	2.14	30,390	13.84	2.04	28.3	5.0	10.22	399	39	2,060
Conn. Co. statewide	19,129	32,653	1.13	13.06	0.478	0.141	1.71	28,868	11.54	2.37	27.3	3.4	8.05	370	46	2,160
Sample of 52 cities under 1 million	19,800	34,100	1.16	14.00	0.410	n.a.	1.72	29,400	12.00	2.58	29.9	n.a.	n.a.	n.a.	44	1,950
Light Rail																
Newark Subway	20,712	43,846	1.98	28.50	0.484	0.193	2.66	22,150	14.20	4.09	58.9	2.5	10.22	296	29	1,970
Light Guideway Transit																
Airtrans Dallas	n.a.	n.a.	n.a.	n.a.	n.a.	n.a.	3.12	66,431	12.00	0.85	10.2	1.0	0.85	58	68	1,676
Rail Rapid Transit																
NYCTA	20,829	91,600	1.92	35.30	0.558	0.078	4.40	47,554	18.32	3.45	63.2	7.2	24.8	744	30	2,850
PATH*****	19,500	68,456	1.94	36.12	0.540	0.138	3.51	35,258	18.60	3.59	66.8	3.9	14.0	392	28	2,160
PATCO Lindenwold	23,310	78,947	1.37	41.11	0.533	0.063	3.39	57,520	30.00	2.57	77.2	8.5	21.9	964	46	5,810
Commuter Rail																
LIRR	29,000	167,380	3.51	107.35	2.816	0.104	5.80	47,711	30.6	1.25	38.1	27.0	33.7	774	23	3,200
PC New Haven	28,177	170,606	3.11	105.78	3.111	0.099	6.05	54,839	34.0	1.00	34.0	31.5	31.5	787	25	3,530
Erie-Lackawanna	25,991	70,854	2.18	68.78	1.689	0.082	2.73	32,565	31.6	1.29	40.7	20.7	26.7	881	33	4,640

Metric conversion: 1 vehicle mile of travel (VMT) or 1 passenger mile (PMT) = 1.609 vehicle kilometers or passenger kilometers

Notes:

* CUMT—Capacity-unit miles of travel; 1 capacity unit assumed at 6 sq. ft. (0.557m2) of gross vehicle floorspace

** Operating "cost" of taxicabs = Gross revenue − 10% depreciation & interest + 15% tips; Long Island data from Davis, Frank W.: *Economic Characteristics of Privately Owned Shared Taxi Systems*, USDOT October, 1974, adjusted by data from operator; NYC estimated on the basis of various sources. Taxi employees include *part-time* workers, as well as drivers under lease arrangements who are technically self-employed

*** Based principally on *Lea Transit Compendium*, "Para-transit", Vol 1, No. 8, 1974; 1973 costs expanded by 1.07 for 1974 estimate; excludes Canadian systems; trip length based on Haddonfield, average probably less than 2 miles

**** NYCTA data from *NYCTA Transit Record* for 1973-74 fiscal year, Vol LIV, No. 8, August 1974; National bus sample—median (not average) figures from Institute for Defense Analyses, *Economic Characteristics of the Urban Public Transportation Industry*, USDOT February 1972; National 1969 bus costs expanded by 1.84 per vehicle-mile for 1974 estimate other data from Tri-State Regional Planning Commission or directly from operating agencies.

***** PATH operating cost recalculated on a basis comparable to NYCTA, excluding in particular the share of Port Authority overhead assigned to PATH

n.a.—not available

Products of columns may vary due to rounding.

EXHIBIT 3.2

Illustrative Operating Costs and Characteristics of Selected Public Transportation Systems, 1974

Note: Column 1 shows cost per employee, which is the total annual operating cost of a transit property divided by the number of its employees. The next ratio is annual cost per vehicle (Column 2), which represents cost per employee multiplied by labor intensity, or the number of employees per vehicle (Column 7). Cost per vehicle divided by the annual miles operated per vehicle (Column 8) equals cost per vehicle mile (Column 3). Cost per vehicle mile multiplied by the average speed (Column 9) equals cost per vehicle hour (Column 4). Cost per vehicle hour divided by the number of passengers boarding per vehicle hour (Column 11) equals cost per passenger. The same result can be obtained by dividing cost per vehicle mile by the number of passengers boarding per vehicle mile (Column 10). Cost per passenger divided by average trip length (Column 12) equals cost per passenger mile. Number of passengers boarding per vehicle mile multiplied by the average trip length equals average vehicle occupancy (Column 13). This is the instantaneous number of passengers occupying a vehicle at any one time, and should not be confused with passengers boarding. The last three columns give different measures of employee productivity. All three are expressed on a daily basis assuming 365 days in a year (even though the number of "average weekday" equivalents in a year for most transit systems is much lower, about 296). The three productivity measures are passenger miles per employee, vehicle miles per employee, and a measure that is meant to compensate for the fact that vehicles of different public transit modes vary in size. This last measure is called capacity-unit miles of travel; each capacity unit is assumed as 6 square feet of gross vehicle floorspace. It can be taken to represent an average comfort standard, typical of a 40-foot, 53-seat bus, where each passenger has about 4.1 square feet of net seating space, less than 1 square foot of aisle space, and about 1 square foot devoted to the driver compartment, vehicle walls, and such. This module is intended to be a common denominator for measures of "capacity" which sometimes assume less than half that space per passenger on subway cars and nearly twice as much on railroad trains.

may cost as much as eight feet, if lumber comes in eight-foot lengths, so may five vehicle hours. This kind of detail cannot be adequately handled in a generalized discussion.

Operating Cost Per Employee. Within the category of pure operating costs, the dominant components are wages and fringe benefits. These vary widely between different transit operations. For example, in major cities of the United States in late 1974, top hourly bus operator rates varied from a high of $6.70 in Chicago to a low of $4.45 in Houston, a difference of 50 percent, with New York City and San Francisco at $6.23. Even within the New York Region, however, some small bus operations paid as little as $3.50. Differences in wage rates larger than these are present between different transit modes.

As is evident from the first column in Exhibit 3.2, annual operating costs for a sample of properties in 1974 were in the range of $8,000 to $12,000 per employee for taxicabs, around $15,000 per employee for dial-a-bus, $16,000 to $22,000 for scheduled buses, between $20,000 and $23,000 for rapid transit, and $24,000 to $29,000 for suburban rail. The absolute figures should not be memorized by the reader, since by the time the book is read they will have changed due to inflation. Between 1965 and 1974 inflation and rising real wages and benefits were raising transit operating costs per worker nationwide about 9 percent each year. Rather, the important thing is the *relative* magnitudes, the fact that cost per employee varies as much as *three and a half times* between a suburban taxi operation and some suburban rail properties.

Components of the annual operating cost per employee for five selected taxi and mass transit operations for which data were readily available are detailed in Exhibit 3.3. This shows that non-labor types of expenses, such as fuel and power, parts and materials, insurance and miscellaneous payments amounted to between 15 and 30 percent of the total operating cost per worker in 1974. In absolute terms, the non-labor expense ranged only between $2,500 and $6,000 per worker, more or less equally divided among the three categories of power, materials, and miscellaneous payments. The latter include, aside from insurance and accident costs, non-labor related taxes.

The remaining 70 to 85 percent of the annual operating cost per employee represented direct and indirect labor expense. Pure wages (including tips in the case of taxi workers) were in the range of $5,500 to $9,300 for taxi employees, in the $10,700 to $13,900 range for bus and subway employees, and around $16,500 for suburban railroad employees. For the urban mass transit operations, some 27 percent must be added to direct wages and salaries to account for pensions and other social insurance benefits. For suburban railroad workers this proportion is higher, 37 percent. For taxi systems this category is very small due to different labor arrangements. For example, the lowest labor cost suburban taxi operation shown does not pay its drivers wages but technically leases the taxicabs to them, thus avoiding payroll taxes for any but its few direct employees, while affording its drivers the status of self-employment.

Excluding the indirect benefits, one can roughly say that taxicab workers in 1974 made about $3.10 an hour (including tips) in the suburban case, and about $3.80 an hour in the New York City case. Transit workers made on the order of $5.50 an hour in the Connecticut bus example and $7.50 an hour in the New York City example (including overtime). Railroad workers made on the order of $9 an hour on Long Island. Such wage differentials are to some extent related to the productivity of the different systems. Despite their high wages, railroad workers, as will be shown shortly, are able to deliver passenger miles of travel at one seventh the cost of taxi drivers. Nevertheless, wage differences of this magnitude can make a crucial difference in the viability of planned public transit systems. For example, it is of basic importance whether a dial-a-ride system can pay its workers taxi

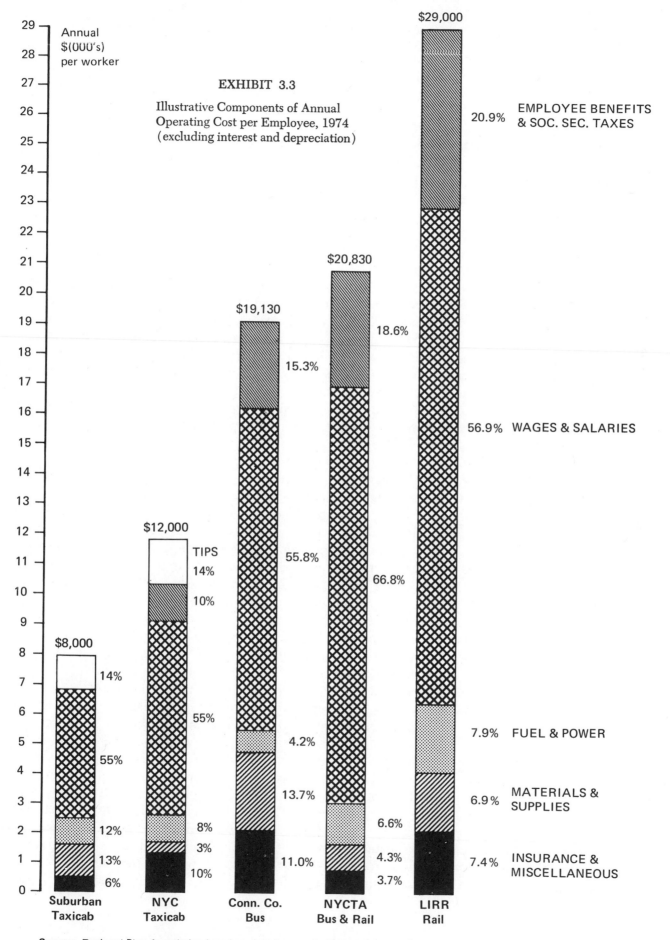

EXHIBIT 3.3

Illustrative Components of Annual
Operating Cost per Employee, 1974
(excluding interest and depreciation)

Annual
$(000's)
per worker

Suburban Taxicab — $8,000: 14%, 55%, 12%, 13%, 6%

NYC Taxicab — $12,000: TIPS 14%, 10%, 55%, 8%, 3%, 10%

Conn. Co. Bus — $19,130: 15.3%, 55.8%, 4.2%, 13.7%, 11.0%

NYCTA Bus & Rail — $20,830: 18.6%, 66.8%, 6.6%, 4.3%, 3.7%

LIRR Rail — $29,000: 20.9% EMPLOYEE BENEFITS & SOC. SEC. TAXES, 56.9% WAGES & SALARIES, 7.9% FUEL & POWER, 6.9% MATERIALS & SUPPLIES, 7.4% INSURANCE & MISCELLANEOUS

Source: Regional Plan Association based on data from various operating agencies

drivers' wages, or whether it has to pay bus drivers' wages for what is basically a taxicab type of service. Likewise, it is of basic importance whether a new rail transit operation is classified as suburban rail, and must pay railroad wages, or whether it is urban rapid transit, with its lower pay scales.

Labor Intensity and Operating Cost Per Vehicle. Transportation employees use vehicles to move people. Generally, the fewer employees needed to operate one vehicle, the greater their productivity, other things being equal. Column 7 in Exhibit 3.2 lists typical ratios of employees to vehicles. With the exception of commuter railroads, the ratio of employees to vehicles stays generally in the range between 1.7 and 4.

Somewhat contrary to popular lore, the lowest ratio of employees to vehicles—around 1.7—is found on some bus systems. This is largely due to the concentration of service during peak hours and very sparse operations during off-peak and weekend periods when many buses are idle and not manned. Bus systems that provide more of a round-the-clock service, such as those shown for New Jersey, Nassau County, and New York City, have employee-to-vehicle ratios of 2.1 to 3.5. This range is also representative of the two taxicab operations shown, which likewise provide 24-hour, 7-day-a-week service. The lower suburban ratio is, once more, indicative of lower vehicle utilization. One might add that the taxi employees listed include part-time workers who do not work full shifts, but only in response to periods of high demand. In this way the taxi industry, with its more flexible labor practices, is able to achieve economies that are foreclosed to mass transit operations. It is also notable that the employee-to-vehicle ratio for eight dial-a-bus operations averages 2.3, characteristic of the taxicab range but substantially above the typical scheduled bus in the nation's smaller cities.

The employee-to-vehicle ratio of rapid transit systems tends to be higher than that of buses. Exhibit 3.4 explains the reasons why. It compares, by way of the first two bars, the employees per bus with the employees per subway car on the New York City transit system, and allocates them by major function. Some 2.2 employees out of a total of 3.53 per bus are bus drivers (vehicle attendance and operation); about 0.81 take care of vehicle maintenance; about 0.28 are off-vehicle operating personnel such as dispatchers and schedulers; some 0.24 are administrators. The major labor saving of rapid transit occurs because of the reduced need for on-vehicle personnel, achieved by operating vehicles in trains. Only 0.97 employees per subway car are motormen and conductors. The vehicle maintenance, general operations, and administrative personnel are somewhat higher than on the bus but generally similar. Two new categories appear, however, on rapid transit which are absent on the bus: fare collection (0.62 station agents per subway car) and the maintenance of way and of power systems (1.18 employees per car). These cancel the savings in vehicle operators compared to the bus and raise the total employee-to-vehicle ratio to 4.40.

A natural question that arises at this point is to what degree this labor intensity can be reduced by automation. The PATCO Lindenwold line from Philadelphia to southern New Jersey is widely regarded as the most efficient rapid transit operation in the United States, hence its experience is instructive. As evident from Exhibits 3.2 and 3.4, its labor-to-vehicle ratio is 3.39, about 23 percent below subways and 4 percent below buses in New York City. PATCO has automatic fare collection and automatic train operation, with only one attendant on each train. The effect of the former is dramatically evident in Exhibit 3.4: only 0.1 fare collection personnel per car on PATCO, versus 0.62 on the NYCTA. This represents roughly a 12 percent labor saving. The vehicle operation and attendance category is also reduced by about one third (PATCO runs shorter trains, so its per-car requirements for operating personnel are inherently somewhat higher), but the saving is negated by higher

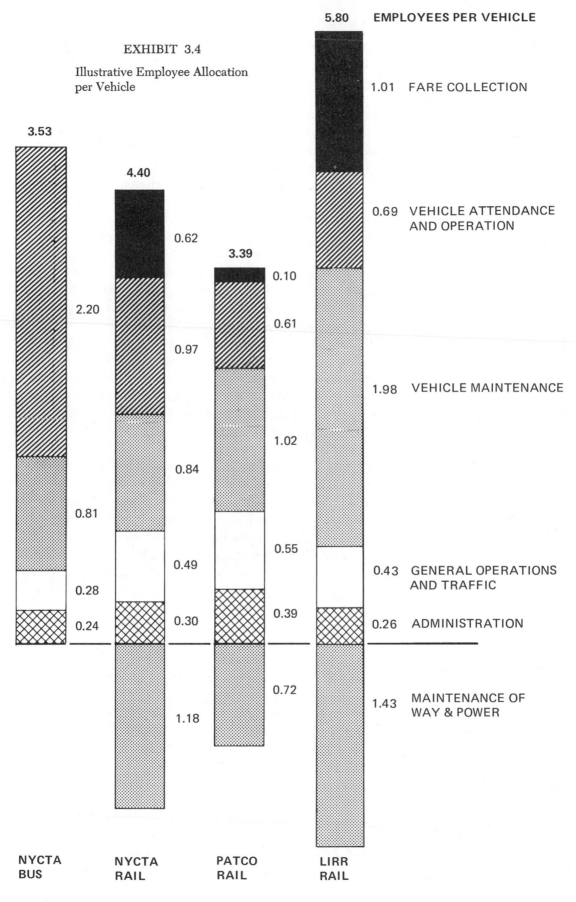

5.80   **EMPLOYEES PER VEHICLE**

EXHIBIT 3.4

Illustrative Employee Allocation per Vehicle

1.01   FARE COLLECTION

3.53

4.40

0.62

3.39

0.10

0.69   VEHICLE ATTENDANCE AND OPERATION

2.20

0.97

0.61

1.98   VEHICLE MAINTENANCE

0.84

1.02

0.81

0.49

0.55

0.43   GENERAL OPERATIONS AND TRAFFIC

0.28

0.39

0.26   ADMINISTRATION

0.24

0.30

0.72

1.43   MAINTENANCE OF WAY & POWER

1.18

NYCTA BUS   **NYCTA RAIL**   **PATCO RAIL**   **LIRR RAIL**

Note: All data exclude transit police

Source: Regional Plan Association based on data from various operating agencies

requirements for vehicle maintenance, general operations, and administration. Half the labor saving on PATCO vis-à-vis the NYCTA has nothing to do with automation but occurs in the area of maintenance of way and power, at the bottom of the bar chart. This is largely because PATCO is a new line and runs for most of its length above ground, where mechanized track maintenance equipment can be easily deployed. All told, however, a combination of moderately lower labor requirements per car, more car miles per car due to higher speed, and larger car size enables PATCO to achieve a rather dramatic increase in labor productivity which will be shown later.

Further on the subject of automation, available operating characteristics for the Dallas-Ft. Worth airport Airtrans light guideway transit system are also listed in Exhibit 3.2. It has totally unmanned vehicles, about one fifth the size of the PATCO cars, operating singly or in two-car trains. For 51 passenger and 17 utility vehicles, the system required 181 employees, averaging about 2.7 per vehicle, of whom 1.8 were maintenance workers, 0.5 passenger service employees, and 0.4 central control and supervisory personnel. It was expected that as the system shakes down, the manpower requirements might be reduced to 1.8 per vehicle by eliminating the passenger service and some of the maintenance personnel.

The highest ratios of employees per vehicle are found on the commuter railroads. One must emphasize that the allocation of labor to passenger operations in systems that carry both passengers and freight will always remain controversial. Data reported by railroads will inevitably vary due to differences of accounting, which may have influenced the New Haven and Erie-Lackawanna figures in Exhibit 3.2. The Long Island Railroad is singled out in Exhibit 3.4 because it is predominantly a passenger operation. Freight accounts for roughly 18 percent of its fully allocated cost, reported according to ICC rules; the employees were allocated on the same basis. It can be seen that its employees in maintenance-of-way exceed those on rapid transit; this is plausible, because the railroad operates more trackage per car. The categories of administration, general operations, and train operation (which includes motormen and conductors) are rather similar. The big excess is in two areas: vehicle maintenance and fare collection. Fare collection includes assistant conductors, ticket collectors, and station ticket agents, of whom there are about 1.0 per car. Vehicle maintenance, with nearly 2.0 employees per car, is about twice as labor intensive as on rapid transit. This is partly due to Interstate Commerce Commission rules, which require much more stringent inspection than on rapid transit; it is also due to the labor practices in the maintenance shops. All this adds up to an employee-to-vehicle ratio of 5.80, some 30 to 70 percent more than on the two rapid transit systems shown in Exhibit 3.4. On the basis of that exhibit one can estimate that two measures, namely automatic station fare collection and bringing the vehicle maintenance practices to the standard of those on PATCO, might reduce the manpower needs and costs of a railroad such as Long Island by about 25 percent.

Returning now to Exhibit 3.2, the total operating cost per vehicle, shown in the second column, is the product of the cost per employee and the number of employees per vehicle.

Vehicle Utilization and Vehicle Speed. A stationary vehicle, needless to say, is of little use for passenger transportation. Rather, the number of miles a vehicle moves during a year is a measure of how many passengers it can help to transport how far. This indicator is listed in Column 8 of Exhibit 3.2. It shows that taxicabs run 40,000 miles a year in suburban territory (which is about the national average) and up to 75,000 miles a year in New York City. Buses rather consistently clock 30,000 miles a year; nationally, this figure tends to be about 6,000 miles lower for the smallest systems and an equal number of miles higher for the largest systems. Rapid transit cars run 30,000 to 60,000 miles a year, and commuter rail cars are in the same range. The highest miles per vehicle tend to be achieved by the two automated systems shown—PATCO Lindenwold and Dallas Airtrans. Thus, *while automatic train operation reduces the manpower per vehicle only modestly, it does improve vehicle utilization: automated vehicles work harder,* once they are "de-bugged."

For the manually operated systems, annual miles per vehicle tend to increase with labor intensity. Conversely, both low employees per vehicle and low miles per vehicle are related to sparse off-peak service, as illustrated by the taxicabs on Long Island, buses in Connecticut, and Erie-Lackawanna trains. For any given level of labor input, annual miles per vehicle are further affected by the operating speed. The systems which run faster also tend to clock more miles per vehicle per year. Conversely, the low annual use of New York City buses, as an example, which occurs despite a high labor intensity, is due to the extremely slow operating speeds on city streets.

Dividing annual cost per vehicle by the number of miles it travels each year, we obtain cost per vehicle mile, shown in the third column of Exhibit 3.2. This gives quite a different picture than cost per vehicle, and even the ranking of different systems is sometimes reversed. The cost per vehicle mile is shown at 40 to 55 cents for taxicabs; $1.10 to $3.60 for buses; $1.40 to $1.90 for rapid transit cars; and $2.20 to $3.50 for commuter rail cars. The national average for buses in smaller cities is at the lower end of the range shown, about $1.20, largely due to differences in wage rates. The rapid transit figures for other U.S. cities are similar to the range shown; however, adjusted for differences in wage rates, a study for the U.S. Department of Transportation found New York City Transit Authority costs per vehicle mile to be the lowest in the nation in 1969.[7]

In Exhibit 3.5 the operating cost per vehicle mile is plotted against the average operating speed, as listed in Column 9 of Exhibit 3.2. The curved lines are lines of equal cost per vehicle hour (cost per vehicle mile times average speed). It is evident that most observations fall quite neatly on or near these arithmetical lines of equal cost per vehicle hour. This can also be seen in Column 4 of Exhibit 3.2. *Within each mode, the differences in cost per vehicle hour are small.* In particular, the very large differences in bus operating cost are reduced dramatically, when costs are presented per vehicle hour. The reasons for this consistency were explained earlier—labor is paid by the hour and most of the operating cost is labor cost. The relative constancy of costs per vehicle hour within each public transit mode leads to two important conclusions.

First, costs per vehicle mile can be substantially reduced by operating the vehicles at a higher speed. For example, even at the extreme cost of $105 per vehicle hour, commuter rail expense per car mile can be reduced roughly 25 percent (from $3.50 to $2.60) by increasing operating speed from 30 to 40 miles per hour. This is within the capabilities of existing equipment if the track is upgraded and station stops are judiciously selected. With potential labor savings in fare collection and equipment maintenance indicated earlier, it is not unreasonable to envisage cost savings per car mile in excess of 40 percent compared to 1974 conditions on a passenger railroad such as the Long Island.

The potential for increased speed is extremely limited on existing subways because of close station spacing, existing track geometry, and signalling. On new lines, however, operating speed can be raised from about 20 to over 30 miles per hour, as the experience of PATCO and BART demonstrates. This can reduce costs per vehicle mile on the order of one third. As can be seen in Exhibit 3.5, PATCO's lower cost per vehicle mile, compared to the NYCTA or PATH, is mostly due to its higher speed.

Bus costs per bus mile can likewise be reduced through higher operating speed, though one should stress that in practice, costs per vehicle mile in the higher speed range do not de-

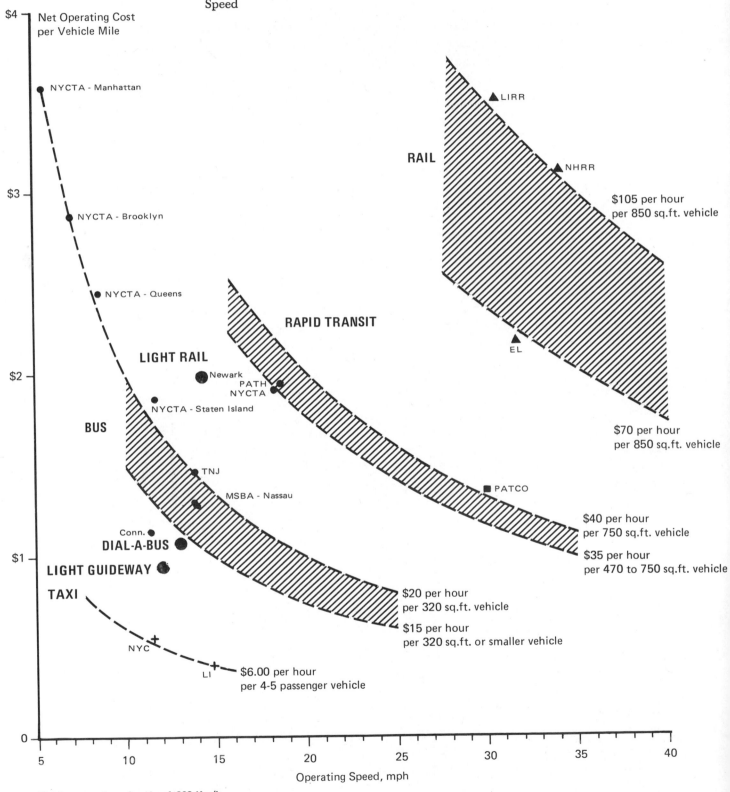

EXHIBIT 3.5

Operating Cost per Vehicle Mile in
1974 Dollars Related to Operating
Speed

Net Operating Cost
per Vehicle Mile

$4

NYCTA - Manhattan

RAIL

▲ LIRR

▲ NHRR

$105 per hour
per 850 sq.ft. vehicle

$3

NYCTA - Brooklyn

NYCTA - Queens

RAPID TRANSIT

LIGHT RAIL

▲ EL

$2

Newark

PATH
NYCTA

NYCTA - Staten Island

BUS

$70 per hour
per 850 sq.ft. vehicle

TNJ

MSBA - Nassau

PATCO

$40 per hour
per 750 sq.ft. vehicle

Conn.

DIAL-A-BUS

$35 per hour
per 470 to 750 sq.ft. vehicle

$1

LIGHT GUIDEWAY

TAXI

$20 per hour
per 320 sq.ft. vehicle

$15 per hour
per 320 sq.ft. or smaller vehicle

NYC

LI

$6.00 per hour
per 4-5 passenger vehicle

0

5   10   15   20   25   30   35   40

Operating Speed, mph

Metric conversion: 1 mph = 1.609 Km/h

Source: Exhibit 3.2

cline as fast as the illustrative curves in Exhibit 3.5 would suggest. Still, exclusive bus lanes and other ways of preferential bus treatment offer significant possibilities for reducing costs per bus mile, and intercity buses remain a for-profit operation largely because of their speed. Even taxicabs reduce their costs per vehicle mile in places (such as lower density neighborhoods) or at times (such as at night) when higher speeds are possible.

The second major conclusion is that cost per vehicle hour is a convenient yardstick for matching travel supply to travel demand. Travel demand occurs in time—one speaks of trips generated "per average day," "per average hour," "per peak hour." By comparing the number of trips demanded per hour to the cost of supplying service per hour the cost of a passenger trip becomes apparent. Or, conversely, one can say how many passengers are needed to support what kind of service at what fare.

For example, at a cost of $100 per hour, and at a fare of, say, $2.00, a commuter rail car needs 50 passengers to board it each hour in order to cover its operating cost. *This approach —how many passengers are needed to "rent" a vehicle for an hour at what fare and subsidy cost—is used in this book as a basis for relating transportation modes to levels of development density and the respective levels of travel demand.*

In addition to the four major modes of public transportation, the position of three intermediate modes is also indicated in Exhibit 3.5. Light rail is represented by the Newark subway, with a 1974 cost of $28.50 per vehicle hour. This is comparable to the Shaker Heights line in Cleveland, which has similar characteristics; San Francisco light rail costs appear to be slightly lower. In any case, light rail costs per vehicle hour fall about halfway between bus and rapid transit, and so does its break-even passenger load per hour.

Dial-a-bus operating costs are on the average in the lower range of regular bus costs, around $13.50 per vehicle hour. It will be shown later that this average conceals wide variation from system to system, with some costing only moderately more than a taxicab and others as much as the highest-cost regular bus operations. Still, the fact that the average cost is more than twice as high as that of the taxicab means that, on the average, dial-a-bus must attract more than twice as many passengers per hour to break even at taxicab kinds of fares—$2 per passenger trip. Given the attainable loadings, this is about what it does. Its cost per passenger averages only slightly less than a taxi, and its low fares are very heavily subsidized.

Costs for full-scale light guideway systems were not available because neither the Morgantown, West Virginia line nor Airtrans at the Dallas-Ft. Worth airport were fully operational as of this writing. However, operating characteristics for the latter, as shown in Exhibit 3.2, were available, based on more than a year of experience. If one assumes employee pay scales in the upper bus range, with a total operating cost per employee of $20,000, then cost per vehicle hour can be estimated at $9.60 and cost per vehicle mile at 80¢. The known costs of some of the short-link automated airport "peoplemovers" are in the 75¢ to $1.25 per vehicle mile range, so the estimate seems reasonable. At this rate and at a fare of 25¢, the system would need 38 riders per vehicle hour to break even, about four times as many as the Dallas system actually attracted. The projected 1976 costs for the Morgantown system were lower—they can be indirectly estimated at $5.70 per vehicle hour, and 30¢ per vehicle mile.

The ability of the different vehicles to carry the passenger load necessary to pay for them depends, of course, on their size. Size is usually specified in terms of seats, but for vehicles that are designed also to carry standees the capacity unit of 6 square feet of gross floorspace is a better common denominator.

In Exhibit 3.6, the costs per vehicle hour shown in the previous Exhibit are recalculated in terms of seat-units for those vehicles that have no provision for standees, and in terms of

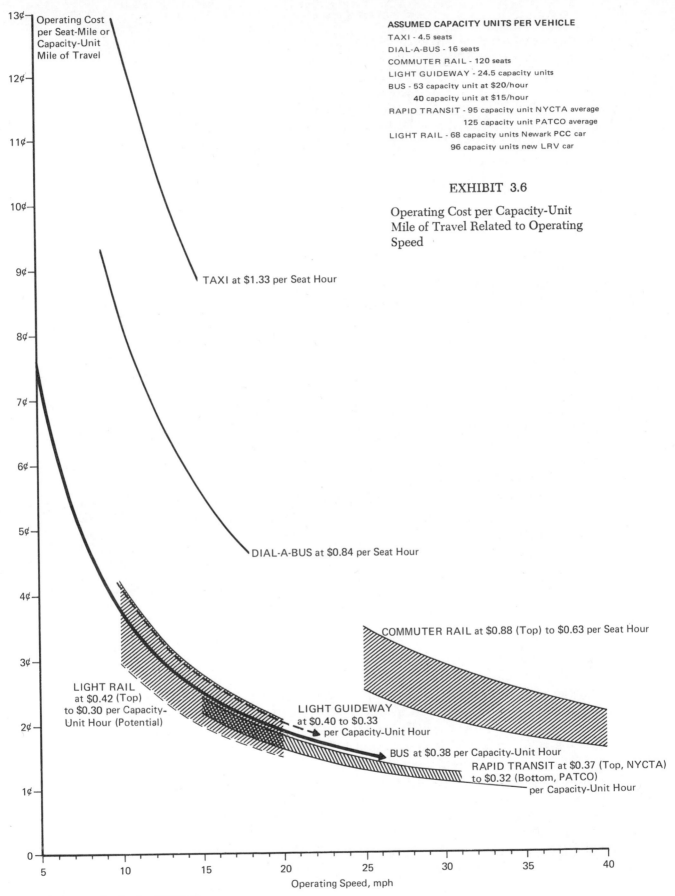

ASSUMED CAPACITY UNITS PER VEHICLE

TAXI - 4.5 seats
DIAL-A-BUS - 16 seats
COMMUTER RAIL - 120 seats
LIGHT GUIDEWAY - 24.5 capacity units
BUS - 53 capacity unit at $20/hour
 40 capacity unit at $15/hour
RAPID TRANSIT - 95 capacity unit NYCTA average
 125 capacity unit PATCO average
LIGHT RAIL - 68 capacity units Newark PCC car
 96 capacity units new LRV car

EXHIBIT 3.6

Operating Cost per Capacity-Unit
Mile of Travel Related to Operating
Speed

Operating Cost
per Seat-Mile or
Capacity-Unit
Mile of Travel

TAXI at $1.33 per Seat Hour

DIAL-A-BUS at $0.84 per Seat Hour

COMMUTER RAIL at $0.88 (Top) to $0.63 per Seat Hour

LIGHT RAIL
at $0.42 (Top)
to $0.30 per Capacity-
Unit Hour (Potential)

LIGHT GUIDEWAY
at $0.40 to $0.33
per Capacity-Unit Hour

BUS at $0.38 per Capacity-Unit Hour

RAPID TRANSIT at $0.37 (Top, NYCTA)
to $0.32 (Bottom, PATCO)
per Capacity-Unit Hour

Operating Speed, mph

Metric conversion 1 mph = 1.609 Km/h

Note: Operating speed includes turn-around time and station dwell-time

Source: Exhibit 3.2

capacity-units for the others. Per unit of capacity per hour, the cost of the taxicab is over three times as high as that of most other systems, and dial-a-bus about twice as high. The commuter rail range follows dial-a-bus quite closely in terms of costs per seat hour; the fact that it can operate at a fraction of its cost per seat mile is due to high speed. All the other systems are clustered closely around the bus. Based on the earlier estimate, light guideway appears slightly more expensive, and rapid transit the same or somewhat less expensive. Light rail is marginally more expensive with old equipment (PCC cars), and may turn out to be among the least expensive to operate if one assumes new equipment (U.S. Standard Light Rail Vehicle) with the same ratios of employees per vehicle and vehicle miles per vehicle as exist today.

Use by Passengers and Employee Productivity. The actual use by passengers experienced in 1974 is listed in Column 11 of Exhibit 3.2, which lists passengers boarding per vehicle hour on the different systems. The fares on some of them were quite different from those mentioned earlier for purposes of illustration and some, such as the PATCO Lindenwold line, did cover their costs. Among buses with 35¢ fares, those in Manhattan came within 9 percent of covering their costs. The cost per passenger that would have to be charged to cover pure operating expenses is listed in Column 5 of Exhibit 3.2.

While cost per passenger is a convenient device for relating transportation demand to the provision of service, what the passenger buys is not just a trip but a trip for a certain distance. The distance varies from a low of 1.5 miles on buses in Manhattan to a high of 31.5 miles on the New Haven Railroad, as Column 12 in Exhibit 3.2 shows. Average trip length multiplied by the number of passengers boarding per vehicle mile equals average vehicle occupancy, shown in Column 13 of Exhibit 3.2. It also represents total passenger miles divided by the total vehicle miles.

Compared to the vehicle capacities listed at the upper right of Exhibit 3.6, the average occupancies are low: 15 to 26 percent on buses, 18 to 28 percent on the rail systems. This is largely the result of extreme peaking of demand, which will be discussed in the next chapter. The peak one-directional load at the maximum load point determines the total number of vehicles that must be deployed; their return trips are largely empty and their use during the rest of the day is sparse. It is unrealistic to expect 50 to 60 percent load factors, typical of the airlines, on urban transit; still, as recently as 1950, load factors of 30 to 36 percent were quite common, because of greater off-peak use as well as greater crowding during peak hours. This contributed significantly to keeping fares per passenger down.

Low as they are, vehicle occupancies do vary dramatically between different systems, from a low of 0.6 to 0.7 passengers per taxicab (which, in the two examples shown, run empty 50 to 45 percent of the time and, when occupied, carry 1.13 to 1.36 passengers, on the average), to more than 30 passengers per rail car. Costs per vehicle mile divided by average occupancies yield costs per passenger mile, and it is the widely different occupancies that make a taxi ride cost 70 cents per passenger mile while a rail ride only costs 10 cents per passenger mile. The high bus occupancies of Manhattan cannot offset the high cost per vehicle mile caused by slow speed, so that the cost per passenger mile is 26 cents, while in suburban areas higher speeds allow the cost per passenger mile to go down to 14 cents or lower despite very low occupancies.

In an inflationary period, dollars and cents represent a rather impermanent way of expressing costs. The labor input required—along with energy and materials input mentioned in the Introduction—is a more constant measure. In Exhibit 3.7, the inverse of labor input, namely, the output per worker, is shown in terms of passenger miles, as well

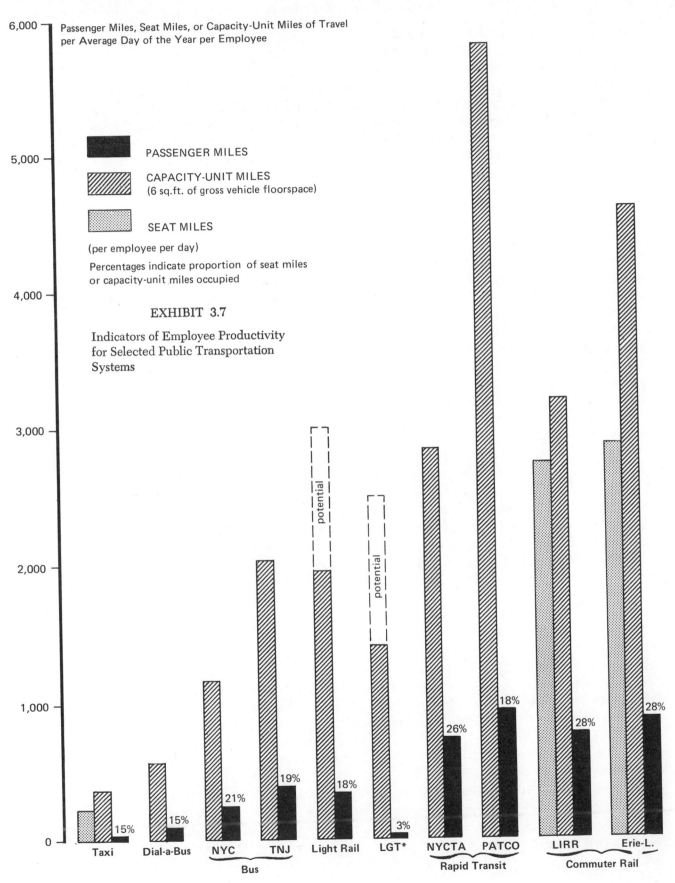

6,000 — Passenger Miles, Seat Miles, or Capacity-Unit Miles of Travel per Average Day of the Year per Employee

- ███ PASSENGER MILES
- ▨▨▨ CAPACITY-UNIT MILES (6 sq.ft. of gross vehicle floorspace)
- ░░░ SEAT MILES

(per employee per day)

Percentages indicate proportion of seat miles or capacity-unit miles occupied

EXHIBIT 3.7

Indicators of Employee Productivity for Selected Public Transportation Systems

potential

potential

15% 15% 21% 19% 18% 3% 26% 18% 28% 28%

Taxi Dial-a-Bus NYC TNJ Light Rail LGT* NYCTA PATCO LIRR Erie-L.

Bus Rapid Transit Commuter Rail

*LGT–Light Guideway Transit, Dallas Airtrans in this case

Source: Exhibit 3.2

as seat miles or capacity-unit miles. The data refer to an average day of the year (not average weekday), largely following the last three columns in Exhibit 3.2.

It is evident that rapid transit and commuter railroads come out at the high end of the scale, with anywhere from about 2,800 to nearly 6,000 capacity-unit miles delivered per employee per day. Moderately high percentages of occupancy also allow them to be high in terms of the passenger miles produced per employee. The difference between the seat-mile bars and the capacity-unit bars is an indicator of the above-average space standard provided by the railroads (up to 10, rather than 6 square feet per passenger), a relationship that also holds true for taxis.

Suburban buses and light rail are in the middle of the productivity range; the dashed bar shows the potential productivity increase with new light rail equipment. The productivity of New York City buses is suppressed by slow operating speed. The productivity of dial-a-buses and taxis is shown to be roughly one sixth to one tenth that of regular buses in terms of passenger miles. It is higher in terms of the vehicle space provided. The productivity of the automated light guideway system shown is in the range between New York City and suburban buses. Its passenger productivity is depressed because of sparse passenger demand at a newly opened airport; potential productivity reflects anticipated future manpower reductions.

Summarizing, the bar chart in Exhibit 3.7 shows that *with an equal labor input, large-scale, capital-intensive rail transit systems deliver substantially more passenger miles and more units of passenger capacity than bus systems and that individualized services are virtually an order of magnitude below the regular buses in terms of productivity.* For the productivity to be used, however, the necessary density of demand must be present. Where it is not, more labor-intensive systems must be resorted to. Also, the capital invested in capital-intensive systems is not free. This leads us to a brief review of the two major components of capital cost, namely the costs of rolling stock and guideway costs.

CAPITAL COSTS

The costs of rolling stock for public transit have undergone an unusually high and rather uneven escalation in recent years. For example, in 1967-68, when the current Long Island Railroad fleet was ordered, the multiple-unit electric cars cost $212,000 each. In 1975, the price quoted for similar equipment was $750,000, representing a 3.5-fold increase in eight years. The price of buses has not escalated nearly as much, and the wholesale price of automobiles has gone up only about 1.4 times. The cost-of-living index rose about 1.6 times during the period.

Part of the reason for the difference is that prices quoted for equipment with long delivery times, such as rail cars, have built into them the manufacturer's estimate of future inflation, while off-the-shelf items, such as taxicabs, are quoted in today's prices. This makes price comparisons between the two types of equipment based on currently quoted prices inaccurate. The inaccuracy becomes even greater if historic prices are used, as they often are, in calculating the capital cost of existing fleets on transit systems. In any practical sense, the value of a five-year-old railroad car is pretty much the same as that of a brand-new one. Yet, with accounting based on historic cost the difference between the two can appear huge, given both price inflation and the increase in interest rates. The difficulty can be corrected with accounting based on the undepreciated replacement cost. For our purposes, however, it is simpler not to deal with empirical equipment costs of existing systems, but rather to assume all-new equipment for all transit modes being compared, keeping in mind that currently quoted prices for heavy equipment with long delivery times are inflated.

Exhibit 3.8 lists selected 1975 prices of typical new vehicles, assumes replacement cycles or amortization periods common to the industry, and shows average annual depreciation as well as average annual debt service on the undepreciated cost; the latter is based on a 12 percent interest rate for vehicles with short life spans, and on an 8 percent interest rate for vehicles with longer life spans. The sum of depreciation and interest appears in Column 6 as the average annual capital cost per vehicle. Since the common denominator in our comparisons is not the vehicle, but rather the capacity unit of a vehicle, cost per capacity unit is shown in Column 10, and cost per capacity-unit mile travelled in Column 11.

What stands out is that, *adjusted for a standard unit of capacity, the capital cost of rolling stock per mile travelled is quite similar for all the modes being compared.* It is in the range of 0.3 to 0.7 cents for taxis and dial-a-buses; in the range of 0.3 to 0.4 cents for buses; between 0.3 and 0.5 cents for rapid transit; around 0.7 cents for both light rail and commuter railroads; only the automated light guideway vehicle stands out above the others, with 1.0 cents per capacity-unit mile travelled.

The initial cost of vehicles is generally related to their weight, to the complexity of the equipment, and to the degree of mass production. The mass-produced auto, used as a taxicab in the first line of Exhibit 3.8, cost only around $1.50 a pound in 1975 prices; buses and rapid transit cars for immediate delivery cost mostly in the range of $3.00 to $3.50 a pound; light rail, heavy rail, and rapid transit cars for future delivery cost on the order of $5.00 to $7.50; the complex automated light guideway vehicle, manufactured in a small order, cost $13.00 per pound; it has been estimated that production in large orders could bring that down to around $10.00. Generally, the capital cost of sophisticated automation alone has been estimated to about equal the cost of a comparable manually operated vehicle.

For vehicles with life spans exceeding 25 years, the initial cost of the vehicle itself is surpassed by the cost of debt service if an 8 percent interest rate is assumed, as evident from Exhibit 3.8. While debt service at an even higher rate comprises only 15 percent of the capital cost of the taxicab, it is 37 percent of the capital cost for the bus with its 15-year assumed lifespan, and 58 percent of the rail vehicles with 35-year life spans. *High interest rates greatly increase the cost of durable equipment with long life cycles.*

In fact, there are sound economic reasons *not* to use an interest rate as high as 8 percent, if the object is to calculate the total cost of a transit system over a span of future years, and if operating costs are treated in constant dollars. The reason is that to a large extent, an 8 percent interest rate represents a hedge against future inflation. The real long-term cost of capital is usually assumed to be 3 percent, or at most 4 to 5 percent if a risk factor is included—such as the possibility that the investment will have to be discarded prematurely. Since we are about to compare capital costs with operating costs, using an interest figure that embodies future inflation—nominal changes in the value of money, not real resource costs— would force us to take into account future inflation in operating costs as well. Since operating expenses per vehicle mile have been rising about 10 percent annually between 1966 and 1974, the present value of a discounted stream of operating expenses over the life cycle of a vehicle would be very much higher than the 1974 operating costs portrayed so far. To avoid the extreme uncertainty of projecting future inflation in labor costs, it is preferable to calculate in constant dollars. If operating costs are presented in constant dollars, then the interest rate should also be one that does not include the effect of future inflation. With a 4 percent interest rate, the amounts shown in column 5 of Exhibit 3.8 for vehicles with life spans of over 10 years are cut in half.

EXHIBIT 3.8

Illustrative Capital Costs of Rolling Stock for Public Transportation, 1975

	New vehicle cost in 1975 $$ (1)	Assumed replacement period, years (2)	Assumed annual VMT/veh (3)	Straight-line depreciation annual $$ (4)	Average annual debt service, at indicated % $$ (5)	Average annual cost per vehicle $$ (6)	Gross floor area per vehicle, sq.ft. (7)	Capacity units @ 6sq.ft. (8)	Empty weight lbs. (9)	Average annual cost: per capacity unit $$ (10)	Average annual cost: per capacity unit mile $$ (11)	Weight per capacity unit, lbs. (12)	Weight of materials consumed per 1,000 capacity-unit miles, lbs., during replacement period. (13)
TAXICAB													
4-passenger car	5,000	3	40,000	1,666	300 (12%)	1,966	45e	7	3,500	281	0.0070	500	4.2 (7.30)**
6-passenger car	6,000	3	60,000	2,000	360 (12%)	2,360	55e	9	4,000	262	0.0044	444	2.5 (3.70)**
DIAL-A-BUS													
11-seat van	12,000	4	30,000	3,000	720 (12%)	3,720	100e	17	5,000	219	0.0073	294	2.45 (3.78)**
19-seat bus (23')	23,000	12	30,000	1,917	920 (8%)	2,837	185	31	7,500	92	0.0031	242	0.67
BUS													
35-seat urban bus (30')	43,000	15	30,000	2,867	1,720 (8%)	4,587	240	40	13,400	115	0.0038	335	0.74
36-seat urban bus (35')	57,000	15	30,000	3,800	2,280 (8%)	6,080	293	48	18,840	127	0.0042	393	0.87
36-seat urban bus (40')	64,000	15	30,000	4,267	2,560 (8%)	6,827	340	57	19,750	120	0.0040	346	0.77
53-seat commuter bus (40')	67,000	15	30,000	4,467	2,680 (8%)	7,147	320	53	29,955	135	0.0045	565	1.25
68-seat two-deck bus (35')	83,500	15	30,000	5,567	3,340 (8%)	8,907	560	93	37,700	96	0.0032	405	0.87
LIGHT RAIL													
68-seat light rail vehicle	350,000	30	40,000	11,667	14,000 (8%)	25,657	576	96	67,000	267	0.0067	698	0.58
LIGHT GUIDEWAY TRANSIT													
8-seat vehicle (Morgantown)	113,000	20	60,000	5,650	4,520 (8%)	10,170	103	17	8,600	598	0.0100	506	0.42
RAPID TRANSIT													
56-seat NYCTA R-46 car*	285,333	35	50,000	8,152	11,413 (8%)	19,565	750	125	81,000	156	0.0031	648	0.37
Same, probable cost for post-1976 delivery	450,000	35	50,000	12,857	18,000 (8%)	30,857	750	125	81,000	247	0.0049	648	0.37
COMMUTER RAIL													
120-seat Multiple Unit electric car	750,000	35	50,000	21,429	30,000 (8%)	51,429	850	142	100,000	362	0.0072	704	0.40 (0.47)**

Notes:

*Cost of cars on a large order (750) delivered in 1975-76; other prices are 1975 quotations for delivery at various times

**Vehicle weight consumed per seat-mile, rather than capacity-unit mile shown in parentheses on systems where extra capacity units are used to provide more comfort to the seated passenger, and not to accommodate standees.

e—estimated

n.a.—not available

Metric conversion: 1 mile = 1.609 Km; 1 sq.ft. = 0.0929 m^2; 1lb. = 0.4536 Kg.

Source: Regional Plan Association based on data from various operating agencies

The effect is portrayed graphically in Exhibit 3.9, which compares the capital costs of new equipment to the operating costs previously shown in Exhibit 3.6 at selected speeds. For taxicabs, the capital cost of the vehicle is indicated to add on the order of 10 percent to the operating cost, which is in keeping with past studies of the industry.[8] Interest is of minimal importance, because of the brief life cycle of the taxicab. For buses, past experience suggests roughly the same share of capital costs;[9] such is shown to be the case at a speed around 10 mph; at higher speeds, the fixed component of capital cost becomes relatively more important, as operating cost declines.

In large part because of operating costs reduced by higher speeds, the capital cost component of equipment plays a much larger role on the various fixed-guideway systems shown; in round figures, it adds in excess of 25 percent to the operating cost if an 8 percent interest rate is assumed, and over 18 percent at the more appropriate 4 percent interest rate.

The relative position of the two prime contenders for the bus market, light rail and light guideway transit, changes only modestly if vehicle capital costs are added to operating costs. Under 1974-75 conditions, the operating costs of light rail and light guideway systems were about the same if measured per capacity-unit at comparable speed; both appeared to be slightly higher, but generally similar to the bus; however, the capital cost of the automated light guideway vehicles is about one third higher than that of light rail vehicles if adjusted per unit of capacity. This puts light guideway at a slight disadvantage, as evident from Exhibit 3.9. Proponents of both systems are hoping for a roughly 30 percent reduction in operating costs based on improved technology, so the two can be expected to continue running neck and neck.

The rolling stock costs of rapid transit per capacity-unit mile travelled are about the same as those of buses if an 8 percent interest rate is used, and lower if a 4 percent interest rate is used. If added to the operating costs shown previously in Exhibit 3.6, rapid transit still remains slightly less expensive than the bus at comparable speed on the average. With both operating costs and equipment costs higher than those of rapid transit, commuter rail remains a rather high-cost operation, and one way for it to compete is through higher speed; Exhibit 3.9 indicates that with a 4 percent interest on equipment it is slightly less expensive, per capacity-unit mile delivered, at a speed of 40 mph than rapid transit is at 20 mph.

While the economics of high interest rates works against long-lived equipment, environmental factors favor it. The auto used as a taxicab has to be thrown away every three years or so, and thereby consumes over 7 pounds of metal and other materials for every 1,000 seat-miles delivered, as the last column in Exhibit 3.8 shows. The bus, replaced every 15 years or so, consumes about 1 pound of vehicle weight for every 1,000 capacity-unit miles delivered; rail and light guideway vehicles generally consume less than 0.5 pounds of weight for every 1,000 capacity-unit miles delivered.

Also of environmental interest is Column 12 in Exhibit 3.8, which shows the net vehicle weight per capacity unit. Energy consumption of different vehicle types, while obviously related to the energy conversion efficiency of the different propulsion systems used, and to the frictional resistance of the guideway—e.g., rubber on concrete versus steel on steel—also depends on the vehicle weight that has to be pushed around. It is apparent that differences in this weight are not very large. The light guideway vehicles weigh about the same per capacity unit as autos; buses of the urban and dial-a-bus variety tend to be lighter; rail vehicles tend to be heavier.

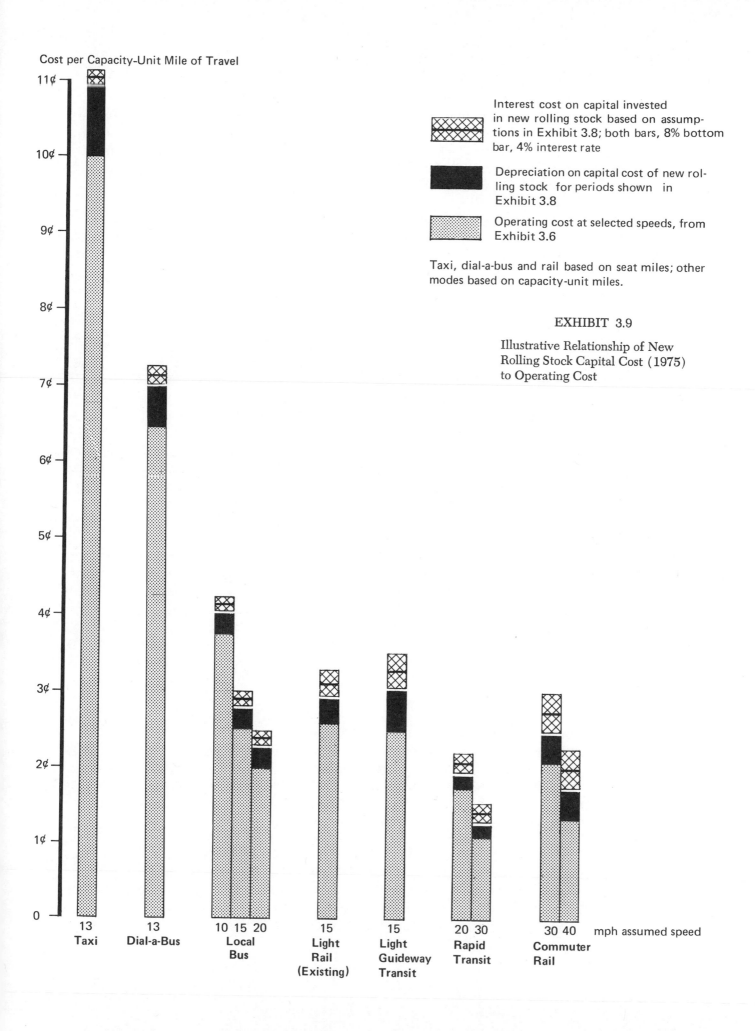

Cost per Capacity-Unit Mile of Travel

Interest cost on capital invested in new rolling stock based on assumptions in Exhibit 3.8; both bars, 8% bottom bar, 4% interest rate

Depreciation on capital cost of new rolling stock for periods shown in Exhibit 3.8

Operating cost at selected speeds, from Exhibit 3.6

Taxi, dial-a-bus and rail based on seat miles; other modes based on capacity-unit miles.

EXHIBIT 3.9

Illustrative Relationship of New Rolling Stock Capital Cost (1975) to Operating Cost

mph assumed speed

13
Taxi

13
Dial-a-Bus

10 15 20
Local
Bus

15
Light
Rail
(Existing)

15
Light
Guideway
Transit

20 30
Rapid
Transit

30 40
Commuter
Rail

In addition to the cost of vehicles, taxicabs, dial-a-buses, and regular buses incur only modest capital costs: they consist principally of garage investment, occasional passenger shelters, and radio transmitting and receiving equipment, which is important for the demand-responsive systems. Roadway costs are typically not calculated for these modes, because they share the roadway with other traffic and represent a very small proportion of it. By contrast, guideway capital costs are of decisive importance for systems which operate on exclusive rights-of-way.

Guideway capital costs are a prime example of fixed costs. An increased amount of traffic does not lead to a proportionate increase in the capital investment needed—except in extreme situations. Therefore, fixed guideway systems are able to realize economies of scale. For the same reason, the direct relationship that was assumed, for the sake of simplicity, between costs and vehicle units of capacity in the preceding discussion cannot be applied to guideway costs. Rather, one has to look for a minimum traffic volume at which an investment in a separate guideway is warranted.

The difficulties with interest rates encountered in calculating the capital cost of vehicles are even more pronounced in the case of guideways. While tracks, signals, and power lines do wear out, the useful life of some guideway structures such as tunnels or embankments is indefinitely long. London's first subway tunnels, opened over a century ago in 1863, still provide benefits to passengers and to the city as a whole and are likely to continue to do so for a long time to come. Meanwhile, the meaning of an 8 percent interest rate is that a 50-year investment has to pay for itself in 12 years. Even a 4 percent rate requires it to pay for itself in 22 years. One can raise the question to what extent such yardsticks of the money economy are applicable to investments that are able to provide real savings in time, energy, and materials virtually in perpetuity. On the other hand, the fact remains that urban guideway construction is very expensive, that capital is scarce, and that the absence of any priorities for allocating it will also lead to a waste of resources.

The resolution of this dilemma is clearly beyond the limits of this study. Yet, its very theme—what densities of urban development can support what kinds of public transportation—requires at least some tentative answers. To approach these, the purposes of a transit guideway on an exclusive or partially exclusive right-of-way can be classified as five-fold: (1) To increase speed, with the resulting benefits of reduced operating cost, time savings to riders, and some ridership diversion from the auto; (2) To attract ridership by the superior ride quality it can offer compared to transit in mixed traffic; (3) To expand transportation capacity in places where traffic cannot be adequately handled by present means; (4) To protect the non-user of the guideway from the negative effects of the traffic it attracts, as well as from visual intrusion; (5) To establish a fixed framework for future land use commitments supportive of public transportation.

We shall briefly go through the exercise of assigning monetary values to the benefits of increased speed. As an example, let us assume a bus line that carries 4,000 daily passengers per mile of route on 400 daily bus trips—a midday frequency of about 10 buses an hour in one direction. Let us further assume that the bus line operates at an average speed of 12.5 miles per hour, and that an exclusive right-of-way would increase its speed to 25 mph. From Exhibit 3.6, assuming 50 capacity-units per bus and 290 full operating days per year, the annual savings in vehicle operation can be calculated at $87,000 per mile from such a speed increase. Assuming further that the riders value their in-vehicle time at 5 cents a minute, the annual per-mile benefit to riders would be an additional $139,000. Lastly, a speed increase to 25 mph will be competitive with the auto, and may attract perhaps 2,000 former auto users. Since the average costs of operating an auto and transit are similar, the savings to be realized are in the extra urban costs of operating an auto, primarily parking charges and tolls, although some reduction in accident costs, in auto ownership, and in the congestion for the remaining auto users will also ensue. Pegging these rather arbitrarily at 15 cents per passenger mile, we get another $87,000 in benefits, for a total of $313,000 annually. This stream of benefits would warrant an investment of $3.8 million per mile if discounted at 8 percent, and $6.7 million per mile if discounted at 4 percent, assuming a 50-year project life. To the extent that some elements will wear out earlier, the allowable investment would be accordingly reduced.

In 1975 prices, the former sum could buy some bus pavement or light rail tracks on an existing right-of-way. The latter sum would allow work closer to light guideway or rapid transit standards in some parts of the country. Thus, if a prepared right-of-way exists, it is possible to visualize a situation where a daily volume of as few as 4,000 to 6,000 passengers would warrant fixed-guideway transit on the basis of speed-related transportation benefits alone.

However, where a ready-made right-of-way does not exist, and continuous grade separation is required, guideway costs rapidly rise into the $30 to $50 million per mile range, requiring volumes for justification that rarely exist in American cities. If tunneling is required, costs rise further into the $70 million to $200 million per mile range which can be beyond the reach of purely transportation-related benefit-cost analysis, even with volumes near a comfortable capacity of 200,000 per day, as may be realized on some of the lines under construction in New York.

Some of the more basic difficulties with benefit-cost analysis applied to public transit systems should be enumerated at this point. The first—illustrated above—is its extreme sensitivity to interest rate assumptions.

The second has to do with the largest single component of the "benefits"—the cost of time. A review of seven studies to justify new transit systems[10] has shown that their assumptions about the cost of time varied from 1 to 6 cents per minute. Empirical studies referred to in Chapter 1 suggest that the topography of values that people attach to time is quite complex, varying over a range from less than 1 to 30 cents per minute depending on travel mode, income, and other variables. Nor can this value be readily escalated in relation to the Cost of Living Index. The implicit valuation of time is usually calculated on the basis of how people trade off time against fares or auto travel costs. Thus, when fares do not go up because of subsidy, or when auto costs lag behind the cost of living, as they used to until 1973, the "value of time" also lags. Meanwhile, in 1965-74 the Construction Cost Index was escalating much faster than the general rate of inflation. As a result, construction that seemed justifiable by time savings a decade ago may not seem so any longer. One may question to what extent such relatively short-term fluctuations in the inflation rate should be allowed to influence basic decisions about the shape of the urban infrastructure which, once in place, tends to outlast generations.

Lastly, existing benefit-cost studies have even greater difficulty dealing with benefits unrelated to time savings and thus throw in with "benefits" such spurious items as increased construction employment, increases in local taxes, or the "savings" from planned freeways no longer needed.

Monetary values are difficult indeed to attach to the four non-time-related benefits of fixed-guideway transit listed earlier. There is ample evidence that new transit facilities induce new travel that would have not taken place without them, but what is the dollar value of this new mobility, given primarily to non-auto owners, and of increased comfort standards? Evidence quoted in the first chapter suggested that both may be quite high, but these values rarely enter traditional calculations. Studies for rapid transit in Seattle[11] hoped for 2.5 percent newly induced traffic, whereas it turned out to be near 35 percent on the BART Trans-Bay tube.

To the extent that transit can reduce auto traffic congestion in selected corridors the benefit is counted as time-saving to non-users, but what about the value of relieving overcrowding on parallel transit lines, which is a significant justification for much of New York's subway construction? Only oblique numerical evidence exists on the benefits of increased space standards on transit, and of relieving subway congestion.

On the issue of the high costs of tunneling, it seems that a "pure" transportation investment, such as an elevated structure, could be amply justified on transportation grounds alone in all places where subways are proposed. A tunnel under a downtown area, however, or under an intimate residential neighborhood, is fundamentally not a transportation investment. It is an urban design investment, and thus not subject to analysis in transportation terms, much like an urban park, which might not withstand benefit-cost analysis purely in terms of recreation. One basic difficulty with bus-only systems, sometimes heralded as a low-cost alternative to rail or rail-like transit, is that they cannot enter closely built-up areas except at very much higher tunneling costs than electrically propelled systems, because of ventilation[12] (as well as passing) requirements. Bus-only proposals typically ignore this community condition of underground distribution in dense activity centers, and thus are not comparing like with like in their benefit-cost analyses.

On the issue of establishing a fixed framework for future land use commitments supportive of public transportation, calculations in current day economic terms are clearly irrelevant, since short-term profit is largely dictating the abandonment of cities in favor of far-flung dispersal. A major purpose of fixed transit investment is to create the preconditions for reversing this trend, so that nodes of potentially high access are created at which concentrations of both residential and nonresidential activities will be able to take place in the future. The basic resource benefits of such a more compact urban pattern will include reduced auto use, reduced overall travel demand, reduced energy, materials, space, and time consumption. They will, however, be the result of development patterns transit will make possible, not the result of a transit system as such. In this way, investment in fixed-guideway transit can be regarded as a down payment on a more resource-conserving urban future.

With all these considerations in mind, we are still left with the issue of how to allocate scarce money resources for transit today. The real-resource benefits of fixed public transit routes are related to their near-term use by people. Future activity nodes are generally more likely where there is some activity today, and the need for protecting the above-ground urban environment from transportation intrusion is also greater where the volume of travel is greater. The need for increased comfort is greater where the number of people is greater, and so are the time-related benefits. Thus *one can rank transit construction proposals in terms of their near-term use by people—in terms of passenger miles of travel—and see to it that those which need the least dollars per passenger mile get them first, without worrying much about how the money is contributing to the various particular hard-to-quantify benefits.* Presumably, these have been weighted in the process of political decision, community consultation, and engineering and architectural design.

Obviously, ranking in terms of construction dollars to be spent per passenger mile is not advanced here as the sole investment criterion. While it does relate prospective investment to prospective use, several caveats concerning such a yardstick are in order. First, both cost and patronage estimates of future systems are often quite imprecise. Second, the approach does not distinguish between passenger miles newly attracted to transit and those diverted from existing facilities. Third, care should be taken not to apply it to particular high-cost links in a system, because such exceptional costs in one place may be offset by below-average costs of other links; also, patronage figures should reflect full development, not partial use of an incomplete system element. Fourth, the approach is directed at long-term investment, with a life span assumed here to be 50 years. Without an explicit time dimension, high-volume facilities could be built, rebuilt, and expanded over and over again with apparent justification but without real merit.

Exhibit 3.10 lists examples of recent fixed-guideway construction costs in relation to passenger use. They include conventional rapid transit, commuter rail, automated light guideway transit, and an exclusive busway. The construction costs are stated in terms which do not deviate too far from 1974 dollars; actual costs are separated from projected costs. The passenger miles reflect either traffic actually attained in 1974-75, or an estimate of the potential traffic for this period. They do not reflect speculative long-term projections. It can be seen from the last column that the investment per daily passenger mile ranges from $240 to $3,200. The anticipated 1974 dollar costs of completing four projects in the New York Region show a narrower spread, $800 to $1,800 per daily passenger mile. San Francisco's BART is about in the middle, with $1,200. Discounted at a 4 percent interest rate over 50 years and apportioned among actual users, the New York range, which includes San Francisco, comes out to be 13 to 28¢ per passenger mile. Some New York City projects which won strong political backing in the late 1960s but which were then deferred had costs up to five times above the range shown.[13]

Following the experience of routes that did gain eventual political and technical support, it appears that rail transit investments up to roughly $1,800 in 1974 prices per passenger mile to be served on an average weekday shortly after completion are warranted.

Apart from this essentially political justification, one can offer an energy justification. One dollar spent on rapid transit construction in 1974 prices required on the order of 60,000 to 77,000 Btu of energy input.[14] One passenger mile per average weekday represents 14,800 passenger miles over 50 years. Prorated over this period, the $1,200 per passenger mile cost of building BART means an indirect energy expenditure of about 6,200 Btu per passenger mile, if one uses the higher Btu value. Similarly, the $1,800 Archer Avenue subway cost shown in Exhibit 3.10 means about 9,400 Btu per passenger mile. Adding, say, 3,200 Btu per passenger mile typical of direct energy expenditures for rapid transit, the total energy cost becomes 9,400 Btu per passenger mile in the first case and 12,600 Btu in the second case. This range does not exceed the total direct plus indirect cost of the auto, which can be pegged at 10,000 to 14,000 Btu per passenger mile in urban weekday use. The figures are obviously subject to variation; thus BART requires about 0.5 kwh or 5,000 Btu per passenger mile to operate; this plus its construction energy expenditure makes it only modestly less energy intensive than the auto. On the other hand, the Chicago Transit Authority uses only 2,300 Btu per passenger mile to operate; it thus might spend more on construction (i.e., build a new downtown subway) and still remain less energy intensive than the average urban auto. Lastly, the total energy costs of the auto on particular, costly urban freeways can be much higher than average; for the planned Westway in Manhattan the direct and indirect cost of auto use can be estimated at around 20,000 Btu per passenger mile.

For purposes of illustration, one can pick an investment yardstick of $1,500 per passenger mile; with this level of expenditure in 1974 prices, total energy costs of transit will on the average not exceed total energy costs of the auto at the present time. At $1,500 per passenger mile, a $100 million-a-mile tunnel would have to carry a daily volume of at least

EXHIBIT 3.10

Illustrative Capital Costs of Guideway Construction Related to Passenger Use

	Dates of constr. starts	Route length miles (track miles in parentheses)	Construction cost, $ million	Cost per route-mile, $ million (per track mile in parentheses)	Average use, passenger miles per route mile per day	Investment per daily passenger mile in circa 1974 dollars
Actual costs:						
Long Island RR, Merrick-Bellmore (elevated on existing right-of-way)	1973	3.7 (7.4)	26.6	7.2 (3.6)	30,000 estimated 1975	$240
El Monte Busway, Los Angeles (surface)	1972	11.2	60.0	5.4	14,600 estimated 1975 @ 10.6 mi. per trip	$366
Second Avenue Subway, Manhattan (tunnel)	1972-74	1.3 (3.4)	92.8	71.4 (27.3)	150,000 potential 1974 demand	$476
63rd Street Subway, Manhattan-Queens (tunnel)	1969-75	2.5 (5.9)	324.5	130.0 (55.0)	215,000 potential 1974 demand	$605
Washington Metro (tunnel and elevated for contracts shown)	1970-75	45.4 (91.0)	1,828.0	40.3 (20.1)	50,000 potential 1975 demand	$806
Light Guideway Transit, Morgantown (68% elevated-32% surface)	1971	2.2 (4.4)	59.0*	26.8 (13.4)	24,000 estimated 1975	$1,112
Bay Area Rapid Transit (36% surface-33% elevated-31% tunnel)	1964-70	71.0 (142.0)	1,400.0**	30.0 (15.0)	25,000 actual 1975	$1,200
Archer Avenue Subway, Queens (tunnel)	1972-75	1.2 (3.3)	125.2	104.3 (37.9)	75,000 potential 1974 demand	$1,390
Light Guideway Transit, Dallas Airport (80% surface-20% elevated)	1971	6.4 (12.8)	43.0	6.7 (3.4)	2,080 estimated 1975	$3,221
Projected costs: * **						
63rd Street & Queens Superexpress line	(Jan. 1974 dollars)	8.8 (18.9)	847	96.3 (46.0)	116,000 potential 1974 demand	$830
PATH Plainfield extension	(Est. 1974 dollars)	17.4 (35.0)	250	14.4 (7.2)	16,588 potential 1975 @ 10 mi. per trip	$887
Second Avenue & Bronx Express line	(Jan. 1974 dollars)	14.0 (33.0)	1,928	137.7 (58.4)	139,000 potential 1974 demand	$991
Archer Avenue & Southeast Queens line	(Jan. 1974 dollars)	5.4 (12.2)	385	71.3 (31.6)	39,000 potential 1974 demand	$1,828
MARTA (Atlanta) Phase A (35% subway-45% elevated-20% surface)	(1975 dollars)	13.7 (27.4)	585	42.7 (21.3)	40,100 official 1981 / 25,000 estimated 1981	$1,069 / $1,670****

Notes:

* Total cost through start of operations in 1975 $64 million; $59 million includes both guideway construction and automated control system.

** Construction cost in 1974 $$ about 2.12 billion; per route-mile and per passenger-mile costs based on this figure; deviation from 1974 cost not sufficiently large to warrant adjustment in other instances.

*** New York use figures based on the assumption that the full system is in operation, including an as-yet undetermined second feeder link into the 63rd street tunnel; contracts shown under "actual costs" exclude track equipment.

**** ... official projection and estimate refer to completion of Phase A only.

66,000 passengers; a $25 million-a-mile aerial structure at least 16,000; and a $10 million-a-mile surface structure at least 6,600. Without considering indirect energy expenditures, the warrants suggested for fixed-guideway transit have typically been much higher. For example, the justification for an exclusive bus lane has been doubted at volumes of less than about 15,000 passengers per day in both directions, because the corresponding one-directional flow of about 2,500 persons per track or lane in the peak hour can be handled by automobiles on one freeway lane.[15] We will return to a discussion of these relationships in greater detail in the summary chapter.

SERVICE CHARACTERISTICS AND RESOURCE USE

A summary of the key characteristics of the eight public transit modes considered is shown in tabular form in Exhibit 3.11. The four qualitative attributes of manner of access, service frequency (on-demand, on-headway, or on-schedule),[16] routing, and type of right-of-way are listed at the top. An indication of the size of the group that travels together is vehicle occupancy, shown next, which should be read in conjunction with the line indicating whether or not the vehicles travel in trains. The larger the vehicle occupancy, the more people share the cost of "renting" a vehicle, but also the higher the development density needed to assemble this group.

Illustrative maximum capacities of the different modes—that is, the maximum number of people that can be carried per lane or track in one direction during one hour—are also shown. This subject typically receives much attention in the literature, but is not emphasized here because outside the largest cities such as New York no public transportation modes in the United States have to operate near their maximum capacity. Furthermore, maximum capacity depends on so many conditions and assumptions that it is a highly relative figure. The assumptions used in the exhibit are spelled out in detail.

Rough ranges of operating speed are also indicated, along with the average door-to-door speeds in the New York Region. The high door-to-door speed of the taxicab, compared to its low operating speed, is a result of very short access time. The average trip length bears some relationship to the average speed.

In addition to the 1974 dollar costs per passenger mile, two kinds of environmental costs are listed for reference: the cost in energy used for vehicle propulsion, and the cost in materials consumed to make and replace the vehicles. Both might be usefully related to those of the private auto, assuming that in urban weekday use it is occupied by 1.5 people (the occupancy is higher for trips outside urban areas and on weekends). Under urban weekday conditions, the direct energy expenditure per passenger mile in an auto which delivers 13.9 miles per gallon is about 6,000 Btu, dramatically less than the expenditure of a taxicab or a dial-a-bus but about twice the expenditure of a regular bus or rapid transit. Commuter rail and light rail show energy expenditures somewhat above those of buses or rapid transit, in the first case because of the high speed, in the second case because of the low passenger occupancy. Energy-storage systems now in experimental use, which aim at retrieving the power lost in braking, can reduce the energy use of the electric transit modes by some 20 percent. If greater savings are attained by the private auto as its weight is reduced and more efficient engines are developed, the energy advantage of the mass transit modes over the private auto may shrink in time.

EXHIBIT 3.11

Illustrative Characteristics of Eight Modes of Public Transportation in the U.S.

	Taxicab	Dial-a-bus	Local Bus	Express Bus	Light Rail	Light Guideway Transit	Standard Rapid Transit	Commuter Rail
Access: Door-to-door service (D to D) or walk to station or auxiliary access mode to get to station?	D to D	D to D	Walk	Walk or Auto	Mostly Walk	Walk or Access Mode	Walk or Access Mode	Access Mode or Walk
Service Frequency: On demand, on schedule or on headway?	Demand	Demand	Schedule or Headway	Schedule	Headway	Demand or Headway	Headway	Schedule
Routing: Direct or with stops for other passengers?	Direct	Stops and route-deviation	Stops	Few Stops	Stops	Direct or Stops	Stops	Some Stops
Operation: In mixed traffic, in reserved lanes, or on exclusive right-of-way?	Mixed Traffic	Mixed Traffic	Mixed Traffic	Mixed Tr. or Res.Lanes	Mixed, or Res. Lanes, or Excl.Row	Excl. Row	Excl. Row	Partially Excl. Row
Vehicle Occupancy: Average daily number of passengers per vehicle (Passenger-miles/vehicle mile)	0.75	1.15	7-12	7-20	13+	(4.4) exist. 1	14-25	27-32
Vehicle Size: Passenger capacity, seats or 6 sq.ft. capacity units for vehicles allowing standees	4-5 (seats)	16+ (seats)	40-57 (cap.units)	53 (seats)	68-(96) (cap.units)	20-25 (cap.units)	90-150 (cap.units)	80-120 (seats)
Vehicle Capability for Trains:	none	none	none	none	1-3 cars	1-3 cars	2-11 cars	1-10+ cars
Illustrative Maximum Line Capacity Per Hour: Passengers per one-way lane or track per hour (with no less than 6 sq.ft. of gross vehicle floorspace per person) under indicated conditions	375 (500 cabs @0.75 pass)	575 (500 vans @ 1.15 pass)	6,800 (120 stopping buses @57 pass)	10,000 (off-line stops 240 buses @45) 33,000 (nonstop 735 buses @ 45)	13,500 (140 stopping cars @ 96 pass)	4000 (off-line stops 240 cars) 9800 (offline stops 200 trains @ 2 cars)	38,000 (32 stopping trains @ 8 large cars)	30,000 (25 trains @10 cars some stops)

EXHIBIT 3.11 continued

Speed: Maximum (mph)	60	60	60	60	55	35	80	100
Average operating (mph) (see exhibits 4.1 and 4.2 for detail)	12-15	13-16	6-20	20±	6-25	12-19	16-45	25-45
Door-to-door (airline, not over-the-road speed in the New York Region)	9	n.a.	5.5		n.a.	n.a.	10	20
Average Passenger Trip Length (miles):	2-3	2	2-4	15±	3+	1+	4-12	15-26
Operation and Maintenance Cost: Per passenger-mile at average vehicle occupancy and speed in 1974 $$)	$0.75	$0.90	$0.14 (outside NYC)	$0.05-0.13 (N.J., Conn.)	$0.16 (old eqpt)	($0.21) (at 18% occup)	$0.06-0.14	$0.08-0.10
Direct Energy Consumption: Per passenger-mile at average vehicle occupancy and speed, N.Y. Region, 1974	15,000 Btu	14,000 Btu (estimated)	2,800 Btu		4,600 Btu	n.a.	3,000 Btu	3,360 Btu
Materials Consumption for Rolling Stock: Per 1000 passenger miles, exclusive of replacement parts	40 lbs	13 lbs	6.0 lbs		4.9 lbs	(2.6 lbs)	1.8 lbs	1.5 lbs

Note: Figures in parentheses are not currently attained in the U.S.; costs for light guideway transit shown assuming the same occupancy (18%) as light rail or automated rapid transit; actual load factors on the experimental systems are lower. Energy consumption data derived from: Tri-State Regional Planning Commission. *Regional Propulsion Efficiency of Tri-State Ground Modes of Passenger Transportation.* ITR 4502-2601, March 1975, Table II, line 9. Also Regional Plan Association and Resources for the Future, Inc., *Regional Energy Consumption.* January, 1974. Table F, p. 15. Other figures from previous exhibits. Bus and light rail capacities from Hoey, William F. and Levinson, Herbert S., *Bus Capacity Analysis.* Wilbur Smith & Associates, January 1975. Dial-a-bus fuel use from Bert Arrillaga "Paratransit Strategies for Energy Conservation" *Traffic Engineering* Nov. 1975; occupancy changed from 1.47 in this source to 1.15 for consistency with other data.

Metric conversion:

1 mile = 1.609 Km

1 Btu = 0.252 Cal

1 lb = 0.454 Kg

Direct energy consumption primarily for vehicle propulsion represents only a part of the total energy used by any transportation mode. Eric Hirst has shown that indirect energy use for such purposes as auto manufacture, highway construction, and producing gasoline is about 70 percent of the direct gasoline consumption per passenger mile.[17] In public transit systems, the major source of indirect consumption is guideway construction. In the case of the San Francisco BART, the energy consumed for construction was estimated to be about equal to the energy requirement for propulsion over a period of 50 years.[18] This figure will vary depending on how intensively a new guideway is used; on existing systems the energy cost of construction can be considered amortized.

A recurring source of indirect energy consumption, however, is the need to replace the vehicles as they wear out. The materials consumption for vehicle replacement is one index of this indirect energy cost. For a passenger auto that weighs 3,500 lbs., is driven 10,000 miles a year, and is thrown away every 10 years, the materials consumption, not including spare parts, amounts to some 23 lbs. per 1,000 passenger miles. It can be seen from the bottom line in Exhibit 0.6 that this figure is about half that of a taxicab, but much higher than that of all other modes of public transportation: about 6 lbs. for the bus and as little as 1.5 lbs. for commuter rail, which uses durable vehicles that may run two million miles before they are discarded.

Obviously, the figures shown are but partial and approximate indicators of environmental costs, and are meant to be only suggestive of the fact that not all public transit modes are superior to the private auto environmentally. While the mass transit modes do have an advantage at present, even if the energy cost of construction is included, an individualized mode such as the taxicab is greatly inferior to the auto, and dial-a-bus may be marginally worse or better. The case for both of these low density modes has to be made on social grounds. A complete accounting of environmental costs—pertaining both to energy use and emissions—must be made in the context of the land-use environment which the different transit systems require, and must take into account the reduced travel demand at higher densities of land use, as well as other energy savings resulting from more compact settlement. For such an assessment, the analysis presented in this book is merely a starting point.

One subject remains to be considered, and that is those operating conditions of public transportation which are influenced by development patterns and which in turn influence operating costs. These conditions include operating speed, the size of the tributary area over which demand densities have to be calculated, and the daily peaking patterns of demand; they are treated in Chapter 4.

Transit Supply:

4. Operating Conditions

OPERATING SPEED AND DEVELOPMENT DENSITY

Foremost among the operating conditions of public transportation which are influenced by the urban environment is operating speed. Exhibit 4.1 displays the relationship between urban density—expressed in dwelling units per net residential acre—and average daily operating speed of selected travel modes in the New York Region. The speeds of three public transit modes—local bus, rapid transit, and commuter rail—are placed in the context of auto speeds on freeways and arterial streets.

The auto's speed advantage is quite evident, but it does decline with rising density. A rise in development density from around 2 to 200 dwelling units per acre causes freeway speed to drop from over 50 to about 35 miles per hour or less, and arterial speed from around 50 to about 13 miles per hour or less. Some of this drop is caused by tighter highway geometry in built-up areas, but most of it is due to traffic interference, either direct, in the form of congestion delays, or indirect, in the form of more intersectional controls per mile of road, which is the major cause of slower movement on arterial surface streets.

Local bus speeds, shown in the lowest curve, are kept low by all of the conditions encountered on arterial streets and, in addition, by passengers loading and unloading. Thus, average local bus speed tends to be about 8 mph lower than that of the auto on an arterial. County-wide average bus speeds, based on operating records, are plotted in Exhibit 4.1, which shows that bus speeds decline in a very consistent manner from around 20 mph in a low density area such as Suffolk county to 5.7 mph in Manhattan.

Density-related operating speeds for taxi and dial-a-bus are not available. The selected averages reported in Exhibit 3.2 include considerable idle time, and therefore are not much better than those of the local bus.

Systems which operate on an exclusive right-of-way, such as subways and railroads, shown by the two curves in the middle, are able to penetrate high density areas with a

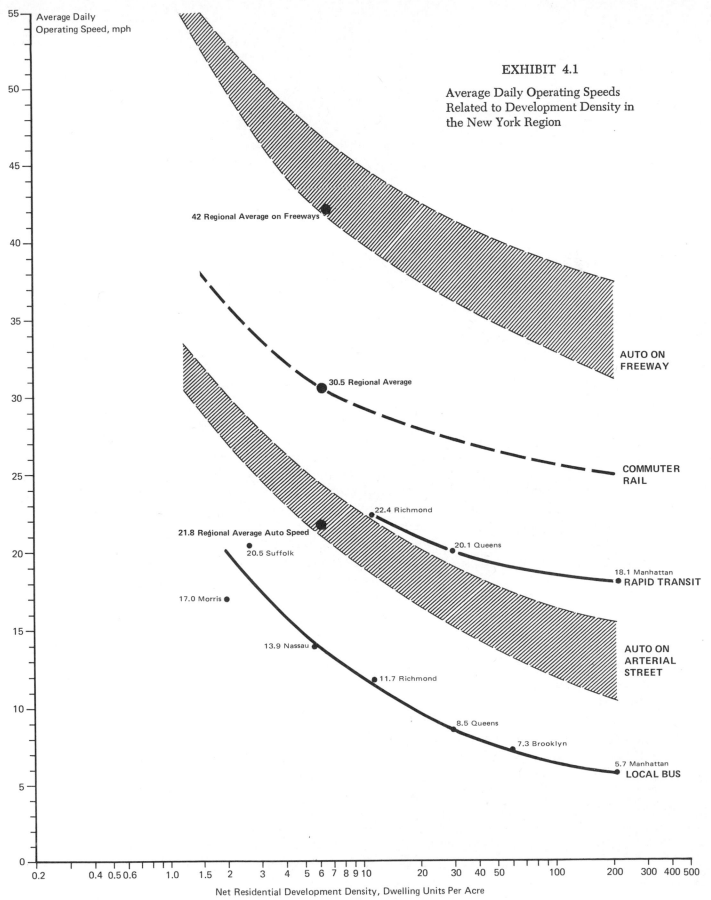

EXHIBIT 4.1

Average Daily Operating Speeds
Related to Development Density in
the New York Region

Average Daily
Operating Speed, mph

42 Regional Average on Freeways

30.5 Regional Average

AUTO ON FREEWAY

COMMUTER RAIL

22.4 Richmond

21.8 Regional Average Auto Speed

20.5 Suffolk

20.1 Queens

18.1 Manhattan
RAPID TRANSIT

17.0 Morris

AUTO ON ARTERIAL STREET

13.9 Nassau

11.7 Richmond

8.5 Queens

7.3 Brooklyn

5.7 Manhattan
LOCAL BUS

Net Residential Development Density, Dwelling Units Per Acre

Sources: Tri-State Regional Planning Commission *Streets and Highways* (1968); *ITR 4337-2104* (1972) and *ITR 4253-1206* (1971); also Transit Authority and other operating data.
Metric conversion: 1 mph = 1.609 Km/h; 1 dwelling, unit per acre = 2.471 dwelling units per hectare.

much smaller reduction in speed than vehicles operating in mixed traffic. Their relative advantage increases with increasing density. However, their operating speed is not completely immune to the density of the surrounding development. They too can be subject to congestion delays due to passenger loading or conflicts with other trains. Even non-stop runs through high density areas can be delayed by track geometry, especially on approaches to terminals. Most importantly, higher density generally calls for closer station spacing.

On the whole, subway operating speeds are shown to be faster than those of the auto on arterial streets, but commuter railroads fall far below freeways on an average daily basis. Only during peak hours do freeway speeds drop to near commuter rail, enabling the latter to be competitive in speed. The absence of consistent data made it impossible to show peak hour speeds in Exhibit 4.1.

OPERATING SPEED AND STATION SPACING

To single out the effect of station spacing on the speed of public transportation, operating speed is plotted against distance between stops in Exhibit 4.2. The broad band represents a range of speeds calculated from a sample of train schedules on New York subways and electrified commuter railroads, while the dots show selected system-wide averages in other cities. The performance of the New York City subways falls roughly in the same range as that of several other old systems, with an average speed (including layover time at terminals) of 18 miles per hour at the system-wide average distance between stops of 0.5 miles, reaching 27 miles per hour on runs where stations are 1.5 miles apart. The electrified commuter railroads essentially continue the same curve. They average about 30 miles per hour at a station spacing of 2 miles and reach 40 miles per hour on runs where stations are more than 10 miles apart, beyond the right edge of the chart.

Two new systems—PATCO and BART, connected by the top curve—are able to achieve, for the same distance between stops, roughly 40 to 45 percent higher speeds than the New York lines and most of the older systems. However, with old but high-acceleration PCC cars, the Newark light rail line attains a speed of 22 mph at a station spacing of 0.43 miles, not counting layover time, and thus falls on the same high-performance curve as PATCO and BART. Including layover time, the Newark PCC speed drops to 14.2 mph and the BART speed to 33.6 mph.

For any public transit system with close station spacing, average speed is primarily determined by a vehicle's ability to accelerate. Initial acceleration and deceleration are governed by the comfort of the standing passenger. An acceleration greater than about one-ninth to one-seventh of gravity will tend to cause people to lose their balance; hence 2.5 to 3.0 miles per hour per second is widely adopted as a limiting value for rail transit equipment, even though the friction of a steel wheel on a steel rail would allow it to accelerate up to 4.7 miles per hour per second. However, the vehicle's ability to sustain acceleration after it has picked up some speed depends on how powerful the vehicle is, roughly indicated by the horsepower-to-weight ratio. The schedules of the New York City transit system are geared to pre-1965 cars, equipped with about 10 horsepower per ton of empty weight. Newer cars are lighter and have more powerful motors but cannot be employed to their full capability until entire lines are suitably re-equipped and provided with more power supply. By contrast, the BART cars are equipped with 19 horsepower per ton.

Top speed is less important as long as stations are fairly closely spaced. For example, with half-mile station spacing, even high acceleration equipment can attain a speed of 50

EXHIBIT 4.2

Average Operating Speed Related to Station Spacing

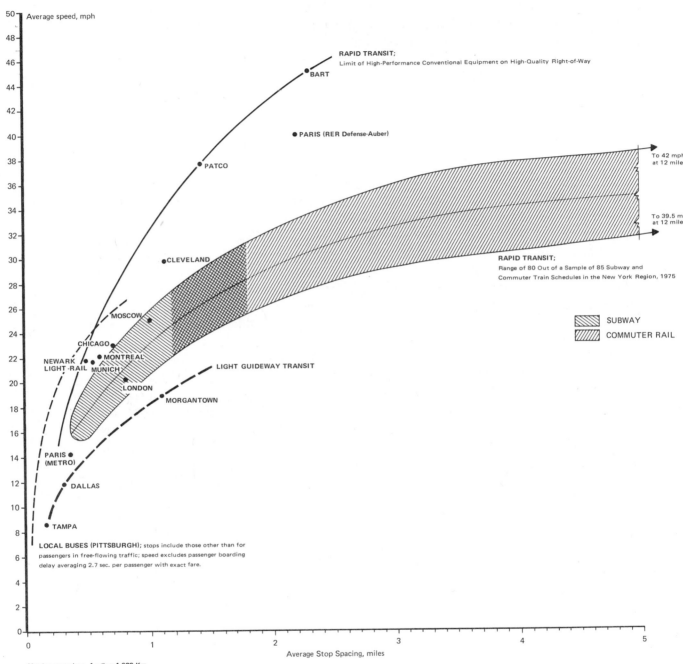

Average speed, mph

50
48
46 RAPID TRANSIT;
    Limit of High-Performance Conventional Equipment on High-Quality Right-of-Way
44 ● BART
42
40 ● PARIS (RER Defense-Auber)
38 ● PATCO
36
34
32
30 ● CLEVELAND
28
26 MOSCOW
24 CHICAGO
22 NEWARK ● MONTREAL
    LIGHT-RAIL MUNICH
20 ● LONDON
18 ● MORGANTOWN
16
14 PARIS ●
    (METRO)
12 ● DALLAS
10
8   ● TAMPA
6   LOCAL BUSES (PITTSBURGH); stops include those other than for
    passengers in free-flowing traffic; speed excludes passenger boarding
    delay averaging 2.7 sec. per passenger with exact fare.
4
2
0

LIGHT GUIDEWAY TRANSIT

To 42 mph at 12 miles

To 39.5 mph at 12 miles

RAPID TRANSIT;
Range of 80 Out of a Sample of 85 Subway and
Commuter Train Schedules in the New York Region, 1975

SUBWAY
COMMUTER RAIL

0   1   2   3   4   5
Average Stop Spacing, miles

Metric conversion: 1 mile = 1.609 Km.

Sources: New York Region—Transit Authority and commuter rail schedules.

Foreign—*Jane's World Railways.*

Buses—Richard Feder, *The Effect of Bus Stop Spacing on Travel Time.* Carnegie-Mellon University, 1973

miles per hour only momentarily; then it has to start braking. With 2 to 3-mile station spacing, a 70 to 80 miles per hour top speed can be useful, if the track is built and maintained to allow such speeds. On the New York City transit system, this will be possible only on new lines under construction or planned. However, on commuter railroads, the 100 miles per hour top speed capability of their new cars could be put to full use much sooner as track is upgraded and additional power supply is provided. This would raise the performance curve of the commuter railroads in Exhibit 4.2 substantially, if not into the BART range, at least close to the Cleveland and the Paris regional express range; suburban rail speeds would begin to approximate the lower range of freeway speeds.

Lastly, time losses in stations can be a major source of delay. High level platforms and wide, automatic doors, designed to expedite passenger boarding and alighting, are becoming standard on both rapid transit and electrified suburban railroads in the New York Region. With their help, rapid transit systems attain station dwell times in the 12 to 30 seconds range. On subways, however, station delays can be caused by passenger overcrowding, and on suburban railroads station dwell times are often still several minutes long due to traditional modes of operation.

On buses, whose performance curve is shown in Exhibit 4.2, exclusive of any time spent standing, dwell time at stops may average 2.7 seconds per passenger boarding with exact fare, about 2.0 seconds per passenger alighting, plus some stopping and starting delay. Signal delay and delay due to traffic conditions must of course be added to these to arrive at actual average operating speed. The performance curve of three light guideway systems is shown to be below the others.

STATION SPACING AND ACCESS MODES

While high speed is important for public transit from the viewpoint of reducing costs and competing with the auto for patronage, it can also mean that the bus or train will speed past potential patrons without picking them up. Any system that does not provide personalized door-to-door service but rather caters to group ridership must consider the basic choice: whether it can attract more passengers by stopping at a few points but offering faster speed to the potential patrons accessible to them, or by stopping at more points accessible to passengers, but offering them slower speed. A detailed consideration of station spacing theory is beyond the scope of this discussion. Suffice it to say that what the potential passengers are after is the shortest overall door-to-door travel time, or lowest travel price in the generalized sense used in the first chapter.

That means that the selection of a desirable station spacing depends on the length of the trips served. On a longer trip, en route time savings from less frequent stops are more likely to offset time losses caused by longer access times to stops. It also means that station spacing depends on the speed of getting to the stations. The faster the access, the less frequent can be the stops, thus further raising overall speed. However, measuring the access time to stops is complicated by the fact that riders weigh en route time and access time differently. One study found that for a 5-mile average bus trip, bus stops should be spaced 0.7 miles apart, if in-vehicle time and walking time to stops are weighted equally. However, if walking time is three times more onerous than in-vehicle time, as some behavioral evidence would suggest, then the desirable spacing becomes only 0.3 miles.[1] If the access to the station is not on foot but by some auxiliary mode, then the inconvenience of a transfer—itself worth several minutes, in addition to the actual delay incurred—must be taken into account. It will be perceived to be worthwhile only on a longer trip.

Montreal, wishing to divert short trips from local buses and to maximize pedestrian access in a city with an average density of 35 dwellings per acre, opted for a station spacing of 0.6 miles, as shown in Exhibit 4.2. Similarly, the Manhattan portion of the Second Avenue Subway, intended to carry both regional and local trips, was, after considerable public debate, designed with a station spacing of 0.6 miles. With high performance equipment, this will allow scheduled speeds in the 22 to 25 miles per hour range, with nearly total dependence on pedestrian access to stations in an area with residential densities in excess of 200 dwellings per acre.

By contrast, the PATCO Lindenwold line, able to achieve nearly 38 miles per hour average speeds with a station spacing in excess of 1.4 miles, is heavily dependent on feeder modes. In the suburban territory it serves, which has a density of less than 5 dwellings per net residential acre, 80 percent of the passengers arrive by auto, 9 percent by bus, and only 11 percent walk. BART, achieving a 45 mile per hour speed with a 2.3 mile station spacing, was designed primarily for auto access, though it has attracted significant patronage by feeder bus, particularly at the nonresidential end of trips. However, the long station spacing does act as a screen which eliminates short trips—the average trip is 13.5 miles.

Express buses in very large cities seek to obviate the need for feeder modes by collecting passengers on foot near their places of origin and delivering them close to their destination with a non-stop run in between. For example, only 16 percent of passengers using the Shirley Express Busway near Washington arrive at the bus stop by auto, while 84 percent walk; similarly, about 89 percent of the passengers using express buses from outer parts of New York City walk to the bus stop at the home end. But the non-stop express run amounts to an extremely long station spacing in practice. Thus, express bus service caters exclusively to particular sets of very long trips and in no way serves the intermediate area. Also, the close-to-door service in a low-density area with limited demand cuts service frequency quite drastically: the Shirley busway generally has 5 to 20 daily departures from any one neighborhood, while the Lindenwold line has 144 daily trains leaving from any station. Thus, trade-offs involving not only access distance but also service frequency must be considered.

Furthermore, of great importance is the ability to interchange between lines and to use the system as a network rather than as a series of discrete and specialized runs. Fixed guideway systems alone, or interchanging with bus lines on a systematic basis, or local bus systems properly laid out, all have this property of connectivity, which enables them to serve trips other than those to the predominant destination. Express buses generally lack this property. Cursory evidence suggests that systems with greater connectivity attract significantly more patronage.[2]

The feasibility of any public transportation system that follows a prescribed route depends on how far people are willing to travel to get to it. If people were to insist on boarding the vehicle at their doorstep, an extremely high population density would be needed to support any transit route. If, by contrast, they were willing to travel relatively far, then more passengers could be collected from a wider tributary area and even a modest population density could support transit service. Under North American conditions, long access distances to transit are generally not tolerated. Tri-State Regional Planning Commission's 1963 Home Interview Survey indicates that, outside downtown areas, people reported their walk to a bus to be, on the average, in the 3-to-4-minute range, their walk to a subway or rail station to be in the 5-to-10 minute range, and their drive to rail stops to average 7 to 15 minutes.[3] More detailed studies of people's behavior in getting to rail stations are regrettably sparse, particularly with respect to non-downtown areas. Still, available evidence does support the notion of very short access links.[4]

In principle, the average travel distance to a transit stop will depend on the distribution of travellers around that stop, their propensity to take the trip, and the location of competing stops. Exhibit 4.3 focuses on this third factor. The top curve shows the average spacing of rapid transit or commuter rail stations in selected counties of the New York Region and relates it to the average density. The distance between stations is expressed as the square root of the total land area divided by the total number of stations, and thus takes into account both the spacing of stops along a route and the spacing of the routes themselves. This measure is quite different from the "scheduled stop spacing" in Exhibit 4.2, which refers only to the stops which a particular train makes along its route. The lower set of curves portrays the median access distance to the rail stops by auto driver, auto passenger, and by the pedestrian. The shaded band shows a range of pedestrian access distances to bus stops, for reference. Access distances by bus or taxi were not available but can be presumed to fall between the auto and the pedestrian range.

The median access distance to stations is chosen in preference to the "average" distance for a good reason: average distances can be influenced in a rather erratic manner by a few very long trips. The outer boundary of the area over which trips take place is quite indeterminate. Meanwhile, the median trip length defines the distance within which 50 percent of the trips are confined. If one knows how many trips originate within the median distance, then one knows that the total number of trips is twice as large, without worrying about the exact distance from which the remaining 50 percent come.

It can be seen from Exhibit 4.3 that the median distance travelled by the auto driver to a station is fairly parallel to the average areawide distance between stations. It is somewhat more than half that distance at low suburban densities of 2 dwellings per acre and somewhat less than half at middle suburban densities of 6 dwellings per acre. The median access distance of the auto passenger (the "kiss-and-ride" trip) involves the time of two people, and double the amount of driving, and hence is more resistant to longer distances. Overall, the relationship shows that where a closely-meshed grid of transit routes with stations is available, access distances to them are short, whereas access distances to an outlying terminal are much longer. There is an outer limit beyond which people will not travel if the access mode is perceived as very costly.

Thus the pedestrian access trip to stations responds to station spacing only in a very limited manner. The median walk to subway stations does increase from 0.17 miles in Midtown Manhattan, where stations are very closely spaced, to about 0.32 miles at the edge of subway-served territory.[5] It appears that no matter how station spacing increases, 50 percent of the people will not walk much more than 6 minutes or 0.3 miles to a non-downtown rail station, even if there is a fraction of 1 percent who will walk over 30 minutes or more than 1.5 miles. This is not inconsistent with the finding that at a distance of 2,500 feet or a 9-minute walking time (assuming, all the while, an average walking speed of 3.1 miles per hour), 50 percent or more of those travelling that distance will prefer a feeder bus to walking, even in a low income area, with a double fare.[6]

The propensity to walk to bus stops is even more limited than that of walking to commuter rail or rapid transit stations. A study of walking distances in residential areas of Washington, D.C.[7] found the median walk to a bus stop to vary from 400 feet among high income passengers to 710 feet among low income passengers. The median walk for all groups was 560 feet. Comparable data are not available for the New York Region, but inference from the walking times reported in Tri-State's Home Interview survey would sug-

EXHIBIT 4.3

Access Distance to Stations Related to Spacing and Development Density in the New York Region

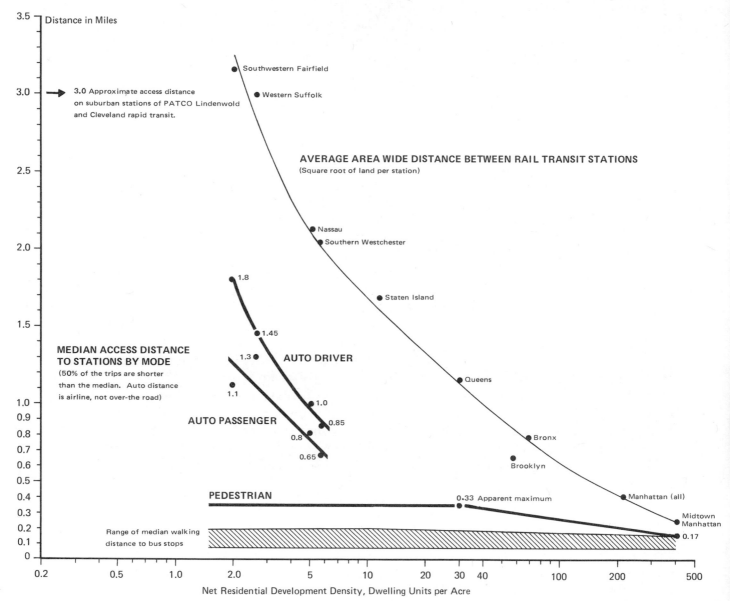

Distance in Miles

3.0 Approximate access distance on suburban stations of PATCO Lindenwold and Cleveland rapid transit.

● Southwestern Fairfield

● Western Suffolk

AVERAGE AREA WIDE DISTANCE BETWEEN RAIL TRANSIT STATIONS
(Square root of land per station)

● Nassau
● Southern Westchester

1.8
● 1.45
1.3 ● **AUTO DRIVER**
1.1
1.0
0.85
0.8
0.65

● Staten Island

MEDIAN ACCESS DISTANCE TO STATIONS BY MODE
(50% of the trips are shorter than the median. Auto distance is airline, not over-the road)

AUTO PASSENGER

● Queens

● Bronx

● Brooklyn

PEDESTRIAN

0.33 Apparent maximum

● Manhattan (all)

Midtown
Manhattan

0.17

Range of median walking distance to bus stops

Net Residential Development Density, Dwelling Units per Acre

0.2   0.5   1.0   2.0   5   10   20   40   100   200   500

Metric conversion: 1 mile = 1.609 Km.; 1 dwelling unit per acre = 2.471 dwelling units per hectare

Sources: Tri-State Regional Planning Commission and Regional Plan Association

gest a median walking distance of around 750 feet, which may increase to 1,000 feet at most in suburban counties such as Bergen and Nassau, with residential densities averaging 5 dwellings per acre. Densities lower than that do not seem to produce longer walking distances to bus stops. On the contrary, the home-interview data imply substantially shorter walking distances at very low densities, perhaps because very large lot subdivisions are simply not laid out for walking. Interestingly, walking distances to bus stops measured by the Paris transportation authority are very close to the distances inferred from Tri-State's home interview data. Within the city of Paris, the median walk to a bus stop is 820 feet, and in the suburban area 1,050 feet.[8]

Assuming diamond-shaped tributary areas, which occur if the street grid is rectilinear, a 1,000-foot median walk means that an isolated bus stop will draw half its walk-in passengers from an area of only 46 acres. Similarly, a rail stop with an 0.3-mile median pedestrian access distance will draw half its walk-in trade from only 142 acres, or 0.22 square miles. Assuming auto tributary areas defined by an airline (rather than over-the-road) distance to be circular, half the drive-in trade will come from an area of 3 square miles at a median driver access distance of 1 mile, and from an area of 10 square miles at the longest median distance shown in Exhibit 4.3, which is 1.8 miles. These tributary areas will become smaller to the extent that they overlap between adjacent stations, but on the whole this illustrates the rapidly increasing role of feeder modes as distance between station increases.

Thus it is that in Manhattan, with stations on the average 0.4 miles apart, about 95 percent of the subway riders walk and only 4 percent use a feeder bus. The proportion of bus users to the subway increases to 16 to 18 percent in Brooklyn and the Bronx, and reaches 37 percent in Queens, where one has to travel 1.2 miles on the average before finding a station. Auto access to stations becomes significant here and rapidly increases with declining density and increasing distance between stations. In the upper suburban density range characteristic of older development, about 25 percent walk to stations while about 70 percent drive or are dropped off. At the edges of the Region, less than 10 percent walk to stations. For example, even at the Trenton station, despite compact urban development around it, only 8 percent of the passengers walk to trains. The reason is that with no competing stations nearby, the station serves a wide tributary area far beyond the city itself.

PEAKING CHARACTERISTICS

An important operating condition that remains to be covered is the peaking pattern of daily passenger use on public transportation. As pointed out earlier, the rolling stock requirements of a system are determined by the peak one-directional load at the highest load point, as well as by the running time in which the vehicle can repeat its trip. To understand why peaking patterns on different public transportation systems are different from each other and from the daily patterns of travel demand in general, one should recall that the choice of public transportation modes is a highly selective process, and that their functions in an auto-oriented society are quite specialized.

To begin with, Exhibit 4.4 displays two characteristic peaking patterns which express the daily variation in total travel demand at the home end. The first graph shows all trips entering and leaving a Manhattan apartment house on foot. Some of these trips remain walking trips, others subsequently become trips by auto, taxi, bus, or rapid transit. The second graph shows all trips entering and leaving a Long Island subdivision by auto. For practical purposes, these auto trips also represent the universe of trips made by the subdivision's residents outside the subdivision. The Manhattan apartment house has more pronounced 8 to 9 and 5 to 6 peaks because, due to the small household size, a much greater proportion of residents travel to work than in the case of the Long Island subdivision. The significant similarity between the two patterns is that for about 9 of the 14 hours between 7:00 A.M. and 9:00 P.M., hourly traffic stays near the level of 4 percent of total daily traffic. For about 5 hours of the day (the rush periods), travel activity is about twice as high, and approaches or exceeds the level of 8 percent of total daily travel per hour. Nevertheless, this base peaking pattern is seen to be quite moderate: the highest hour—5:00 to 6:00 P.M. in both instances—accounts for 10.7 and 8.8 percent of total daily travel, respectively.

The first public transportation mode compared to this base pattern is the taxicab, shown in its suburban application in the bottom graph of Exhibit 4.4. In scale, the pattern is very similar to the suburban auto. The highest hour accounts for 8 percent of total daily trips. Moreover, for nine hours after 10:00 A.M. the traffic level is virtually even, at 6 percent of the daily total per hour. The peaking is not only flatter than that of the auto but reversed in time: the use of this particular taxi fleet is heaviest in the morning, when business travel occurs and auto traffic is fairly light. In contrast to the auto, there is no afternoon peak, but use in the evening hours between 10:00 P.M. and midnight is heavier than auto use. The suppression of the afternoon peak may be indicative of the difficulty of taxi travel during the hours of heavy auto movement. Night-time use between midnight and 5:00 A.M. is virtually nonexistent.

The peaking patterns of suburban taxi use are emphasized here because in many ways the demand for dial-a-bus service is very similar. It also tends to be fairly steady between 7:00 A.M. and 7:00 P.M., with some slack in the late morning. In fact, some of the use patterns reported for dial-a-bus are remarkably level throughout the daytime period.[9] This is largely because trips to work are not served by suburban taxi or dial-a-bus in any major way; the miscellaneous trips that are served are those which cannot be served by auto, and their incidence in time is somewhat different from that of auto trips. Of course, the fairly steady use pattern of the suburban demand-responsive systems enables them to use manpower and equipment in an efficient way, a luxury denied to long-haul fixed-route systems that cater primarily to the work trip.

Exhibits 4.5 through 4.7 present one-directional peaking patterns of commuter railroads, rapid transit, and local buses recorded at the highest load point—crossing entryways into the Manhattan Central Business District. Suburban rail, one of the most specialized transit systems, serving predominantly work trips and overwhelmingly one location—the Central Business District—also experiences the sharpest peaking. As seen in Exhibit 4.5, commuter railroads in the New York Region in 1973 carried 45.8 percent of their inbound daily traffic during the morning peak hour. The figure is not directly comparable to the bi-directional data shown in the earlier exhibit, but recalculated in bi-directional terms, the 8:00 to 9:00 peak hour on suburban rail amounts to 23.7 percent of the daily traffic, a peak three times sharper than that of autos and taxis. Except for the "shoulder" hours on each side of the peak, inbound traffic is generally at a level of 1 to 3 percent of the daily total per hour between 6:00 A.M. and 8:00 P.M. Outbound traffic is somewhat more heavily clustered around the afternoon peak, between 2:00 P.M. and midnight. In any case, peak hour demand is 12 to 15 times greater than the demand throughout most of the day.

Rapid transit displays a moderately more attenuated pattern, with 30 percent of the daily one-directional movement occurring during the peak hour. In bi-directional terms, the peak hour carries 16.7 percent of the daily travel, or twice as much as the peak hour of autos and taxis. Except, again, for the "shoulder" hours on each side of the peak, traffic between

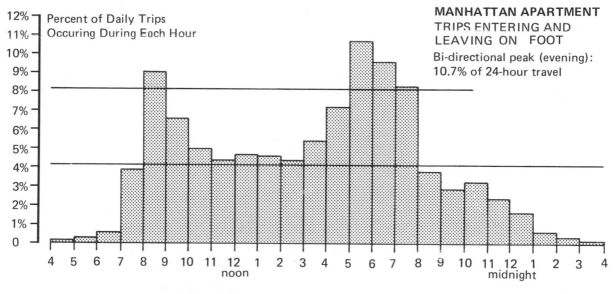

MANHATTAN APARTMENT
TRIPS ENTERING AND
LEAVING ON FOOT

Bi-directional peak (evening):
10.7% of 24-hour travel

EXHIBIT 4.4

Home-Based Bi-Directional Peaking
Patterns of All Trips Compared to
Peaking of Suburban Taxi Travel

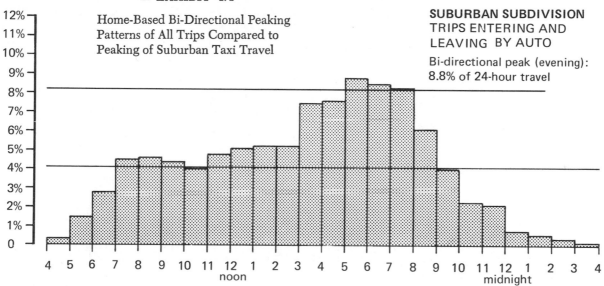

SUBURBAN SUBDIVISION
TRIPS ENTERING AND
LEAVING BY AUTO

Bi-directional peak (evening):
8.8% of 24-hour travel

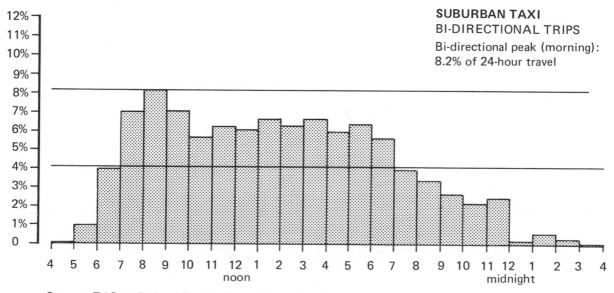

SUBURBAN TAXI
BI-DIRECTIONAL TRIPS

Bi-directional peak (morning):
8.2% of 24-hour travel

Sources: Tri-State Regional Planning Commission and Regional Plan Association

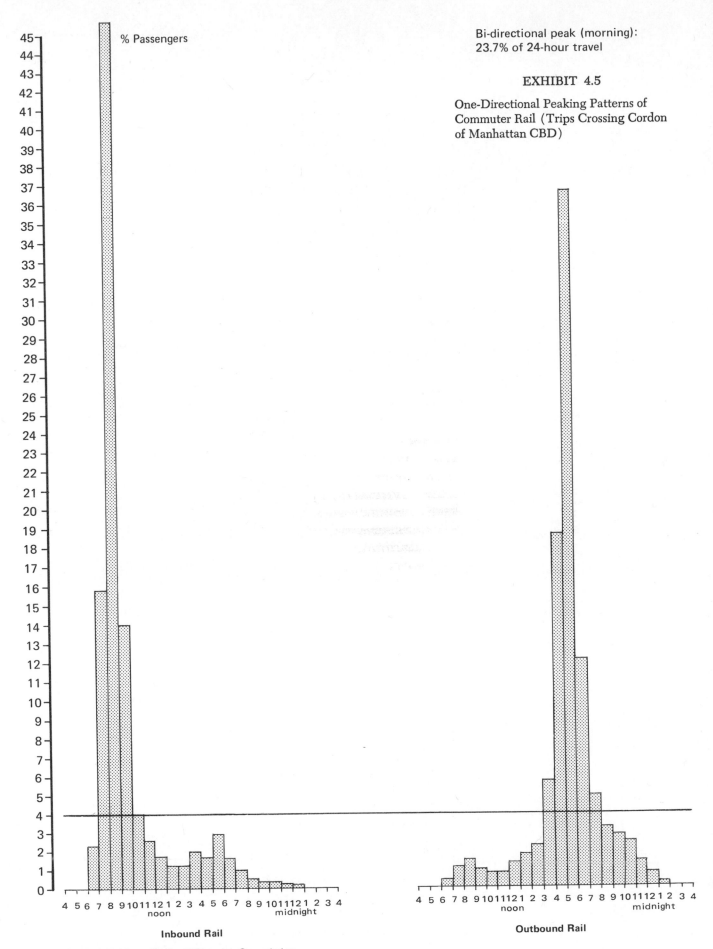

% Passengers

Bi-directional peak (morning):
23.7% of 24-hour travel

EXHIBIT 4.5

One-Directional Peaking Patterns of
Commuter Rail (Trips Crossing Cordon
of Manhattan CBD)

Inbound Rail

Outbound Rail

Source: Tri-State Regional Planning Commission

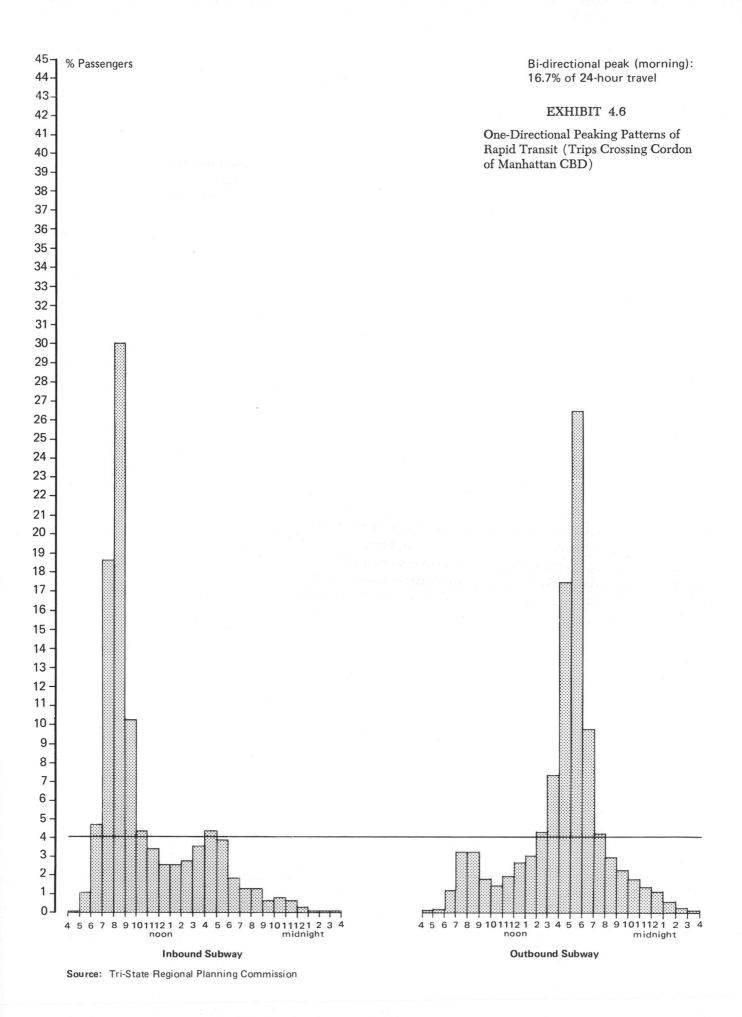

Bi-directional peak (morning):
16.7% of 24-hour travel

EXHIBIT 4.6

One-Directional Peaking Patterns of
Rapid Transit (Trips Crossing Cordon
of Manhattan CBD)

Inbound Subway

Outbound Subway

Source: Tri-State Regional Planning Commission

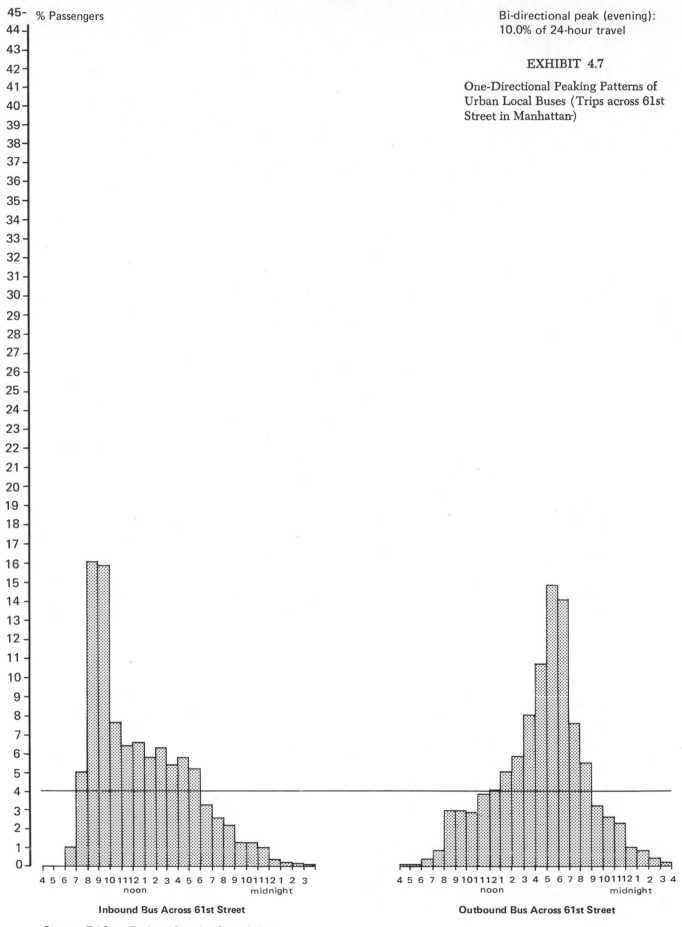

Bi-directional peak (evening):
10.0% of 24-hour travel

EXHIBIT 4.7

One-Directional Peaking Patterns of
Urban Local Buses (Trips across 61st
Street in Manhattan·)

Inbound Bus Across 61st Street

Outbound Bus Across 61st Street

Source: Tri-State Regional Planning Commission

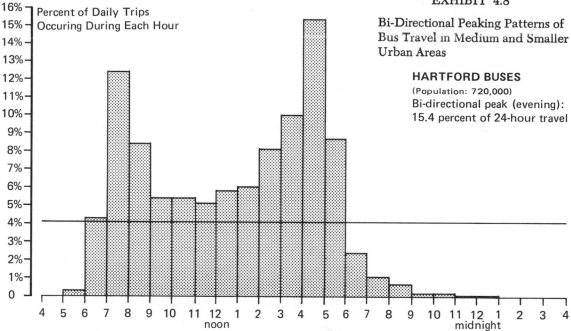

EXHIBIT 4.8

Bi-Directional Peaking Patterns of Bus Travel in Medium and Smaller Urban Areas

HARTFORD BUSES
(Population: 720,000)
Bi-directional peak (evening):
15.4 percent of 24-hour travel

Percent of Daily Trips Occuring During Each Hour

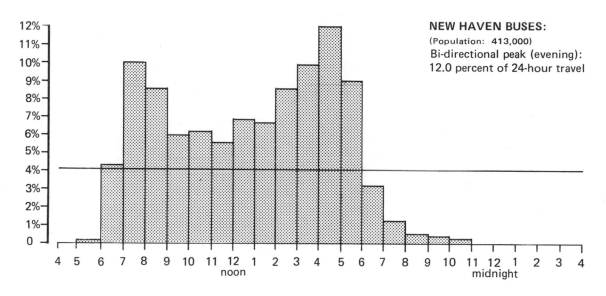

NEW HAVEN BUSES:
(Population: 413,000)
Bi-directional peak (evening):
12.0 percent of 24-hour travel

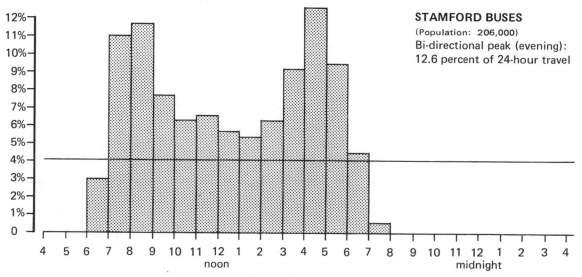

STAMFORD BUSES
(Population: 206,000)
Bi-directional peak (evening):
12.6 percent of 24-hour travel

Source: Connecticut Department of Transportation

6:00 A.M. and midnight is generally at a level between 1 and 4 percent of the daily total per hour. Peak hour demand is roughly 7 times greater than the demand throughout most of the day.

The pattern of local buses in Manhattan is strikingly different. The peak is 10 percent on a bi-directional basis. This means that the peaking pattern of local buses in Manhattan is roughly the same as that of travel demand in general. Particularly on the in-bound trips, hourly demand stays at around 6 percent of the daily total per hour for about 8 hours of the day, a pattern quite reminiscent of the peaking of origins and destinations at the home end of all trips shown in the first graph of Exhibit 4.4.

The explanation is that because of low auto ownership, buses are used in Manhattan for all kinds of local trips, much like the auto in the suburbs. Therefore, the buses' daily pattern approximates the peaking pattern of total travel demand. Rail and rapid transit, by contrast, are used selectively, only for trips which the auto cannot handle. To a considerable extent, their potential off-peak use is handled by the auto. The low peaking pattern of bus travel in Manhattan is rather unusual. In most medium-sized metropolitan areas of the United States, where auto is more widely available, bus use closely approximates the *subway* peaking pattern in New York City. It is not unusual for bus systems to carry close to 30 percent of their one-directional daily load in one hour, though in Canadian cities the proportion is more on the order of 20 percent.

For the three medium-to-smaller-size urban areas depicted in Exhibit 4.8, only bi-directional peaking patterns were available. It can be seen that in Hartford, with a metropolitan population of about three quarters of a million, the bi-directional peak is 15.4 percent, which suggests a one-directional peak of close to 30 percent. In the two smaller areas of New Haven and Stamford, peaking is not quite as sharp, somewhat closer to the Manhattan pattern, because more work trips occur by auto and the bus is left to carry pretty much the full range of trips made by people without an automobile.

When it comes to translating the potential daily trips by transit into hourly rates, necessary to relate ridership to hourly service frequencies and vehicle costs, the data presented in Exhibits 4.4 through 4.8 can be used as a guide. To simplify matters and to relate to actual operating practices, the day can be divided into three periods: the peak period, the base period which lasts throughout the rest of the day and early evening, and the nighttime period when very little travel occurs. Depending on the composition of the ridership (more or less oriented toward the trip to work), appropriate hourly shares of total daily ridership can be chosen for each of the three periods.

5 Matching Supply and Demand at Different Densities

MEASURES OF DEMAND DENSITY AND TRANSIT SERVICE

Now we can put together the material assembled in the preceding four chapters. On the basis of Chapter 2, we can estimate the total number of trips between a nonresidential cluster of a given size and type and a residential area of a given density located at a given distance from it; we can also estimate how many of these trips are likely candidates for public transportation under different assumptions of income, household size, and transit service. These potential public transit trips can be expressed in terms of *density of demand—trip origins per square mile* per day.

From Chapter 3 we know that operating costs relate in a stable manner to vehicle hours of operation; hence we express the *density of supply* in terms of *vehicle hours per square mile*. Trip origins per square mile per day divided by vehicle hours per square mile per day yield *passengers boarding per vehicle hour*, a measure of *vehicle productivity*. Knowing the operating cost per vehicle hour, the number of passenger boardings per vehicle hour tells us the cost per passenger. Some of this will be paid from the fare, some from public subsidy. Based on the material in Chapter 1, we can informally assess the impact of different fare levels on demand.

The remaining issue is how to translate the service density of vehicle hours per square mile per day into more specific terms of service frequency, its distribution over the course of the day, and route spacing. Chapter 4 responds to that; it says, for example, that one bus hour represents different service frequencies at different densities, because speed varies with density. At a density of 2 dwellings per acre, bus speeds average 20 mph, meaning that one bus hour represents 20 bus miles of travel. If parallel bus routes are spaced one half mile apart, then 20 bus miles per square mile per day mean an average frequency of 10 buses per day on each of the two routes in one direction.

121

To explore the feasibility of different modes at different densities, the type of analysis suggested here has to be applied systematically over a broad range of density conditions, mode by mode, which is what the remainder of this chapter is devoted to.

Density of demand is illustrated first in terms of one-way trips per square mile from residential areas to nonresidential clusters in Exhibits 5.1 and 5.2. The exhibits must of necessity be highly selective, singling out relatively few representative values. Procedures for calculating intermediate values, or values based on different assumptions, are given in the Appendix.

Exhibit 5.1 lists per capita trip rates to selected sizes and types of nonresidential clusters from selected distances based on Exhibit 2.21, and in the columns below translates them into trip densities per square mile at selected densities of development. The resulting table illustrates the universe of all trips by mechanical modes from residential to nonresidential areas, some of which will use public transit under various conditions.

The very rapid attenuation of trip densities with distance evident in Exhibit 5.1 is due not just to declining travel propensity and to lower residential densities at greater distances, but also to the geometric quality of concentric rings whose area increases with the square of the radius, thus spreading out patrons who come from longer distances.

The figures shown represent averages under specified assumptions, and in the real world considerable variation around the average values exists. Let us take the trips to a downtown-oriented cluster of 20 million square feet (between Bridgeport and New Haven in size) at a distance of 5 miles, with a per capita trip rate shown as 0.0842. This represents a sum of the work trip and non-work trip rates, each of which exhibits a statistical variation around the mean. One can gain a rough impression of this variation from Exhibit 2.20. Moreover, the work trip rate per worker is converted into a work trip rate per capita on the assumption that the labor force participation rate is 40 percent. This is generally true of suburban areas. In higher density neighborhoods the labor force participation rate can be as high as 70 percent if they are affluent, and as low as 20 percent if they are poor. This represents a second source of variation.

Next, the trip rate is multiplied by the number of residents in a square mile, which is a measure of gross density. This is a third source of variation, for the share of the square mile devoted to net residential use at any density may vary considerably. For a density of 5 dwellings per acre, the gross density is shown as 3,600 persons per square mile, an average for the urbanized portion of the New York Region. The household size at that density averaging 3.2 persons, this means that only 35 percent of the gross square mile is in residential use, and that much of it is vacant. If the square mile were to be exclusively residential, with no vacant land and perhaps 20 percent of the land in streets, the gross density at a net density of 5 dwellings per acre would be as high as 8,190 persons per square mile. In detailed applications to specific neighborhoods, actual density figures reflecting local land use should be used whenever possible.

Lastly, all figures in Exhibit 5.1 are based on the assumption that the nonresidential clusters are independent of Manhattan—that is, located more than 60 miles from Columbus Circle. This makes them useful for illustrating conditions on a national level, but for places within the New York Region, this introduces a fourth source of variation. The reduction in the per capita trip rate in residential areas because of the competing influence of Manhattan is relatively small at large distances; the earlier mentioned trip rate of 0.0842 is only reduced to 0.0720 if the nonresidential cluster in question is located 40 miles from Manhattan; however, it shrinks to 0.0330 if it is 5 miles from Manhattan.

EXHIBIT 5.1 Illustrative Demand Density of Trips by All Modes from Selected Residential Densities at Selected Distances to Nonresidential Clusters of Three Types (clusters assumed to be independent of Manhattan)

Size of cluster, million sq. ft. non residential floor space	Residential density dwellings/acre	Equivalent gross density per / sq. mi.	One-way trips per gross sq. mile to cluster at following distances: (sum of work and non-work trips)						
			1 mi.	3 mi.	5 mi.	10 mi.	20 mi.	30 mi.	40 mi.

Trips to Downtown-oriented clusters:

		Trip attraction rate per capita:	0.609	0.319	0.212	0.0982	0.0360	0.0173	0.0097
200	200	70,600	43,000	22,500	15,000	6,930	--	--	--
	100	46,000	28,000	14,700	9,750	4,520	--	--	--
	50	27,000	16,400	8,610	5,720	2,650	--	--	--
	30	19,000	--	6,060	4,030	1,870	684	--	--
	15	10,200	--	--	2,160	1,000	367	176	--
	10	7,100	--	--	1,510	697	256	122	69
	7	5,600	--	--	1,190	550	202	97	54
	5	3,600	--	--	--	354	130	62	35
	3	2,000	--	--	--	196	72	35	19
	2	1,100	--	--	--	108	40	19	11
	1	360	--	--	--	--	13	6	3

		Trip attraction rate per capita:	0.552	0.272	0.171	0.0744	0.0229	0.0100	0.0055
100	150	60,000	33,100	16,300	--	--	--	--	--
	100	46,000	25,400	12,500	7,870	--	--	--	--
	50	27,000	14,900	7,340	4,620	2,010	--	--	--
	30	19,000	10,500	5,170	3,250	1,410	435	--	--
	15	10,200	--	2,770	1,740	759	234	102	--
	10	7,100	--	--	1,210	528	163	71	39
	7	5,600	--	--	958	417	128	56	31
	5	3,600	--	--	616	268	82	36	20
	3	2,000	--	--	--	149	46	20	11
	2	1,100	--	--	--	82	25	11	6
	1	360	--	--	--	27	8	4	2

		Trip attraction rate per capita:	0.493	0.220	0.1308	0.0506	0.0128	0.0050	0.0024
50	100	46,000	22,700	10,100	--	--	--	--	--
	50	27,000	13,300	5,940	--	--	--	--	--
	30	19,000	9,370	4,180	--	--	--	--	--
	15	10,200	--	2,240	1,330	516	--	--	--
	10	7,100	--	1,560	929	359	91	36	--
	7	5,600	--	--	732	283	72	28	--
	5	3,600	--	--	471	182	46	18	9
	3	2,000	--	--	262	101	26	10	5
	2	1,100	--	--	144	56	14	6	3
	1	360	--	--	--	18	5	2	1

		Trip attraction rate per capita:	0.407	0.157	0.0842	0.0262	0.0049	0.0016	0.0006
20	50	27,000	11,000	--	--	--	--	--	--
	30	19,000	7,733	--	--	--	--	--	--
	15	10,200	4,150	1,600	--	--	--	--	--
	10	7,100	2,890	1,110	598	186	--	--	--
	7	5,600	--	879	472	146	27	--	--
	5	3,600	--	565	303	94	18	6	2
	3	2,000	--	314	168	52	10	3	1
	2	1,100	--	173	93	29	5	2	1
	1	360	--	--	30	9	2	1	0

		Trip attraction rate per capita:	0.338	0.114	0.0544	0.0134	0.0020	0.0005	0.00014
10	30	19,000	6,420	--	--	--	--	--	--
	15	10,200	3,450	1,160	--	--	--	--	--
	10	7,100	2,400	809	386	95	--	--	--
	7	5,600	1,890	638	305	75	11	--	--
	5	3,600	1,220	410	196	48	7	--	--
	3	2,000	676	228	109	27	4	1	0
	2	1,100	372	125	60	15	2	1	0
	1	360	--	41	20	4	1	0	0

		Trip attraction rate per capita:	0.267	0.075	0.032	0.0059	0.00063	0.00011	0.00002
5	10	7,100	1,900	533	227	42	--	--	--
	7	5,600	1,500	420	179	33	4	--	--
	5	3,600	961	270	115	21	2	--	--
	3	2,000	534	150	64	12	1	0	0
	2	1,100	294	83	35	6	1	0	0
	1	360	96	27	12	2	0	0	0

EXHIBIT 5.1 continued

Trips to Spread Clusters with Mixed Use:

			Trip attraction rate per capita: 0.2992	0.1092	0.0582	0.0190	0.0046	0.0018	0.00095
20	50	27,000	8,080	--	--	--	--	--	--
	30	19,000	5,680	--	--	--	--	--	--
	15	10,200	3,050	1,110	--	--	--	--	--
	10	7,100	2,120	775	413	135	--	--	--
	7	5,600	1,680	612	326	106	26	--	--
	5	3,600	1,080	393	210	68	17	6	3
	3	2,000	598	218	116	38	9	4	2
	2	1,100	--	120	64	21	5	2	1
	1	360	--	39	21	7	2	1	0

			Trip attraction rate per capita: 0.247	0.0832	0.040	0.0119	0.0024	0.0010	0.00035
10	30	19,000	4,690	--	--	--	--	--	--
	15	10,200	2,520	849	--	--	--	--	--
	10	7,100	1,750	591	284	84	--	--	--
	7	5,600	1,380	466	224	67	13	--	--
	5	3,600	889	300	144	43	9	4	1
	3	2,000	494	166	80	24	5	2	1
	2	1,100	272	92	44	13	3	1	0
	1	360	--	30	14	4	1	0	0

			Trip attraction rate per capita: 0.2060	0.0594	0.0274	0.0066	0.0012	0.00035	0.00014
5	10	7,100	1,460	422	195	47	--	--	--
	7	5,600	1,150	333	153	37	7	--	--
	5	3,600	742	214	99	24	4	1	1
	3	2,000	412	119	55	13	2	1	0
	2	1,100	227	65	30	7	1	0	0
	1	360	74	21	10	2	0	0	0

			Trip attraction rate per capita: 0.1484	0.0338	0.0132	0.0027	0.00032	0.0001	0.00002
2	7	5,600	831	189	74	15	2	--	--
	5	3,600	534	122	48	10	1	0	0
	3	2,000	297	68	26	5	1	0	0
	2	1,100	163	37	15	3	0	0	0
	1	360	53	12	5	1	0	0	0

Trips to Shopping-Oriented Spread Clusters

			Trip attraction rate per capita: 0.450	0.1656	0.0832	0.0204	0.0025	0.00057	0.00021
10	30	19,000	8,550	--	--	--	--	--	--
	15	10,200	4,590	1,690	--	--	--	--	--
	10	7,100	3,200	1,180	591	145	--	--	--
	7	5,600	2,520	927	466	114	14	--	--
	5	3,600	1,620	596	300	73	9	2	1
	3	2,000	900	331	166	41	5	1	0
	2	1,100	495	182	92	22	3	1	0
	1	360	--	60	30	7	1	0	0

			Trip attraction rate per capita: 0.410	0.1400	0.064	0.0138	0.0015	0.00019	0.0001
5	10	7,100	2,911	994	454	98	--	--	--
	7	5,600	2,300	784	358	77	8	--	--
	5	3,600	1,480	504	230	50	5	1	0
	3	2,000	820	280	128	34	3	0	0
	2	1,100	451	154	70	15	2	0	0
	1	360	148	50	23	5	1	0	0

			Trip attraction rate per capita: 0.346	0.1032	0.040	0.0069	0.00054	0.00011	0.00002
2	7	5,600	1,940	578	224	39	3	--	--
	5	3,600	1,246	372	144	25	2	0	0
	3	2,000	692	206	80	14	1	0	0
	2	1,100	381	114	44	8	1	0	0
	1	360	125	37	14	2	0	0	0

Source: Exhibit 2.21

Note: A dash -- indicates that a given density is generally not found at a given distance from cluster

With these caveats on variability, we can proceed to Exhibit 5.2, where transit trips are singled out from the universe of total trips using procedures described in Chapter 2. Those procedures, it might be recalled, estimate percent transit use by starting with auto ownership per household as a function of residential density, income, household size, and type of transit service territory. Auto ownership at the place of residence is translated into auto ownership in an origin-destination stream based on the density of the nonresidential destination, and the latter is translated into percent travellers coming from zero, one, and two-or-more-car households. Different preferences for auto versus public transit are assigned to each of these three groups depending on the density of the nonresidential destination and the frequency and coverage of transit service by different modes. The composite effect of these factors is listed in the fourth column of Exhibit 5.2, under the heading of percent transit.

Since the type of service territory plays a major role in determining percent transit—affecting both auto ownership and the choice of mode at any auto ownership level—two or three examples of service territory are listed for each residential density and each cluster size. Minimum bus service represents percent transit use at a theoretical minimum peak hour bus frequency (say, 1 bus an hour), which can be raised depending on the actual frequency to be tested. Rapid transit territory is defined as an area 40 percent of which lies within 2,000 feet of subway stations—this is equivalent to a 1-mile band along a rapid transit line, with stations spaced about 0.75 miles apart. Rail service means the presence of a commuter rail station with all-day service within a fairly broad area.

The rapid transit territory exhibits by far the highest percent transit use; rail service occupies an intermediate position and minimum bus is plausibly the lowest; however, at very high service frequencies, the bus can attain comparable percent transit use. For example, for a downtown-oriented cluster of 50 million square feet of nonresidential floorspace (the size of Newark) and a density of 10 dwellings per acre, transit use at minimum bus service is shown to be 35.2 percent; this would be raised to 46.0 percent with a bus frequency of 20 per hour during the peak two-hour period, compared to 57.0 percent in rapid transit territory and 41.7 percent in rail territory.

Not shown in Exhibit 5.2 is the effect of income and household size, which affects the choice of mode indirectly via auto ownership; both variables are assumed about the region-wide median level. Their effect can be illustrated as follows for a 10 dwellings per acre neighborhood near a nonresidential cluster of 50 million square feet. If the income is high (upper fifth) and the adult household size large (2.5 instead of 2.0), transit use in the three service territories drops by 7 to 11.6 percentage points; if income is low (lower fifth) and the adult household size is small (1.5), transit use increases by 5.8 to 6.8 percentage points. The effect is strongest in the bus territory and weakest in the rapid transit territory. If a consideration of the income and household size variables is desired, it can be achieved with the help of the procedures given in the Appendix.

In Chapter 2, the choice of mode was calculated in relation to the nonresidential density of clusters; this is translated in Exhibit 5.2 into cluster size for purposes of illustration. For specific applications, using the actual nonresidential density of the cluster will yield greater accuracy. Also, for the highest density clusters, taxi trips are counted as auto trips; this explains why in the highest density range in Exhibit 5.2, transit use does not exceed 80 percent.

In keeping with the networkless structure of the procedures presented, no account is taken of transit or auto speed; a distribution of these speeds such as it existed in the New York Region in 1963-70 is subsumed in the data. If significant departures from this speed

EXHIBIT 5.2

Illustrative Demand Density of Trips by Public Transit from Selected Residential Densities at Selected Distances to Nonresidential Clusters of Three Types, Assuming Minimum Service Level in Three Territories

MB = Minimum Bus Service; RT = Rapid Transit territory (40% within 2000 feet of stations); RS = Rail Service in Corridor; assumes median income level ($10,000 in 1969 $$) and 2 persons over 16 years per household; percentages of transit use applied to total trips in Exhibit 5.1.

Size of cluster, million sq. ft. non residential floors space	Residential density, dwellings/acre	Transit Service Territory	Percent Transit	One-way trips per gross sq. mile to cluster at following distances: (sum of work and non-work trips)						
				1 mi.	3 mi.	5 mi.	10 mi.	20 mi.	30 mi.	40 mi.
Trips to Downtown-oriented clusters:										
200	200	MB	69.4	29,800	15,600	10,400	4,810	--	--	--
		RT	80.2	34,500	18,000	12,000	5,560	--	--	--
	100	MB	64.7	18,100	9,510	6,310	2,920	--	--	--
		RT	78.1	21,900	11,500	7,610	3,530	--	--	--
	50	MB	60.2	9,870	5,180	3,440	1,600	--	--	--
		RT	76.0	12,500	6,540	4,347	2,010	--	--	--
	30	MB	56.7	--	3,440	2,290	1,060	388	--	--
		RT	74.4	--	4,510	3,000	1,390	509	--	--
	15	MB	52.0	--	--	1,120	520	191	100	--
		RT	72.3	--	--	1,560	723	265	127	--
	10	MB	49.8	--	--	752	347	127	61	34
		RT	71.1	--	--	1,070	496	182	87	49
		RS	55.4	--	--	837	386	142	68	38
	7	MB	47.8	--	--	569	263	97	46	26
		RT	70.0	--	--	812	385	141	68	38
		RS	53.3	--	--	634	293	108	52	29
	5	MB	46.1	--	--	--	163	60	29	16
		RT	69.0	--	--	--	244	90	43	24
		RS	52.2	--	--	--	185	68	32	18
	3	MB	43.0	--	--	--	84	31	15	8
		RS	50.2	--	--	--	98	36	18	10
	2	MB	41.6	--	--	--	45	17	8	5
		RS	48.5	--	--	--	52	19	9	5
	1	MB	37.5	--	--	--	--	5	2	1
		RS	45.5	--	--	--	--	6	3	1
100	150	MB	59.0	19,500	9,620	--	--	--	--	--
		RT	71.5	23,700	11,700	--	--	--	--	--
	100	MB	57.0	14,500	7,130	4,490	--	--	--	--
		RT	70.5	17,900	8,810	5,550	--	--	--	--
	50	MB	52.7	7,850	3,870	2,430	1,060	--	--	--
		RT	68.9	10,300	5,060	3,180	1,380	--	--	--
	30	MB	49.5	5,200	2,560	1,610	698	215	--	--
		RT	67.3	7,070	3,480	2,190	948	293	--	--
	15	MB	45.1	--	1,250	785	342	106	46	--
		RT	66.3	--	1,840	1,154	503	155	68	--
	10	MB	42.6	--	--	515	225	69	30	17
		RT	64.1	--	--	776	338	104	46	25
		RS	48.2	--	--	583	254	79	34	19
	7	MB	40.9	--	--	392	171	52	23	13
		RT	63.1	--	--	604	263	81	35	20
		RS	47.8	--	--	458	199	61	27	15
	5	MB	38.4	--	--	237	103	31	14	8
		RT	62.1	--	--	383	166	51	22	12
		RS	45.8	--	--	282	123	38	16	10
	3	MB	36.5	--	--	--	54	17	7	4
		RS	43.7	--	--	--	65	20	9	5
	2	MB	34.7	--	--	--	28	9	4	2
		RS	42.2	--	--	--	35	11	5	3
	1	MB	31.6	--	--	--	9	3	1	1
		RS	39.6	--	--	--	11	3	2	1
50	100	MB	49.0	11,100	4,950	--	--	--	--	--
		RT	62.2	14,100	6,280	--	--	--	--	--
	50	MB	45.0	5,990	2,670	--	--	--	--	--
		RT	61.0	8,110	3,620	--	--	--	--	--
	30	MB	41.7	3,910	1,740	--	--	--	--	--
		RT	59.9	5,238	2,500	--	--	--	--	--
	15	MB	36.7	--	822	488	189	--	--	--
		RT	58.0	--	1,300	771	299	--	--	--
	10	MB	35.2	--	549	327	126	32	13	--
		RT	57.2	--	890	530	205	52	21	--
		RS	41.7	--	651	387	150	38	15	--
	7	MB	33.2	--	--	243	94	24	9	--
		RT	56.0	--	--	410	158	40	16	--
		RS	40.0	--	--	293	113	29	11	--
	5	MB	32.0	--	--	151	58	15	6	3
		RT	55.0	--	--	259	100	25	10	5
		RS	38.9	--	--	183	71	18	7	4
	3	MB	29.9	--	--	78	30	8	3	1
		RS	37.3	--	--	98	38	10	4	2
	2	MB	28.4	--	--	41	16	4	2	1
		RS	35.8	--	--	52	20	5	2	1
	1	MB	25.3	--	--	--	5	1	1	0
		RS	33.5	--	--	--	6	2	1	0

EXHIBIT 5.2 continued

20	50	MB	35.8	3,940	--	--	--	--	--	--
		RT	52.0	5,720	--	--	--	--	--	--
	30	MB	32.8	2,540	--	--	--	--	--	--
		RT	51.1	3,950	--	--	--	--	--	--
	15	MB	28.9	1,200	462	--	--	--	--	--
		RT	49.9	2,070	798	--	--	--	--	--
	10	MB	26.9	777	299	177	50	--	--	--
		RT	48.3	1,400	536	289	90	--	--	--
		RS	32.7	945	363	196	61	--	--	--
	7	MB	25.2	--	222	119	37	7	--	--
		RT	47.2	--	415	223	69	13	--	--
		RS	30.6	--	269	145	44	8	--	--
	5	MB	23.4	--	132	71	22	4	1	0
		RT	46.4	--	262	141	44	8	3	1
		RS	30.1	--	170	91	28	5	2	1
	3	MB	21.5	--	68	36	11	2	1	0
		RS	28.8	--	90	48	15	3	1	0
	2	MB	20.0	--	35	19	6	1	0	0
		RS	27.7	--	48	26	8	1	1	0
	1	MB	17.4	--	--	5	2	0	0	0
		RS	26.1	--	--	8	2	1	0	0
10	30	MB	26.1	1,680	--	--	--	--	--	--
		RT	44.5	2,860	--	--	--	--	--	--
	15	MB	23.0	793	267	--	--	--	--	--
		RT	43.0	1,480	499	--	--	--	--	--
	10	MB	21.7	521	176	84	21	--	--	--
		RT	42.0	1,010	340	162	40	--	--	--
		RS	26.2	629	212	101	25	--	--	--
	7	MB	18.8	355	120	57	14	2	--	--
		RT	41.1	777	262	125	31	5	--	--
		RS	25.0	473	160	76	19	3	--	--
	5	MB	17.5	214	72	34	8	1	--	--
		RT	40.2	490	165	79	19	3	--	--
		RS	24.0	293	98	47	12	2	--	--
	3	MB	15.6	105	36	17	4	1	0	0
		RS	22.6	153	52	25	6	1	0	0
	2	MB	14.1	52	18	8	2	0	0	0
		RS	21.6	80	27	13	3	0	0	0
	1	MB	11.9	--	5	2	0	0	0	0
		RS	19.7	--	8	4	1	0	0	0
5	10	MB	14.1	268	75	32	6	--	--	--
		RT	35.0	665	187	79	15	--	--	--
		RS	20.0	380	107	45	8	--	--	--
	7	MB	12.6	189	53	23	4	1	--	--
		RT	34.1	512	143	61	11	1	--	--
		RS	18.8	282	79	34	6	1	--	--
	5	MB	11.4	110	31	13	2	0	--	--
		RT	33.3	320	90	38	7	1	--	--
		RS	18.0	173	49	21	4	0	--	--
	3	MB	09.7	52	15	6	1	0	0	0
		RS	16.7	89	25	11	2	0	0	0
	2	MB	08.4	25	7	3	1	0	0	0
		RS	16.0	47	13	6	1	0	0	0
	1	MB	06.4	6	2	1	0	0	0	0
		RS	14.6	14	4	2	0	0	0	0

Trips to Spread Clusters with Mixed Use:

20	50	MB	26.1	2,110	--	--	--	--	--	--
		RT	44.8	3,620	--	--	--	--	--	--
	30	MB	23.7	1,346	--	--	--	--	--	--
		RT	43.5	2,470	--	--	--	--	--	--
	15	MB	20.6	628	229	--	--	--	--	--
		RT	42.1	1,280	467	--	--	--	--	--
	10	MB	18.9	401	146	78	26	--	--	--
		RT	41.1	871	319	170	55	--	--	--
		RS	18.6	394	144	77	25	--	--	--
	7	MB	17.3	291	106	56	18	4	--	--
		RT	40.1	674	245	131	43	10	--	--
		RS	17.5	294	107	57	19	5	--	--
	5	MB	16.1	174	63	34	11	3	1	0
		RT	39.1	422	154	82	27	7	2	1
		RS	16.5	178	65	35	11	3	1	0
	3	MB	14.4	86	31	17	5	1	1	0
		RS	15.0	90	33	17	6	1	1	0
	2	MB	13.1	--	16	8	3	1	0	0
		RS	13.9	--	17	9	3	1	0	0
	1	MB	11.3	--	4	2	1	0	0	0
		RS	12.1	--	5	3	1	0	0	0
10	30	MB	20.0	938	--	--	--	--	--	--
		RT	39.3	1,840	--	--	--	--	--	--
	15	MB	17.2	433	146	--	--	--	--	--
		RT	37.9	955	322	--	--	--	--	--
	10	MB	15.9	278	94	45	13	--	--	--
		RT	36.8	644	217	105	31	--	--	--
		RS	15.2	266	90	43	13	--	--	--
	7	MB	14.6	201	68	33	10	2	--	--
		RT	35.9	495	165	80	24	5	--	--
		RS	14.3	197	67	32	10	2	--	--
	5	MB	13.4	119	40	19	6	1	1	0
		RT	35.0	311	105	50	15	3	1	0
		RS	13.5	120	41	19	6	1	1	0
	3	MB	12.0	59	20	10	3	1	0	0
		RS	12.1	60	20	10	3	1	0	0
	2	MB	10.7	29	10	5	1	0	0	0
		RS	11.1	30	10	5	1	0	0	0
	1	MB	09.0	--	3	1	0	0	0	0
		RS	09.6	--	3	1	0	0	0	0

EXHIBIT 5.2 continued

5	10	MB	12.9	188	54	25	6	--	--	--
		RT	33.0	481	139	64	16	--	--	--
		RS	13.7	200	58	27	6	--	--	--
	7	MB	11.9	137	40	18	4	1	--	--
		RT	32.0	368	107	49	12	2	--	--
		RS	11.9	137	40	18	4	1	--	--
	5	MB	10.9	81	23	11	3	0	0	0
		RT	31.4	233	67	31	8	1	0	0
		RS	11.0	82	24	11	3	0	0	0
	3	MB	09.6	40	11	5	1	0	0	0
		RS	09.9	41	12	5	1	0	0	0
	2	MB	08.5	19	6	3	1	0	0	0
		RS	09.0	20	6	3	1	0	0	0
	1	MB	06.7	5	1	1	0	0	0	0
		RS	07.3	5	2	1	0	0	0	0
2	7	MB	09.8	81	19	7	1	0	--	--
		RT	28.1	234	53	21	4	1	--	--
		RS	08.8	73	17	7	1	0	--	--
	5	MB	08.0	43	10	4	1	0	0	0
		RT	27.2	145	33	13	3	0	0	0
		RS	08.0	43	10	4	1	0	0	0
	3	MB	06.8	20	5	2	0	0	0	0
		RS	07.0	21	5	2	0	0	0	0
	2	MB	05.9	10	2	1	0	0	0	0
		RS	06.2	10	2	1	0	0	0	0
	1	MB	04.5	2	1	0	0	0	0	0
		RS	05.0	3	1	0	0	0	0	0

Trips to Shopping-oriented Spread Clusters:

10	30	MB	20.0	1,710	--	--	--	--	--	--
		RT	39.3	3,360	--	--	--	--	--	--
	15	MB	17.2	789	291	--	--	--	--	--
		RT	37.9	1,740	641	--	--	--	--	--
	10	MB	15.9	509	188	94	23	--	--	--
		RT	36.8	1,178	434	217	53	--	--	--
		RS	15.2	486	179	90	22	--	--	--
	7	MB	14.6	368	135	68	17	2	--	--
		RT	35.9	905	333	167	41	5	--	--
		RS	14.3	360	133	67	16	2	--	--
	5	MB	13.4	217	80	40	10	1	0	0
		RT	35.0	567	209	105	26	3	1	0
		RS	13.5	218	80	41	10	1	0	0
	3	MB	12.0	108	40	20	5	1	0	0
		RS	12.1	109	40	20	5	1	0	0
	2	MB	10.7	53	19	10	2	0	0	0
		RS	11.1	55	20	10	2	0	0	0
	1	MB	09.0	--	5	3	1	0	0	0
		RS	09.6	--	6	3	1	0	0	0
5	10	MB	12.9	376	128	59	13	--	--	--
		RT	33.0	961	328	150	32	--	--	--
		RS	13.7	399	136	62	13	--	--	--
	7	MB	11.9	274	93	43	9	1	--	--
		RT	32.0	736	251	115	25	3	--	--
		RS	11.9	274	93	43	9	1	--	--
	5	MB	10.9	161	55	25	5	1	0	0
		RT	31.4	465	158	72	16	2	0	0
		RS	11.0	163	55	25	6	1	0	0
	3	MB	09.6	79	27	12	3	0	0	0
		RS	09.9	81	28	13	3	0	0	0
	2	MB	08.5	38	13	6	1	0	0	0
		RS	09.0	41	14	6	1	0	0	0
	1	MB	06.7	10	3	2	0	0	0	0
		RS	07.3	11	4	2	0	0	0	0
2	7	MB	09.8	190	57	22	4	0	--	--
		RT	28.1	545	162	63	11	1	--	--
		RS	08.8	171	51	20	3	0	--	--
	5	MB	08.0	100	30	12	2	0	0	0
		RT	27.2	339	101	39	7	1	0	0
		RS	08.0	100	30	12	2	0	0	0
	3	MB	06.8	47	14	5	1	0	0	0
		RS	07.0	48	14	6	1	0	0	0
	2	MB	05.9	22	7	3	0	0	0	0
		RS	06.2	24	7	3	0	0	0	0
	1	MB	04.5	6	2	1	0	0	0	0
		RS	05.0	6	2	1	0	0	0	0

Source: Percent transit use developed from Exhibit 2.12 (with the help of nomographs shown in the Appendix) and applied to total trips in Exhibit 5.1

Note: A dash -- indicates that a given density is generally not found at a given distance from a cluster.

pattern are to be tested, the material presented in Chapter 1, dealing with diversion of auto owners to transit, based on travel time differences and with the magnitudes of induced travel, can be informally applied. The same goes for different levels of transit fare.

Lastly, it should be emphasized that for purposes of determining the viability of any particular transit route, the transit trip densities such as those portrayed in Exhibit 5.2 should be considered to be cumulative. For example, the 200 million square foot nonresidential cluster size illustrated comes rather close to representing Midtown Manhattan, with about 260 million square feet of nonresidential floorspace. However, if the influence of all of the Manhattan Central Business District is to be taken into account, the trip end densities generated by the 130 million square feet in Lower Manhattan and by some 150 million in the valley between the two peaks must be added. Similarly, the trip end densities generated by any intervening nonresidential clusters that happen to be located on the route from a residential area being investigated must be added as well. The same holds true for smaller downtowns and their surrounding nonresidential clusters. In a large metropolitan area, this "coattail" effect allows many smaller subcenters to have transit service which they would not justify on their own.

The transit trips illustrated in Exhibit 5.2 represent strictly one-way trips from *residential origins* to nonresidential clusters, and as such are useful for estimating demand for line-haul systems, be they buses or trains. They are not useful for estimating highly localized multidirectional trips, such as those by taxi or dial-a-bus. To assess the demand for these modes in relation to residential density, Exhibit 5.3 is presented.

This is a modified enlargement of Exhibit 2.7 and focuses on the lower range of densities. It shows trips from all origins (not merely from residential origins as do Exhibits 5.1 and 5.2) and thus the trip densities shown may be more than twice as high as those just discussed. The top curve shows trips by all public transit modes in the New York Region for reference. The second curve shows only those public transit trips which are *not* destined to the Central Business Districts of Manhattan, Brooklyn, and Newark; these local transit trips are in scale with those of several medium-sized urban areas across the country. They reflect two-way per capita transit trip rates averaging between about 0.04 and 0.16 at the densities shown. For comparison with the line of averages based on 1963 data, actual 1974 observations for local bus trips in a suburban county and in five smaller cities of the Region are also shown. While Nassau County and the cities of Bridgeport and Long Beach are close to the line of averages, the other three towns show a wide dispersion. The bottom line shows New York Region trips by taxi; it reflects a per capita trip rate of about 0.01.

Also shown are observed trip densities of several taxi and dial-a-bus operations in North America, described in greater detail in Exhibit 5.4. The dial-a-bus data fall into two distinct groups: suburban and poverty-area oriented. The trip densities of the suburban operations are generally between those of local buses and taxicabs in the New York Region; they reflect per capita trip rates of 0.01 to 0.06, averaging about 0.03. The poverty area dial-a-bus densities are similar to those of taxicabs.

Density of supply is related to the density of demand in the beginning of this chapter simply by relating vehicle hours of operation per square mile per day to passengers boarding per square mile per day. Obviously, in the real world, tailoring transit supply to demand is a more complex matter. It means, first of all, taking account of the shape of the daily peak which, as Chapter 4 has shown, can vary over a substantial range; it means taking account of the average passenger trip length, so that the product of passengers boarding per vehicle mile and their trip lengths (which spells vehicle occupancy) does not exceed available vehicle capacity. It means taking account of the cumulative distribution of passen-

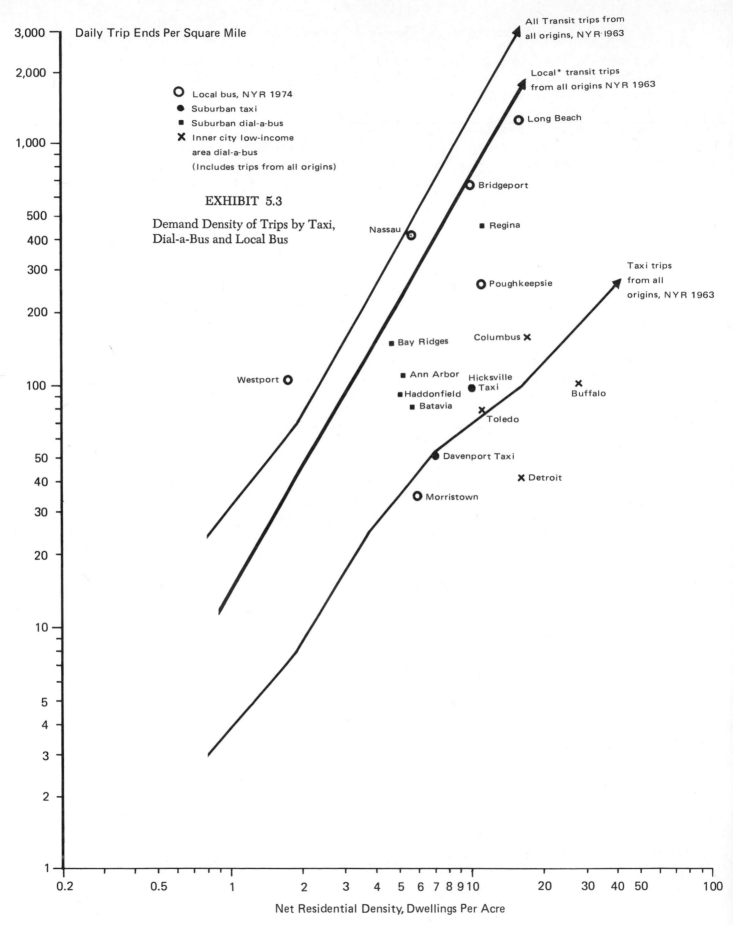

EXHIBIT 5.3

Demand Density of Trips by Taxi,
Dial-a-Bus and Local Bus

Daily Trip Ends Per Square Mile

○ Local bus, NYR 1974
● Suburban taxi
■ Suburban dial-a-bus
✗ Inner city low-income
  area dial-a-bus
  (Includes trips from all origins)

All Transit trips from all origins, NYR 1963

Local* transit trips from all origins NYR 1963

Taxi trips from all origins, NYR 1963

Long Beach
Bridgeport
Regina
Nassau
Poughkeepsie
Columbus
Bay Ridges
Ann Arbor
Hicksville Taxi
Haddonfield
Batavia
Toledo
Buffalo
Westport
Davenport Taxi
Detroit
Morristown

Net Residential Density, Dwellings Per Acre

* Transit trips other than to the Central Business Districts of Manhattan, Brooklyn, and Newark

Sources: Tri-State Regional Planning Commission and Exhibit 5.4

ger boardings and debarkations along a route, which depends on the distribution of densities along the route, and builds up to the passenger volume at maximum load point. It means taking account of the route length and the average speed of each transit line, for these determine whether, for instance, two runs during the peak hour can be made by the same vehicle, or whether one vehicle is needed for each peak hour run. It means taking account of such institutional arrangements as work rules, which determine whether a vehicle operator must work a straight shift, or can split shifts; in the former case, frequent off-peak service can be provided at little additional cost, in the latter case, service frequency can be tailored more closely to demand. It may also mean taking account of an entire system, not just individual lines, and balancing income from heavily used routes against losses on lightly used ones.

In dial-a-bus systems, tailoring vehicle supply to demand also starts with the peak load and must take into account passenger trip length, but instead of route length, the extent of the service area becomes a critical factor, and additional elements enter the picture, such as the amount of waiting time and route-deviation that passengers will tolerate.

In train operations, further variables enter the picture. Thus, a 30 percent one-directional peak would suggest that if the same space standards and waiting time standards were to be maintained throughout the day, 7 times more vehicle units of capacity would have to be operated during the peak hour than during most of the rest of the day. Ideally, this might mean 7-car trains during the peak hour and 1-car trains during most of the rest of the day, running at the same high frequency. This does not usually happen in the real world, where both peak hour space standards and off-peak service frequency are often sacrificed in an effort to cut costs.

For the sake of arriving at a generalized relationship between development density and the feasibility of different transit modes, important details of this kind cannot be adequately treated. We shall deal with service frequency first on an *average daily* basis, relating vehicle hours of operation to the total number of runs over a 20-hour period. Only when it comes to an analysis of individual routes will peaking characteristics and capacity constraints be considered.

To introduce the discussion of the individual modes, Exhibit 5.4 deals with empirical examples of taxi, dial-a-bus, and fixed route bus operations. It shows the service density expressed in vehicle hours per square mile, gives some indication of the average waiting times these service densities imply, shows the demand densities served in each case and the resulting "vehicle productivity", i.e., passengers boarding per vehicle hour. It is these passengers who must share the cost of furnishing one vehicle hour of service.

THE TAXICAB

Of all public transit modes, the taxicab operates over the broadest range of densities and provides the highest level of service at a cost that is, except for some dial-a-bus operations, also the highest. A brief look at the relationship between passenger demand and the supply of taxi service is instructive primarily as a benchmark for comparison with other modes.

As was shown in Chapter 3, the cost of operating a taxicab can be generally assumed at around $6.00 per vehicle hour in 1974 prices, though some operations manage to be cheaper. At that cost and an average fare of $2.00 per passenger, the cab needs to pick up 3 passengers per hour to operate. A demand density of 3 daily trips per square mile (typi-

EXHIBIT 5.4

Comparison of Demand Densities and Service Densities of Selected Public Transportation Modes

	Gross population density per/sq.mi.	Net dwellings/acre	Area of operation, sq.mi.	Daily Hours of operation	AVERAGE DAILY DEMAND DENSITY — Passenger trip ends/sq.mi.	AVERAGE DAILY SERVICE DENSITY — Vehicle-miles per sq.mi.	Vehicle-hours per sq.mi.	AVERAGE DAILY VEHICLE PRODUCTIVITY — Psgrs. boarding per veh-hr	Operating cost per veh-hr $	Operating cost per passenger $	Ave. Fare $	Waiting Time	Ride Time
SHARED-RIDE TAXI (1973-74)													
Davenport, Iowa	5,000	6.9	19.7	24	52	170	13.5	3.85	4.27	1.11	1.11	20 min.	11 min.
Hicksville, N.Y.	7,100	10.0	6.8	24	99	495	33.7	2.94	5.70	1.94	1.94	10 min.	9 min.
DIAL-A-BUS (1973-74)													
Bay Ridges, Ont.	3,500	4.6	4.0	20	150	n.a.	15.5	9.7	7.75	0.80	0.25	54 min.	7 min.
Haddonfield, N.J.	3,680	4.9	10.9	24	91	n.a.	17.6	5.4	20.48	3.81	0.28	19 min.	13 min.
Ann Arbor, Mich.	3,857	5.1	2.3	11.5	109	n.a.	15.6	6.0	10.51	1.74	0.48	9 min.	13 min.
Batavia, N.Y.	4,032	5.5	4.3	12	81	n.a.	7.0	11.7	7.14	0.61	0.50	11 min.	11 min.
Toledo Model Cities	7,650	11.0	3.5	15	78	n.a.	17.1	4.6	8.75	1.90	0.00	30 min.	30 min.
Regina, Sask.	7,733	11.0	7.5	18.5	453	n.a.	21.6	19.5	13.13	0.67	0.35	23 min.	18 min.
Detroit Model Cities	10,810	16.0	9.5	16	42	n.a.	6.7	6.3	10.22	1.62	0.00	20 min.	20 min.
Columbus Model Cities	11,640	17.0	2.5	15.3	158	n.a.	18.0	8.8	15.24	1.73	0.17	27 min.	19 min.
Buffalo Model Cities	17,950	27.0	3.0	17	100	n.a.	11.3	8.9	22.80	2.56	0.00	18 min.	37 min.
FIXED-ROUTE LOCAL BUS (1974)													
Long Beach, N.Y.	15,775	15.4	2.1	19	1,279	342	32.0	40.0	11.84	0.296	0.197	15 min.	
Poughkeepsie N.Y.	5,910	11.2	6.6	11.5	264	106	9.2	28.7	11.25	0.392	0.223	15 min.	
Bridgeport, Conn.*	8,521	9.8	21.8	17	671	282	23.5	28.6	12.27	0.429	0.483	5 to 30	
Nassau County, N.Y.**	6,703	5.6	144.1	20	417	212	15.3	27.3	17.97	0.659	0.507	5 to 17	
Morristown, N.J.***	5,887	5.9	3.0	7	35	16	1.1	31.8	13.10	0.412	0.000	42 min.	
Westport, Conn.	1,378	1.7	19.9	14	106	78	3.7	28.6	18.59	0.650	0.154	17 min.	

Sources: Frank W. Davis et.al., *Economic Characteristics of privately-owned Shared-ride Taxi Systems,* The University of Tennesse Transportation Center, October 1974 Bert Arrillaga, George E. Mouchahoir, *Demand-Responsive Transportation System Planning Guidelines,* McLean, Va., The MITRE Corporation, April 1974

Local bus, Tri-State Regional Planning Commission, *Interim Technical Reports 4441-3308* and *4510-3308,* "City Transit Profiles I and II," April 1974 and July, 1975; population and density data from U.S. Census and Regional Plan Association; annual data converted to daily on the assumption of 290 equivalent operating days per year in the section on local buses.

Note: Waiting time for fixed-route buses taken as one-half average service frequency.

*Bridgeport data for 1972; cost per bus hour includes profit of 5.4 cents per passenger.

**Metropolitan Suburban Bus Authority (MSBA) service area only; trips include feeder service to New York City subways.

***Local Colonial Coach service only; excludes extensive county-wide and regional services

cal of one-acre lot densities) can thus be satisfied with a supply of one vehicle hour per square mile per day, meaning that one cab working a 15-hour day may be sufficient to cover 15 square miles. At a density of 5 dwellings per acre, with 30 daily demands per square mile (per Exhibit 5.3), a supply of 10 vehicle hours per square mile may be necessary, and so on.

The feasibility threshold of taxi service is very low (probably in the rural density range of fewer than 100 people per gross square mile), but taxi use does increase with the density of development. In suburban areas, taxi operations are typically based near local trip generators of above-average density, such as shopping centers, bus or rail stations. Exhibit 5.3 shows that the average rate of 0.01 taxi trips per person per day (typical of the New York Region outside Manhattan as well as of Davenport, Iowa) is raised to 0.014 in Hicksville, Long Island, where more than one third of all taxi trips are to or from the local railroad station.[1] Among cities, those with higher densities tend to have higher taxi use per capita,[2] largely because of the concentration of taxi travel in major Central Business Districts. In the New York Region, this concentration reaches its apex in the central square mile of Midtown Manhattan, where a demand density of over 100,000 daily trips is satisfied by a service density of nearly 30,000 vehicle hours per square mile.

One effect of increased service density, to be dealt with more explicitly in connection with other modes, is reduced waiting time. Exhibit 5.4 suggests that the higher service density of Hicksville results in a much shorter waiting time compared to Davenport; in downtown areas, where the service density is sufficiently high for cabs to be flagged in the street rather than summoned by telephone, waiting time is reduced to a few minutes. The vehicle productivity of a taxicab (number of passengers boarding per vehicle hour) seems to rise moderately with rising density, though accurate data are lacking. Nevertheless, *the taxi is able to service selected trips over the full range of urban and suburban densities.*

DIAL-A-BUS

The aim of dial-a-bus is to increase vehicle productivity compared to the taxicab and thereby to lower the cost per passenger. However, ride sharing presupposes a demand density substantially higher than the minimum needed to support the individualized taxi service. At a density of one dwelling per acre, where only 3 to 10 potential local transit trips originate in any square mile over an entire day, the chances of shared riding are clearly minimal.

Dial-a-bus systems shown in Exhibits 5.3 through 5.5 operate at suburban densities of 4.6 to 11 dwellings per acre, and up to 27 dwellings per acre in poverty areas, serving demand densities between 40 and 400 daily trips per square mile. Their vehicle productivities are on the whole only moderately higher than those of taxicabs. The differences in dial-a-bus productivity are in part explained by differences in operation: service from many origins to many destinations, in the manner of a taxicab; or service from many origins to a few destinations, e.g., to fixed stops in a downtown area; or from many origins to one destination, e.g., a railroad station; or subscription service, where a fixed number of patrons and their departure times are known in advance.

The productivities of the nine dial-a-bus systems listed in Exhibit 5.4 are plotted against development density in Exhibit 5.5. While there is a general tendency for vehicle productivity to rise with rising density of development, two distinct patterns are apparent. The system with the highest vehicle productivity, the one in Regina, Sask., carries 90 percent

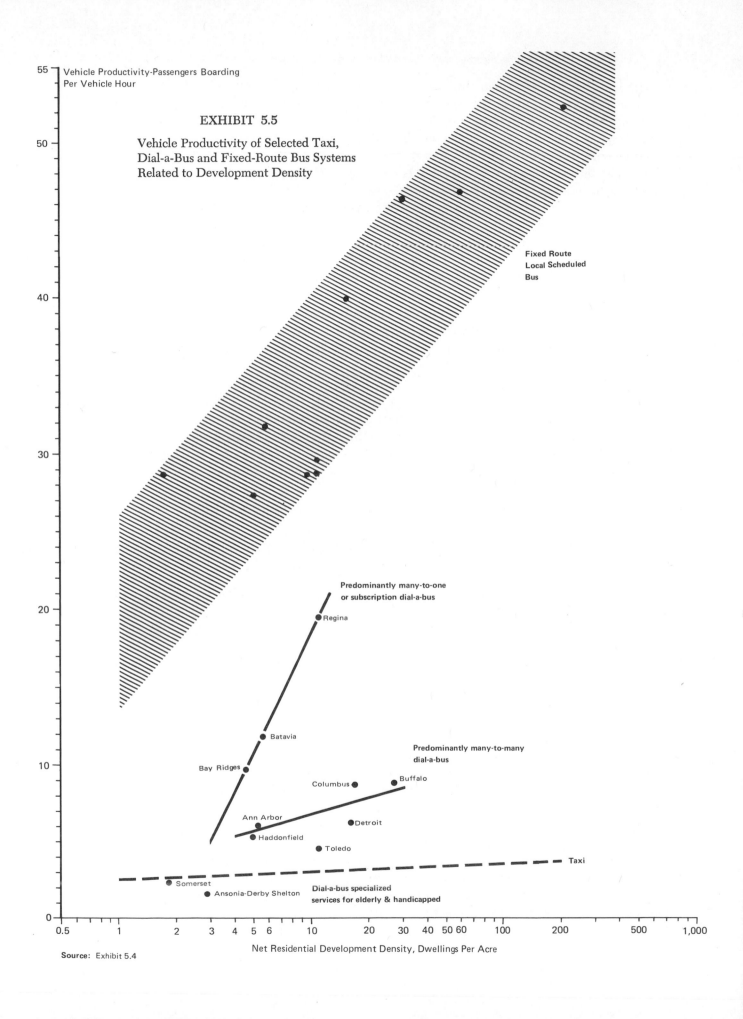

EXHIBIT 5.5

Vehicle Productivity of Selected Taxi,
Dial-a-Bus and Fixed-Route Bus Systems
Related to Development Density

Vehicle Productivity-Passengers Boarding
Per Vehicle Hour

Fixed Route
Local Scheduled
Bus

Predominantly many-to-one
or subscription dial-a-bus

Regina

Predominantly many-to-many
dial-a-bus

Batavia

Bay Ridges

Columbus

Buffalo

Ann Arbor

Detroit

Haddonfield

Toledo

Taxi

Somerset

Ansonia-Derby Shelton

Dial-a-bus specialized
services for elderly & handicapped

Net Residential Development Density, Dwellings Per Acre

Source: Exhibit 5.4

of its passengers in the many to-few and many-to-one modes; in Bay Ridges, Ont., 85 percent of the trips are many-to-one, destined for the railroad station; and in Batavia, N.Y., vehicle productivity is enhanced by subscription services. By contrast, the discontinued Haddonfield, N.J., system with 5.4 passengers boarding per vehicle hour had over 90 percent of the service in the taxi-like many-to-many mode, and the productivities of the other five predominantly many-to-many services do not exceed 9 passengers boarding per vehicle hour, even at fairly high urban densities.

Factors other than the type of service and development density also influence dial-a-bus productivity. If the trips are short, more of them can be handled per vehicle hour. The service areas of many systems are very small (2 to 5 square miles), implying very short trips. Until 1975, the Haddonfield, N.J., system served the largest area—about 11 square miles—and its average passenger trip was only 2.0 miles. Moreover, vehicle productivity is inversely related to the level of service, as measured by waiting time and route deviation time; it can be increased at the expense of letting passengers wait longer for a pickup and taking them farther out of their way before delivery. Conversely, if short waiting and route deviation times are desired, more service (more vehicle hours per square mile) must be provided, and the number of passengers boarding per vehicle hour drops. Increasing the size of the service area may amplify this phenomenon. As service area expands, route deviation time for the individual pickups also increases, as does the uncertainty of meeting promised pickup times, so that more vehicle hours may be needed to maintain the same service level.[3] It can be seen from Exhibit 5.4 that despite a service density in the high range, the waiting time in Haddonfield still averaged 19 minutes. The difficulty of providing an adequate service level over a wide area is perhaps best illustrated by the collapse of the San Jose, Calif., system in 1975: despite a low density of demand (fewer than 30 trips per square mile), the huge area served required much higher vehicle densities than those being provided; as a result, waiting times stretched to several hours.

The expense of providing vehicle hours per square mile can be reduced by curtailing the service period and by eliminating nighttime hours of low productivity. Of all the systems listed, only the discontinued one in Haddonfield provided 24-hour service; some systems that gained a reputation of success, notably Ann Arbor and Batavia, provide service for only 12 hours. They offer waiting times in the 9 to 11 minute range at costs of $0.60 to $1.75 per passenger over areas as small as 2 to 4 square miles.

As with any new service, dial-a-bus did increase public transit ridership in the areas served. On a very low base, the increases have been in the range of 40 to 100 percent or more, though Exhibit 5.3 and the accompanying discussion place them in a better perspective on a per square mile or per capita basis; dial-a-bus trips typically account for 1 to 3 percent of all mechanical trips in the areas served. The gains in ridership are mostly attributable to two factors: 1) the low, heavily subsidized fare, ranging from about one quarter of the taxi fare to nothing, and 2) the very introduction of an additional, premium transit service with virtually no walking and indoor, rather than outdoor, waiting.

The fare elasticity of dial-a-bus has been found generally in the same range as that of regular buses in small urban areas shown in Exhibit 1.1, that is between −0.6 and −0.8. Of all the service quality issues, waiting time and its reliable estimation by the dispatcher have been found to be the most sensitive. It has been estimated that a pickup within 15 minutes results in a 5 percent ridership loss, one within 15 to 30 minutes in a 22 percent loss, and one in more than 30 minutes in a 45 percent loss.[4] Surveys have found that compared to fixed-route transit, a larger proportion of dial-a-bus passengers are riders by choice; in rough terms, over one third have been diverted from buses and taxis, one quarter to one half have been diverted from the auto, and one tenth to one quarter have been newly induced.[5] However, the money costs of this gain in ridership have been generally very high, as will be shown shortly.

The operating cost of dial-a-bus, which in Chapter 3 was treated in terms of average figures, is shown in Exhibit 5.4 to vary over a broad range, from around $7.00 per vehicle hour (only moderately more than a taxicab) to over $20.00 per vehicle hour, which is in the upper range of regular bus costs. Apart from different operating conditions, the difference is due mainly to different wage rates and labor arrangements. Batavia, with the lowest cost per vehicle hour, employed nonunion labor at around $3.40 per hour. The driver cost (including overtime and benefits) in Haddonfield in 1974 was $10.90 per hour.[6] It is clear that if dial-a-bus drivers were to be paid taxi driver wages, a moderate vehicle productivity increase compared to the taxicab, attained through shared riding, would result in a cost per passenger lower than that of a taxicab. Exhibit 5.4 shows this is in fact what happened in Batavia, N.Y. and Bay Ridges, Ont. On the other hand, if dial-a-bus drivers are to be treated the same as regular bus drivers on systems with some of the better pay scales, then vehicle productivity must be in excess of about 10 passengers boarding per vehicle hour for the cost per ride to be below that of a taxi. As evident from Exhibits 5.4 and 5.5, only three of the nine systems reviewed attained such high productivity, due either to a many-to-few service pattern or heavy reliance on subscription service. On the other six systems, cost per rider ranged from $1.62 to $3.81 and the subsidy per rider from $1.26 to $3.53; in the short-lived San Jose project mentioned earlier, the subsidy per rider was estimated at $4.00 or more.[7] In other words, not counting the two Canadian systems and the low-wage Batavia system, the average subsidy per rider alone was about equal to the average cost of a taxi ride ($2.07 in 1973-74 prices).

These operating results led an authority on the subject to "conclude that for the types of areas being served, demand responsive transportation systems can be most useful and economically viable when operated in a many-to-one or many-to-few mode, as a feeder to line-haul fixed-route transportation modes or to other major trip generators. . . . Unless currently observed demand densities for many-to-many trips increase, it does not appear that vehicle productivity will ever be high enough to justify continuation of this type of service . . . the most economical way to provide this service would appear to be by using taxicabs that are allowed to carry several passengers at the same time. . . ."[8]

To pinpoint the feasibility threshold of dial-a-bus operations in relation to the density of development more closely, we return to the productivity vs. development density relationships in Exhibit 5.5. If we assume dial-a-bus operating cost at $12.00 per vehicle hour (equivalent to a total driver cost, including fringes and overtime, of no more than about $6.50 an hour), then 6 passenger boardings per hour are needed to attain the same per passenger cost as that of a taxicab. Taking many-to-many service first (the second curve from the bottom), we note that this productivity is reached on the average at a density of *6 dwellings per acre*. At lower densities, dial-a-bus at the assumed cost per vehicle hour will be more expensive than a taxicab. If dial-a-bus labor rates are such that operating cost is $14.00 per vehicle hour, the feasibility threshold quickly moves to *about 12 dwellings per acre*, a density range that is fairly well defined as fixed-route bus territory.

Generalizing, we may say that dial-a-bus in many-to-many service can carry passengers at a cost lower than the taxicab *only if the wage scales are such that its cost per vehicle hour is less than twice that of the local taxi service;* in that case, it may be applicable at densities between about 6 and 12 dwellings per acre. Failing that, the social purposes of dial-a-bus, such as providing mobility to the elderly, the indigent, and the handicapped, can be more effectively served by providing them with subsidized rides in local taxicabs.

In fact, dial-a-bus services designed for the exclusive use of the elderly and handicapped, and operated usually by social agencies, tend to attain vehicle productivities no higher than those of taxicabs; two such examples are shown at the bottom of Exhibit 5.5. This is what one would expect, given the inherently low demand densities of the special trips in question. Since the costs per vehicle hour of these services are in no way lower than those of taxis, the costs per passenger tend to be higher. Once again, in areas where other public transportation is lacking, subsidizing the taxi fares of the people to be helped is likely to be more effective than maintaining separate services.

The situation is quite different for dial-a-bus many-to-one and subscription services, which appear able to attain roughly triple the productivity of a taxicab at a density of 4 dwellings per acre, and roughly six times its productivity at 10 dwellings per acre, as evident from the admittedly sparse data on which the third curve from the bottom in Exhibit 5.5 is based. Thus, *at operating costs of $12.00 per vehicle hour, many-to-one and subscription services appear to be competitive with the taxicab at densities above about 3.5 dwellings per acre, and even at $20.00 per vehicle hour at densities above 5 dwellings per acre.*

Obviously though, such semi-fixed route operations are a far cry from the ubiquitous service systems originally envisaged by dial-a-bus advocates, and have in fact preceded the concept, for example in the form of one-man private bus lines feeding suburban commuter rail stations. They should be recognized as a *necessary adjunct of regional public transit networks, but they do not represent a major element* in the total public transportation picture.

LOCAL BUS

The operating cost of regular fixed-route buses was shown in Exhibit 3.2 to be in the range between $13 and $22 per vehicle hour in 1974 prices. The lower part of Exhibit 5.4 amplifies that range somewhat by showing that some smaller operations were still able to keep it near $11 per vehicle hour due to driver wages in the range of $3.25 to $3.90 an hour, not much different from those of taxi drivers. If costs on the order of $2.00 per passenger trip (customary for taxicabs, and tolerated with a huge subsidy on dial-a-buses) were acceptable on regular buses, then regular buses could be supported with vehicle productivities as low as 5 to 10 passengers boarding per vehicle hour. This could extend fixed-route bus service at high frequencies (competitive with dial-a-bus) into the density range of less than 5 dwellings per acre.

However, the whole purpose of fixed-route buses is to provide public transportation at a cost substantially below that of taxis and dial-a-buses, and the key to that is substantially higher vehicle productivity. Exhibit 5.5 shows that passenger boardings per vehicle hour on fixed route buses in the New York Region increase from about 27 in suburban areas to 52 in Manhattan; the national average shown earlier in Exhibit 3.2 is about 30, a figure that is sometimes viewed as a standard for local services.[9] With a $12.00 operating cost per vehicle hour, 30 passengers boarding per vehicle hour mean a 40¢ cost per passenger; with a $20.00 operating cost, the per passenger cost becomes 67¢. Vehicle productivity of course is merely the quotient of demand density and service density, with the latter being our first concern at this point.

EXHIBIT 5.6

Illustrative Minimum Demand Densities
Needed to Support Selected Service
Frequencies of Fixed-Route Buses

One-directional service frequency:		10-minute average (120 departures/20 hrs.) (5 minute waiting time)									Implicit veh.productivity, pass. boarding per veh. hr.
Density, DU's/acre:		1	2	5	7	10	15	30	50	100	
Assumed speed (Exh. 4.1) mph:		24	20	15	13.3	12	10.3	8.5	7.7	7.0	
Needed veh-hrs/sq.mi. per day: at ½ mile route spacing		10	12	16	18	20	23.3	28.2	31.2	34.3	
Cost/sq.mi. @ 20 $ Veh-hr $:		200	240	320	360	400	466	564	624	686	
Needed pass. boarding per sq. mi. (one-directional)	@ $1/pass:	200	240	320	360	400	466	564	624	686	20
	@ 0.75/pass:	267	320	427	480	533	621	752	832	915	26.7
	@ 0.50/pass:	400	480	640	720	800	932	1,128	1,248	1,372	40
Cost/sq.mi. @ $15/Veh.hr. $:		150	180	240	270	300	350	423	468	514	
Needed pass. boarding per sq. mi. (one-directional)	$2/pass:	75	90	120	135	150	175	212	234	257	7.5
	$1/pass:	150	180	240	270	300	350	423	468	514	15
	0.75/pass:	200	240	320	360	400	467	564	624	685	20
	0.50/pass:	300	360	480	540	600	700	846	936	1,028	30

One-directional service frequency:		30-minute average (40 departures/20hrs.) (15 minutes waiting time)									Implicit veh.productivity, pass. Loading per veh. hr.
Density, DU's/acre:		1	2	5	7	10	15	30	50	100	
Assumed speed (Exh. 4.1) mph:		24	20	15	13.3	12	10.3	8.5	7.7	7.0	
Needed veh-hrs/sq.mi. per day: at ½ mile route spacing		3.3	4	5.3	6	6.7	7.8	9.4	10.4	11.4	
Cost/sq.mi. @ 20 $ Veh-hr $:		66	80	106	120	134	156	188	208	228	
Needed pass. boarding per sq. mi. (one-directional)	@ $1/pass:	66	80	106	120	134	156	188	208	228	20
	@ 0.75/pass:	88	107	141	160	179	208	251	277	304	26.7
	@ 0.50/pass:	132	160	212	240	268	312	376	416	456	40
Cost/sq.mi. @ $15/Veh.hr. $:		50	60	80	90	101	117	141	156	171	
Needed pass. boarding per sq. mi. (one-directional)	$2/pass:	25	30	40	45	51	59	71	78	86	7.5
	$1/pass:	50	60	80	90	101	117	141	156	171	15
	0.75/pass:	67	80	107	120	135	156	188	208	228	20
	0.50/pass:	100	120	160	180	202	234	282	312	342	30

EXHIBIT 5.6 continued

One-directional service frequency:		1-hour average (20 departures/20 hrs.) (30 minutes waiting time)									Implicit veh. pro-ductivity, pass.
Density, DU's/acre:		1	2	5	7	10	15	30	50	100	
Assumed speed (Exh. 4.1) mph:		24	20	15	13.3	12	10.3	8.5	7.7	7.0	Loading per veh. hr.
Needed veh-hrs/sq.mi. per day: at ½ mile route spacing		1.7	2.0	2.7	3.0	3.3	3.9	4.7	5.2	5.7	
Cost/sq.mi. @ 20 $ Veh-hr $:		34	40	54	60	66	78	94	104	114	
Needed pass. boarding per sq. mi. (one-directional)	@ $1/pass:	34	40	54	60	66	78	94	104	114	20
	@ 0.75/pass:	45	53	72	80	88	104	125	139	152	26.7
	@ 0.50/pass:	68	80	108	120	132	156	188	208	228	40
Cost/sq.mi. @ $15/Veh.hr. $:		26	30	41	45	50	59	71	78	86	
Needed pass. boarding per sq. mi. (one-directional)	$2/pass:	13	15	21	23	25	30	36	39	43	7.5
	$1/pass:	26	30	41	45	50	59	71	78	86	15
	0.75/pass:	35	40	55	60	66	79	95	104	115	20
	0.50/pass:	52	60	82	90	100	118	142	156	172	30

Source: Regional Plan Association

Service density—vehicle hours per square mile—is related to the quality of service on dial-a-bus systems only in a rather complex and indirect manner. On fixed-route systems, coverage and frequency of service are translated into service density very directly. Full bus coverage can be assumed to exist at a half-mile spacing between bus routes, in which case one bus run per day in one direction in a square mile means two vehicle miles per square mile. Similarly, a service frequency of one bus every hour for 20 hours on two routes means 40 vehicle miles per square mile. Of course, if two perpendicular routes with half-mile spacing are added, 80 vehicle miles per square mile will be required. Dividing vehicle miles by the operating speed gives us the *vehicle hours* per square mile necessary to maintain a selected service frequency at a selected route spacing.

Three illustrative service frequencies are shown in Exhibit 5.6: service every 10 minutes, service every half hour, and service every hour on the average during a 20-hour operating day, with two bus routes per square mile. The prevailing average speeds at each of the nine residential densities are listed, derived from Exhibit 4.1, followed by the number of vehicle hours per square mile per day needed to obtain a given service frequency at a given residential density. The service density of vehicle hours per square mile represents one-directional trips and does *not* include return trips; in this respect, it differs from the service densities listed earlier in Exhibit 5.4. This is done because in subsequent discussion the service density will be related to demand density expressed in *trip origins only*, on the assumption that in the course of a day travel is symmetrical.

Next, the service density is multiplied by two illustrative costs per vehicle hour—$20.00 and $15.00; the resulting dollar costs per square mile needed to provide a given service frequency at a given density of development are shown. Thus, with the higher of the two bus costs, providing a 10-minute service *in one direction only* requires anywhere from $200 to $686 per square mile per day, depending on development density; an hourly service costs one sixth as much.

The dollar costs of providing different service frequencies per square mile are of intrinsic interest. For example, they suggest that even if the residents of an area with development densities as low as one dwelling per acre wish to have a bus service every 10 minutes with nobody walking more than 5 minutes, they can have it—provided each resident contributes $1.14 per day (there being about 350 residents in a gross square mile at a net density of 1 dwelling per acre, and the costs of service in both directions being double those shown). With half-acre lots, the cost of a 10-minute service with half-mile route spacing declines to 48¢. Above 10 dwellings per acre, the cost per resident becomes less than 10¢ per day. Lower costs would result from assuming a lower cost per bus hour, a shorter service period, and greater spacing between bus routes. On the other hand, if one assumes a grid service of perpendicular routes, the costs would double.

In the absence of subsidies of the magnitude implied by these per capita figures,* the cost of providing service has to be related to ridership. Below the cost of service per square mile, Exhibit 5.6 lists the number of passenger boardings per square mile necessary to cover it at selected costs per passenger. The implicit vehicle productivities are listed to the right. A range of costs per passenger other than those shown can be easily calculated.

To determine the feasibility of different service frequencies at different densities of development, the remaining step is to find at what densities of development the passenger demand—the passenger boardings per square mile listed in Exhibit 5.6—actually occurs. One method of doing that is displayed in Exhibit 5.7.

The heavy diagonal line shows one-way local transit trips per square mile (i.e., trips not oriented to the three major Central Business Districts) in the New York Region as a function of development density. It is derived from Exhibit 5.3, but its trip definition is basically comparable to the trips from residential origins only given in Exhibit 5.2. As noted several times earlier, local transit trips in the lower and middle density ranges in the Region are not substantially different from those in middle-sized urban areas across the nation.

The set of curves intersecting the heavy diagonal represents the "needed passenger boardings" from Exhibit 5.6. For each service frequency—one hour, 30 minutes, and 10 minutes—two curves are shown; the upper curve reflects a cost per passenger of 50¢, and a cost per bus hour of $15.00; the lower curve reflects a 75¢ cost per passenger, and a $20.00 cost per bus hour. Of course, any number of other cost combinations could have been drawn, but these two adequately represent the middle and upper range of bus operating costs, as well as realistic minimum vehicle productivities—from 26.7 to 30 passengers boarding per vehicle hour.

It is evident that the upper two curves intersect the diagonal demand line *at about 15 dwellings per acre,* indicating that above that density *10-minute bus frequency is feasible* on the average, at the costs indicated. The second two curves intersect the demand line *at about 7 dwellings per acre,* indicating that above that density *30-minute service is feasible.* The third set of curves intersect the demand line *at about 4.5 dwellings per acre,* indicating that above that density *hourly service is feasible.*

We might recall that in Exhibits 2.4 and 2.5 transit trips per capita increased sharply at densities above 7 dwellings per acre in a number of urban areas; that threshold is confirmed here analytically, as representing an approximate limit of half-hourly bus frequency in local service.

---

* Transit subsidies by all levels of government in U.S. urban areas in 1974 averaged just under 2¢ per capita per day, with just under 4¢ contributed from fares.

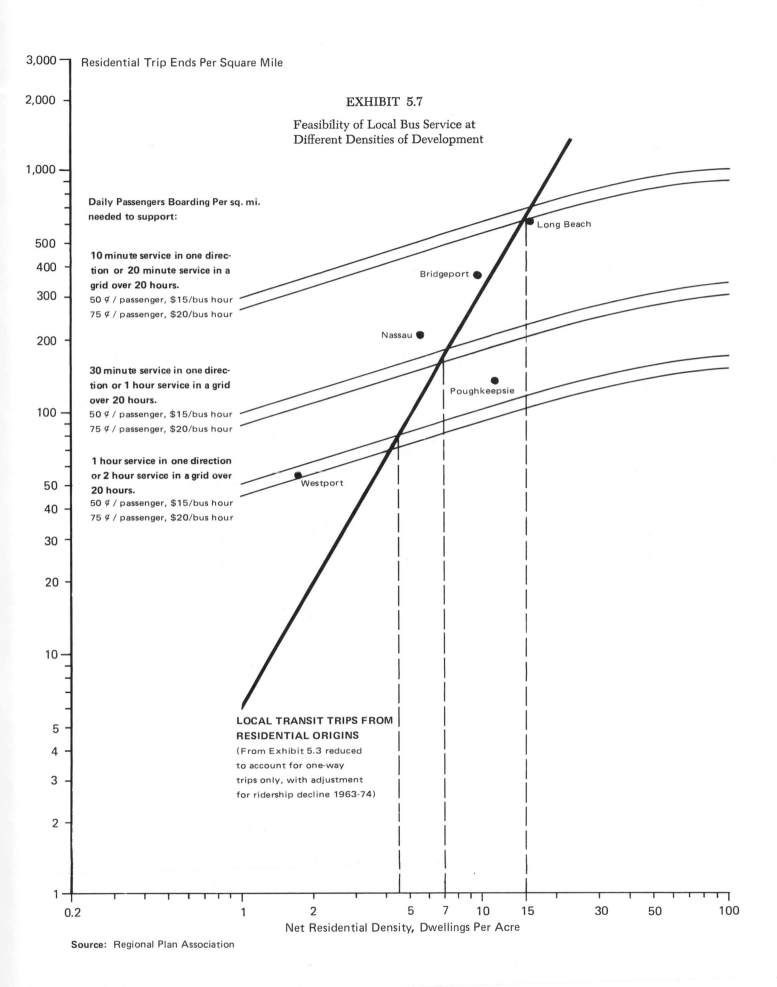

3,000 — Residential Trip Ends Per Square Mile

EXHIBIT 5.7

Feasibility of Local Bus Service at
Different Densities of Development

**Daily Passengers Boarding Per sq. mi.
needed to support:**

**10 minute service in one direc-
tion or 20 minute service in a
grid over 20 hours.**
50 ¢ / passenger, $15/bus hour
75 ¢ / passenger, $20/bus hour

**30 minute service in one direc-
tion or 1 hour service in a grid
over 20 hours.**
50 ¢ / passenger, $15/bus hour
75 ¢ / passenger, $20/bus hour

**1 hour service in one direction
or 2 hour service in a grid over
20 hours.**
50 ¢ / passenger, $15/bus hour
75 ¢ / passenger, $20/bus hour

Long Beach

Bridgeport

Nassau

Poughkeepsie

Westport

**LOCAL TRANSIT TRIPS FROM
RESIDENTIAL ORIGINS**
(From Exhibit 5.3 reduced
to account for one-way
trips only, with adjustment
for ridership decline 1963-74)

Net Residential Density, Dwellings Per Acre

Source: Regional Plan Association

It is always useful to compare analytically derived magnitudes with empirical observations. The demand densities of three bus systems shown earlier in Exhibit 5.4 fall very close to the independently derived demand line: Long Beach, Bridgeport, and Nassau County. Neither route spacing, nor service periods, nor costs of these systems are quite the same as assumed in Exhibits 5.6 and 5.7, but their service frequency indeed is between 10 and 30 minutes, as Exhibit 5.7 would indicate. One should note in comparing Exhibits 5.4 and 5.6 that the service densities in the former represent two-way trips, hence are twice those in the latter; also that the route spacing in Long Beach is much closer than in Bridgeport, which largely explains why service frequency is lower in Long Beach despite more bus hours per square mile.

Two empirical observations depart far from the line of averages: Poughkeepsie has only about one third of the local transit trips per square mile that would seem to be expected at its density, while the affluent commuter suburb of Westport has more than three times as many. Despite widely different densities, incomes, and age characteristics, Long Beach, Bridgeport, and Westport all produce 0.08 two-way bus trips per capita daily, while Poughkeepsie only produces 0.045. The ridership level in Westport is in part inflated by numerous access trips to the local railroad station, that is, trips that are not local in nature; other reasons for the deviations will become apparent shortly.

Even with demand densities such as they have, Poughkeepsie and Westport could only support service roughly once an hour, according to Exhibits 5.6 and 5.7. In reality, Exhibit 5.4 shows them to have 30- to 35-minute service. The explanation lies in their curtailed service periods, which are 11.5 and 14 hours daily, instead of the 20 hours assumed here. Prorated over 20 hours, their service frequencies turn out to be 50 to 52 minutes, which is in scale with what Exhibit 5.7 shows. Still, the two exceptions demonstrate that *under certain conditions, the feasibility threshold of half-hourly fixed-route bus service may lie at a density as low as 2 dwellings per acre, or as high as 11 dwellings per acre.*

In large part, this wide spread is due to the variety of demand conditions which the average demand line in Exhibit 5.7 covers. Embedded in the range of residential densities shown in that Exhibit are different types of nonresidential clusters, ranging in size from less than 1 million to 30 million square feet. The residential areas are located at different distances from clusters of various sizes and types. The service frequency likewise varies. A more detailed consideration of bus feasibility thresholds requires that these factors be taken into account. The procedures established so far in this book and summarized in the beginning of this chapter allow us to do this.

Exhibit 5.8 is based on the same passenger boardings per square mile needed to support 10-minute, 30-minute, and hourly service with the same cost, service period, and route spacing assumptions used in the previous exhibit. It addresses the question: at what residential density and at what distance from a nonresidential cluster of what size and type do these passenger boardings per square mile begin to occur?

Thus, while Exhibit 5.7 indicated that 10-minute bus service under the stated conditions is feasible at densities above 15 dwellings per acre, Exhibit 5.8 details that statement by saying that it is feasible, if the residential area in question is closer than 5 miles to a downtown of 50 million square feet, or closer than 3 miles to a downtown of 20 million square feet, or closer than about 2 miles to a downtown of 10 million square feet.

Similarly, while the threshold of 30-minute service was previously indicated at a density of 7 dwellings per acre, Exhibit 5.8 shows this to be true if the residential area is closer than about 7 miles to a downtown of 50 million square feet, or closer than 4 miles to a downtown of 20 million square feet, or closer than 1.4 miles to a downtown of 5 million square feet.

The downtown of Poughkeepsie happens to contain 5.7 million square feet of nonresidential floorspace; referring to Exhibit 5.2, the low trip density of its surrounding area is explained in this light by the small downtown size. At an average density of 10 dwellings per acre, Exhibit 5.8 predicts the feasibility of hourly full-day service within a radius of 2.9 miles. In fact, its equivalent, namely half-day half-hourly service, is provided within a radius of about 3 miles.

Generally, given the prevailing residential densities, Exhibit 5.8 suggests that 10-minute bus service throughout the day (or its equivalent) is feasible in residential areas around downtowns larger than about 50 million square feet. Downtowns in the 10 to 20 million square foot range can support this service frequency only in their immediate vicinity. For them, a 30-minute full day service or its equivalent are more appropriate, being applicable in the 1 to 5 mile range, depending on density. The equivalent of hourly service throughout the day appears supportable by downtowns as small as 5 million square feet, but it would work at distances of over 2 miles only at residential densities of more than 5 dwellings per acre.

One should stress that while a fixed demand line is used in Exhibit 5.7, the demands calculated for Exhibit 5.8 do respond dynamically to increased service frequency, following the relationships shown in Exhibits 2.14 through 2.16. The response is based on peak hour travel, assuming that 25 percent of all one-directional bus runs during 20 hours occur in the course of a two-hour peak period. This generally reflects operating practices in the New York Region, even though the proportion varies from 10 percent (meaning equal frequency throughout the day) to 75 percent (typical of some express operations). Because no comparable data on the patronage-inducing effect of greater off-peak frequency are available within the context of the procedure used, it may well be that the response to higher frequency is understated. Exhibit 1.2 suggests that such is the case.

Also, the reader should be reminded that the data in Exhibit 5.8 are conservative in another way—they are based only on residence-based trips from residential areas to the nonresidential clusters in question. In real life, numerous intermediate nonresidential destinations will be interspersed between the residential area of origin and the major nonresidential destination. This coattail effect must be included in any realistic analysis of a specific place, but cannot be handled in the generalized framework of Exhibit 5.8. The effect is particularly important on long local bus routes, where the number of trips debarking short of the final destination is large.

Exhibit 5.8 also explores the feasibility of bus service to spread nonresidential clusters of the mixed-use and shopping-oriented types. It is evident that the service which can be provided to shopping-oriented spread clusters is not too different from that to small downtowns; however, spread clusters of mixed use have a very limited potential for bus service, unless they are surrounded by high residential densities, or unless they can ride the coattails of a nearby downtown.

Neither Exhibit 5.7 nor Exhibit 5.8 deal explicitly with fares. Fares are assumed to be at generally prevailing average levels, with perhaps up to one third of the stated cost per passenger covered by subsidy. To the extent that the effects of sharply different fare levels are to be explored, the elasticities shown in Exhibit 1.2 can be used to make rough estimated adjustments. For example, while the average fare level in Bridgeport was around 50¢, the fare level in the nearby Westport transit district averaged 15¢, collected mostly from

EXHIBIT 5.8

Maximum Distances from Nonresidential Clusters at Selected Residential Densities at Which Passenger Boardings per Square Mile to the Clusters in Question Cover the Cost of Local Buses at Stated Service Levels

(Distances in Miles)

DOWNTOWN-ORIENTED CLUSTERS

Bus cost: $20 per vehicle hour, $0.50 per passenger (40 boardings per vehicle hour)

Service frequency for 20 hrs. at ½ mi. route spacing

Cluster size, million sq.ft.	10 minutes				30 minutes				1 hour			
	50	20	10	5	50	20	10	5	50	20	10	5
Residential density, du's/acre: 1	--	--	--	--	--	--	--	--	--	--	--	--
2	--	--	--	--	1.2	--	--	--	2.8	1.3	--	--
5	1.2	--	--	--	4.2	2.2	1.3	--	7.0	3.9	2.4	1.2
7	1.8	1.0	--	--	5.3	3.0	1.8	1.0	8.6	5.0	3.1	1.6
10	2.5	1.3	--	--	6.1	3.8	2.5	1.3	10.2	6.1	4.1	2.2
15	3.3	1.8	1.2	--	7.9	4.8	3.0	1.8	11.6	7.2	4.7	2.8
30	5.6	3.3	2.2	1.2	11.1	6.8	4.6	2.8	15.3	9.7	6.4	4.1
50	7.2	4.3	2.8	1.7	13.0	8.3	5.6	3.5	17.8	11.3	7.6	5.0
100	10.0	6.2	4.2	2.6	16.8	10.8	7.3	4.9	23.0	14.1	9.8	6.6

Bus cost: $15 per vehicle hour, $0.50 per passenger (30 boardings per vehicle hour)

Service frequency for 20 hrs. at ½ mi. route spacing

Cluster size, million sq.ft.	10 minutes				30 minutes				1 hour			
	50	20	10	5	50	20	10	5	50	20	10	5
Residential density, du's/acre: 1	--	--	--	--	--	--	--	--	--	--	--	--
2	--	--	--	--	1.8	--	--	--	3.8	1.8	1.1	--
5	1.8	1.0	--	--	5.5	3.0	1.8	1.0	8.6	4.9	3.1	1.6
7	2.6	1.3	--	--	6.8	3.9	2.4	1.3	10.3	6.1	3.8	2.1
10	3.5	1.9	1.3	--	8.3	4.8	3.2	1.7	11.9	7.3	4.9	2.8
15	4.5	2.6	1.7	1.0	9.6	5.8	3.8	2.3	13.4	8.4	5.5	3.4
30	7.0	4.3	2.7	1.6	12.8	8.2	5.4	3.4	17.6	11.2	7.4	4.9
50	8.8	5.4	3.6	2.2	15.1	9.7	6.4	4.3	20.7	12.8	8.7	5.8
100	11.7	7.3	5.1	3.2	19.7	12.3	8.4	5.7	26.2	15.9	11.0	7.5

Bus cost: $20 per vehicle hour, $0.75 per passenger (26.6 boardings per vehicle hour)

Service frequency for 20 hrs. at ½ mi. route spacing

Cluster size, million sq.ft.	10 minutes				30 minutes				1 hour			
	50	20	10	5	50	20	10	5	50	20	10	5
Residential density, du's/acre: 1	--	--	--	--	--	--	--	--	1.2	--	--	--
2	--	--	--	--	2.1	1.0	--	--	4.3	2.2	1.2	--
5	2.2	1.1	--	--	6.0	3.3	2.1	1.1	9.3	5.4	3.3	1.8
7	3.0	1.6	1.1	--	7.3	4.3	2.7	1.4	10.8	6.5	4.2	2.3
10	3.9	2.2	1.5	--	8.8	5.3	3.5	1.9	12.6	7.8	5.2	2.9
15	4.9	2.9	1.8	1.1	10.2	6.3	4.2	2.5	14.2	9.0	5.8	3.7
30	7.7	4.7	3.0	1.7	13.7	8.7	5.8	3.6	18.7	11.7	7.8	5.1
50	9.4	5.8	3.9	2.4	15.9	10.3	6.9	4.5	21.7	13.4	9.2	6.2
100	12.4	7.8	5.3	3.4	20.7	12.8	8.9	6.0	27.5	16.7	11.5	7.8

Bus cost: $15 per vehicle hour, $0.75 per passenger (20 boardings per vehicle hour)

Service frequency for 20 hrs. at ½ mi. route spacing

Cluster size, million sq.ft.	10 minutes				30 minutes				1 hour			
	50	20	10	5	50	20	10	5	50	20	10	5
Residential density, du's/acre: 1	--	--	--	--	--	--	--	--	1.7	--	--	--
2	--	--	--	--	3.1	1.4	--	--	5.6	2.7	1.7	--
5	3.1	1.6	1.0	--	7.5	4.4	2.7	1.4	10.8	6.4	4.2	2.3
7	4.0	2.3	1.5	--	8.9	5.3	3.4	1.8	12.6	7.8	5.1	2.9
10	5.2	3.0	1.8	1.1	10.4	6.3	4.3	2.4	14.6	9.1	6.1	3.6
15	6.4	3.8	2.4	1.4	11.9	7.5	4.9	3.1	16.3	10.4	6.8	4.4
30	9.3	5.7	3.8	2.3	15.8	10.1	6.7	4.3	21.4	13.3	9.0	6.0
50	11.5	6.8	4.8	2.9	18.4	11.7	7.9	5.3	24.7	15.2	10.4	7.1
100	14.4	9.2	6.3	4.2	23.6	14.6	10.2	6.9	30.8	18.7	12.8	8.8

EXHIBIT 5.8 continued

RETAIL-ORIENTED SPREAD CLUSTERS

Bus cost: $15 per vehicle hour, $0.50 per passenger (30 boardings per vehicle hour)

Service frequency for 20 hrs. at ½ mi. route spacing		10 minutes		30 minutes		1 hour	
Cluster size, million sq.ft.		10	5	10	5	10	5
Residential density, du's/acre:	1	--	--	--	--	--	--
	2	--	--	--	--	1.1	--
	5	--	--	2.1	1.4	3.3	2.3
	7	--	--	2.7	1.9	4.2	3.0
	10	1.6	1.2	3.4	2.5	5.1	3.9
	15	2.2	1.5	4.2	3.1	5.8	4.3
	30	3.4	2.5	5.8	4.3	7.9	6.3

SPREAD CLUSTERS WITH MIXED USE

Bus cost: $15 per vehicle hour, $0.50 per passenger (30 boardings per vehicle hour)

Service frequency for 20 hrs. at ½ mi. route spacing		10 minutes		30 minutes		1 hour	
Cluster size, million sq.ft.		10	5	10	5	10	5
Residential density, du's/acre:	1	--	--	--	--	--	--
	2	--	--	--	--	--	--
	5	--	--	--	--	1.8	1.1
	7	--	--	1.3	--	2.3	1.5
	10	--	--	1.8	1.3	3.1	2.2
	15	--	--	2.3	1.6	3.7	2.4
	30	1.8	1.3	3.7	2.4	5.6	3.8

Derivation: Using the operating speed-residential density relationship of Exhibit 4.1, the cost of providing the frequency of service at the stated costs per vehicle-hour in a square mile is determined for each residential density and translated into the required daily passengers needed at the assumed fare. Next, for each given combination of residential density, non-residential floorspace size, non-residential concentration (NRC) type, and bus frequency, the percent of trips by transit is found (using Exhibits 7.14 through 7.20), assuming "neither" territory, median family income equal to $10,000 (1969 dollars), and adult household size of 2.0. The percent transit is divided into the daily passengers required calculated earlier to derive an estimate of the total number of trip-makers required between the residential area and the NRC. When divided by the population per gross square mile for the appropriate net residential density (using Exhibit 0.2), the required trip rate per capita from the residential square mile to the NRC is found. By assuming a labor force participation rate of 0.4 and using Exhibits 6.2 through 6.7, a plot of trips per capita versus distance to NRC is drawn. From it the distance to provide that trip rate is estimated.

the sale of annual passes. This 70 percent fare reduction, compared to prevailing levels, would suggest a 42 percent higher ridership level, assuming the small-town elasticity of −0.6, and keeping all other conditions constant. This may mean that nearly a third of the ridership on the Westport system is there due to the low fare. More than that may be explained by service frequency, which is unusually high for the density in question. The convenience of an annual pass undoubtedly further encourages ridership. One might note that the per passenger subsidy on the Westport system in 1974 was 50¢, about double the average in the New York Region, but only one quarter of the average subsidy on dial-a-buses.

The foregoing discussion addressed the reasonableness of bus service related to densities in a square mile. To make a particular service level feasible, the necessary density of demand must prevail, *on the average, over an entire route*, not over one square mile. The distances shown in Exhibit 5.8 represent the limit of a particular service *only if it is assumed that all square miles along a route have the same density*. In reality, residential densities tend to be higher near a downtown and fall off with distance, in a pattern known as the density gradient. As a result, square miles closer to downtown which straddle a bus route are likely to supply boarding passengers in excess of the required productivity, and the resulting surplus revenue may make it possible to extend the route much beyond the distances shown in Exhibit 5.8.

Because density gradients come in all kinds of shapes, one must either deal with each specific route individually or else assume a hypothetical density gradient and deal with an illustrative route. The gradients assumed for the exercise in Exhibit 5.9 for downtown sizes of 50, 35, and 20 million square feet of nonresidential floorspace are identical to those spelled out later in this chapter in Exhibit 5.14. Those for the downtowns of 10 and 5 million square feet are drawn in a similar manner. The passenger demand in bus route corridors for the five downtown sizes is calculated in the same way as in Exhibit 5.8, except that

EXHIBIT 5.9

Illustrative Local Bus Route Characteristics to Downtowns of Selected Sizes under Assumed Conditions

Downtown cluster size, millions sq.ft. nonres. floorspace	50	35	20	10	5
Assumed route length, miles	12	9	6	5	5
One-way travel time, minutes	52.0	37.5	23.1	17.4	16.0
Overall speed, miles per hour	13.8	14.4	15.6	17.2	18.8
Service frequency for 20 hours at ½ mile route spacing			10 minutes		
1. Daily one-way passengers	7,310	4,120	2,162	759	n.c.
2. Peak hour frequency to provide capacity at maximum load point	25	14	7	3	n.c.
3. Daily cost of providing required service including peak hour demand	5,200	2,250	1,386	1,044	n.c.
4. Passenger miles, one-way	23,226	12,537	5,825	2,023	n.c.
5. Cost per passenger mile, $	0.22	0.18	0.24	0.52	n.c.
6. Route length that provides cost per passenger mile at $0.20, miles	11	11	5	0	n.c.
Service frequency for 20 hours at ½ mile route spacing			30 minutes		
1. Daily one-way passengers	6,886	3,847	2,003	687	241
2. Peak hour frequency to provide capacity at maximum load point	23	14	7	3	1
3. Daily cost of providing required service including peak hour demand	4,784	2,100	647	348	320
4. Passenger miles, one-way	21,816	11,683	5,348	1,829	616
5. Cost per passenger mile, $	0.22	0.18	0.12	0.19	0.52
6. Route length that provides cost per passenger mile at $0.20, miles	11	11	11	5	0
Service frequency for 20 hours at ½ mile route spacing			1 hour		
1. Daily one-way passengers	6,423	3,576	1,845	614	205
2. Peak hour frequency to provide capacity at maximum load point	22	12	6	2	1
3. Daily cost of providing required service including peak hour demand	4,576	1,800	555	174	160
4. Passenger miles, one-way	20,259	11,040	4,915	1,684	502
5. Cost per passenger miles, $	0.22	0.16	0.12	0.10	0.32
6. Route length that provides cost per passenger mile at $0.20, miles	10	12	14	13	3

the passengers boarding are accumulated over the route's length. In the nature of the demand procedures used, all passengers originating in a residential area are going to the non-residential cluster that is being examined.

The costs are calculated either for one of the three assumed service frequencies or for the frequency that is necessary to serve peak hour demand at the highest load point, whichever is greater. The cost per vehicle hour is assumed to be $15, and it is assumed that the labor agreement allows split shifts of 4 and 4 hours each. To be able to compare the different routes, average cost per passenger mile is calculated for each downtown size and for each service level. Obviously, this cost is strongly affected by the assumptions used, particularly those about route length, about the shape of the density gradient, about the peaking pattern and the cost per vehicle hour. Nevertheless, a consistent pattern emerges.

For the 10-minute average service frequency during a 20-hour period (equivalent to 15 buses in the peak hour), the lowest cost per passenger mile is calculated at a downtown size of 35 million square feet. For smaller downtowns, the lower demand requires fewer than 15 buses in the peak hour and the consequent oversupply results in higher costs per passenger mile. For larger downtowns, both costs and passenger miles increase. Costs, however, rise somewhat faster since the buses are travelling slower through higher density areas surrounding the downtown.

For the 30-minute average service frequency for 20 hours (equivalent to 5 buses in the peak hour), the lowest cost per passenger mile is calculated at a downtown of 20 million square feet. Smaller downtowns have insufficient passenger demand to fill buses in the peak hour, while bus routes to larger downtowns show costs rising with slower speeds.

Similarly, a 10 million square foot downtown appears to provide the lowest cost for once-an-hour service on the average for 20 hours.

One can examine these findings from a different perspective: what size downtown can provide for what level of local bus service at a reasonable cost per passenger mile? If we assume 20¢ per passenger mile as a cutoff point, an answer can be suggested; moreover, one can estimate how long a route can be at what downtown size to stay within that limit.

Referring to Exhibit 5.9, downtowns of 5 million square feet cannot be supplied with either 10- or 30-minute headways for 20 hours at a cost of 20¢ per passenger mile or less. Hourly service becomes reasonable only if the initially assumed 5-mile route length is pared down to 3 miles.

A 10 million square foot downtown can support a 30-minute service at the postulated cost per passenger mile. Hourly service can be provided at a substantially lower cost, or, al-

EXHIBIT 5.9 continued

Derivation: Line 1 — cumulated public transit trips for each square mile on route's length calculated on the basis of gross population density as shown in Exhibit 7.1; per capita trip rates as shown in Exhibit 7.8 and 7.9 assuming a 40% labor force participation rate; and percent transit use as shown for "neither" territory in Exhibit 7.14 with adjustment for peak period frequency in Exhibit 7.16

Line 2 — assumes 30 percent of travel in peak hour and 45 passengers per vehicle for 2 routes within mile wide corridor.

Line 3 — assumes operating speeds as per Exhibit 4.1, $15 per vehicle-hour and split shift labor agreement of 4 hours—4 hours.

Line 4 — sum of products of one-way passengers at each mile interval times the distance from the downtown.

Line 5 — line 3 divided by line 4.

Line 6 — trial-and-error recalculation of cost per passenger mile for longer or shorter assumed routes.

n.c. —   not calculated

ternatively, the route of a once-hourly service can be extended to 13 miles. Ten-minute service is unreasonable.

A 20 million square foot downtown can provide all three frequencies of local bus service, although the 10-minute frequency requires a slight cropping of the route length, down to 5 miles. But at either 30-minute or one-hour frequencies, costs can be much lower or routes can be extended to 11 miles or more.

With a downtown of 35 million square feet, all three service levels are also possible, and routes can be extended by two or three miles beyond the nine miles assumed, still remaining below the 20¢ per passenger mile criterion. However, their costs cannot drop as low as for the smaller downtowns due to lower speeds over longer distances.

For downtowns of 50 million square feet or more, costs per passenger mile are calculated to be above 20¢, reflecting the higher vehicle costs of travel through higher densities over longer and slower routes. Cropping the routes somewhat will reduce their cost per passenger mile.

Exhibit 5.10 represents the relationships calculated in Exhibit 5.9 graphically. It emphasizes the point that each downtown size tends to have an "optimum" service frequency, one that results in the lowest cost per passenger mile. It also shows that as downtown size increases, any particular selected service frequency eventually becomes insufficient to meet the demand; more buses have to be added, until hourly service becomes half-hourly, half-hourly service becomes 10-minute service—on the average, in the course of the entire day—and so on. This is why the three curves eventually merge into one in the upper left hand part of the graph.

To recapitulate, the answer to the question, "What residential density can support what level of bus service?" depends on how far away from a nonresidential concentration of what size the residential area in question is located; but, very importantly, it also depends on the density of the neighboring residential areas through which the route in question passes (the density gradient), and on the length of the route. Because of the multitude of values which these variables can assume, *the feasibility of service in any particular residential area can, in principle, be only determined case-by-case.* For purposes of illustration, some arbitrary but reasonable assumptions about route lengths and density gradients were made in Exhibits 5.9 and 5.10. The specific values shown in these Exhibits are valid only under the assumptions used. However, the relationships illustrated do have general validity: service frequency increases with increasing downtown size; but the cost of supplying bus service also increases as speed declines with rising city size and density. For example, under the conditions assumed, a 12-mile route to a downtown of 50 million square feet would have a 50-minute running time. This leads to a consideration of express service.

EXPRESS BUS

The methodology of measuring the density of supply in terms of vehicle hours per square mile and relating it to demand density—passengers boarding per square mile—is suitable for vehicles which traverse a continuous demand surface. It is not directly applicable to express buses, which pick up passengers from an isolated collection area and then run nonstop. In this case, vehicle hours have to be calculated based on round-trip distance (including the usually empty return run) and its speed. The speed is not neatly related to development density as in the case of local buses, but varies depending on how much of the run is on freeways and on congested streets.

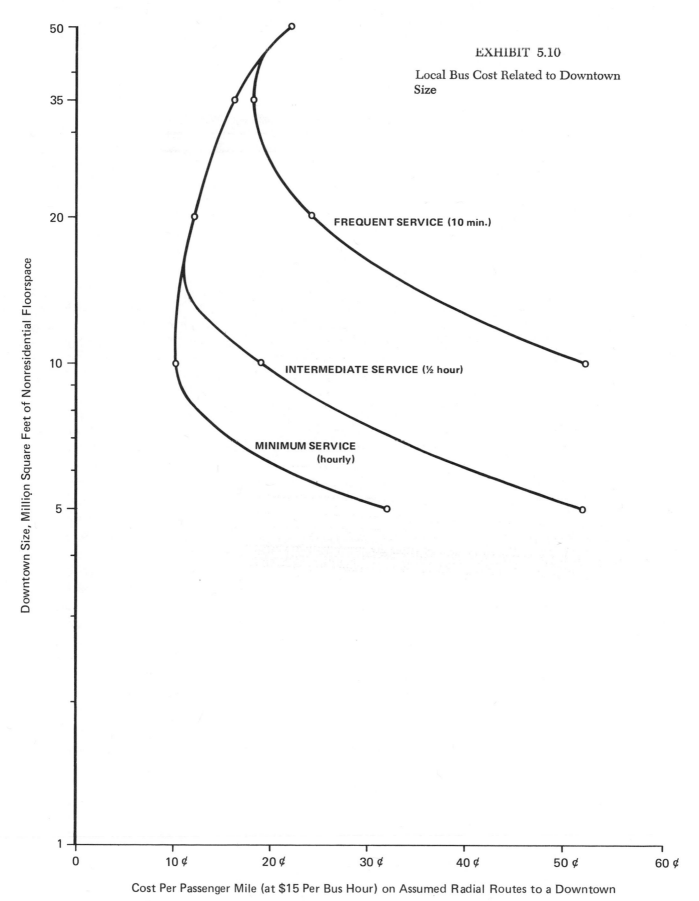

EXHIBIT 5.10

Local Bus Cost Related to Downtown Size

FREQUENT SERVICE (10 min.)

INTERMEDIATE SERVICE (½ hour)

MINIMUM SERVICE (hourly)

Downtown Size, Million Square Feet of Nonresidential Floorspace

Cost Per Passenger Mile (at $15 Per Bus Hour) on Assumed Radial Routes to a Downtown

Source: Exhibit 5.9

The vehicle hours must be related to passenger boardings within the entire collection area of the route. That area may be quite small if all passengers walk to the bus, or very large if all arrive by auto. Chapter 4 has shown that the proportion of passengers arriving by auto may range from 10 to 90 percent or more, depending on whether the express bus service is from residential streets or from commuter parking lots.

Two types of collection areas will be examined here. In the first case, the bus is assumed to circulate through a neighborhood to insure that every resident is within a quarter mile of a bus stop before it makes the express run to a downtown. It is assumed that this collection area is 2 square miles and that the bus requires 15 minutes to collect the passengers. In the second case, park-and-ride access is assumed: most riders drive or are driven from a 20-square-mile tributary area to a single location before the bus makes its express run. For both exercises a cost of $15 per bus hour is assumed with a 4 and 4-hour split shift permissible; on the demand side, it is assumed that the trips are exclusively trips to work, and that they take place only over a two-hour period inbound and a two-hour period outbound.

The purpose of the illustrative calculations is to find out what minimum residential densities in the collection areas will provide sufficient passenger volume to keep costs per passenger mile within predetermined limits. This is done for three assumed operating speeds (35, 25, and 15 mph), three peak hour service frequencies (5, 10, and 30 buses in two hours), four downtown sizes (50, 35, 20, and 10 million square feet of nonresidential floorspace), and four distances between the beginning of the express run and the downtown (5, 10, 15, and 20 miles). Two limits of cost per passenger mile are assumed: 10¢ and 20¢. The former appears to be in scale with many existing express bus operations, as well as with rail operations with which the express bus may be in competition. The latter is in scale with local bus operations, which express buses might replace on particular routes.

One further point must be borne in mind for a proper understanding of the required residential densities shown in Exhibits 5.11 and 5.12. Many densities are unlikely to occur in the given situations even over a two-square-mile collection area, on the average, given empirically encountered density gradients. This is even more true in the case of collection areas as large as 20 square miles, where average densities are likely to be quite low. In the Exhibits, density ranges that are likely to exist in reality are boxed in.

Turning to Exhibit 5.11, which deals with the case of the two-square-mile pedestrian collection area, we see in the upper part of the table that at a cost of 10¢ per passenger mile or less only a frequency of 5 buses during the two-hour peak period can be supported, only from a downtown of 50 million square feet, at 25 to 35 mph speeds, at a distance of 10 miles, and at densities in the 12 to 14 dwellings per acre range.

However, if costs of 20¢ per passenger mile are acceptable—which converts to a cost per passenger of $2 at 10 miles, $3 at 15 miles, and so on—then there is a somewhat wider variety of situations that can support express buses with pedestrian collection. These include:

5 buses during the two-hour peak period
  if downtown size is 20 million square feet and at 5 miles residential densities are 8 to 10 dwellings per acre;
  or if downtown size is 35 million square feet and at 5 miles densities are 6 to 7 dwellings per acre, at 10 miles densities are 8 to 10 dwellings per acre;
  or if downtown size is 50 million and at 15 miles densities are 8 to 11 dwellings per acre, at 10 miles densities are 6 to 10 dwellings per acre, at 5 miles densities are 5 to 6 dwellings per acre.

EXHIBIT 5.11

Express Bus Operations with Local Collection: Minimum Average Residential Density in Collection Area That Provides Stated Costs per Passenger Mile at Stated Distances from Downtown Cluster Sizes for Selected Line Haul Speed and Service Levels (residential density in dwelling units per acre)

Distance from downtown, miles	5			10			15			20		
Line Haul Speed, miles per hour	35	25	15	35	25	15	35	25	15	35	25	15

$0.10 per Passenger Mile, 5 Buses During Two-Hour Peak

Downtown size, millions sq.ft.												
50	--	--	--	12	14	--	18	25	--	27	--	--
35	--	--	--	19	24	--	--	--	--	--	--	--
20	--	--	--	--	--	--	--	--	--	--	--	--
10	--	--	--	--	--	--	--	--	--	--	--	--

$0.10 per Passenger Mile, 10 Buses During Two-Hour Peak

50	--	--	--	24	28	--	--	--	--	--	--	--
35	--	--	--	30	--	--	--	--	--	--	--	--
20	--	--	--	--	--	--	--	--	--	--	--	--
10	--	--	--	--	--	--	--	--	--	--	--	--

$0.10 per Passenger Mile, 30 Buses During Two-Hour Peak
not possible to provide at 30 du/acre or less

$0.20 per Passenger Mile, 5 Buses During Two-Hour Peak

50	5	5	6	6	7	10	8	11	15	14	18	27
35	6	6	7	8	10	14	13	16	25	23	28	--
20	8	10	13	15	18	26	28	--	--	--	--	--
10	19	22	27	--	--	--	--	--	--	--	--	--

$0.20 per Passenger Mile, 10 Buses During Two-Hour Peak

50	7	8	10	10	13	19	16	22	29	29	--	--
35	9	11	14	15	20	27	25	--	--	--	--	--
20	14	19	26	28	--	--	--	--	--	--	--	--
10	30	--	--	--	--	--	--	--	--	--	--	--

$0.20 per Passenger Mile, 30 Buses During Two-Hour Peak

50	22	24	29	--	--	--	--	--	--	--	--	--
35	27	29	--	--	--	--	--	--	--	--	--	--
20	--	--	--	--	--	--	--	--	--	--	--	--
10	--	--	--	--	--	--	--	--	--	--	--	--

BOXED IN RESIDENTIAL DENSITIES SUGGEST THOSE THAT ARE LIKELY TO BE ENCOUNTERED

Note: A dash -- indicates either more than 30 dwelling units per acre is required, or that it is impossible to supply the service at the stated cost per passenger mile at any residential density.

Source: Regional Plan Association

EXHIBIT 5.12

Express Bus Operations with Park and Ride: Minimum Average Residential Density in Tributary Area That Provides Stated Costs per Passenger Mile at Stated Distances from Downtown Cluster Sizes for Selected Line Haul Speed and Service Levels (residential density in dwelling units per acre)

Distance from downtown, miles	5			10			15			20		
Line Haul Speed, miles per hour	35	25	15	35	25	15	35	25	15	35	25	15

$0.10 per Passenger Mile, 5 Buses During Two-Hour Peak

Downtown size, millions sq.ft.	35	25	15	35	25	15	35	25	15	35	25	15
50	2	2	--	3	3	--	4	4	--	4	5	--
35	2	2	--	3	4	--	4	5	--	6	7	--
20	3	3	--	5	5	--	7	10	--	13	20	--
10	5	5	--	13	16	--	30	--	--	--	--	--

$0.10 per Passenger Mile, 10 Buses During Two-Hour Peak

Downtown size	35	25	15	35	25	15	35	25	15	35	25	15
50	3	4	--	4	5	--	5	5	--	7	8	--
35	3	4	--	5	5	--	6	7	--	10	15	--
20	4	5	--	7	8	--	10	14	--	29	--	--
10	8	10	--	23	30	--	--	--	--	--	--	--

$0.10 per Passenger Mile, 30 Buses During Two-Hour Peak

Downtown size	35	25	15	35	25	15	35	25	15	35	25	15
50	5	5	--	7	8	--	12	15	--	23	--	--
35	6	7	--	9	13	--	21	27	--	--	--	--
20	8	12	--	23	30	--	--	--	--	--	--	--
10	--	--	--	--	--	--	--	--	--	--	--	--

$0.20 per Passenger Mile, 5 Buses During Two-Hour Peak

Downtown size	35	25	15	35	25	15	35	25	15	35	25	15
50	2	2	2	2	2	3	2	3	4	3	4	5
35	2	2	2	2	2	3	3	3	4	4	4	6
20	2	2	2	3	4	5	5	5	7	6	7	12
10	3	4	5	5	7	12	15	19	30	28	--	--

$0.20 per Passenger Mile, 10 Buses During Two-Hour Peak

Downtown size	35	25	15	35	25	15	35	25	15	35	25	15
50	2	2	2	2	2	3	3	4	5	5	5	7
35	2	2	2	3	3	4	4	5	6	5	7	11
20	3	3	3	4	5	6	6	8	14	11	16	30
10	5	5	6	10	13	23	25	--	--	--	--	--

$0.20 per Passenger Mile, 30 Buses During Two-Hour Peak

Downtown size	35	25	15	35	25	15	35	25	15	35	25	15
50	3	4	5	4	5	6	6	7	12	9	13	24
35	4	4	5	5	6	9	7	11	25	15	24	--
20	5	6	7	8	12	21	17	30	--	--	--	--
10	9	12	17	30	--	--	--	--	--	--	--	--

BOXED IN RESIDENTIAL DENSITIES SUGGEST THOSE THAT ARE LIKELY TO BE ENCOUNTERED

Note: A dash -- indicates either more than 30 dwelling units per acre is required, or that it is impossible to supply the service at the stated cost per passenger mile at any residential density.

Source: Regional Plan Association

10 buses during the two-hour peak period
>   *if* downtown size is 35 million square feet and at 5 miles densities are 9 to 11 dwellings per acre;
>   *or if* downtown size is 50 million square feet and at 10 miles densities are 10 to 19 dwellings per acre, at 5 miles densities are 7 to 10 dwellings per acre.

There are no reasonable densities that can support a service of 30 express buses during the peak period from a two-square-mile collection area.

In sum, *while there are circumstances where express bus operations with local collection are possible, they are largely confined to a narrow range.* At 10¢ per passenger mile, a 15- to 20-mile run to a downtown of 50 million square feet requires the rather high residential density of 12 to 14 dwellings per acre. For lower residential densities, still larger downtown size would be needed to attain the same trips per square mile. Nonresidential clusters of over 50 million square feet are mostly found in urban areas of over one million people, which suggests that our hypothetical *express bus service remains confined to very large cities, if it is dependent on pedestrian access.* In fact, the major existing walk-to-express-bus services are located in the Washington area, in New York City, and in New Jersey.

An express bus service of the park-and-ride variety is applicable more broadly, as Exhibit 5.12 indicates. However, one should bear in mind that the larger collection area of 20 square miles is less likely to have the average densities that may be encountered in a 2 square mile area. Therefore, the range of realistic densities for the collection areas is narrowed a great deal, as evident from the boxes in the Exhibit.

At 10¢ per passenger mile the services that can be supported, following the top part of Exhibit 5.12, are:

5 buses during the two-hour peak period
>   *if* the downtown size is 20 million square feet and at 5 miles the density is 3 dwellings per acre;
>   *or if* the downtown size is 35 million square feet and at 5 miles the density is 2 dwellings per acre, at 10 miles the density is 3 to 4 dwellings per acre, at 15 miles the density is 4 dwellings per acre;
>   *or if* the downtown size is 50 million square feet and at 5 miles the density is 2 dwellings per acre, at 10 miles the density is 3 dwellings per acre, at 15 miles the density is 4 dwellings per acre, and at 20 miles (and a speed of 35 mph) the density is 4 dwellings per acre.

10 buses during the two-hour peak period
>   *if* the downtown size is 20 million square feet or more and at 5 miles the residential density is 4 to 5 dwellings per acre;
>   *or if* the downtown size is 35 million square feet and at 5 miles the residential density is 3 to 4 dwellings per acre;
>   *or if* the downtown size is 50 million square feet and at 5 miles the residential density is 3 to 4 dwelling units per acre, and at 10 miles the residential density is 4 dwellings per acre, provided that operating speeds are 35 mph or more.

If a cost of 20¢ per passenger mile is acceptable, then express bus service of a park-and-ride type can cover a still wider range of conditions, including fairly slow speed (15 mph) and higher service frequencies.

Summarizing, park-and-ride express bus services generally can provide low and medium service frequencies (about 10 buses in a two-hour period or less) to downtowns larger

EXHIBIT 5.13

Characteristics of Express Bus Services to Two Medium-Sized Cities

	Daily passengers (two directions)	Daily bus hours (two directions)	Demand density daily trips per sq.mi.* (one direction)	Veh. productivity passengers per bus hour	Buses assigned to route (morning-evening)	Daily bus hours per assigned bus	Service period, hours (one direction)	Number of runs (one direction)	Running time minutes	Approximate distance miles	Approximate scheduled speed, mph
To Hartford from:	(Hartford urbanized area population 465,000; CBD office floorspace 7.4 million sq.ft.; Nonres. floorspace in cluster over 35 million sq.ft.)										
Manchester	1,064	24.15	22.7	44.0	5-7	4.0	2	14	20	8	24
West Hartford	783	19.02	17.8	40.2	4-5	4.2	2	13	20	5	15
Enfield	709	23.43	10.7	30.3	7-7	3.3	1.6	9	30	17	34
Avon	526	27.50	11.2	20.8	5-7	4.6	1.5	7	35	12	20
Glastonbury	328	13.50	3.2	24.3	4-4	3.3	1.5	7	25	7	17
Middletown	255	11.40	3.1	22.4	3-3	3.8	1.2	4	30	17	34
Simsbury	244	11.00	3.5	22.2	5-4	2.4	1.3	4	30	12	24
Newington	204	11.40	7.7	17.9	3-3	3.8	1.5	6	20	10	30
Total	4,113	139.22		29.5						10.3	
To New Haven from:	(New Haven urbanized area population 348,000, CBD office floorspace 3.6 million sq.ft.; Nonres. floorspace in cluster 26.6 million sq.ft.)										
Branford	447	14.42	10.4	31.0	3-3	4.8	2	9	15	7	28
Milford	98	10.00	2.2	9.8	2-2	5.0	1.5	4	25	10	24
Total	545	24.42		22.3						7.5	

Note: * Demand density arbitrarily calculated over gross land area of each municipality, which ranges from 13.2 to 51.7 square miles; actual tributary area not known.

Source: May, 1975 operating data from Paul B. Hoar, Connecticut Department of Transportation

than about 20 million square feet, for distances up to 15 miles or so, from residential areas with densities as low as 2 dwellings per acre. But, while *park-and-ride express bus service is broadly applicable to medium-sized cities, it becomes questionable for downtown sizes of less than 20 million square feet.*

It is useful, once more, to relate analytical conclusions to empirical observations. Exhibit 5.13 shows some characteristics of express bus routes instituted in 1973-75 to serve the downtowns of two medium-sized cities in Connecticut, Hartford and New Haven. All of these routes are of the park-and-ride type, served either by existing church-owned parking lots or by newly constructed commuter lots. It can be seen that the suburban routes operate mostly over a distance of 5 to 12 miles; the two 17-mile routes go essentially beyond the suburbs, to neighboring small cities. Based on municipal boundaries, the demand densities range from 2 to 23 daily trips per square mile. The average scheduled speed varies from 15 to 34 mph, with the higher speeds generally occurring in corridors with freeways. The service period does not exceed 2 hours in each direction, with 4 to 14 departures. The productivity varies greatly from route to route, but averages 28.4 passengers per vehicle hour. The fare in May, 1975 averaged 44¢ per passenger for a trip just under 10 miles. How much of the cost this fare covered is not clear. On the Hartford and New Haven bus systems as a whole, the operating cost was $14.32 per bus hour, suggesting a cost of 50¢ per passenger. However, this average cost may not be applicable to the express bus routes, with their below-average vehicle utilization. As evident from the sixth column in Exhibit 5.13, buses assigned to the service operated an average of only about 4 hours a day. Whether they could be used elsewhere during off-peak hours is questionable, though the labor agreement did permit 4-hour split shifts for bus drivers.

More generally it is evident that Hartford, with a downtown nonresidential concentration in excess of 35 million square feet (about one third of it in the Central Business District proper) supports a healthy array of express bus services, with the two most heavily used close-in routes perhaps operating at a profit. By contrast, New Haven, with a concentration of 26 million square feet, supports only one reasonably used route, with the other carrying fewer than 100 people per day, or only 10 passengers boarding per bus hour. It may well be, as with rapid transit patronage shown in Exhibit 2.3, that express bus patronage is more a function of Central Business District office floorspace than of total nonresidential floorspace in a more broadly defined cluster. The CBD office floorspace is 7.4 million square feet in Hartford, with additional large office buildings outside the CBD proper, while in New Haven it is 3.6 million square feet. Furthermore, one should keep in mind that a heavy commuter market to the north of New Haven's downtown is not exploited by commuter buses because of the lack of convenient freeway access. Nevertheless, the Connecticut data seem to support the proposition that a *downtown cluster size on the order of 20 million square feet may represent the lower limit of park-and-ride express bus feasibility.*

LIGHT RAIL

Light rail is the first of the fixed-guideway systems to be discussed, and certain methods of approach common to all of them must be stated at the outset. In exploring the appropriateness of different fixed-guideway systems to different land use configurations, a distinction should be made between areas which already have fixed guideways in place and those where the construction of new ones is at issue. In the first case, the cost comparisons are rather straightforward even though in dealing with fixed guideway operations vehicle hours are no longer a very clean cost indicator. Fixed operating and maintenance costs subsumed in the cost per vehicle hour cause it to vary depending on the scale of operations, and the importance of vehicle capital costs increases as operating speed increases. To keep things simpler, we will not introduce these corrections. In the second case, where new construction is involved, the investment per passenger mile becomes of paramount importance, making it necessary to deal with traffic volumes on a route. This subject will be treated below.

Historically, light rail has been used in applications as diverse as slow operation in mixed traffic serving local trips in high density areas, and high speed interurban operation on reserved rights-of-way through rural areas. Most surviving operations in North America represent line-haul service to downtowns at moderately high speeds, a kind of junior rapid transit. Current proposals also focus on this application, though some involve the replacement of local buses on high density routes, and others the replacement of conventional railroad equipment in suburban service on lightly used lines. We will focus on the line-haul service to downtown areas, after some general remarks about the others.

Concerning facilities already in place, it is instructive to refer back to Exhibits 3.6 and 3.9. Equalized for units of capacity and for operating speed, existing light rail appears to be only marginally more expensive than buses. If able to attain higher speed than buses on a comparable route, it has an advantage of lower cost per mile even today. The advantage will increase with the introduction of the larger Standard Light Rail Vehicle, which promises to drop costs substantially below the bus average per hour of a unit of capacity. *This would argue for keeping existing light rail operations with exclusive or partially reserved rights of way in place* on cost grounds alone. On the grounds of patronage one can surmise, by analogy with rapid transit and commuter rail, that light rail does have an attractive power greater than that of a bus under conditions of equal fares and equal time savings.

From Exhibit 3.6 one can further see that, equalized for units of capacity and for operating speed, the Standard Light Rail Vehicle is likely to cost one third to one half as much to operate as present heavy commuter rail equipment. This strongly suggests that *on sparsely used rail lines* where present operating speeds are slow and where there is no significant interference from other traffic, such as freight trains, *the substitution of light rail cars for commuter rail equipment looks very promising.* For the same operating cost, two to three times the service frequency might be provided with a marked effect on patronage. Among proposals of this type in the New York Region one might mention the conversion of certain north-south feeder branches of the Long Island Railroad in Nassau County, and of the shore line south of Long Branch in Monmouth County. Of course, the cost differences between conventional rail and light rail are not just technological, but largely institutional. Any such conversion hinges on labor agreements that would make the savings possible. The capital costs involved are modest, since light-rail type electrification is inexpensive and signalling not very elaborate.

As for the return of light rail vehicles to street operations in downtown areas, three observations are in order. First, since the light rail vehicle is nearly twice as large as a bus, its substitution for a bus can mean cutting service frequency. This can lead to reductions in patronage unless compensating improvements are introduced. Second, a major reason for the demise of the traditional streetcar in North America was its conflict with auto traffic, particularly near intersections and island platforms. Should the attitude toward allowing the auto to go anywhere in a downtown area change, one could visualize streets set aside for pedestrians and streetcars only, where the conflicts of mixed traffic would be eliminated. Intersecting streets would be controlled by streetcar-actuated signals to assure priority at intersections. This could provide the kinds of speed and amenity advantages that would help compensate for lesser service frequency. Third, while bus frequencies on some heavily travelled downtown streets might seem higher than necessary to provide adequate service, this is less likely to be the case on specific bus routes as they fan out from the downtown area. A substitution of streetcars for buses on the heavily travelled segment alone would necessitate transfers from buses to streetcars—a travel impediment that is unlikely to be worthwhile, unless the streetcar route is long. This then leads us to consider the feasibility of light rail as a junior rapid-transit type service to downtowns of different sizes. To do that, we must deal not only with demand densities and service densities as before, but with traffic volumes in prospective rail corridors.

Calculating corridor volumes for any "typical" downtown cluster and its surrounding urban area is a highly conjectural exercise, because the volumes depend on the distribution of residential densities around the cluster. They depend both on the residential density gradient—how steeply densities decline as distance from the downtown increases—and on the geographic shape of the residential areas; for example, a city strung out along a valley or a peninsula is likely to have heavier corridor volumes than a city with the same size downtown that spreads equally in all directions on a plain.

Quite obviously, these two factors of density gradient and shape vary widely from city to city. The illustrative urban areas with downtowns of 100, 50, 35, and 20 million square feet of nonresidential floorspace presented in Exhibit 5.14 are assumed to be more or less circular in shape, and to have residential gradients as shown in the first line for each downtown size. These assumed gradients bear a consistent relationship to downtown size and resemble the gradients around urban centers in the New York Region outside Manhattan, but they do not portray any actual cities.

A third essential factor for calculating the feasibility of any transit system which, unlike the local bus, does not depend on pedestrian access alone is the size of the tributary area. With wide route spacing typical of fixed-guideway systems, the relationship between vehicle hours of service provided and passenger boardings must be calculated over the entire tributary area of a route, not over one square mile. Unfortunately, the size of the tributary area is typically not known. The relationships shown in Exhibit 4.3 are helpful for estimating rail and rapid transit tributary areas in the New York Region, but are of little relevance to smaller centers with different distance-density relationships, different relative speed advantages, and a different spacing of routes. In addition, the relationships can vary depending on local practices. For example, in Boston, local buses are excluded from entering the downtown, thus expanding the tributary area of rail facilities.

In Exhibit 5.14 the tributary area of a downtown-bound fixed guideway is assumed to be 1 mile wide for the first two miles near the downtown, and then to fan out gradually, encompassing roughly a one-seventh segment of a circle; it is also assumed to bulge out beyond the outer terminal. The trips originating within a 1-mile band along the guideway are calculated on the basis of "rapid transit territory" choice-of-mode relationships, while those originating from beyond the 1-mile band follow the "minimum bus service" relationships. Trips from each of these two territories are listed separately, then added, and cumulated to represent the downtown-bound flow. The flow at the beginning of the second mile can be viewed as the flow at the maximum load point, which determines rolling stock requirements; trips from the first square mile with the highest density are assumed to

EXHIBIT 5.14

Illustrative Fixed Guideway Corridor
Flows to Downtowns of Selected Sizes
under Assumed Conditions

Distance to downtown, miles		2	3	4	5	6	7	8	9	10	11	12	13	14	15
Downtown cluster size, million sq.ft. nonres. floorspace...........	100														
1. Assumed net residential density, dwellings/acre		70	40	25	18	13	10	8	6	5	4.4	3.9	3.5	3.1	2.8
2. Assumed tributary area beyond 1-mile band, sq.mi.		0	0.5	1.6	2.7	3.9	5.0	6.1	7.2	8.4	9.5	10.6	11.7	12.9	14.4
3. Residence-based transit trips to downtown from 1-mile band		9,653	4,254	2,290	1,354	818	534	367	236	166	127	93	69	53	40
4. Residence-based transit trips to downtown from beyond 1-mile band		0	1,564	2,461	2,549	2,159	1,793	1,433	1,077	855	737	602	487	411	1,320
5. Total residence-based transit trips to downtown from given distance		9,653	5,818	4,751	3,903	2,977	2,327	1,800	1,313	1,021	864	695	556	464	1,360
6. Cumulative volume, one-way daily trips in corridor		37,502	27,849	22,031	17,280	13,377	10,400	8,073	6,273	4,960	3,939	3,075	2,380	1,824	1,360
7. Daily PMT in corridor, both directions.................................	395,650	Average two-way flow 26,377 PMT/mile; average trip 5.3 miles; sector area 150 sq.mi.													

Distance		2	3	4	5	6	7	8	9	10	11	12	13	14	15
Downtown cluster size, million sq.ft. of nonres. floorspace......	50														
1. Assumed net residential density, dwellings/acre		40	23	14	10	8	6	5	4	3.5	3.2	2.8			
2. Assumed tributary area beyond 1-mile band, sq.mi.		0	0.5	1.5	2.7	3.9	5.0	6.1	7.2	8.4	9.5	10.6x4			
3. Residence-based transit trips to downtown from 1-mile band		4,388	1,947	971	529	337	209	137	96	66	50	32			
4. Residence-based transit trips to downtown from beyond 1-mile band		0	644	991	878	798	653	488	401	306	263	778			
5. Total residence-based transit trips to downtown from given distance		4,388	2,591	1,962	1,407	1,135	862	625	497	372	313	810			
6. Cumulative volume, one-way daily trips in corridor		14,962	10,574	7,983	6,021	4,614	3,479	2,617	1,992	1,495	1,123	810			
7. Daily PMT in corridor, both directions.................................	141,264	Average two-way flow 11,772 PMT/mile; average trip 4.7 miles; sector area 98.3 sq.mi.													

Distance		2	3	4	5	6	7	8	9
Downtown cluster size, million sq.ft. of nonres. floorspace......	35								
1. Assumed net residential density, dwellings/acre		25	15	10	7.5	6.5	4.5	3.5	3
2. Assumed tributary area beyond 1-mile band, sq.mi.		0	0.5	1.6	2.7	3.9	5.0	6.1	7.2x4
3. Residence-based transit trips to downtown from 1-mile band		2,517	1,095	553	314	218	115	70	47
4. Residence-based transit trips to downtown from beyond 1-mile band		0	335	518	473	475	315	226	729
5. Total residence-based transit trips to downtown from given distance		2,517	1,430	1,071	787	693	430	296	776
6. Cumulative volume, one-way daily trips in corridor		8,000	5,483	4,053	2,982	2,195	1,502	1,072	776
7. Daily PMT in corridor, both directions.................................	68,126	Average two-way flow 7,570 PMT/mile; average trip 4.2 miles; sector area 56.6 sq.mi.							

EXHIBIT 5.14 continued

Downtown cluster size, million sq.ft. of nonres. floorspace......	20				
1. Assumed net residential density, dwellings/acre		20	10	7	5	4
2. Assumed tributary area beyond 1-mile band, sq.mi.		0	0.5	1.6	2.7	3.9x4
3. Residence-based transit trips to downtown from 1-mile band		1,631	535	276	139	73
4. Residence-based transit trips to downtown from beyond 1-mile band		0	150	235	188	568
5. Total residence-based transit trips to downtown from given distance		1,631	685	511	327	641
6. Cumulative volume, one-way daily trips in corridor		3,795	2,164	1,479	968	641
7. Daily PMT in corridor, both directions.............................	25,684	Average two-way flow 4,280 PMT/mile; average trip 3.4 miles; sector area 25.4 sq.mi.				

Derivation: Line 1 — density gradient assumed with reference to Exhibits 7.3 and 5.1

Line 2 — assumed with some reference to Exhibit 4.3; including the 1-mile band containing the fixed guideway, the area shown represents approximately one-seventh the area of a circle with distance to downtown as a radius; i.e. it is assumed that no more than 7 radial lines serve the downtown

Line 3 — trip end density calculated on the basis of gross population density as shown in Exhibit 7.1; per capita trip rates as shown in Exhibit 7.8 and 7.9, assuming a 40% labor force participation rate; and percent transit use as shown for "rapid transit" territory in Exhibit 7.15, with adjustment for 40% coverage in Exhibit 7.18

Line 4 — trip end density calculated on the basis of Exhibits 7.1, 7.8 and 7.9 as above, with percent transit use as shown for "neither" territory in Exhibit 7.14, multiplied by line 2.

Line 5 — equals sum of lines 3 and 4

Line 6 — volumes at each distance equal sum of preceding figures to the right in line 5

Line 7 — daily PMT equals sum of columns in line 6 + column 1 (for 1-mile distance, where volume assumed equal to 2-mile distance) X 2 for return trips.

reach downtown by modes other than fixed guideway transit and are therefore not shown. Total passenger miles per day in the corridor—a measure to which potential capital investment can be related—is shown for each downtown size in line 7.

Evaluating the possibilities for light rail in the context of Exhibit 5.14, we observe that for downtowns between 20 and 50 million square feet in size, the estimated corridor volumes at maximum load point range from 3,800 to 15,000 daily trips in one direction. This is in scale with existing light rail operations largely on reserved rights-of-way. Typical daily one-directional volumes on these are: Norristown line in Pennsylvania—4,750; Newark, N.J., and Shaker Heights, Ohio—7,000; Riverside and Beacon Street lines in Boston at their junction—17,200 (the latter line includes some service not on exclusive right-of-way). Obviously, the estimated corridor volumes in Exhibit 5.14 are strongly influenced by the rather broad tributary area assumed; with the area confined to a 1-mile band along the line, they would shrink by 30 to 40 percent. However, there seems to be no reason to confine the tributary area this way; experience with the Newark line, which is fed largely by 12 intersecting bus routes, indicates that it receives passengers from an area in excess of 100 square miles, even though the line is only 4.3 miles long, bounded by a park on one side and by a neighborhood averaging about 15.5 dwelling units per acre on the other. The latter density impedes parking at stations. Because of their origin-destination patterns, only a part of the bus users in the 100 square mile area near Newark find it to their advantage to transfer to the light rail line.[10] With competition from nearby bus routes, or with a light rail line that does not provide adequate downtown distribution, the same would occur in the hypothetical tributary areas of Exhibit 5.14, thereby reducing ridership. Thus the volumes shown might be considered attainable if *all* transit patrons in the corridor who are destined to downtown would use the facility in question.

Under this assumption, the volumes would assure good service frequencies. If 30 percent of the one-directional flow occurs during the peak hour, then the flow at the maximum load point would require 12 Standard Light Rail Vehicles per hour at a comfortable loading (1 passenger per 6 sq. ft. capacity unit) for a downtown of 20 million square feet (somewhat larger than Bridgeport); 25 vehicles per hour for a downtown of 35 million square feet (about the size of Hartford); and 47 vehicles per hour for a downtown of 50 million square feet (representative of a million-sized city); the latter flow might be handled by two-car trains.

To calculate operating costs, the speed must be known. Data are insufficient to develop any relationship between operating speed and development density, of the type portrayed in Exhibit 4.1, for light rail. One can assume that in local street operation its speed is similar to that of the bus. However, on an exclusive right-of-way (with only one intersection at grade) the Newark line attains an average scheduled speed of 22 mph with a station spacing of 0.43 miles—a point which falls on the high-performance rapid transit curve in Exhibit 4.2 alongside PATCO and BART. The operating speed shown in Exhibit 3.2 is 14.2 mph because layover time accounts for a large share of total operating time on the short route. To simplify things, we will assume that on a separate right-of-way, the scheduled speed for all three downtown sizes is 25 mph, corresponding to a station spacing of 0.5 miles, and that layover time is a generous 9 minutes, resulting in operating speeds of 15.4, 17.6, and 19.0 mph for the three sizes respectively on 6, 9, and 12-mile-long routes as shown in Exhibit 5.14.

For the 20 million square foot downtown, 120 one-way vehicle runs during a 20 hour daily operating period can be assumed, as was done with local buses. This represents an average peak period headway of one vehicle every 4 minutes, and an average off-peak headway of a vehicle every 16 minutes. For the two larger downtown sizes, peak period capacity requirements necessitate increasing total daily vehicle runs if the 16 minute off-peak headway is to be maintained. The number of daily one-way vehicle runs becomes 172 for the 35 million square foot downtown and 260 for the 50 million square foot downtown. With the route lengths and speeds assumed, this translates into 93.5, 176.0, and 328.5 vehicle hours in both directions. At $28.50 per vehicle hour from Exhibit 3.2, the three illustrative light rail routes will cost $2,665, $5,016, and $9,362 per day to operate. Dividing these by the daily passengers from Exhibit 5.14 we find that the operating cost per passenger boarding ranges from 34¢ to 31¢, substantially below the 50¢ to 75¢ per passenger costs we were dealing with when exploring the feasibility of local buses. The operating cost per passenger mile ranges from 10¢ in the smallest of the three downtowns to 7¢ in the largest.

Not only are the operating costs per passenger for light rail under assumed conditions substantially lower than for local buses, but light rail can also serve substantially lower development densities at a longer distance from downtown than local buses, given the same service frequency.

The mechanisms which account for that bear some elaboration. To begin with, the vehicle productivity which underlies the figures cited is very high: in the range of 85 to 90 passengers boarding per vehicle hour. Such a productivity is not out of line with existing performance: the Newark light rail line was shown to have close to 60 passengers boarding per vehicle hour in Exhibit 3.2, and the vehicles in our examples are 40 percent larger. This high productivity is attained by a combination of high speed and sparse route spacing. Whereas the local bus routes were spaced half a mile apart, in the light rail examples we have routes serving tributary areas of 25 to 100 square miles. Averaged over the entire tributary area, the demand densities are not very high: around 150 residence-based trip ends per square mile. But averaged in the same way the supply density is extremely low (fewer than 2 vehicle hours per square mile in one-way terms) resulting in the high productivity.

Such low supply density can attract the necessary demand because the assumed speed and service features of the routes are rapid transit-like. They cause above-average trip densities within the one-mile band of what we have called "rapid transit service territory," and they attract residents from the rest of the tributary area by feeder modes. The dependence on feeder modes means, of course, that the total average cost per passenger in reality is higher than just the cost of using the light rail route; some passengers have to pay for feeder buses, others for access by auto. This is a feature common to all systems that involve access by feeder modes, including express buses in all but the largest cities.

After this encouraging discussion[11] of the operating costs of light rail, we must turn to its capital costs, assuming a reserved, even if not fully grade separated, right-of-way, for without it our speed and patronage assumptions do not hold. Using a rough investment yardstick of $1,500 per daily passenger mile scaled at the close of Chapter 3 so as not to exceed the energy cost of the auto, the 25,700 daily passenger miles estimated for a 6-mile-long light rail route to a downtown of 20 million square feet might warrant an investment of $38.5 million. The 10 vehicles needed to provide the desired peak-hour service will cost $3.5 million, and installing track, drainage, overhead power, station platforms, a storage and maintenance shed and other incidental items might cost $4 million a mile on *an existing right-of-way* in 1974 prices outside New York City. This leaves only $11 million, or less than $2 million per mile, for right-of-way acquisition or heavy construction, if such are needed. Unfortunately, existing prepared rights-of-way, while often available, are not often useful. For example, an unused railroad will often go through a decaying industrial area and not be at all attractive for pedestrian access; or a wide freeway median may end abruptly at an interchange, from which it is impossible to reach the main downtown street without extensive construction. Opportunities of an unused right-of-way in the right place are rare, and without them a truly high-speed light rail line to a downtown of 20 million square feet will tend to incur unreasonably high construction costs per passenger mile.

By the same reckoning, a downtown of 35 million square feet might warrant spending $102 million for a hypothetical 9-mile route, or $11 million a mile. This does leave some room for heavy construction. For example, if an unused railroad, otherwise suitable for conversion to light rail, does not quite reach the center of downtown, this sum would make it possible to build a 1-mile tunnel under the main street (for, say, $50 million) and have enough left to rehabilitate the rail line. A downtown of 50 million square feet might warrant spending $212 million on its 12-mile route, or $18 million per mile. This might allow a short downtown tunnel and a grade-separated elevated structure of some length.

Obviously, there should be no rule that every urban area must invest $1,500 per daily passenger mile in rail transit facilities; the examples are merely intended to show how the scale of construction might change if it is related to passenger use in a consistent manner. The advantage of light rail, compared to the next systems we will discuss, lies in its flexibility. A downtown tunnel, for example, may not be a desirable alternative if the main street can be converted into a pedestrian mall with a reserved light rail right-of-way in the middle. The slight reduction in speed might be compensated for by easier and more pleasant pedestrian access. With a changed attitude toward the auto, arterial streets in residential areas might be likewise converted to exclusive light rail use, delivering transit service where it is needed without the heavy intrusion of elevated structures or the huge cost of tunnels, at a speed superior to buses in mixed traffic.

In sum, *light rail does seem to be promising for downtowns in the 35 to 50 million square foot range,* generally found in cities of about three quarters of a million people or more; *under fortuitous circumstances of existing rights-of-way, individual lines may be workable to downtowns as small as 20 million square feet. A line might extend into residential areas with densities substantially lower than those which can be served by local buses of comparable frequency.*

LIGHT GUIDEWAY TRANSIT

Light guideway transit is a new transportation mode, dating back only to 1966 when the Westinghouse "Transit Expressway" demonstration opened in South Park in Pittsburgh. Not counting installations at exhibitions, amusement parks, and test facilities, most systems in service in the United States operate at airports and represent short links or loops with the equivalent of less than one mile of two-track guideway. Our interest here is not in such specialized uses, but in broader urban applications in competition with established urban travel modes. Several large cities with low densities of development have been looking at light guideway transit as a possible answer to their rapid transit needs. The operating experience of the short airport "peoplemovers" does not seem to be readily transferable to such larger urban installations. The only two prototypes which begin to approach an urban scale are the Morgantown, W. Va. and Dallas-Ft. Worth Airport systems, with the equivalent of 2.2 and 6.5 miles of two-track guideway respectively. Yet, even here "it is difficult to derive any useful conclusions from experience to date because neither system has been in operation long enough to establish a sound basis for projecting operation and maintenance costs," a Congressional study reported in 1975.[12]

Using some assumptions, we have estimated the light guideway operating cost as being around 40¢ per capacity unit of a vehicle per hour on the Dallas system, and around 33¢ on the Morgantown system, in 1974-75 prices. The former cost happens to be about 2¢ lower than the existing operating cost of light rail, and the latter about 3¢ higher than the assumed operating cost of light rail with new vehicles. Until harder evidence becomes available, it is not unreasonable to assume that, equalized for speed and vehicle size, the operating costs of light guideway are about in the same range as light rail, automation notwithstanding.

To further quote the Congressional study, "Dramatic economies through the substitution of computers and electronic equipment for operating personnel are unlikely in the foreseeable future. To provide . . . service without human operators requires much electronic and mechanical equipment that must be monitored and maintained by skilled technicians. As the complexity of such systems increases, opportunities for equipment malfunction increase correspondingly, necessitating additional specialized personnel."[13]

If light guideway and light rail costs per capacity unit per hour are roughly equal, the next question is what number of capacity-unit miles can be delivered per hour. The scheduled speeds of the Dallas and Morgantown systems are relatively slow—12 mph with 0.3 mile station spacing in the first case and 19 mph with 1.1 mile average spacing in the second case. Operating speeds including layover time, which were used in the cost calculations of all the other systems in Exhibit 3.2, are not available; layover time may not be a very meaningful concept for unmanned vehicles. Recognizing this lack of precise comparability, we can still say that today light guideway speeds are slower than those of light rail at comparable station spacing.[14]

Top speeds of the present generation of light guideway equipment generally do not exceed 35 mph, compared to 55 mph for light rail. This is conditioned by the very close headways of the small vehicles, which make higher speeds impractical with present control technology. To the extent that light guideway systems are designed for demand-responsive rather than headway-type operation during off-peak hours, as is Morgantown, some of the time lost because of slower speed can be made up by skipping intermediate stops. During peak periods, however, light guideway costs per capacity-unit mile must be assumed to be higher than those of light rail because of lower speed.

A key difference between the two systems is in vehicle size. The capacity of the Dallas vehicle is roughly one quarter and that of the Morgantown vehicle less than one fifth the capacity of the standard light rail car, meaning that, other conditions being equal, automated light guideway transit could provide four to five times the service frequency of light rail. Of course, this is only possible at volumes which do not exceed the capacity of the system. With two-car trains on 18-second headways, the capacity of the Dallas system with 6 square feet of gross vehicle floorspace per passenger is 9,800 passengers per hour per direction, and that of the Morgantown system, with single vehicles on 15-second headways, is 4,080 passengers per hour per direction. If 30 percent of the one-directional traffic occurs during the peak hour, the Morgantown-type system would be adequate for the corridor volume shown in Exhibit 5.14 for a downtown of 35 million square feet (about the size of Hartford), and the Dallas type system for a downtown of 50 million square feet (about the size of Newark).

The high service frequencies offered would undoubtedly raise the traffic volumes shown. Exactly how much is difficult to say, for the procedures used for fixed systems are not sensitive to service frequencies. We can say, though, that the peak hour frequencies provided by light rail under our assumed conditions for the two downtown sizes just mentioned are already quite high, 25 and 47 vehicles per hour, meaning average waiting times, calculated at half the headway, of 72 and 38 seconds. It is doubtful that reducing them further would add many riders. The average assumed off-peak waiting time of 8 minutes could stand improvement, and off-peak ridership could be increased. The increase might be greater than the loss in ridership suffered because of the slower speed of light guideway compared to light rail. The increase will be bought at the price of a higher operating cost, given the present slow speeds of light guideway transit.

It seems that the capability of the small light guideway vehicles to provide frequent service would best be utilized at low traffic volumes which, when carried by the large light rail vehicles at acceptable loadings, result in headways that are too long. If we consider peak hour headways of more than 4 minutes as "too long," then light guideway transit appears useful at volumes of 1,500 or fewer people per peak hour per direction, corresponding to daily flows of 5,000 to 6,000 or fewer people per direction at the maximum load point. In the context of Exhibit 5.14, such flows would occur in corridors leading to downtowns of about 25 million square feet of nonresidential floorspace or less.

At this point, we come to the issue of capital costs. The construction costs of the present generation of light guideways are inherently much higher than those of light rail. Light rail on an existing right-of-way involves installing drainage, scraping some earth, bringing in ballast, placing ties and tracks, paving grade crossings and passenger platforms, and stringing electrical wire. Wayside signalling, essential in rapid transit operations, is often not needed, and grade crossings can be protected by ordinary traffic signals actuated by the streetcar. By contrast, light guideway transit requires an elaborate control system with a central building that houses computers and monitoring equipment. On a prepared right-of-way, it typically requires a continuous reinforced concrete trough, with support surfaces for wheels carrying the vehicle and for guide wheels, with contact surfaces for power supply, and with cables transmitting the automatic control information. Since present-day light guideway systems run on rubber tires, a heating system is necessary in cold climates to melt snow and ice. Stations are fairly substantial structures, with high-level platforms and automatic fare collection equipment. This kind of structure cannot be crossed by intersecting traffic at grade, and whenever street crossings occur they must be either elevated or in a tunnel.

Construction of the relatively inexpensive Dallas airport system cost close to $7 million per double-track mile. It runs mostly at grade, with the new airport built around it. Construction of the Morgantown system, which uses elevated guideways extensively, cost $27 million a mile. The Morgantown cost is burdened with difficult topographic and geological conditions,[15] but it is more representative of the costs of inserting a light guideway into an existing urban environment. Both costs exclude the cost of vehicles, but include the cost of designing and installing the automatic control system.

Averaging the Dallas and the Morgantown construction and design costs, we come up with $17 million per double-track mile in circa 1974 dollars, which in all probability is too modest. For example, given community resistance to elevated structures in downtown areas, the cost of a light guideway of existing configuration in a tunnel might well be in the $35 to $40 million per mile range. Now, applying the illustrative investment scale of $1,500 per daily passenger mile, we find that spending even $17 million per mile would be justified with a passenger flow upward of 11,300 passengers per day per two directions. Under the assumptions of Exhibit 5.14, such flows (averaged over the route length) occur to downtowns of 50 million square feet or more, and exceed the peak-hour capability of the present generation of single-vehicle light guideway transit; the Dallas-type system might be appropriate for this downtown size. It has the capability of running vehicles in trains and in this way resembles standard rapid transit. Yet, at this scale of passenger volume and downtown size, light rail could provide a very good service frequency at much lower capital cost.

If light guideway transit is to be employed at volumes below 5,000 to 6,000 passengers per direction per day at the maximum load point (at flows that, averaged over the entire route, add up to about 5,500 in both directions, where the frequent service capability of small vehicles would be most useful), then the investment per passenger mile becomes in excess of $3,000. This is three times as much as the projected per passenger mile cost of the Second Avenue subway in Manhattan.

We thus come to the paradox that *in those line-haul applications where the unique attributes of light guideway transit would be most useful, the capital cost per passenger mile of the present generation of light guideways is so high as to be out of a reasonable range. Where passenger volume could justify its high cost, the system does not have the capacity to carry the volume at the present state of the art,* unless it adopts traditional transit attributes, such as operation in trains. *At these high volumes, traditional transit can provide satisfactory service frequencies at a lower capital cost,* and at a generally similar or lower operating cost.

This is not to say that there is no room at all for automated light guideway transit on the present urban scene. Where peak requirements are low, but total daily flow is high, the high investment may be justified. Such is the case in Morgantown, where the peak 20-minute demand is about 1,100 rides per direction, but the projected daily flow is 24,000 passenger miles per mile of route, in scale with the 1975 use of BART. This occurs because most of the passengers are students moving between campuses during class breaks: peak hour flow does not occur twice a day, but once every hour as long as classes are in session. Thus, Morgantown's capital cost per passenger mile projected is around $1,000, about the same as that of the Second Avenue subway. *The present generation of light guideway transit appears limited to special applications, not to line-haul use with its very high peaks.*

The major research thrust of automated guideway technology has been to reduce the headways below the present 18 to 15 seconds, closer to the 2 seconds that are attained by autos on a freeway, and thereby to increase peak capacity. The result would be to make automated light guideway transit more competitive in the relatively high volume market of traditional transit systems. The high off-peak service frequencies possible with automatic vehicles would presumably attract more riders than are willing to use traditional systems, and non-stop routing between origin and destination could be an added advantage. However, the logistics of handling even moderately high passenger flows with a multitude of small vehicles, each following its own route, are formidable indeed. The tendency in studies of area-wide urban systems has been to lean toward traditional transit operating modes while using automatic control.[16] Furthermore, the service frequency elasticities, discussed in Chapter 1, while appreciable, are substantially below unity, indicating that the number of passengers attracted will lag behind the expension of service. This means, in turn, that vehicle productivity will drop and cost per passenger will increase.

While the exact shape of these relationships remains unclear, it does seem that a more *promising research thrust would be to greatly simplify the design of light guideways and of the appurtenant hardware.* The aim would be to reduce capital costs to a level where light guideways could economically serve modest traffic volumes which are below the reach of traditional fixed systems. This could increase service frequencies where such an increase is needed most, and also enable closer route spacing, reducing the need for auto access. Another aim would be to reduce the visual bulk of the guideways, thus improving their community acceptance. The concept of a prefabricated "two-in-one" guideway, mentioned in Chapter 3, appears to be the only current effort in this direction.

STANDARD RAPID TRANSIT

Similar to light guideway transit, standard rapid transit is distinguished from light rail by an exclusive guideway with no grade crossings. This feature is made necessary by its high speed, its frequency, and by the fact that electric current collection is usually near the ground, rather than overhead, to reduce the headroom in tunnels. Rapid transit also requires an extensive signalling system, may have automatic train operation, and has large station areas which provide off-vehicle fare collection. This elaborate physical plant incurs operating and maintenance costs which must be offset by the lower cost of operating vehicles at high speed, and by operating them in trains rather than singly. Thus, *rapid transit comes into its own where travel distances are such as to require speeds higher than those which light rail can provide, and where travel volumes are such that vehicle operation in trains can still provide reasonably high service frequencies.*

Referring back to Exhibit 5.14, we note that for the assumed 9-mile run into a downtown of 35 million square feet, a 22-minute travel time attainable by light rail seems reasonable. Also, that if 125 capacity units are assumed for a modern rapid transit car, then the 30 percent of the daily one-directional flow at the maximum load point that occurs in the peak hour can be handled by 10 two-car trains. At 6-minute headway may not be bad in itself, but it is significantly worse than the 2.4 minutes that would have been provided in the situation by light rail.

Proceeding to the downtown of 50 million square feet, we find that on the assumed 12-mile run, time savings on the order of 5 to 10 minutes, compared to the light rail operation previously discussed, could be attained with rapid transit type operation at 30 to 38 mph. These two rapid transit speeds correspond to station spacings of 0.9 and 1.5 miles. We also find that the peak hour volume could be handled by 12 three-car trains or 18 two-car trains, beginning to indicate an acceptable service frequency, compared to the unnecessarily high frequency of 47 light rail cars per hour.

Lastly, for the assumed 15-mile run into a downtown of 100 million square feet, rapid transit-type speeds are clearly more attractive. The peak hour flow of 11,250 in one direction at the maximum load points would be near capacity for light rail, but could be easily handled by 15 six-car rapid transit trains, providing a very good service frequency of 4 minutes.

Comparisons between light rail and rapid transit in terms of vehicle hours within our framework become somewhat vague, since they hinge on rather arbitrary assumptions about off-peak train lengths. Generally, one can say that for a downtown as large as 35 million square feet, rapid transit trains would tend to provide excessive capacity, which would result in low vehicle productivity. At the 50-million square foot size, assuming a 30-mph scheduled and a 23-mph operating speed (i.e., including layover time) with three-car trains throughout the day and the same 16-minute off-peak frequency as assumed earlier, a vehicle productivity of 80 passengers boarding per vehicle hour might be attained, comparable to the PATCO Lindenwold line. At a cost of $40 per vehicle hour, the 374 vehicle hours needed would cost 50¢ per passenger or about 10¢ per passenger mile. At the 100-million square foot downtown size, the cost per passenger mile might be lower under comparable assumptions.

In sum, our rough scaling of operating characteristics suggests that *a downtown size of about 50 million square feet of nonresidential floorspace with 15,000 one-directional rides per day at the maximum load point on a route is about the lower threshold of rapid transit*.

Just as in the case of light rail, we note that *as long as the attraction of a large downtown is present, and as long as access by feeder modes is possible, relatively low demand densities can support rapid transit at the residential end of the trip*. The demand density, averaged over the entire tributary area, is about 150 residence-based downtown-oriented trips per square mile for the 50-million square foot downtown, and about 250 for the 100-million square foot downtown. At the outer extremities of the lines to both downtowns, the assumed residential densities in Exhibit 5.14 drop as low as 3 dwellings per acre.

Of course, the operating costs per passenger at these outer extremities are much higher than those in close-in areas. While we scaled the *average* cost per passenger for the assumed route to a downtown of 50 million square feet at 50¢, it will range from about 30¢ per passenger boarding in the second mile to $4.30 per passenger boarding in the eleventh mile, if an equal speed with a service density of 34 vehicle hours per route mile is assumed. With a flat fare, the riders boarding in the second and third miles would be subsidizing the riders boarding in miles 4 through 12. While this may be an argument for a graduated fare, it is distinctly *not* an argument for chopping the route off after three miles; by doing so, as one can see in Exhibit 5.14, we would lose half the passengers, and the route would no longer be viable as a rapid transit route. In the real world, balancing fares, costs, and patronage to decide where to terminate a route is a delicate exercise, which we cannot engage in here.

Rather, we will proceed to see if rapid transit routes to downtowns of 50 million square feet of nonresidential floorspace or larger are supportable from the viewpoint of capital costs. These costs are high because rapid transit needs a continuously grade-separated right-of-way, a signalling system which, even without automatic train operation, is likely to cost twice as much as installing the track itself, and relatively heavy structures to support the axle loads of large cars. The geometric design requirements of large cars operating at high speeds are rather stringent. For example, the Morgantown light guideway vehicles climb grades as steep as 10 percent; light rail vehicles can ascend 10 percent grades for short stretches, but can easily handle 4 to 6 percent grades; by contrast, the maximum grade of 5 percent on the New York subway system is handled with great difficulty at slow speed, and the desirable design grade for rapid transit is 2 to 3 percent. Similarly, 150-foot turning radii more than adequate for light rail do survive on old rapid transit systems, but neither the 15-mph speed restrictions nor the wheel squeal they produce with long cars are assets. To sustain a 50-mph speed, desirable horizontal radii for rapid transit are 1,500 to 2,000 feet. These design requirements translate into high construction costs. In 1974 New York City prices—which were above the national average—placing a rapid transit line on an existing right-of-way cost on the order of $15 million a mile for two tracks, while the cost of tunnels started at about $60 million a mile and went much beyond $100 million under some conditions.

If one were to apply the investment scale of $1,500 per passenger mile to the passenger miles and route lengths in Exhibit 5.14, one would see that for a downtown of 35 million square feet about $11 million per mile might be spent, which clearly will not buy rapid transit, though it might buy a very respectable light rail line. For a downtown of 50 million square feet, $18 million per route mile might be spent, which might be adequate only if the right-of-way is mostly in existence. For a downtown of 100 million square feet, $40 million per mile might be spent, which will buy a rapid transit system. For example, the central area of Washington, D.C., defined more narrowly than the "nonresidential downtown clusters" in this book, contains about 90 million square feet of nonresidential floorspace, of which 71 million are office space. The Washington Metro as of 1975 was costing on the order of $40 million a mile. Its proposed extent (98 miles) is in scale with the system implied for a downtown of 100 million square feet in Exhibit 5.14, namely seven spokes at 15 miles each for a total of 105 miles.

On the grounds of capital cost as well as on operating grounds, *rapid transit to a downtown of 50 million square feet appears to be a touch-and-go proposition. Generally speaking, a downtown size larger than that seems needed both from the viewpoint of capital investment, and to achieve good service frequencies with reasonably long trains.*

We might recall that, in Exhibit 2.3, empirical figures for rapid transit use in United States cities were related to downtown office floorspace, yielding a rather consistent picture. One should expect that rapid transit use is better related to office floorspace than to total nonresidential floorspace used in our hypothetical examples. It is difficult to establish any equivalences between total nonresidential floorspace and office floorspace. Nor is actual rapid transit use equivalent to our corridor volumes, unless all public transit trips to downtown in hypothetical corridor use rapid transit. However, from Exhibit 2.3 one can deduce that, under existing conditions, downtowns with 15 million square feet of *office* floorspace or less would tend to generate rather meager rapid transit usage (about 80,000 daily riders or less) which is enough to fill two rather lightly used transit spokes. There are only about half a dozen downtowns in the United States which have more than 15 million square feet of office space, and which do not already have rapid transit. Actual volumes per two-track line on approaches to Manhattan in 1973 (after a sharp decline in ridership) were in the range of 75,000 to 375,000 daily riders; in Chicago, on the order of 120,000; in Boston,

35,000 to 90,000. Of course, at the outer extremities of lines even in New York, daily volumes of 3,000 to 10,000 riders could be encountered.

While it is clear that downtown size, measured by total nonresidential floorspace or by office building floorspace, is the prime determinant of rapid transit feasibility at least under North American conditions, floorspace statistics are scanty and, in the popular mind, rapid transit feasibility is still largely associated with metropolitan area population. Equivalencies between downtown area size and metropolitan population are difficult to establish in part because of data deficiencies, in part because the two are often only loosely related. Nevertheless, relating existing rapid transit systems to the population of the metropolitan areas they serve is of interest. Exhibit 5.15 shows that, world-wide, of the 51 rapid transit systems in existence as of early 1976, half served areas with 2 to 10 million inhabitants. To be sure, several systems served cities with fewer than a million people, but most of these are essentially light rail systems, sometimes designated a pre-metro (PM) in the Exhibit. It is also notable that most of the 51 rapid transit systems, serving as they do cities of high density, are quite short: the average route length is just 13 miles per million population, and only London, Stockholm, Oslo, and San Francisco provide more than 30 route miles per million population served.

Also of interest in Exhibit 5.15 is annual per capita use of the systems, what used to be known as the "riding habit." It strongly reflects levels of auto ownership in the different cities, as well as city size. Moscow and Osaka rank highest, with over 250 annual trips per resident; one might note that New York City's figure was identical in 1925, but was down to 127 in 1973; Cleveland and San Francisco rank lowest, with fewer than 10 rides per resident of the area served in 1973.

Summarizing the historic detail of Exhibit 5.15, the growth of rapid transit mileage in the United States and the world over the past century is portrayed in Exhibit 5.16. What some have called "the second youth of rapid transit" in the period after 1960 is readily apparent.

COMMUTER RAIL

Commuter rail is a highly specialized mode of public transit; significant use, in excess of about 15,000 rides per day, is limited in North America to only seven urban areas—New York, Chicago, Philadelphia, Montreal, Boston, Toronto, and San Francisco. All of these have more than 25 million square feet of office floorspace in their major downtowns. The only two downtowns which exceed that size but have very little commuter rail traffic are Washington and Los Angeles; their sparse use is in part related to the geography of their rail networks, just as the above-average rail use in Philadelphia is related to an extensive and closely meshed network. Detroit, with 23 million square feet of office space, was expanding its fledgling commuter service in 1976.

Inflated by institutional arrangements, commuter rail operating costs are high, whether calculated per vehicle hour, or equalized per unit of capacity or per seat. However, commuter rail is the fastest mode of public transportation, and it does attain above average load factors. As a result, its costs per passenger mile are not out of line with those of rapid transit and sometimes even express buses. In the New Jersey sector of the New York Region during 1974, both commuter rail and express bus were delivering passenger miles at about 8¢. Aside from the fact that in an area such as the New York Region facilities for replacing heavy commuter rail flows with buses simply do not exist, the patronage inducing ability of

EXHIBIT 5.15

Rail Rapid Transit Systems, 1863-1975

	Year opened	Route miles of Line							1973 Annual Rides in millions	1970 Approximate Population in area served in millions	Approximate Annual rides per capita	Approximate Route-miles per 1 million population
		1880	1900	1920	1940	1960	1970	1975				
1. London	1863	35	110	157	200	244	254.5	257.0	644	7.4	87	34.7
2. N.Y. Region	1867	32.2	64.6	216.1	281.5	269.3	269.7	263.1*	1,138	8.9	128	29.6
3. Chicago	1892		34.0	68.0	82.0	64.0	87.0	87.0	116	3.4	34	25.6
4. Budapest	1896		2.3	2.3	2.3	2.3	6.3	8.6	n.a.	1.9	n.a.	4.5
5. Glasgow	1897		6.6	6.6	6.6	6.6	6.6	6.6	14	0.9	16	7.3
6. Boston	1897		1.5	24.1	26.5	42.1	42.1	50.5**	100	2.7	36	18.7
7. Vienna	1898		16.7	16.7	16.7	16.7	16.7	18.0	73	1.9	38	9.5
8. Paris	1900		6.4	59.6	107.4	117.1	143.2	157.2	1,303	8.2	159	19.2
9. Berlin	1902			22.1	47.2	51.3	62.1	68.8***	333	3.2	104	21.5
10. Philadelphia	1907			24.3	40.7	38.0	48.4	49.6****	115	3.0	38	16.5
11. Hamburg	1912			20.3	40.1	44.4	55.0	61.2	207	1.8	115	34.0
12. Buenos Aires	1913			5.0	14.0	17.4	19.6	19.6	n.a.	2.9	n.a.	6.8
13. Madrid	1919			1.6	18.0	18.0	28.3	34.6	550	3.1	177	11.2
14. Barcelona	1924				10.0	11.7	18.8	24.8	249	1.7	146	14.6
15. Athens	1925				8.2	16.2	16.2	16.2	n.a.	0.9	n.a.	18.0
16. Tokyo	1927				8.9	25.0	85.3	124.2	1,850	11.5	161	10.8
17. Osaka	1933				4.7	10.4	39.8	43.5	756	3.0	252	14.5
18. Moscow	1935				16.4	50.7	91.0	102.2	1,800	7.1	254	14.4
19. Stockholm	1950					24.8	40.0	43.7	200	1.3	154	33.6
20. Toronto	1954					4.6	20.7	25.7	174	2.3	76	11.2
21. Cleveland	1955					15.3	19.3	19.3	13	2.0	7	9.6
22. Leningrad	1955					8.9	30.2	39.0	530	4.0	133	9.8
23. Rome	1955					6.8	6.8	6.8	25	2.7	9	2.5
24. Nagoya	1957					4.0	20.1	23.6	179	2.0	90	11.8
25. Lisbon	1959					4.5	5.3	7.5	78	1.6	49	4.7
26. Kiev	1960					3.3	9.7	11.5	179	1.7	105	6.8
27. Milan	1964						13.1	21.5	112	1.7	66	12.6
28. Oslo	1966						18.1	24.2	n.a.	0.5	n.a.	48.4
29. Montreal	1966						16.3	16.3	125	2.5	50	6.5
30. Tbilisi	1966						6.5	7.8	100	0.9	111	8.6
31. Stuttgart (PM)	1966						0.8	3.2	n.a.	0.6	n.a.	5.3
32. Baku	1967						6.5	15.3	63	1.3	48	11.8
33. Cologne (PM)	1968						2.8	12.5	n.a.	0.9	n.a.	13.9
34. Frankfurt	1968						12.0	12.3	n.a.	0.7	n.a.	17.6
35. Rotterdam	1968						4.7	4.7	n.a.	1.1	n.a.	4.3
36. Brussels (PM)	1969						3.8	5.0	n.a.	1.1	n.a.	4.6
37. Mexico	1969						26.2	26.2	490	7.3	67	3.6
38. Peking	1969						13.9	13.9	n.a.	7.6	n.a.	1.8
39. Munich	1971							16.8	n.a.	1.3	n.a.	9.2
40. Sapporo	1971							7.5	n.a.	1.0	n.a.	7.5
41. Yokohama	1972							8.6	n.a.	2.2	n.a.	3.9
42. San Francisco	1972							71.0	20	2.3	9	30.8
43. Sao Paolo	1974							10.6	- - -	5.2	- - -	3.5
44. Santiago	1974							9.4	- - -	2.7	- - -	1.8
45. Kharkov	1974							6.5	- - -	1.2	- - -	5.4
46. Seoul	1974							5.9	- - -	5.5	- - -	1.1
47. Prague	1974							4.3	- - -	1.1	- - -	3.9
48. Bonn	1975							4.6	- - -	0.3	- - -	15.3
49. Hannover	1975							3.0	- - -	0.5	- - -	6.0
50. Kobe	1975							3.5	- - -	1.3	- - -	2.7
51. Washington	1976							4.6	- - -	2.9	- - -	1.6
World Total		67.2	242.1	623.7	931.2	1,117.4	1,567.4	1,889.0		144.8		13.2
U.S. Total		32.2	100.1	332.5	430.7	428.7	466.5	545.1		25.2		21.8

Route-miles without duplication (or first-track miles) of grade-separated urban rapid transit; excludes commuter or suburban railroads, and portions of them which may operate in tunnels in inner urban areas; includes those portions of light rail or streetcar lines which operate in tunnels and are sometimes known as pre-metro (marked PM). Not all mileages conform exactly to years shown.

Sources: *Jane's World Railways* (London, 1975 and earlier editions); Union Internationale des Transports Publics: *Les Transports Publics dans les Principales Villes du Monde* (1963); Howson, Henry F.: *World's Underground Railways* (London, 1964); Josef Otto Slezak, *Die Untergrundbahnen der Sowjetunion* (Vienna, 1967) Regional Plan Association (correspondence with selected operating agencies and file data).

*Includes NYCTA 230.6 mi., SIRTOA 14.3 mi., PATH 13.9 mi. and Newark Subway 4.3 mi.

**Includes 18 miles of streetcar routes in tunnel or on grade-separated right-of way

***Includes 3.1 miles which are inoperative due to partition of the city

****Includes SEPTA subway-elevated 22.1 mi., SEPTA Norristown line 13.5 mi., PATCO Lindenwold 14.0 mi.

Metric conversion: 1 mile = 1.609 Km.

EXHIBIT 5.16

Route Miles of Rail Rapid Transit
Systems, U.S. and World Total, 1863-
1975

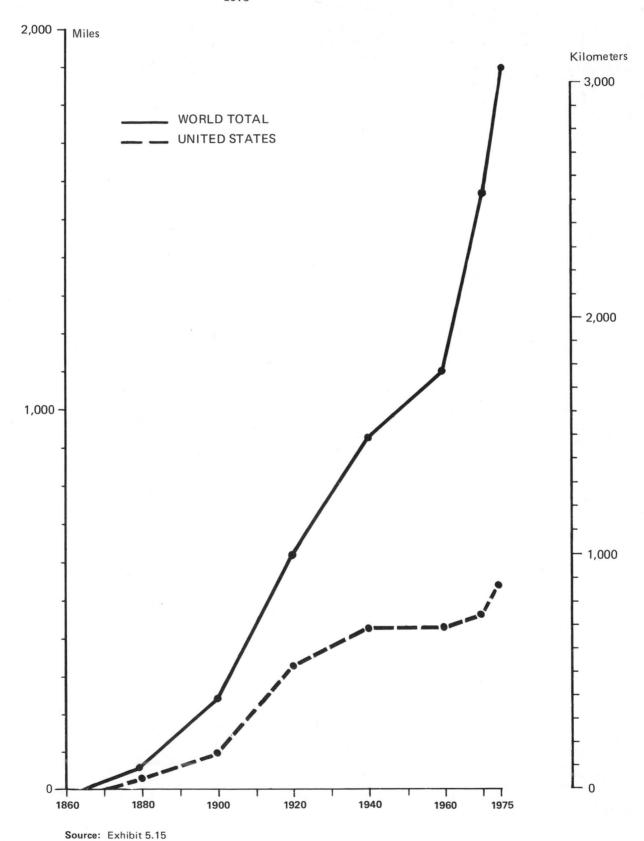

Source: Exhibit 5.15

commuter rail, emphasized several times earlier, must be considered. Whether or not buses could carry a given volume becomes irrelevant, if they are unable to attract it.

There exists a clear need to reduce rail operating costs both through changed labor arrangements and through technology, such as still higher speeds and automatic fare collection, if a new round of commuter line abandonments is to be avoided. However, opportunities for the expansion of commuter rail into presently unserved territory appear limited; they depend on the presence of existing lines which do not require any high-cost reconstruction, which traverse areas not served by other nearby lines, and which serve a very large downtown. If these conditions are met, the density of trip ends needed to support a commuter rail line is quite low, because of its dependence on auto access, because of the relatively infrequent nature of the service, and because of its speed.

For example, in commuter rail terms, a service frequency of 20 trains a day can be considered quite good. Assuming six-car trains, it represents a service density of 120 vehicle miles per route mile in one direction. In an area with an average density of 2 dwellings per acre, Exhibit 4.1 suggests the average commuter rail speed in the New York Region to be around 37 mph, which means that the 120 vehicle miles represent 3.2 vehicle hours. Commuter rail vehicle productivity, following Exhibit 3.2, is on the order of 40 passengers boarding per vehicle hour. At the high cost of $100 per vehicle hour, this reflects a cost of $2.50 per passenger boarding, which on a system with a 25-mile average trip length represents 10¢ per passenger mile. To match the expenditure of 3.2 vehicle hours per route mile, 3.2 × 40 = 128 passengers per route mile must be boarding the train at that density. This would be a fairly high demand density if all the 128 passengers were to come from the square mile adjacent to the route. In reality, of course, they do not. Our ability to estimate the size of tributary areas in a generally applicable manner is weak because of the lack of data on access distances. In the case of the New York Region and commuter rail access we can lean on Exhibit 4.3 and estimate that at a density of 2 dwellings per acre, the tributary area of one rail route mile over which an equal average density of trips prevails is about 7.2 square miles. Spread over this area, the 128 passenger boardings represent a demand density of about 18 trip ends per square mile. If at a density of 1 dwelling per net residential acre the tributary area expands to 12 square miles, then the necessary demand density, considering increased rail speed, drops to about 9 trip ends per square mile. Thus, residential densities as low as 1 to 2 dwellings per acre can support commuter rail, if 10 to 20 downtown-bound trips per gross square mile can be found in the area, and if the downtown in question has at least 25 million square feet of office floorspace—equivalent to perhaps 50 to 70 million square feet of total nonresidential floorspace.

As is the case throughout this chapter, the examples presented are conceptual and illustrative, and in no way a substitute for detailed analyses of specific conditions. However, insofar as possible, they are in scale with observed relationships.

6 Summary and Interpretation

TRANSIT USE AND DEVELOPMENT DENSITY

With existing urban development patterns in the United States, it is possible to expand the use of public transit by improving transit service, but the costs are high and the results relatively modest because transit demand elasticities are low.

Cutting *fares* by 50 percent tends to increase the number of transit riders anywhere from 7 to 43 percent, depending on the type of trip and on the size of the urban area. Non-work trips are more sensitive to fares than work trips, and small places with sparse transit use are more sensitive than large cities. This, however, does not mean that fare subsidies are better spent in small, low density places. Riders are concentrated in large and dense cities to such an extent that, with an equal subsidy per rider, the absolute gain in ridership will be much greater there.

Cutting *running time* by 50 percent tends to increase ridership by 14 to 20 percent, while doubling *service frequency* (thereby cutting waiting time by 50 percent) tends to increase ridership by 24 to 77 percent, depending on existing service frequency. On the whole, passengers are more responsive to travel time reductions than to fare reductions. However, if the cost of service improvements is high, situations can arise when more riders per dollar of subsidy can be attracted by lowering fares.

Ridership response to improved amenity is not well quantified, but evidence suggests that fixed rail systems attract more riders than buses under comparable conditions.

Whether a transit agency attracts extra riders by lowering fares or by providing more frequent service, it will as a rule lose more money. Lowering fares has the advantage that the total cost per rider (fare plus subsidy) is lowered. More frequent service means, other things being equal, higher cost per rider. Only higher operating speed offers the intriguing possibility of both greater ridership and lower cost per rider. Yet, attaining higher speed often requires large capital investment, as does replacing buses with a rail line. Thus, expanding service is a rather expensive way of gaining riders. From the transit viewpoint, it

172

is much more "profitable" to gain riders either from restraints on automobile use or from increased density of urban development.

Higher density of urban development acts both to restrain auto use and to encourage the use of public transit. Higher density has two related aspects—greater downtown size and higher residential density. Average figures from a number of urban areas in the United States suggest that:

· At densities between 1 and 7 dwellings per acre, transit use is minimal.

· A density of 7 dwellings per acre appears to be a threshold above which transit use increases sharply.

· At densities above 60 dwellings per acre, more than half the trips tend to be made by public transportation.

· The reduction in auto trips (and total trips) per person and the increase in transit trips with rising density are most pronounced among middle income households. They are somewhat less pronounced among upper income households, who buy more transportation at any density. Low income households make only the most essential trips to begin with, so that rising density affects their total travel least of all; but they do substitute transit trips for auto trips more than others.

Reasons why transit use increases with rising density. The number of cars owned by a household makes by far the greatest difference in its transit use. However, the number of autos per household, in turn, depends not only on family income and the number of persons of driving age, but also on several aspects of development density and transit service:

· Higher residential density tends to cut auto ownership. Comparing households of the same income and size, a tenfold increase in residential density reduces ownership by about 0.4 autos per household. This is so because at higher densities, auto storage and use are less convenient and more costly, and alternative means of travel—including walking—are available.

· The presence of rail transit further suppresses auto ownership. A nearby rapid transit station can have an effect equivalent to more than a tenfold increase in residential density. Proximity to commuter rail in upper income, low density areas also has an effect, though much smaller.

· Auto ownership is further influenced by the habitual destination of the trips a household makes. Two households residing at the same density will own different numbers of autos depending on the nonresidential density at their place of work.

In addition to auto ownership, two further factors affect transit use: the density of the nonresidential destination (the higher it is, the more likelihood that auto owners will use transit); and the quality of transit service (availability of commuter rail, proximity to a rapid transit station, and the frequency of bus service attract auto owners to transit).

The cumulative effect of these interrelated factors explains the *proportion* of travellers who will choose transit between a particular residential area and a nonresidential destination. However, in assessing the *absolute number* of trips to which this proportion is applied, the *distance* between these two places is of key importance. The willingness to make trips falls off very sharply with distance. As a result, trips to a downtown will be found in large numbers only from fairly close proximity to that downtown. In sum, residents will be more likely to use public transportation:

· The higher the density and the larger the size of a downtown or another cluster of nonresidential activity

· The closer their neighborhood is to that nonresidential concentration

· The better the transit service

The higher the residential density of the neighborhood.

The density (which is usually related to size) of the nonresidential concentration is most important, because of its multiple effect of reducing auto ownership of habitual travellers there, restraining auto use by auto owners, and providing conditions for convenient transit service in two ways: by high frequency of service that is necessary to serve large numbers of riders, and by short access walks made possible by compact land use arrangement. The distance from the nonresidential concentration is second in importance. High residential density by itself does little for transit if there is no dominant place to go to.

Examples of land use policies affecting transit use.

The relationships outlined make it possible to estimate the effect of different land use policies on transit use. The figures should be taken as roughly indicative of the magnitude of the effects; the following examples will illustrate.

1. *Clustering or dispersing nonresidential space.* Suppose 10 million square feet are to be added to a growing urban area. One option is to put the floorspace into two highway-oriented nonresidential clusters, each 5 million square feet in size. Another is to create a new downtown of 10 million square feet. In the second case, per capita trips by transit within a 3 to 5 mile radius will be *50 to 70 percent higher* than in the first case, keeping residential density the same.

2. *Enlarging downtown size or raising nearby residential density.* Suppose the options are to double the size of a downtown from 10 to 20 million square feet, or to double the residential density within a few miles of it from 15 to 30 dwellings per acre. The former will increase per capita trips by transit *three to four times more* than the latter.

3. *Increasing residential density near downtown or farther away.* Suppose the options are to double residential density from 5 to 10 dwellings per acre either within one mile of a downtown of 10 million square feet, or at a distance of 10 miles from it. In the first case, public transit trips per capita in the affected area will increase *seventeen times* as much as in the second case.

4. *Scattering apartments or concentrating them near transit.* Suppose a rapid transit station is located 5 miles from a downtown of 50 million square feet of nonresidential floorspace (the size of Newark, N.J.). At a density of 15 dwellings per acre, the square mile surrounding the station will send about 620 trips a day to the downtown by transit. Suppose speculative development scatters apartments throughout the square mile, raising its density by 20 percent. This will increase transit ridership at the station by about 24 percent. Yet, if the apartments are clustered within 2,000 feet of the station, preserving the rest of the neighborhood intact, transit ridership will increase by 34 percent or more; at least a carload of 62 people a day will be added not from any increase in average density within the square mile, but only from a different arrangement of the new development within it.

Thus land use policies which will do most for public transportation are those which will help cluster nonresidential floorspace in downtowns and other compact development patterns. Downtowns of 10 million square feet of gross nonresidential floorspace (the size of White Plains, N.Y. or Stamford, Conn.), if confined within less than one square mile, begin to make moderately frequent bus service possible and to attract an appreciable proportion of trips by transit. By contrast, downtowns of 5 million square feet (between Poughkeepsie, N.Y. and Middletown, N.Y. in size) can support only meager bus service. Spread suburban clusters of nonresidential use can only occasionally support meager bus service, i.e., if they contain shopping centers, or if they are surrounded by residential densities in excess of about 7 dwellings per acre.

Newark, New Jersey, a downtown of 50 million square feet of nonresidential floorspace, of sufficient size for extensive and frequent local bus service, express bus park-and-ride, and a light rail operation.

Photo Public Service Electric & Gas

Bridgeport, Connecticut, a downtown of almost 20 million square feet of nonresidential floorspace, enough for frequent (every 10 minutes) local bus service. Express bus park-and-ride and light rail are questionable.

White Plains, New York, a downtown of over 10 million square feet of nonresidential floorspace. Adequate in size for only intermediate (half-hourly) local bus service.

Paramus, New Jersey, a loose string of highway-oriented shopping centers totalling about 9 million square feet, only partially shown here. Such clusters can support half-hourly local bus service if they are as large as Paramus and hourly service if half as large.

Residential density is less important for transit use than residential location, i.e., proximity to a downtown of substantial size or proximity to a rail transit line. If greater transit use is the goal, it is more important to put housing close to a downtown than to make it high density. In fact, moderate residential densities in the range of 7 to 15 dwellings per acre can support moderately convenient transit service by any of the transit modes reviewed in this book. Of course, densities higher than this will support better service, as well as more trips on foot. Thus, a strongly transit-oriented city such as Montreal has an average density of 35 dwellings per acre; attached two-family houses form an important part of its newly developed neighborhoods. Evidence from the New York Region suggests that the shift from auto to transit diminishes, and reductions in total travel per capita cease, at densities above about 100 dwellings per acre. This density can be represented by 13-story apartment houses covering 20 percent of their site; on transportation grounds, there appears to be no need to exceed this density. It is important to emphasize, though, that a 13-story building located amid open fields will make no contribution to transit; it will only make a contribution if embedded in an existing urban fabric, close to a downtown or to a rail transit station.

TRANSIT COSTS BY MODE

In the near term, the most important policies necessary to control rapidly rising transit costs are not in the area of land use, but rather in the area of labor relations: preventing wages and salaries, but especially pensions and other benefits in the transit industry, from rising at a much faster pace than in the economy as a whole. While great differences in remuneration among different transit operations may make some further adjustments equitable, this has to occur within the framework of some firmly articulated incomes policy.

In the long term, however, if the survival of public transportation is desired, it will be essential to prevent further erosion of ridership by policies other than service expansion, which insures declining productivity, given present elasticities of demand; such alternative policies will have to be sought in areas of auto restraints and land use changes. In the meantime, it is important to see to it that service expansion by different transit modes is tailored to development densities which the different modes can serve most effectively.

Operating and maintenance costs in dollars. Generally, between 70 and 85 percent of the operating and maintenance cost of public transportation is labor cost. The remainder is split about evenly among three categories: energy, materials, and miscellaneous, which includes insurance and non-labor-related taxes.

The all-important labor cost varies widely both geographically and among transit modes. Bus driver wages on the larger systems in the Tri-State New York Region were twice as high as on some small operations. Earnings of railroad employees were two to four times higher than those of taxi drivers. Often, the cost advantage of a particular mode, such as taxicab versus dial-a-bus, or rapid transit versus commuter rail, results not from the technology of the system but from the labor arrangements peculiar to it.

Automation is often advanced as a way of reducing labor costs. In fact, the number of employees per vehicle on automated systems is not much lower than on similar manual ones. Savings in on-board personnel tend to be cancelled by the more demanding maintenance of the complex equipment. However, the automated vehicles do work harder, and with the same labor produce more vehicle miles than manually operated ones, once their various "bugs" are worked out. Still, manpower savings much greater than those of complete automation can be attained on some overstaffed commuter railroads by changing labor rules and by automating fare collection alone.

Because transit operating cost is mostly labor cost and labor is paid by the hour, the *cost per vehicle hour* is a rather stable index which characterizes different transit modes. Adjusting this cost for differences in vehicle *size*, one finds that the operating cost of buses, rapid transit, light rail, and automated light guideway transit vehicles falls into the same range—between about 32¢ and 42¢ per hour to operate a space needed to carry one passenger comfortably (about 6 sq. ft.) in 1974 prices. One might call this the operating cost per seat hour, except the seat is not a physical seat but a space necessary to comfortably accommodate one passenger, seated or standing. On the average, rapid transit tends to be slightly cheaper than the bus in these terms, light guideway transit slightly more expensive, and light rail more expensive than the bus for old equipment, and, it is hoped, less expensive for new. *The important point is that the differences are marginal.* The three modes which stand out above that range are commuter rail (about one and one half times more expensive), dial-a-bus (about twice as expensive), and taxicab (over three times more expensive).

Given similar costs of supplying one unit of capacity for one hour, there are two ways in which the different modes can compete to provide the end product of transportation, namely passenger miles of travel, at the lowest cost: they can attain higher speed; or they can attain higher passenger occupancy.

At higher speed, more miles per hour are produced, so cost per mile is lowered. Yet speed is affected by density of the surrounding development and by the availability of an exclusive right-of-way. Thus, New York City buses in Manhattan operate at 5.7 mph, while on Staten Island they run at 11.7 mph and therefore cost only half as much per mile. Commuter railroads, averaging over 30 mph, deliver capacity-unit miles at an even lower cost, despite their high labor intensity and high wages.

At higher occupancy, more passengers are carried for each vehicle mile, so the cost per passenger mile is lowered. Average transit occupancies are low because of much idle capacity in the reverse direction during peak hours and in both directions during off-peak hours: they range from about 15 percent of total capacity on taxis and some local buses to 28 percent on some commuter rail lines. Obviously, the chances of attaining higher occupancy are greater as development density increases.

With speed and occupancy related to density in opposite ways, the ultimate cost at which a transit system delivers passenger miles depends not just on the system but on the urban environment in which it is used. In the three-state area of New York, New Jersey, and Connecticut in 1974, the *operating cost per passenger mile* stacked up about as follows: taxicabs—about 75¢; dial-a-bus (now defunct)—$1.90; local buses—14¢ to 26¢; light rail—19¢; rapid transit—6¢ to 14¢; express bus—about 8¢ on the average; commuter rail—8¢ to 10¢. Of course, such cost ranges are affected by local circumstances and can change quickly in an inflationary period.

Costs in resources. The dollar cost of the basic resources used for public transportation varies by geography and is extremely volatile over time. Therefore, Exhibit 6.1 portrays selected costs in units of labor, energy, materials, and space. These are mostly based on operating conditions and passenger use typical of the three-state area, which accounts for more than 45 percent of the nation's transit travel.* The resource costs cited are most sensitive to passenger occupancies, listed at the top of Exhibit 6.1, as well as, in the case of land requirements, to overall system use. Both reflect empirical conditions and as such can be preferable to values calculated under assumed conditions.

From the top set of bars it is evident that taxi and dial-a-bus are extremely labor intensive. To produce 1,000 passenger miles of travel, they require 20 to 30 calendar man-days (i.e., man-days including days off) of paid operating and maintenance personnel, compared to 2.5 to 4.0 man-days on local buses and only 1.0 to 2.5 on rapid transit and commuter rail. Because workers on the more productive systems get paid more, the contrast is not so stark when costs are measured in dollars. Of course, the advantage of the auto with regard to paid labor stands out dramatically—as a drive-it-yourself mode, it requires a fraction of one man-day to produce 1,000 person miles of travel.

The second set of bars shows that direct energy consumption for 1,000 person miles travelled by taxicab or dial-a-bus is about twice as high as by auto; by the mass transit modes, it is generally about half as high as by auto. The bus is indicated to be somewhat less energy-intensive than present-day electric modes because it does not have the handicap of thermal energy loss in the production of electricity. With equipment to recover energy losses in braking, such as that tested on New York City subways, efficiency of the electric modes can be improved, perhaps by as much as 20 percent.

The third set of bars shows materials consumption for the replacement of vehicles. Again, the taxicab has the highest cost, much above the auto, while dial-a-bus does better than the auto. The bus consumes about one quarter of the materials used by the auto to produce 1,000 passenger miles of travel. The more durable vehicles of rapid transit and commuter rail, in turn, use only about one quarter of the materials needed for bus replacement.

The fourth set of bars shows space consumption. The space is that occupied by roadway pavement or tracks and excludes both pavement used for off-street parking of autos and the space used by bus garages and rail yards. No distinction is made between space at

---

* For national data on transit energy consumption, see Philip S. Shapiro and Richard H. Pratt, "Energy Conservation Through Transit" (Kensington, Md.: R. H. Pratt Associates, July 1976). The ranges shown in the second set of bars in Exhibit 6.1 are between this source and the New York Region data summarized earlier in Exhibit 3.11. Most other data in Exhibit 6.1, particularly those on land consumption, are specific to the New York Region. To derive the land consumption figures, the 31-county Region was taken to contain 397,952 acres of street and road pavement (60 percent of total land in street rights-of-way), of which 20 percent is assigned to trucks and the remainder allocated similarly, following the relationship space = speed/flow, to autos, buses and taxis. There are also 14.6 acres of light rail trackage and 1,323 acres of rapid transit trackage; 3,270 acres of commuter rail trackage were assumed by assigning a 27-foot average width of route to passenger service. For other sources see Exhibit 3.11.

EXHIBIT 6.1

Resource Use of Transportation Systems

Exhibit assumes the following average occupancies (persons per vehicle):
Auto, 1.5; Taxicab, 0.7; Dial-A-Bus, 1.2; Bus, 11; Light Rail, 10; Rapid Transit, 24; Commuter Rail, 31.

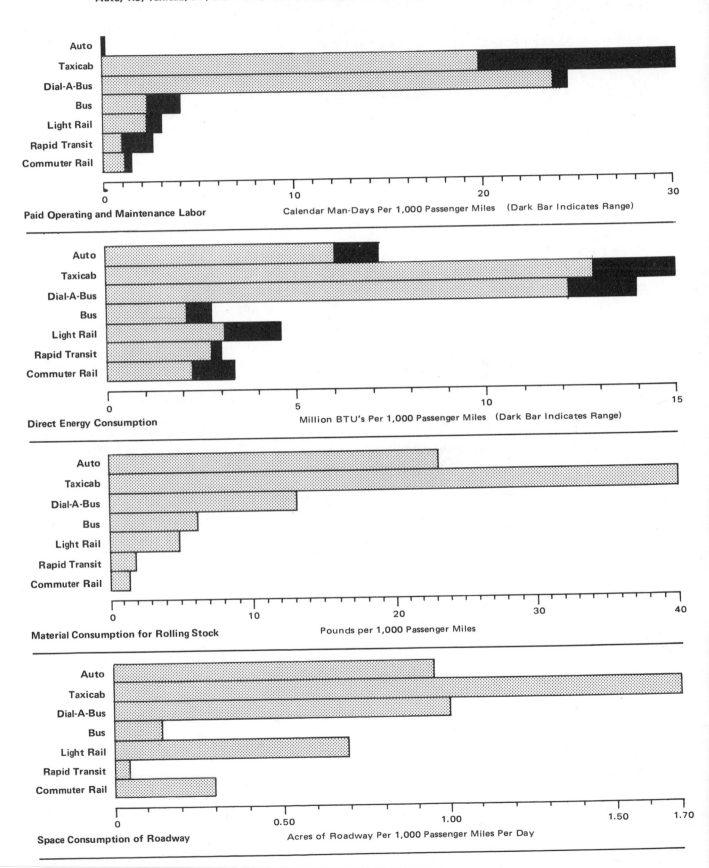

Paid Operating and Maintenance Labor   Calendar Man-Days Per 1,000 Passenger Miles   (Dark Bar Indicates Range)

Direct Energy Consumption   Million BTU's Per 1,000 Passenger Miles   (Dark Bar Indicates Range)

Material Consumption for Rolling Stock   Pounds per 1,000 Passenger Miles

Space Consumption of Roadway   Acres of Roadway Per 1,000 Passenger Miles Per Day

Sources: Principally Exhibits 3.2 and 3.11

grade, above grade or underground. The figures reflect average use over the year, not space needs at maximum capacity, which are much smaller. The space is allocated to exclude freight use of highways and railroads. Once again, the taxicab leads the list with 1.7 acres of pavement used to produce 1,000 passenger miles per weekday. The auto uses just under one acre, commuter rail about one third of an acre, the bus about one sixth, and rapid transit only one twentieth. Light rail, represented in this case by the Newark subway, does worse than other mass transit modes in this instance because of the relatively sparse use of that facility.

Generally, the modes suitable for areas of low density and low demand, namely taxi and dial-a-bus, are very costly in terms of manpower and tend to be actually costlier than the auto in terms of energy and to some extent in terms of materials, at least at currently attainable occupancies. The case for them in preference to the auto cannot be made on environmental grounds, but rather must be made on social grounds, i.e., serving passengers who cannot drive.

By contrast, large-scale systems such as rapid transit and commuter rail tend to be extremely efficient in the use of manpower and materials for vehicles, and quite efficient in the use of energy and space. Yet, for this efficiency to be used, high passenger demand must be present, which requires high density. Where public pressure achieves transit service in low density areas, it is quite possible that resources will be wasted, compared to complete reliance on the auto.

Evaluating capital investment. To determine the full money costs of different modes of transportation, the capital cost of vehicles and guideways must be added to operating cost. Particularly for long-lived equipment, this capital cost will vary greatly depending on the interest rate. Interest rates of 8 to 10 percent, widely used at present, include a hedge against future inflation, against the fact that loans will be repaid in cheaper dollars. In dollars of constant value, the long-term cost of capital is usually reckoned to be around 3 percent, or 4 to 5 percent if a risk that the investment will be abandoned prematurely is accounted for. Yet, inflation affects not only the money with which loans will be repaid, but, so far even more strongly, the transit operating costs. Therefore, if the interest rate is to account for inflation, inflation in operating costs over the lifetime of the investment would have to be accounted for as well, if one wishes to add like and like, operating costs and capital costs. However, calculating future inflation in operating costs is a highly conjectural exercise. It is simpler to work in constant dollars: take operating costs at a point in time as being fixed and add capital costs at an interest rate that does not include future inflation. This certainly rules out interest rates in the 8 to 10 percent range.

Adjusted for a unit of capacity and for length of use, the difference in *dollar costs* between different types *of transit vehicles* is not too great. Generally, the capital cost of rolling stock adds about one tenth to the operating cost per mile of taxis, dial-a-buses, and local buses. For equipment running at high speeds, which has a low operating cost per mile, the capital cost per mile becomes relatively more important; it may add one third to operating cost if a 4 to 5 percent interest rate is assumed. However, these additions essentially leave unchanged the ranking of the different modes based on operating costs alone.

The critical difference in capital costs is in the *costs of building new guideways* for systems which run on exclusive rights-of-way. If that cost is very high and passenger use very low, such systems can become by far the most costly per passenger mile. Therefore, capital investment in guideways must be related to prospective passenger use.

One way of doing that is benefit-cost analysis. However, it can quantify only some of the more obvious transportation-related benefits. Even there, different assumptions about the value of time (a figure that varies in a complex manner over a broad range of values) and about interest rates can lead to widely different conclusions. Broader community-related benefits such as result from placing guideways in tunnels are more difficult to quantify. One can argue that the large extra cost of tunneling is not a transportation investment but an urban design investment and not subject to analysis in transportation benefit-cost terms, much like an urban park, which might not withstand such analysis in recreation terms alone. Also, long-term benefits such as enabling the eventual development of a higher density, resource-conserving urban environment are beyond the reach of benefit-cost analysis in today's dollars.

To avoid the issues of interest rates and hard-to-quantify benefits, one can compare the cost-effectiveness of capital investment among different systems simply by relating it to daily passenger use expected or attained after completion of the project. A sampling of fixed guideway projects recently completed or underway in the United States shows their capital cost to range from $240 to $3,200 per daily passenger mile in constant 1974 dollars. Assuming present ridership levels, New York City subway construction is in the range of $800 to $1,800; BART in San Francisco cost about $1,200 converted into 1974 dollars. This can be a helpful reference for investment elsewhere; presumably the various benefits of the projects have been weighed in the process of political and design decisions.

To get a feel for what investment might be excessive, one can check if a particular route would use more energy indirectly (for construction) and directly (for operation) than would be used if all prospective passengers travelled by auto. Both the energy use per dollar of heavy construction and the direct and indirect energy costs of the auto are approximately known. On that basis one can estimate that if guideway construction cost exceeds about $1,800 per daily passenger mile in constant 1974 dollars, the route will be less energy-efficient than the auto over a 50-year period. Apportioned among travellers over the 50-year period and assuming a 4 percent interest rate, the $1,800 works out to about 27¢ per passenger mile, a yardstick that might seem high unless full energy costs are taken into account. Obviously, both future cost estimates and future patronage estimates can be wrong by a large margin, and decisions cannot be based on cost-effectiveness yardsticks alone; saving energy is not the only purpose of rapid transit.

Because the volumes of transit travel (passenger miles per route mile) vary depending on downtown size, the amount of money that can be invested in one route mile of fixed guideway depends on city size, once a criterion such as $1,800 or any other per-passenger mile figure is assumed. Exhibit 6.2 illustrates how allowable investment per mile of fixed guideway might vary with downtown size assuming $2,000, $1,500, and $1,000 per daily passenger mile as investment yardsticks. Using the middle figure, one can see that a city with a moderate-size downtown of 30 million square feet (about the size of Hartford, Connecticut) might justify only an investment of $10 million per route mile in 1974 dollars; a city with a downtown of close to 100 million square feet of nonresidential

EXHIBIT 6.2

Downtown Size and Estimated per-Mile Expenditure for Fixed Guideways at Three Investment Levels

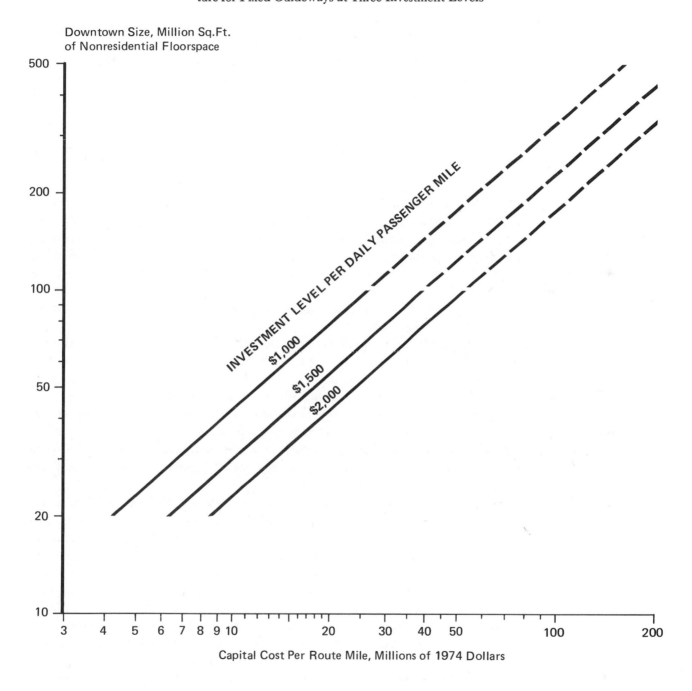

Downtown Size, Million Sq.Ft.
of Nonresidential Floorspace

Capital Cost Per Route Mile, Millions of 1974 Dollars

Note: Based on travel volumes assumed in Exhibit 5.14 for a series of hypothetical cities; dashed lines show extrapolated range.
Costs pertain to full-length radial routes; individual segments may be higher or lower.

floorspace (close to the size of Washington, D.C.) might justify an investment of close to $40 million a mile (which is about what the Washington Metro system actually cost); and in New York City, with the Manhattan Central Business District containing over 500 million square feet of nonresidential floorspace, costs in excess of $200 million per route mile are not out of line. One should emphasize that these relationships are based on the series of hypothetical cities constructed for analyzing fixed-guideway systems in Chapter 5 earlier; travel volumes in specific corridors of real cities may depart widely from the assumed figures, especially if topography concentrates travel only in a few corridors. Exhibit 6.2 is in no way definitive, but is only designed to illustrate how the scale of construction might change if it is related to passenger use in a consistent manner.

WHAT TRANSIT MODE FOR WHAT DENSITY?

The question, "What density of transit service can be supported by what density of development?" cannot be answered in general terms, but only after a large number of variables defining the particular context have been specified. Nevertheless, one can construct more or less "average" hypothetical situations and calculate what transit mode and what level of service fit what density under specified assumptions. One can also compare these to empirical examples. The answers are not precise, but they do show relationships that are useful. The underlying methodology, detailed in the Appendix, allows the interested reader to pursue further analysis on his own.

The Taxicab. While taxis are most conspicuous in dense downtown areas where they in large part compete with other public transportation, their services are more essential in low density areas and small communities, where they often represent the only feasible mode of public transit. At an operating cost of about $6.00 per vehicle hour in 1974 prices, and at a typical cost per passenger of $2.00, a taxicab needs a productivity of 3 passenger boardings per hour to break even. Within a service area of more than a dozen square miles, 3 boardings per hour can be found even at very low rural-suburban densities. Even in such environments, however, taxi stands are typically located near points of highest demand, such as shopping places, rail or bus stations.

The dial-a-bus. This represents an effort to lower the high per passenger cost of a taxi by encouraging group riding. This presupposes a density sufficiently high so that several people with similar origins and destinations can be found at any one place and time. In practice, in an operation between many origins and many destinations, dial-a-bus productivities are not much higher than those of taxis—between 4 and 9 passenger boardings per vehicle hour. This would lead to a lower cost per passenger only if the operating cost per vehicle hour were no different from that of a taxicab. In reality, it tends to be higher because of the need for more supporting personnel, but mostly because of different labor contracts with the more professional drivers; this high labor cost tends to cancel out the gains from greater productivity.

Based on existing experience, *dial-a-bus in a service between many origins and many destinations* can carry passengers at a cost lower than the taxi only if the wage rates are such that the cost per vehicle hour is less than twice that of local taxis. In that case, such dial-a-bus service may be applicable at residential densities *above 6 dwellings per acre,* which is about where 6 passengers can be found by a vehicle in an hour within a relatively confined service area (typically less than a dozen square miles). If wage rates are higher, then social purposes, such as providing mobility to transit-dependents in areas where other public transit is inadequate, could be served at a lower cost by offering them subsidized rides on local taxis. One might note that allowing ride-sharing on taxis in service from many origins to many destinations will not lower taxi costs appreciably, because the probability of shared rides is low.

Conditions are quite different for *fixed-destination and subscription services*. These begin to resemble a fixed-route, rather than completely demand-responsive service, and can attain substantially more passenger boardings per vehicle hour. In the first case, groups of passengers are assured at such places as shopping centers or railroad stations; in the second case, a predictable pattern of trips is served each day and vehicles can be scheduled to use their capacity most effectively. At costs per vehicle hour twice those of taxicabs, fixed-destination and subscription services appear to be competitive with taxis in cost per passenger at *densities above 3.5 dwellings per acre;* at operating costs thrice those of taxis, above about 5 dwellings per acre. Also, allowing ride-sharing on taxis in situations where many people are going to or from one place can lower their cost appreciably.

In sum, dial-a-bus, a new mode that has received much public and technical attention, offers little promise for ubiquitous, taxi-like service, given present labor arrangements. The densities it requires for such service are higher than most new suburbs have, and at such densities, acceptable fixed-route bus service becomes possible, except in very small urban places. The application of dial-a-bus seems to be mostly limited to feeder service to other public transit, and to prearranged subscription services. In many low density suburban situations, subsidizing taxicabs for particular groups of riders would be more effective than introducing new dial-a-bus systems. Among the numerous dial-a-bus systems that have been tried, only those with a heavy emphasis on fixed-destination and subscription service have attained costs per passenger lower than those of taxis.

Jitney service. A nonscheduled operation along a fixed route, jitney service is not investigated in this study. Conceptually, however, jitneys are *not a mode for low density areas.* They require densities similar to those of local buses with a rather frequent schedule, otherwise the waiting time becomes excessive. Surviving jitneys in the United States operate in such higher density environments as downtown San Francisco, Pittsburgh, and Atlantic City.

Local bus. Scheduled local buses cost $11 to $22 per vehicle hour to operate in 1974 prices, but provided travel at a cost between 30¢ and 75¢ per passenger—substantially lower than taxicab or dial-a-bus for a trip of similar length. The key to keeping this cost low is high vehicle productivity—the ratio of density of demand to the density of service. Empirically, local bus productivities in the New York Region range from a low of 27 passenger boardings per vehicle hour in some suburban areas to a high of 52 in Manhattan.

A vehicle productivity of about 30 passenger boardings per vehicle hour is widely accepted as a minimum standard for local buses, but the question at what density a bus can find 30 passengers, on the average, within an hour is not a simple one to answer; empirically, it ranges from 2 to 10 dwellings per acre, depending on numerous conditions, such as fare, service frequency, size of downtown, distance from downtown, length of a route, the shape of the density gradient along it, and the presence of nonresidential use other than that in the major downtown.

With average demand densities prevailing in the New York Region outside New York City, enough bus passengers can be found to provide *"minimum" bus service* (20 runs per direction per day with half-mile parallel route spacing) at a density of *4 dwellings per acre;*

"intermediate" bus service (40 runs under the same conditions) at 7 dwellings per acre; and "frequent" bus service (120 runs or 10-minute average service frequency) at 15 dwellings per acre.

In any particular municipality, however, conditions may depart significantly from these region-wide averages. Thus the town of Westport, Conn., provides the equivalent of "minimum" service (one bus every half hour over 14 hours with 1.5 route miles per square mile) at a density as low as 2 dwellings per acre. This is due to exceptional demand conditions, including, among others, the fact that the rider pays only 15¢ of the 65¢ cost per ride in 1974 prices, and mostly through pre-purchased annual passes. Though the subsidy for the fixed-route, scheduled "minny-buses" in Westport is high, it is substantially below that of most dial-a-bus services, which operate in areas of much higher density.

In contrast to Westport, the city of Poughkeepsie, N.Y., was able to support the equivalent of "minimum" service (half-hourly over only 12 hours with denser spacing of 2.4 route miles per square mile) at a density of 11 dwellings per acre and at a cost lower than Westport (39¢ per ride) not because of higher vehicle productivity but only because of lower wage rates. The demand level in Poughkeepsie is only moderately below "average" conditions, considering that it is, unlike Westport, outside the Manhattan commutershed and that its downtown is small, about 5 million square feet of nonresidential floorspace.

An effort to relate the "minimum," "intermediate," and "frequent" bus service levels to residential densities located at different distances from downtowns of different sizes is presented in Exhibit 5.8 in the preceding chapter. As stated in the accompanying discussion, the Exhibit deals only with trips to the downtowns in question, omitting possible intermediate travel opportunities, and the distances for feasible bus service it lists are only valid if the density gradient is flat. If residential density changes with distance from a downtown, local bus service to areas substantially beyond the distances shown there is possible.

Under some arbitrary but realistic assumptions about density gradients and route lengths, the costs of local bus service to downtowns of different sizes are explored in Exhibits 5.9 and 5.10. Such an exercise suggests that downtown sizes of less than 5 million square feet can only support very low service frequencies over very short route lengths. In the downtown size range between 5 and 35 million square feet, a variety of services become reasonable.

The "minimum" frequency (20 runs per day with half-mile route spacing or its equivalent) appears to provide service at the lowest cost to a downtown of about 10 million square feet (White Plains, N.Y.). Smaller downtowns have insufficient demand to fill the buses at that frequency, so cost rises, but it is still within reason for a downtown of 5 million square feet.

As downtown size rises above 10 million square feet, "minimum" service becomes insufficient to satisfy peak hour demand; more buses must be added, until the service becomes an "intermediate" one. At about 35 million square feet (Hartford, Conn.) "frequent" service becomes necessary.

With rising downtown size, the surrounding residential density rises, so bus operating speed declines, making local bus operations to the larger downtowns more costly. This rise in local bus costs to downtowns above about 20 million and particularly to those above 50 million square feet leads to the consideration of transit modes other than local buses for the larger downtowns.

One should add that the ability of shopping-oriented spread clusters of nonresidential use to support local bus service does not differ much from that of small downtowns (generally below 5 million square feet of nonresidential floorspace). By contrast, highway-oriented spread clusters of mixed use (factories, offices, as well as some retailing and wholesaling) attract only about half as many transit trips as downtowns do and therefore cannot support any bus service on their own unless surrounded by residential densities in excess of about 7 dwellings per acre. They can, of course, receive some service from routes serving a nearby downtown.

Express bus. The bus hours needed to provide any given frequency of peak-period express service are not neatly related to density, as in the case of local buses, but depend on freeway availability, the degree of downtown congestion, and on the length of a route. The density at which enough passengers—predominantly peak-period travellers to work—can be found to use the buses strongly depends on whether access to the buses is on foot or by auto.

Under different assumptions of downtown size, distance from downtown, operating speed, and cost per passenger mile (to account for differences in trip length), the feasibility of different express bus frequencies from areas of different residential density is explored in Exhibit 5.11 for buses approached on foot, and in Exhibit 5.12 for park-and-ride arrangements.

These calculations suggest that express buses with access on foot can operate only at very low frequencies, require residential densities of around 15 dwellings per acre in the collection area, and can, at prevailing costs per passenger mile (not over 10¢ in 1974 prices) serve only very large downtowns, those with more than 50 million square feet of nonresidential floorspace. In fact, the major existing walk-to-express-bus operations are located in the Washington area and in the Manhattan commutershed in New York and New Jersey.

By contrast, the park-and-ride express bus operation collects passengers from a large tributary area and can be supported in a variety of situations. The minimum frequency of 5 buses in a two-hour peak period will work for residential densities of around 4 dwellings per acre up to 20 miles distant from a downtown of 50 million square feet (the size of Newark, N.J.), 15 miles distant from a downtown of 35 million square feet (Hartford, Conn.), or 5 miles from a downtown of 20 million square feet (Bridgeport, Conn.). A higher frequency of 10 buses in the two-hour peak period can also be supported for this range of downtown sizes if residential densities are higher and distances to downtown shorter. Thus, park-and-ride service by express bus appears broadly applicable to a wide range of medium-sized downtowns; however, it becomes difficult for downtown sizes of 20 million square feet or less.

Empirical evidence in Connecticut supports these calculations. Hartford, with a downtown of some 35 million square feet (including 7.4 million square feet of office space) supports a healthy array of park-and-ride express bus routes; by contrast, New Haven, with 26 million square feet of nonresidential floorspace (of which 3.6 million square feet are offices) supports two express routes, only one of which has developed reasonable patronage. Other Connecticut downtowns, with fewer than 20 million square feet, do not have express bus service.

Light rail. The promise of reduced operating cost with new, larger vehicles and the amenity of tracked, electric operation have led to a renewed interest in light rail. One possible application is the substitution of light rail cars for ordinary railroad equipment on some lightly used commuter lines. With their much lower operating cost (due largely to different labor arrangements), light rail cars on such routes could attain greater frequency and attract more passengers. The conversion of the Riverside Line in Boston in 1959 is often cited as a prototype: it increased ridership on the line tenfold.

More broadly, light rail on reserved rights of way is viewed as a junior form of rapid transit, one that can be built at a lower cost because there is no need for full grade separation, geometric standards are less stringent, stations are much less elaborate, power supply and signalling are simpler. In exploring the suitability of light rail to different size downtowns, three questions must be asked: Do the large vehicles provide adequate service frequency? What is their operating cost per passenger mile? Can the line be built at a cost that is within reason?

The answers are based on the hypothetical travel corridors to four downtown sizes portrayed in Exhibit 5.14. It appears that even a downtown of 20 million square feet (somewhat smaller than New Haven, Conn.) can support a respectable service frequency, i.e., 12 runs in the peak hour, of the new Standard Light Rail Vehicles on a radial route. A downtown of 50 million square feet would require 24 two-car trains during the peak hour. Thus, even with vehicles twice the size of buses, insufficient frequency does not seem to be a problem at any of the downtown sizes tested.

Assuming speeds (including an allowance for layover time at terminals) in the 15 mph to 20 mph range and a cost per vehicle hour of $28.50 in 1974 dollars, the cost per passenger mile falls into a reasonable range of 7¢ to 10¢, and the cost per passenger into the 31 to 34¢ range, much superior to local buses. These results stem from a large number of boardings per vehicle hour, attained by a combination of high speed, high passenger demand in the band adjoining the route (rapid transit-like demand levels are assumed for this band), and a large tributary area beyond: roughly one third of the patrons are calculated to arrive from outside the one-mile band within which access to stations on foot is possible. Averaged over the entire tributary area, the demand densities for the downtowns of 20, 35, and 50 million square feet are moderate: about 150 passengers originating per square mile. However, averaged the same way, the supply density is very low: less than 2 vehicle hours in one direction per square mile. This results in high vehicle productivity and low cost per passenger. One might note that on light rail and rapid transit systems, vehicle productivities in the range between 60 and 80 passenger boardings per vehicle hour are quite common.

The promising findings outlined above are dampened, however, if one looks at capital costs of guideway construction. As indicated in Exhibit 6.2, a downtown of 20 million square feet will hardly warrant an expenditure of more than $7 million a mile, which will build a light rail line only if a conveniently located right-of-way is in place. By contrast, a downtown of 50 million square feet might warrant an expenditure of $17.5 million a mile, which might allow some heavy construction such as a short tunnel for downtown access.

Thus, light rail seems promising for downtowns in the 35 to 50 million square foot range, generally found in metropolitan areas of more than three-quarter million inhabitants. Under fortuitous circumstances of existing rights-of-way, individual lines may be workable to downtowns as small as 20 million square feet. Averaged over the length of the route, residential densities of 9 to 12 dwellings per acre can be served.

Light Guideway Transit. In line-haul applications, the present generation of light guideway transit would appear to fit downtowns in the 35 to 50 million square foot range, the same as light rail. Ideally, the key advantage of the small cars, namely their ability to provide very frequent (or even demand responsive) service, particularly during off-peak hours, would be even more useful for downtowns of less than 25 million square feet. However, at any of these downtown sizes, the capital cost of light guideway construction is far above an acceptable range. For larger downtown sizes, where the passenger volume could justify the high capital cost, the present generation of light guideway systems lacks the capacity to carry these higher volumes.

For the time being, light guideway systems seem to be limited to special applications over fairly short distances which lack sharp peaks in demand, not to line-haul use with its high peaks. Much research in light guideways is directed toward attaining shorter headways between vehicles and hence peak period capacity competitive with traditional rail systems. A more promising thrust would seem to be to greatly simplify the design of the guideways and of the appurtenant hardware so that capital costs can be reduced to a level where light guideways could economically serve modest traffic volumes below the reach of traditional transit. A related aim would be to reduce the visual bulk of the elevated guideways to improve their community acceptance.

Standard Rapid Transit. Standard rapid transit comes into its own where travel volumes are sufficiently high so that vehicle operation in trains, rather than singly, can still provide a reasonably attractive frequency, and where travel distances are such as to require speeds higher than those light rail or light guideway can provide. It becomes necessary when travel volumes exceed the capacity of these other modes.

Thus, rapid transit appears inappropriate for downtowns of less than 50 million square feet of nonresidential floorspace, because at these downtown sizes the economies of train operation cannot be fully realized without sacrificing service frequency. On the grounds of capital cost, referring to Exhibit 6.2, rapid transit to a downtown of 50 million square feet of total nonresidential floorspace appears to be a touch-and-go proposition. Generally speaking, a downtown size larger than that, closer to 100 million square feet, seems needed both to attain frequent service with reasonably long trains and to make the capital investment cost effective. At downtown sizes above 100 million square feet of nonresidential floorspace, the travel volume on a radial trunkline just about reaches the capacity of light rail, making rapid transit necessary above that point. Just as with light rail, as long as the attraction of a large downtown is present and as long as access to stations by feeder modes exists, moderate residential densities—averaging perhaps 12 dwellings per acre over the tributary area of a route—can support rapid transit.

Among American downtowns served by rapid transit, Chicago has over 280 million, Washington about 95 million, Montreal 91 million, and Toronto over 75 million square feet of *total nonresidential floorspace.* Because total nonresidential floorspace figures for many downtowns are not readily available, and because rapid transit ridership may be more closely related to *office floorspace,* empirical comparisons of rapid transit ridership and office floorspace in Central Business Districts can be useful. (Downtown, as defined in this study, represents a contiguous area of nonresidential use; Central Business Districts are typically smaller and represent the core of a downtown.) Under existing conditions, Central Business Districts with less than 15 million square feet of *office floorspace* tend to generate rather meager transit use—about 80,000 daily riders or less, which is enough to fill two rather lightly used transit spokes. As of 1970, there were only about half a dozen Central Business Districts in North America which had more than 15 million square feet of office space and which did not have rapid transit in operation or under construction. One of them was Atlanta, which started construction in 1975; the others were Los Angeles, Detroit, Pittsburgh, Dallas, and Houston. Baltimore was on the borderline, but had above-average residential density.

One should add that while downtown size is a much better criterion of transit feasibility than population size, it is by no means the only one. The shape of the urbanized area plays an important role: if topography squeezes settlement and travel into a few narrow corridors, the chances for fixed guideway transit are better than when development is spread over a featureless plain.

Commuter Rail. Opportunities for the expansion of commuter rail into presently unserved territory depend on the presence of rail lines which can be upgraded at moderate capital expenditure and which lead to a very large central business district—one with more than 20 to 25 million square feet of *office floorspace*. Where such lines can be found, the residential density needed to support a commuter rail line is very low because of dependence on auto access to stations and of the relatively infrequent nature of the service.

For example, to provide 20 six-car trains a day at a speed of 37 mph requires the expenditure of 3.2 car hours per route mile. At a vehicle productivity of 40 passenger boardings per hour, typical of commuter rail, this train frequency would require 128 passenger boardings per route mile to support it. The residential density would have to be fairly high if all of the 128 passengers were to live within walking distance. In reality, they may come from an area of 7 square miles if the density is 2 dwellings per acre, and 12 square miles if the density is 1 dwelling per acre. As a result, residential densities as low as 1 to 2 dwellings per acre can support commuter rail if about 10 to 20 trips per day can be found originating per square mile in a residential area and destined to a very large downtown.

In conclusion, the approximate ranges of downtown size for which different transit modes and service levels appear worthy of consideration are summarized in Exhibit 6.3. The dashed bars suggest feasibility under unusual conditions. Specific cities are listed in the Exhibit only to give examples of different downtown sizes; the relationships are derived from average land use-travel relationships within the New York Region, and no effort was made to compare them systematically to actual downtown-bound travel volumes in different cities across the nation; nevertheless, the results closely resemble downtown-bound travel analyses by others, as for example Herbert S. Levinson.[1]

The lower thresholds of residential density which can support a given transit service are much more variable than downtown sizes; approximate indications of the ranges and of the conditions on which they depend are summarized briefly in Exhibit 6.4.

The findings of the study generate some skepticism about the future of two new modes which have received wide publicity: dial-a-bus and light guideway transit. They also indicate the very limited applicability of commuter rail, conventional rapid transit, and express buses with access on foot; under North American conditions, all three of these modes are limited to the very largest cities, most of which have systems in being.

By contrast, express buses with park-and-ride access have very broad potential application throughout the range of medium-sized cities; also, the possibilities for light rail with only partially grade-separated rights-of-way appear much greater than commonly assumed. There may be 30 or so urban areas in the United States where light rail could merit consideration. Whether or not it turns out to be feasible will strongly depend on local conditions, such as the shape of the city and the existence of conveniently located rights-of-way. New, simplified models of light guideway transit, such as the two-in-one guideway, may well be competitive with light rail in these urban areas.

In view of the limited possibilities for full-scale new rapid transit systems in the United States, focusing rapid transit investment on the extension and upgrading of existing systems in the largest cities with heavy transit use would appear to be much more cost effective. The needs for track rehabilitation, station reconstruction,[2] and the completion of several remaining routes, which would bring old systems in New York, Chicago, Philadelphia, and Boston up to the level of the newest ones, are huge, and can usefully absorb very large amounts of money, benefiting large numbers of urban residents.

The construction costs of new rail lines—whether rapid transit or light rail—are high in conventional transportation terms. But they are justifiable, up to a point, by long-term conservation of energy and other physical resources that will come about both from the use of

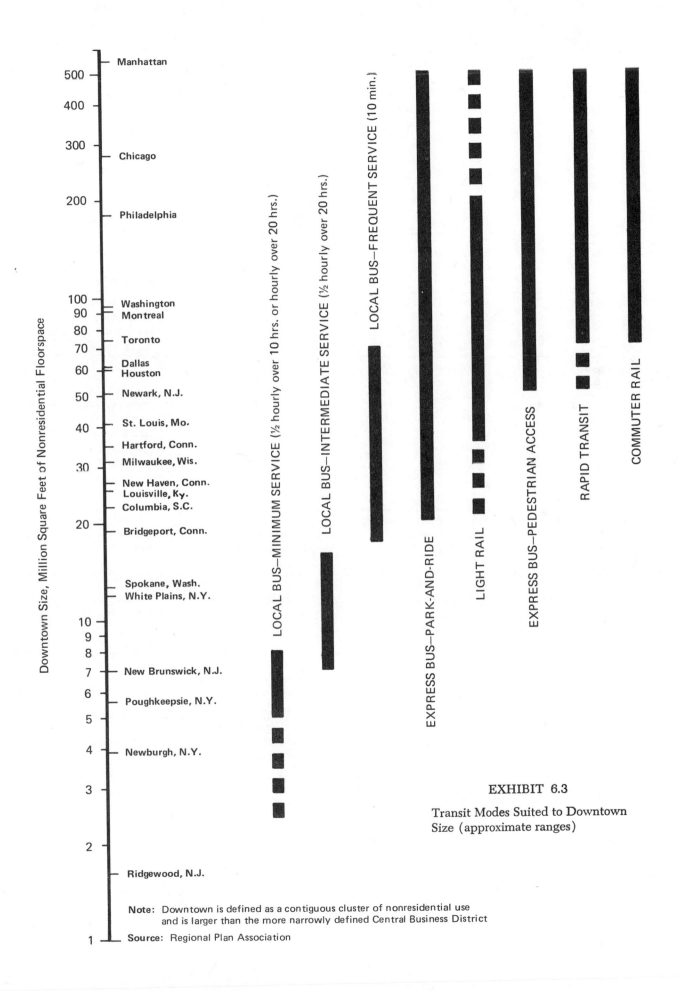

EXHIBIT 6.3

Transit Modes Suited to Downtown Size (approximate ranges)

Downtown Size, Million Square Feet of Nonresidential Floorspace

500 — Manhattan

300 — Chicago

200 — Philadelphia

100 — Washington
90 — Montreal
80 —
70 — Toronto
60 — Dallas / Houston
50 — Newark, N.J.
40 — St. Louis, Mo.
      — Hartford, Conn.
30 — Milwaukee, Wis.
      — New Haven, Conn. / Louisville, Ky.
      — Columbia, S.C.
20 — Bridgeport, Conn.

      — Spokane, Wash.
      — White Plains, N.Y.
10 —
9 —
8 —
7 — New Brunswick, N.J.
6 — Poughkeepsie, N.Y.
5 —
4 — Newburgh, N.Y.
3 —

2 —

      — Ridgewood, N.J.

LOCAL BUS—MINIMUM SERVICE (½ hourly over 10 hrs. or hourly over 20 hrs.)

LOCAL BUS—INTERMEDIATE SERVICE (½ hourly over 20 hrs.)

LOCAL BUS—FREQUENT SERVICE (10 min.)

EXPRESS BUS—PARK-AND-RIDE

LIGHT RAIL

EXPRESS BUS—PEDESTRIAN ACCESS

RAPID TRANSIT

COMMUTER RAIL

1 —

Note: Downtown is defined as a contiguous cluster of nonresidential use and is larger than the more narrowly defined Central Business District

Source: Regional Plan Association

EXHIBIT 6.4

Transit Modes Related to Residential
Density

Mode	Service	Minimum Necessary Residential Density (dwelling units per acre)	Remarks
Dial-a-bus	Many origins to many destinations	6	Only if labor costs are not more than twice those of taxis
Dial-a-bus	Fixed destination or subscription service	3.5 to 5	Lower figure if labor costs twice those of taxis; higher if thrice those of taxis
Local bus	"Minimum," ½ mile route spacing, 20 buses per day	4	Average, varies as a function of downtown size and distance from residential area to downtown
Local bus	"Intermediate," ½ mile route spacing, 40 buses per day	7	
Local bus	"Frequent," ½ mile route spacing, 120 buses per day	15	
Express bus —reached on foot	Five buses during two hour peak period	15 Average density over two square mile tributary area	From 10 to 15 miles away to largest downtowns only
Express bus —reached by auto	Five to ten buses during two hour peak period	3 Average density over 20 square mile tributary area	From 10 to 20 miles away to downtowns larger than 20 million square feet of nonresidential floorspace
Light rail	Five minute headways or better during peak hour.	9 Average density for a corridor of 25 to 100 square miles	To downtowns of 20 to 50 million square feet of nonresidential floorspace
Rapid transit	Five minute headways or better during peak hour.	12 Average density for a corridor of 100 to 150 square miles	To downtowns larger than 50 million square feet of nonresidential floorspace
Commuter rail	Twenty trains a day	1 to 2	Only to largest downtowns, if rail line exists

Source: Regional Plan Association

Two views of low density single-family housing with fewer than three dwellings per acre—a residential density generally too low to support any transit except taxicabs or park-and-ride express bus or commuter rail to a very large downtown.

Seven dwellings per acre, represented by single-family houses on 60 × 100 foot lots. On the average, this represents the threshold of transit-supporting density, allowing about half-hourly local bus service.

the facilities themselves and from the more compact urban environment that they will make possible. To insure that this result comes about, it behooves the public to see to it that land use policy is made supportive of transportation policy.

A good place to start would be with transportation subsidies, not only for capital construction, but also for operating assistance. These are disproportionately available to areas of low density and low riding per capita. Thus, in 1975 the so-called Section 5 funds allocated under the 1974 National Mass Transportation Assistance Act provided 2.8¢ per passenger for the New York portion of the New York-Northeastern New Jersey urbanized area and 45.0¢ per passenger for the Grand Rapids, Michigan urbanized area. Transit-oriented cities such as Pittsburgh, Baltimore, New Orleans, Atlanta, Boston, Philadelphia, Chicago all received less than the national average allocation.[3] Hand in hand with this policy of favoring transit use in those areas where it is least feasible is the emphasis on "para-transit" such as dial-a-bus systems, some of which required over three times as much subsidy per passenger mile as the most expensive rapid transit construction. High-frequency local public transit service is possible even in very low density areas. It is just that the amount of subsidy would have to be 10 to 50 times more than it is at present. A basic decision must be made about whether to perpetuate or to change ongoing land development patterns.

Thus, a report prepared by the U.S. Congress Office of Technology Assessment states: "Federal actions could seek to establish strong linkages between existing community development programs and transit programs in order to effect a coordinated national urban growth management policy. . . . Capital grants for sewerage systems and water supply systems could be tied to the availability of transit services. . . . Mortgages and subsidies for community development in fringe areas could be oriented toward multiuse, clustered activity centers related to transit. . . . Organized and systematic policies for public investment in infrastructure . . . could serve as an effective lever to guide and manage growth. . . .

Ten dwellings per acre, shown here as either detached houses on 40 × 100 foot lots or attached units with pooled open space. This density can generally support half-hourly or more frequent local bus service; if it prevails over a wide area in a corridor leading to a major downtown, a light rail or rapid transit line may be supported. The suppression of auto ownership tends to become pronounced at densities above this level.

Fifteen dwellings per acre, shown here in attached units and in garden apartments with pooled open space, can support a wide array of transit services, if there is a downtown to go to.

Even six-story apartment houses will not support any transit if they are isolated, far from a nonresidential concentration, as shown here in a semi-rural area of northern New York. In an urban context, however, the same six-story buildings with enough open space to average 25 dwellings per acre begin to provide enough ridership to support walk-to-rapid-transit service, as shown in outer Queens.

An ideal arrangement is an alternation of highs and lows that relates directly to bus routes and rapid transit stations while offering a choice of housing types, as seen in the upper view in Toronto. Densities of 140 dwellings per acre can still be pleasantly designed, as in the Manhattan development in the lower view. The 20-story buildings, inhabited by small households, leave 84 percent of the site in a park-like setting. However, both the reduction in auto use and the increase in transit use appear to diminish at densities above 100 dwellings per acre.

Major public policy initiatives are required which would respond to the interrelationship between development and transit."[4]

Such policy initiatives will most likely require both legal prohibitions against spreading potentially transit-supporting development—such as office buildings and multi-family housing—through low density areas, and changes in real estate taxes, with a shift toward land value taxation: "Rapid transit development is inevitably an act of restructuring the city. Knowing this, . . . traction magnates became wealthy in the early years of this century not so much through revenues from their trolleys . . . but mainly by selling and developing real estate along the routes. Allowing the implementing agency to share in the increased value created by . . . transportation investment . . . could help insure that transit is effective in two important respects—meeting broad urban transportation needs and acting as a catalyst for a beneficially restructured urban environment."[5]

Appendix

Procedures for Estimating Public Transit Demand

MEASURES OF DEVELOPMENT DENSITY

By far the most common measure of development density is gross population density, that is, the total population of a political jurisdiction divided by the total land area within its boundaries. Widely used in Census statistics, it is useful for portraying population distribution on a national basis, but its use for urban analysis can be misleading, as indicated in the Introduction. The total land area of a political jurisdiction may include widely varying amounts of open land, depending on where the boundaries are drawn. Hence gross density is a poor estimator of the density of land which is actually in urban use. Only if the boundaries are totally within the built-up area of an urban region does gross population density approximate the density of developed land.

Population density of developed land excludes from the denominator land which is not in urban use, such as forest, agricultural, or vacant land. If public open space, such as parks and semi-public reservations, is also excluded, then the term usually employed is *density of built-up land.* This is the measure shown within the box in Exhibit 0.1. It defines quite well the character of urban development and the nature of transportation requirements, subject of course to the caveat that the *average* built-up density of an entire urban area says nothing about the internal distribution of people and activities. Since the distribution of residential and nonresidential uses is uneven, further differentiation of the density of built-up land is useful.

Net residential density excludes from the denominator the area in streets and other rights of way (rail, etc.), and the area in lots with nonresidential buildings. Typically, the remaining area in residential lots represents anywhere from 30 to 70 percent of the built-up land, averaging 62 percent in the New York Region. The share of the built-up land devoted to residential use increases with declining density, so that the relationship between built-up density and residential density is relatively predictable, as seen in Exhibit 7.1.

EXHIBIT 7.1

Conversion Chart for Selected
Measures of Development Density

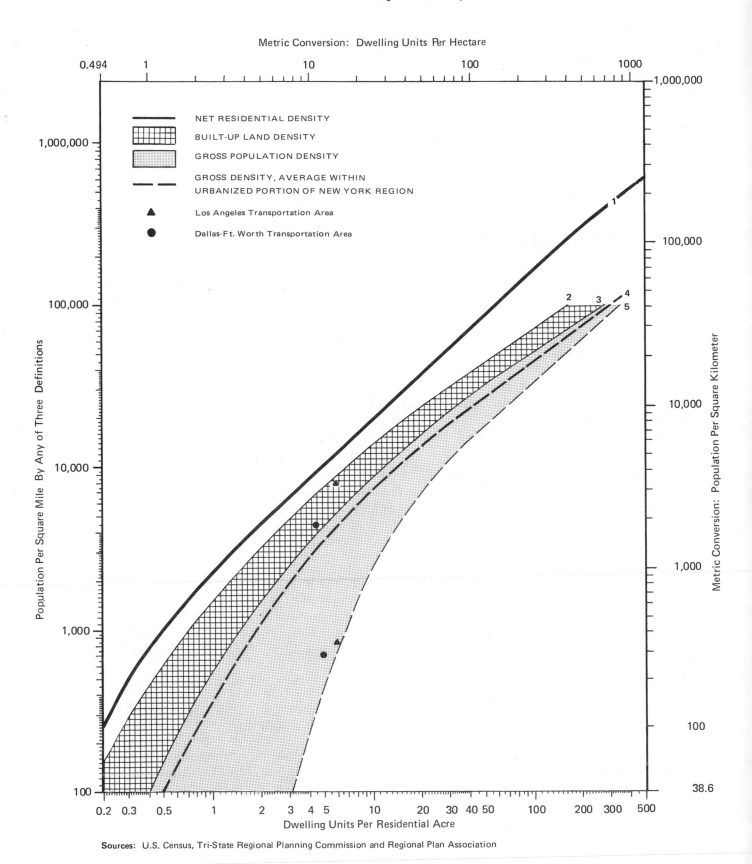

Metric Conversion: Dwelling Units Per Hectare

NET RESIDENTIAL DENSITY

BUILT-UP LAND DENSITY

GROSS POPULATION DENSITY

GROSS DENSITY, AVERAGE WITHIN
URBANIZED PORTION OF NEW YORK REGION

▲ Los Angeles Transportation Area

● Dallas-Ft. Worth Transportation Area

Population Per Square Mile By Any of Three Definitions

Metric Conversion: Population Per Square Kilometer

Dwelling Units Per Residential Acre

Sources: U.S. Census, Tri-State Regional Planning Commission and Regional Plan Association

Dwelling unit density shows net residential density in terms of dwelling units, rather than people, per unit of land. Two variables influence its relationship to the population density. One is the average household size, which may vary from 3.4 persons per household on one-acre lots in the United States of the 1970s, to as few as 1.6 persons per household in apartment neighborhoods, such as some in Manhattan. The other variable is the vacancy rate, which is low in single-family houses, but can be substantial in multi-family apartments. Building and zoning regulations are typically expressed in dwelling units per acre; because of their greater permanence and predictability, dwelling units are generally a more tangible measure for planning purposes and have been widely used in this book.

Exhibit 7.1 enables the reader to convert the density measures enumerated into dwelling units per net residential acre, or per net residential hectare, since metric scales are also included in the exhibit. The chart is calibrated on 1963 and 1970 population and land use data for the New York Region, but is also applicable to other urban areas in the United States at present, as the observations for Los Angeles and Dallas-Ft. Worth (shown by dots) suggest.

The chart* makes three points. First, the population density of net residential land is very firmly related to the dwelling unit density, and the two can be used interchangeably, with the help of the top curve in Exhibit 7.1. That curve, of course, is largely a function of the average U.S. household size in 1970 (as well as of the distribution of household sizes and vacancy rates over the range of densities), and has dropped over time, pushing the other curves downward as well. Hence, the curves should not be applied to historical statistics or to data from other countries without appropriate adjustment. Second, the built-up land density can be predicted, with a moderate amount of leeway, from the density of dwellings. The upward bulge in the built-up density curve is indicative of the greater share of land devoted to residential purposes at middle and lower densities. Third, gross population density is, as was stressed before, a very poor estimator of residential density because of the widely varying amounts of vacant land encompassed. However, within largely urbanized areas, the proportion of non-built-up land (mostly parks and vacant areas) increases on the average quite regularly with declining density and therefore the fourth curve in Exhibit 7.1 can be used fairly reliably for converting gross density into net. Residential density measures of counties and other sub-areas of the New York Region are listed for reference in Exhibit 7.2.

Floorspace density of nonresidential land. Apart from residential lots, built-up land consists of circulation areas (mostly streets) and nonresidential areas. Nonresidential areas are those where people come together for purposes which brought them into an urban area to begin with—work, study, shopping, and so on. While the people density of residential areas is easy to determine, the people density of nonresidential land is more difficult to pinpoint.

---

* An example of using the conversion chart is as follows. Entering at left say at 1,000 and reading across to the first curve and then down, we see that 1,000 people per square mile means 0.5 dwellings per acre if the density refers to net residential land only. Similarly, reading to the second and third curves and then down we see that 1,000 people per square mile of *built-up land* can mean anywhere from 0.8 to 1.5 dwellings per acre of net residential land. Lastly, by reading across to the fourth and fifth curves and then down, we see that 1,000 people per *gross square mile* means 2 dwellings per acre on the average in predominantly urbanized areas, but it can mean as much as 7 dwellings per acre if the boundary of the gross land area is more loosely defined. Reading the chart from the bottom up and then across to the left, one can see what ranges of gross density or built-up land density correspond to what net residential densities.

EXHIBIT 7.2

Average Residential Densities in
Sub-Areas of the New York Region,
1970

	Dwellings per acre of residential land*	Persons per square mile of built-up land**	Persons per square mile of gross land area	Total Population 1970 Census (thousands)	Percent Transit residential work trips 1970 Census ***
1. Manhattan	210.67	85,989	69,333	1,539.2	86.1
2. The Bronx	68.53	50,229	34,067	1,471.7	71.4
3. Brooklyn	58.76	48,007	35,989	2,602.0	71.7
4. Hudson County	36.47	18,687	12,879	609.2	42.5
5. Queens	29.67	23,324	18,298	1,987.2	59.6
6. Staten Island	11.16	9,146	5,164	295.4	37.8
7. Essex County	10.17	11,191	7,181	930.0	28.6
8. Passaic County	6.69	7,745	3,567	460.8	13.0
9. Union County	6.16	7,127	5,288	543.1	15.2
10. Nassau County	5.19	7,376	4,950	1,428.0	21.9
11. Mercer County	5.16	6,117	1,334	304.0	8.9
12. Bergen County	4.83	6,280	3,838	898.0	17.4
13. Westchester County	4.43	5,641	2,019	894.1	27.3
14. Middlesex County	4.27	5,085	1,869	583.8	10.0
15. Central Naugatuck (Waterbury) Plng. Reg.	3.99	5,000	724	223.0	7.2
16. Bridgeport Planning Region	3.72	5,032	2,221	311.0	9.5
17. South Central (New Haven) Plng. Reg.	3.03	3,972	1,385	508.0	8.2
18. Orange County	2.87	2,853	266	221.7	4.8
19. Monmouth County	2.86	3,705	965	459.4	13.1
20. Ocean County	2.75	2,240	325	208.5	4.8
21. Suffolk County	2.58	3,484	1,211	1,125.0	9.6
22. Rockland County	2.53	3,930	1,304	229.9	6.9
23. Housatonic (Danbury) Planning Region	2.46	3,077	417	136.0	3.1
24. Dutchess County	2.36	2,850	273	222.3	2.5
25. Valley (Ansonia) Planning Region	2.35	3,610	1,314	74.0	1.8
26. Putnam County	2.09	2,232	245	56.7	7.0
27. Morris County	2.01	3,010	819	383.5	8.3
28. Southwestern (Stamford) Plng. Reg.	1.96	3,017	1,593	334.0	15.4
29. Sullivan County	1.88	943	53	52.6	n.a.
30. Hunterdon County	1.85	2,068	161	69.7	n.a.
31. Somerset County	1.81	2,649	647	198.4	7.7
32. Ulster County	1.75	2,043	123	141.2	n.a.
33. Warren County	1.57	2,036	204	73.9	n.a.
34. Rest of Litchfield County	1.43	1,606	124	95.9	n.a.
35. Sussex County	1.28	1,438	147	77.5	n.a.

*Includes seasonal dwellings.

**Land in residential uses, nonresidential uses and streets; excludes public open space and reservations.
For land use detail, see *The State of the Region* Regional Plan News 97, March 1975, p. 35.

***Transit defined as sum of subway, rail, bus, taxi. Excludes worked at home, "other" from total. From Tri-State Regional Planning Commission, 1970 County-to-County Travel, Interim Technical Report 4549-1302, December 1975.

Sources: Tri-State Regional Planning Commission and Regional Plan Association

EXHIBIT 7.3

Nonresidential Floorspace Density
Related to Adjoining Residential
Density (in 53 nonresidential clusters
in the New York Region)

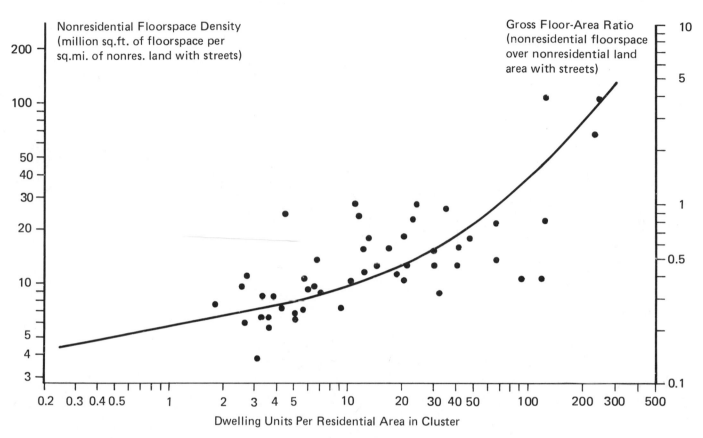

Source: Exhibit 7.4

EXHIBIT 7.4

Characteristics of Nonresidential
Concentrations in the New York Region

Name	1970 Non-Residential Floorspace (millions sq.ft.)	1970 Net Non-Residential Floorspace Density (Millions sq.ft. per nonresidential sq. mi.)	1963 Non-Residential Floorspace (millions sq.ft.)	1963 Gross Non-Residential Floorspace Density (millions sq.ft. per sq. mi.)	Distance to Columbus Circle (miles)
Downtowns					
1. Midtown Manhattan	267.5	102.9	251.0	66.9	1
2. Manhattan Valley	148.7	66.4	151.6	28.9	3
3. Lower Manhattan	131.5	108.7	129.4	65.0	5
4. Newark	51.1	27.6	51.5	17.2	11
5. Downtown Brooklyn	38.8	44.6	33.0	16.5	5
6. Jersey City	29.2	25.6	27.4	13.7	6
7. New Haven	26.6	28.0	23.4	11.7	67
8. Bridgeport	19.1	18.7	17.9	9.0	50
9. Waterbury	13.0	23.6	12.6	6.3	73
10. Paterson	11.9	22.9	10.7	10.7	15
11. Stamford	11.6	15.7	9.8	4.9	29
12. Passaic	11.4	21.9	11.1	11.1	10
13. Hackensack	11.2	10.3	7.4	3.7	8
14. White Plains	10.0	11.1	9.2	4.6	21
15. Yonkers	9.3	15.5	8.9	4.5	12
16. Elizabeth	7.9	13.0	7.8	3.9	15
17. Jamaica Center	7.9	15.8	6.6	6.6	10
18. New Brunswick	7.1	15.1	6.6	6.6	32
19. Meriden	6.5	17.6	6.5	6.5	81
20. Poughkeepsie	5.7	7.3	6.1	3.1	64
21. Hempstead	5.7	11.9	5.0	5.0	19
22. Plainfield	4.5	12.9	4.5	4.5	26
23. Middletown	4.4	6.4	4.3	2.2	52
24. Newburgh	3.9	4.5	3.7	1.9	51

EXHIBIT 7.4 continued

Spread clusters, mixed

1.	South Brooklyn	33.5	13.6	32.5	5.4	8
2.	Bergen Meadows	30.6	10.4	9.7	1.4	7
3.	Long Island City	28.7	22.2	25.9	13.0	3
4.	Greenpoint	25.3	12.8	19.2	6.4	4
5.	Williamsburg	19.8	17.8	15.0	7.5	4
6.	Central Nassau	18.6	9.1	15.2	2.5	17
7.	Maspeth	15.3	12.8	10.2	5.1	4
8.	Springfield	12.6	8.6	6.2	1.6	18
9.	Hicksville	12.2	10.6	10.7	5.4	25
10.	Clifton Rt. 3	11.8	13.7	8.3	2.8	11
11.	Huntspoint	11.1	10.9	8.6	3.9	4
12.	Port Newark	8.1	6.2	6.0	3.0	10
13.	Saddle Brook	6.4	24.6	3.5	3.5	12
14.	South Plainfield	5.6	6.4	2.5	0.8	27
15.	Plainview	5.5	7.2	2.6	1.3	26
16.	Fairfield	4.9	3.9	4.5	2.3	18
17.	Elmsford	3.8	7.2	1.6	0.8	21
18.	Tarrytown	2.7	10.6	3.3	1.7	23
19.	Union	2.3	9.6	1.4	1.4	16
20.	Ridgewood	1.6	6.7	1.5	1.5	17
21.	Englewood Cliffs	1.0	8.3	0.6	0.6	9
22.	Greenwich	0.9	4.7	0.0	0.0	26

Spread clusters, retail

1.	Wayne-Totowa	9.1	9.7	1.6	0.8	17
2.	Paramus	8.8	6.1	4.6	0.9	12
3.	Valley Stream	4.9	8.9	3.9	2.0	16
4.	Bayshore	4.5	5.7	3.4	1.1	38
5.	Jericho	3.8	6.6	2.9	1.5	24
6.	Stamford Fringe	3.7	7.7	2.2	0.7	32
7.	Nanuet	2.3	11.0	0.7	0.7	22
8.	Rego Park	2.2	10.5	2.1	2.1	6
9.	Norwalk	1.3	6.5	0.5	0.5	35

Source: Tri-State Regional Planning Commission and Regional Plan Association

EXHIBIT 7.5

Nonresidential Floorspace Density Related to Nonresidential Cluster Size (23 downtowns and 30 spread clusters in the New York Region; 7 CBDs outside the Region)

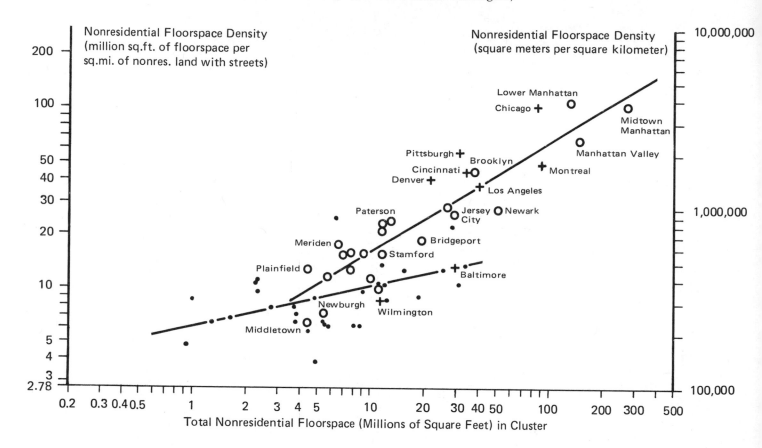

○ DOWNTOWN-ORIENTED NONRESIDENTIAL CLUSTERS
IN THE NEW YORK REGION

• SPREAD NONRESIDENTIAL CLUSTERS
IN THE NEW YORK REGION

+ OTHER DOWNTOWNS

Note: Only selected downtowns in the New York Region are named due to space limitations.
For full listing see Exhibit 7.4

Sources: Tri-State Regional Planning Commission and Regional Plan Association

EXHIBIT 7.6

Floorspace Use in Selected Downtowns, 1963-1975

	Gross Land area, sq.mi.	Total Non-Residential (Non-Residential, million sq.ft.)			Office Buildings			Retail Stores			Residential, million sq.ft.		
		1963	1970	1975	1963	1970	1975	1963	1970	1975	1963	1970	1975
Manhattan*	9.0	532.0	547.8	588.0	200.0	240.0	290.0	40.0	37.0	36.0	187.5	197.0	207.0
Newark	3.0	51.5	51.1	n.a.	12.1	13.8	14.2	7.1	6.5	6.3	24.7	22.5	23.3
Downtown Brooklyn	2.0	33.0	38.8	n.a.	6.6	8.6	9.4	4.3	4.4	n.a.	16.2	17.2	17.3
Jersey City	2.0	27.4	29.2	n.a.	1.8	2.1	2.3	4.6	4.6	4.6	28.1	28.1	29.1
New Haven	2.0	23.4	26.6	n.a.	2.8	3.6	n.a.	2.4	n.a.	n.a.	9.8	9.4	n.a.
Bridgeport	2.0	17.9	19.1	n.a.	1.5	1.9	2.4	3.2	3.6	3.2	9.5	8.7	8.5
Paterson	1.0	10.7	11.9	n.a.	1.2	1.4	1.6	2.9	2.9	2.8	9.4	10.1	9.9
Stamford	2.0	9.8	11.6	n.a.	1.2	1.6	2.6	2.4	2.4	2.3	6;7	7.0	6.9
Hackensack	2.0	7.4	11.2	n.a.	1.3	1.7	1.7	1.5	1.5	1.5	4.4	5.0	5.0
White Plains	2.0	9.2	10.0	n.a.	1.4	2.9	4.8	2.4	3.4	4.0	6.9	7.6	7.8
Jamaica Center	1.0	6.6	7.9	n.a.	1.2	2.1	n.a.	2.2	n.a.	n.a.	5.9	6.2	n.a.
New Brunswick	1.0	6.6	7.1	n.a.	1.0	1.3	1.4	1.8	1.8	1.8	6.0	5.8	5.8
Outside New York Region													
Chicago**	13.6	277.6	n.a.	n.a.	75.2	n.a.	n.a.	31.4	n.a.	n.a.	84.3	n.a.	n.a.
Washington, D.C. ***	1.7	n.a.	n.a.	89.3	n.a.	n.a.	71.0	n.a.	n.a.	7.0	n.a.	n.a.	n.a.
Montreal****	2.1	71.5	81.6	n.a.	25.5	32.9	n.a.	10.1	9.7	n.a.	19.0	20.7	n.a.
Los Angeles	3.5	n.a.	n.a.	79.2	n.a.	32.4	41.4	n.a.	n.a.	13.4	n.a.	n.a.	n.a.
Dallas	1.4	n.a.	n.a.	61.2	17.3	20.5	23.7	n.a.	n.a.	2.8	n.a.	n.a.	n.a.
Houston	1.5	n.a.	n.a.	60.7	n.a.	25.4	36.6	n.a.	n.a.	7.4	n.a.	n,a.	n.a.
Indianapolis	4.5	n.a.	n.a.	30.5	n.a.	10.4	12.5	n.a.	n.a.	5.3	n.a.	n.a.	n.a.
Milwaukee*****	1.7	n.a.	n.a.	28.5	n.a.	8.6	10.2	n.a.	n.a.	3.5	n.a.	n.a.	n.a.
Louisville	1.1	n.a.	n.a.	25.5	n.a.	7.8	10.0	n.a.	n.a.	3.6	n.a.	n.a.	n.a.
Columbia, S.C.	1.7	n.a.	n.a.	22.7	n.a.	2.5	4.0	n.a.	n.a.	2.1	n.a.	n.a.	n.a.
Orlando, Fla.	1.2	n.a.	n.a.	10.0	n.a.	2.3	2.9	n.a.	n.a.	5.2	n.a.	n.a.	n.a.

Notes:

*Includes area south of 60th street, i.e. Midtown, Valley and Lower Manhattan as defined in Exhibit 7.4; other downtowns in Region within same aereal definition as in Exhibit 7.4

**Data actually for 1956; include the Loop (1.2 sq.mi.) and district 11 of the Chicago Area Transportation Study (12.4 sq.mi.); offices assumed to include "service" floorspace plus "public" floorspace within the Loop

***Data actually for 1973

****Data actually for 1962 and 1972 within 1962 definition of "centre-ville"; 1972 definition includes 2.7 sq.mi. with 91 million sq.ft. of non-residential floorspace, of which 35.1 million are in offices and 12.2 in retail.

*****Data actually for 1972

Sources: Tri-State Regional Planning Commission and Regional Plan Association

It may be zero at 4 o'clock in the morning, but very high at 2 o'clock in the afternoon. It also varies greatly depending on the type of building. To sidestep these complexities, a useful aggregate index of the density of nonresidential uses is the density of floorspace. A measure of it widely employed in this book is gross square feet of nonresidential floorspace per square mile of land in nonresidential use.

To show what nonresidential densities are likely to be encountered near what densities of residential development, the two are related to each other in Exhibit 7.3. The residential density scale is the same as in Exhibit 7.1. The places for which the comparison is made are 53 nonresidential clusters in the New York Region, defined as contiguous areas of nonresidential use with at least one million square feet of nonresidential floorspace per gross square mile, and with at least 50 percent of total floorspace in nonresidential use. The gross land area of these clusters varies from 1.0 to 7.0 square miles. Their full listing is given in Exhibit 7.4.

It can be seen that nonresidential densities vary over a narrower range than residential ones—on the average from 5 million to 100 million square feet of nonresidential floorspace per square mile of land in nonresidential use. Expressed in perhaps more familiar terms of Floor-Area Ratios (FAR) shown in the right-hand scale of Exhibit 7.3, the variation is from about an FAR of 0.2 to 4.0. Such densities may appear very low. There are two explanations for this. First, the nonresidential land area as defined here includes adjacent streets. Second, the clusters are rather broadly delineated, and include development at the edges. For example, the Midtown Manhattan cluster as shown has an average Floor-Area Ratio just under 4.0, meaning that the nonresidential floor area of its buildings is about 4 times greater than the land area on which they stand, which is 3.75 square miles. If one takes only the central square mile of Midtown Manhattan, then its average Floor-Area Ratio is roughly 6.0 by the definition used here, i.e., including streets, and about 10.0 excluding streets. The average hides the fact that a few skyscrapers may have an FAR as high as 30.

As one would expect, the density of nonresidential clusters is related to their size—the larger the cluster, the higher the floorspace density. This relationship is portrayed in Exhibit 7.5, which separates the nonresidential clusters into two groups. One group consists of those that are focused on the downtowns of established cities. The other is spread clusters, which are the more amorphous concentrations of nonresidential activity such as occur in suburban areas, or in industrial districts of older cities. The density of the downtown-oriented clusters increases steeply with their size, whereas the variation in density among the spread clusters is much more narrow. The vertical scale in Exhibit 7.5 is the same as in Exhibit 7.3; metric equivalents are included at the top and right-hand margins.

In addition to 24 nonresidential clusters identified as downtown-oriented in the New York Region, 8 Central Business Districts of other urban areas in North America for which relatively comparable data were readily available are also shown. It can be seen that the size-density relationship valid for the New York Region applies to these other downtowns in the nation reasonably well. One should stress that the nonresidential clusters are *not* identical with the more narrowly defined Central Business Districts.

Floorspace statistics in many American urban areas are deficient. Often, only the floorspace of selected building types, such as retail stores or office buildings, is known. These account for varying proportions of total floorspace. Generally speaking, retail is more important in smaller downtown-oriented clusters, where it may account for up to one third of all nonresidential floorspace. This proportion declines as size of downtown increases, to less than one tenth in the largest downtowns. Conversely, office space may amount to about one tenth of total nonresidential floorspace in the smaller areas, but increases steeply with downtown size. It may comprise up to three fifths of the total nonresidential floorspace in large downtown areas. Since office workers are more prominent among transit users than either factory workers or shoppers, *office space alone* can be a useful measure of downtown concentration in large cities. It is used in this manner on occasion, but should not be confused with total nonresidential floorspace.

In spread nonresidential clusters, even approximate relationships of this type do not prevail, because these clusters often tend to be single-purpose. Some may be 90 percent industrial, some over 70 percent retail-oriented, some over 50 percent office-oriented, while still others are quite mixed. Examples of the composition of selected downtowns of the New York Region and outside are given in Exhibit 7.6.

ESTIMATES OF TRANSIT DEMAND

This section will spell out the steps necessary to estimate the demand for public transit trips between two places within the framework of the relationships presented in Chapter 2. Except when necessary to explain their application, no attempt will be made here to describe either the derivation of the relationships used or their rationale. For that, the reader is directed to the appropriate pages in the text.

For some of the relationships to be applied, it will be possible for the user to bypass some of the steps outlined here. He may already possess data for which derivation procedures are given here.

Exhibit 7.7 presents the flow of procedures used to estimate the demand for public transit trips per square mile originating in a residential area and destined for a nonresidential concentration (NRC). The bold type throughout the flow chart indicates the illustrative example later used in this section.

Estimating the Total Number of Trips between Two Places. To estimate the daily number of one-way trips per square mile from a residential area to a nonresidential concentration the user must possess the following data:
· Population of the residential area
· Gross area of the residential area in square miles
· Distance from the residential area to the NRC in miles
· Nonresidential floorspace of the NRC in millions of square feet
· Classification of NRC either as a downtown, a spread mixed use cluster, or a spread retail cluster
· If the NRC is in the New York Region, the distance from the NRC to midtown Manhattan (Columbus Circle) in miles.
In addition, the number of people in the labor force living in the residential area is a desirable item of data for added refinement.

The next step is to refer to the six nomographs, Exhibits 7.8 through 7.13. The derivation of the underlying relationships is fully described on pages 56 through 63. These nomographs are designed to quickly determine the trips per worker for work trips and trips per capita for non-work trips. They graphically display the solution to the six equations described in Exhibit 2.21. Exhibits 7.8 and 7.9 are to be used if the NRC is classified as a downtown, Exhibits 7.10 and 7.11 if the NRC is a spread mixed use cluster, and Exhibits 7.12 and 7.13 if the NRC is a spread retail cluster. After having selected the appropriate nomographs, connect the values of the left-hand M (miles from Manhattan) scale and the right-hand D (distance from residential area to the NRC) scale to locate a point on the pivot line. If the NRC is outside the New York Region, use a value of 60 for M. Having located that point on the pivot line, connect it to the proper value of the F scale, the nonresidential floorspace of the NRC measured in millions of square feet, thus creating a second line. Read off the work trips per worker or the non-work trips per capita where this line intersects the Y scale. Examples of these steps are shown by the dashed lines for Exhibits 7.8 and 7.9 for values of M = 60, D = 5, F = 10, yielding 0.050 work trips per worker and 0.034 non-work trips per capita.

Having derived the work trips per worker from either Exhibits 7.8, 7.10, or 7.12 and non-work trips per capita from Exhibits 7.9, 7.11, or 7.13, the next step is to multiply the work trip rates by the labor force of the residential area and the non-work trip rates by the population of the residential area. In the absence of labor force data for the residential area it can be assumed that the labor force participation rate is 0.40, i.e., the labor force is equal to 40% of the population. If we assume, in our example, a net residential density of 10 dwelling units per acre corresponding to 7,100 persons per square mile (using Exhibit 7.1) and assume also a labor force to population ratio of 0.40, then the volume of work trips per square mile to the NRC equals 0.40 × 7,100 × 0.050, or 142, and the volume of non-work trips equals 7,100 × 0.034, or 241. With the number of work trips and non-work trips known, we can turn our attention to estimating how many are likely to be made by public transit.

Estimating the Percent of Work Trips Using Public Transit. To estimate the percent of work trips between a residential area and an NRC that will be made by public transit, the user must possess the following data:

· The net residential density of the residential area measured in dwelling units per acre
· Classification of the residential area by transit service territory, either "rapid transit" if 50% or more of the area is within 2,000 feet of a rapid transit station, "rail" if 25% of the area is within 2,000 feet of a rail station, or "neither" if neither the "rapid transit" or "rail" criteria apply. If the criteria for both rapid transit and rail are met, the area is classified as rapid transit.
· Classification of the NRC as either a downtown or spread (either mixed or retail) cluster
· The median family income of the residential area in 1969 dollars
· The average number of "adults" per household, i.e., persons 16 years or older per household
· The arithmetic average peak period frequency of bus routes to the NRC
· The percent of residential area within 2,000 feet of a rapid transit station with service to the NRC
· The presence or absence of a rail service in the corridor in question (this is not to be confused with the second point above which classifies the transit station proximity of the residential area).

For further refinement it is desirable to estimate the net nonresidential floorspace density of the NRC, measured in millions of square feet of nonresidential floorspace per square mile of nonresidential area. The description of the rationale for procedures below is found on pages 43 to 51.

Having assembled the data, the next step is to select the appropriate set of curves from Exhibits 7.14 through 7.16. These exhibits graphically portray the solution to the work trip mode choice equations for any net residential density for selected values of NRC floorspace. Exhibit 7.14 indicates the base percent public transit use for work trips from residential areas categorized as "rail" and "neither" territory to downtown NRCs as a function of net residential density and nonresidential floorspace. Exhibit 7.15 shows similar sets of curves

EXHIBIT 7.7

Estimating Public Transit Trips per Square Mile

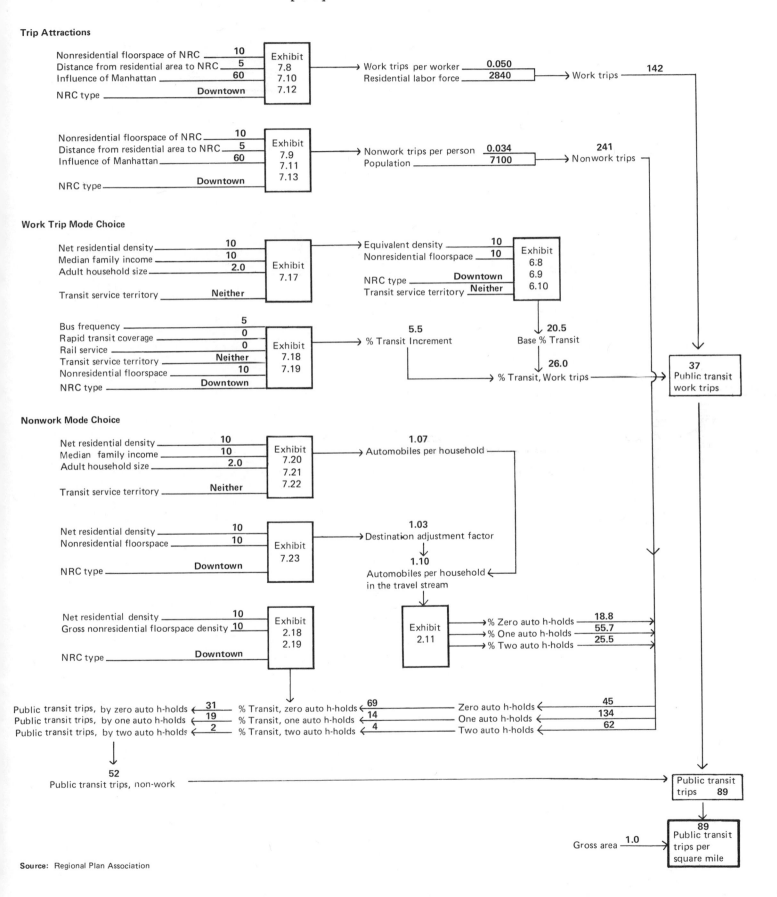

Trip Attractions

Nonresidential floorspace of NRC — 10
Distance from residential area to NRC — 5
Influence of Manhattan — 60
NRC type — Downtown

Exhibit 7.8 7.10 7.12

Work trips per worker — 0.050
Residential labor force — 2840

Work trips — 142

Nonresidential floorspace of NRC — 10
Distance from residential area to NRC — 5
Influence of Manhattan — 60
NRC type — Downtown

Exhibit 7.9 7.11 7.13

Nonwork trips per person — 0.034
Population — 7100

Nonwork trips — 241

Work Trip Mode Choice

Net residential density — 10
Median family income — 10
Adult household size — 2.0
Transit service territory — Neither

Exhibit 7.17

Equivalent density — 10
Nonresidential floorspace — 10
NRC type — Downtown
Transit service territory — Neither

Exhibit 6.8 6.9 6.10

Bus frequency — 5
Rapid transit coverage — 0
Rail service — 0
Transit service territory — Neither
Nonresidential floorspace — 10
NRC type — Downtown

Exhibit 7.18 7.19

% Transit Increment — 5.5
Base % Transit — 20.5
% Transit, Work trips — 26.0

37 Public transit work trips

Nonwork Mode Choice

Net residential density — 10
Median family income — 10
Adult household size — 2.0
Transit service territory — Neither

Exhibit 7.20 7.21 7.22

Automobiles per household — 1.07

Net residential density — 10
Nonresidential floorspace — 10
NRC type — Downtown

Exhibit 7.23

Destination adjustment factor — 1.03
Automobiles per household in the travel stream — 1.10

Net residential density — 10
Gross nonresidential floorspace density — 10
NRC type — Downtown

Exhibit 2.18 2.19

Exhibit 2.11

% Zero auto h-holds — 18.8
% One auto h-holds — 55.7
% Two auto h-holds — 25.5

Public transit trips, by zero auto h-holds — 31 — % Transit, zero auto h-holds — 69 — Zero auto h-holds — 45 — 134
Public transit trips, by one auto h-holds — 19 — % Transit, one auto h-holds — 14 — One auto h-holds — 62
Public transit trips, by two auto h-holds — 2 — % Transit, two auto h-holds — 4 — Two auto h-holds

52 Public transit trips, non-work

Public transit trips 89

Gross area — 1.0

89 Public transit trips per square mile

Source: Regional Plan Association

EXHIBIT 7.8

Work Trips to Downtown Nonresidential Concentrations

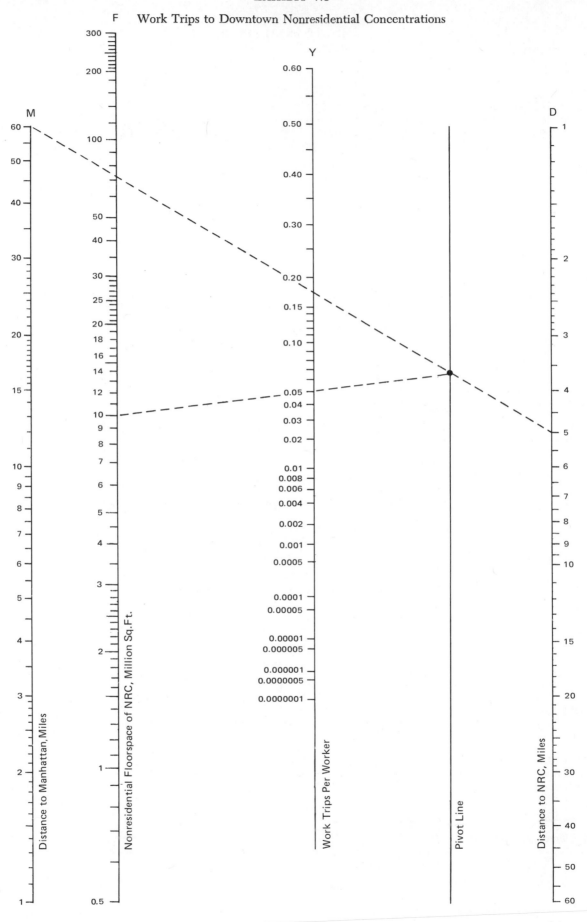

EXHIBIT 7.9

Nonwork Trips to Downtown Nonresidential Concentrations

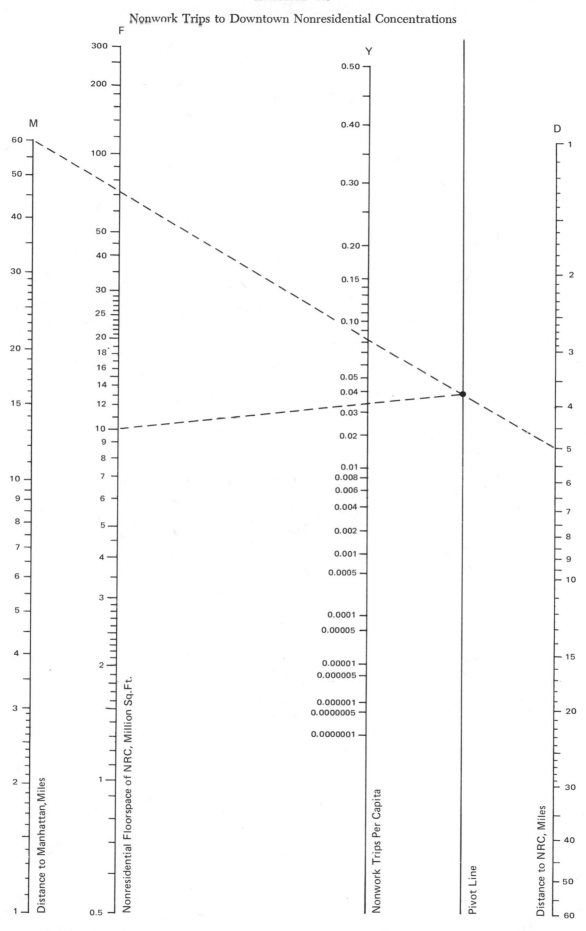

EXHIBIT 7.10

Work Trips to Spread Mixed Use Nonresidential Concentrations

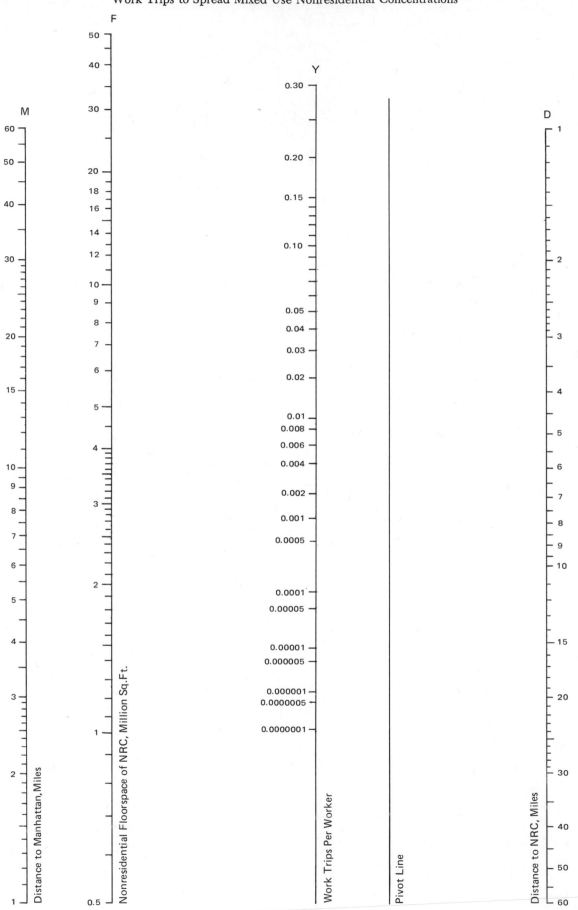

Source: Exhibit 2.21

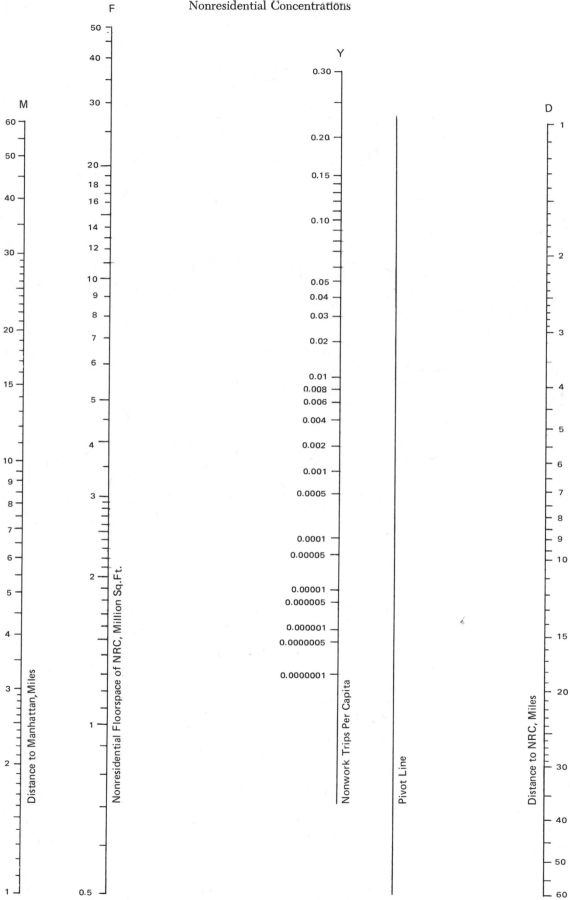

Source: Exhibit 2.21

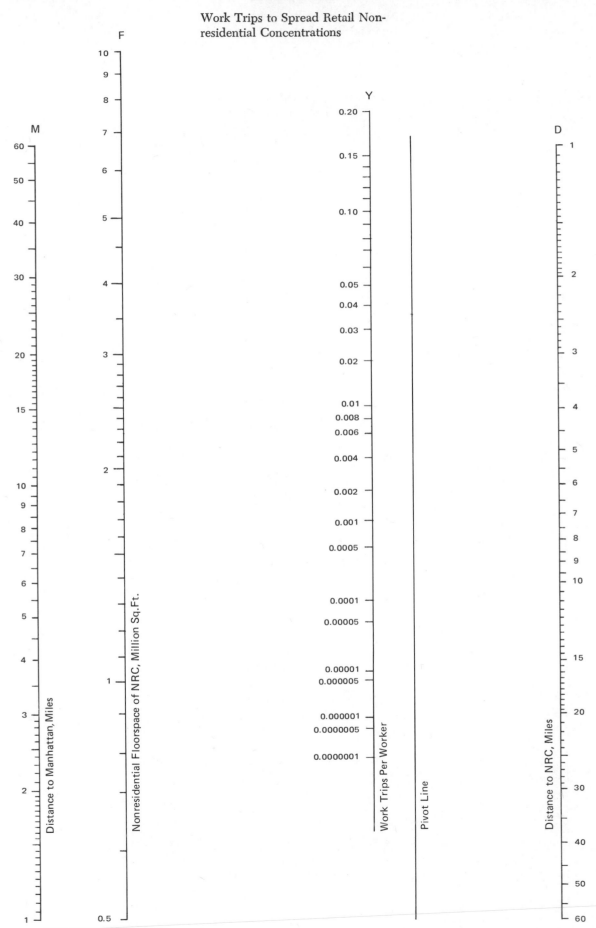

EXHIBIT 7.12

Work Trips to Spread Retail Nonresidential Concentrations

F
10
9
8
7
6
5
4
3
2
1
0.5

Nonresidential Floorspace of NRC, Million Sq.Ft.

M
60
50
40
30
20
15
10
9
8
7
6
5
4
3
2
1

Distance to Manhattan, Miles

Y
0.20
0.15
0.10
0.05
0.04
0.03
0.02
0.01
0.008
0.006
0.004
0.002
0.001
0.0005
0.0001
0.00005
0.00001
0.000005
0.000001
0.0000005
0.0000001

Work Trips Per Worker

Pivot Line

D
1
2
3
4
5
6
7
8
9
10
15
20
30
40
50
60

Distance to NRC, Miles

Source: Exhibit 2.21

EXHIBIT 7.13

Nonwork Trips to Spread Retail
Nonresidential Concentrations

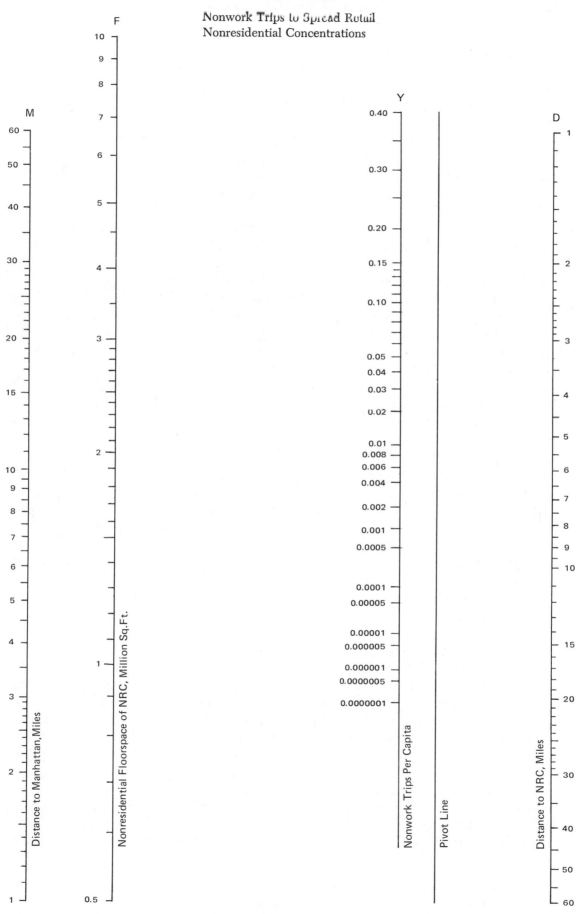

for "rapid transit" territories. Finally, in Exhibit 7.16 the base percent public transit use to spread clusters is indicated for all three territories, "rail" and "neither" above, and "rapid transit" below. By way of example, if the net residential density is 10 dwelling units per acre, the base percent of work trips that will be public transit is 20.5% for an NRC of 10 million square feet of nonresidential floorspace in a non-rapid transit, non-rail territory. This is shown by the dashed line in Exhibit 7.14.

These exhibits were drawn by assuming automobile ownership levels for the particular residential density based on median family income of $10,000 in 1969 dollars and 2.0 adults per household. Since this combination will seldom be the case it is desirable to have a procedure for adjusting the percent public transit use if $10,000 and 2.0 are not the actual values. Exhibit 7.17 presents factors to use for the three territories to determine the equivalent net residential densities to use to enter Exhibits 7.14 through 7.16 if the median family income is not $10,000 and/or the adult household size is not 2.0. Suppose the median family income in the example above (dwelling units per acre = 10, F = 10) is $15,000 and the adults per household are 2.2. As shown by the dashed line in Exhibit 7.17 ("neither" territory), an equivalent residential density factor of 0.22 is determined. This factor is multiplied by the actual net residential density, 10 dwelling units per acre in this example, and an equivalent net residential density of 2.2 is found. This value is then used in Exhibit 7.14 to find the base percent transit use when median family income is $15,000 and adult household size is 2.2. In this example, the new base percent transit use would be 13.2. Thus, the difference in base percent total transit use for two residential densities of the same actual densities but with different incomes and different adult household sizes can be determined.

The base percent public transit use values found by using Exhibits 7.14 through 7.17 do not yet reflect the influence of the transit service characteristics. In Exhibits 7.18 and 7.19 the increments that transit service adds to the base percent public transit use are given. Exhibit 7.18 shows the increment in *percentage points* for downtown NRCs for varying frequencies of bus service during the peak period in the upper portion of the Exhibit, for varying rapid transit coverages in the middle portion of the Exhibit, and for the existence of rail service in the lower portion for the three transit service territories. For example, 5.5 percentage points should be added if there are five buses per hour in the peak two-hour period from a "neither" residential territory of net residential density of ten dwelling units per acre to a downtown NRC of 10 million square feet, as shown by the dashed line in Exhibit 7.18. When added to the base percent public transit use of 20.5% determined earlier, a percent public transit use of 26.0% is found. As can be seen from that Exhibit, this increment is rather independent of downtown size, varying only slightly for residential densities above 10 dwelling units per acre.

Also shown in Exhibit 7.18 is a dashed line for a residential area with ten dwelling units per acre and a downtown of 10 million square feet which will have 20.0 percentage points added to its base percent public transit use if the residential area has 80% of its area within 2,000 feet of a rapid transit station with service to that downtown. If that residential area has rail service to the downtown, an increment of 5.9 percentage points can be determined, as shown by the dashed line in the lower part of Exhibit 7.18. Similarly, Exhibit 7.19 shows the increments to be added for spread clusters for bus frequency depending on applicable service territories. The rail service increment is omitted since it was not a significant factor for mode choice to spread clusters. Note that the rapid transit coverage for "rail" or "neither" territory, depicted in the center of Exhibit 7.18, does not exceed 50 percent, since if it did, it would be classified as "rapid transit" territory, not as "rail" or "neither."

EXHIBIT 7.14

Percent Transit Use for Work Trips vs.
Net Residential Density, "Neither,"
and Rail Territories to Downtown NRCs
for Selected Nonresidential Floorspace (F)

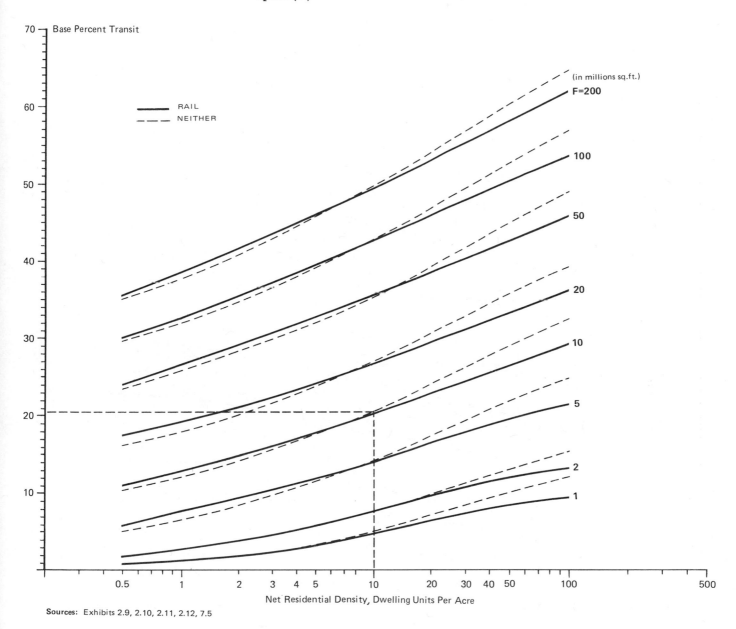

Sources: Exhibits 2.9, 2.10, 2.11, 2.12, 7.5

EXHIBIT 7.15

Percent Transit Use for Work Trips
vs. Net Residential Density, Rapid
Transit Territory to Downtown NRCs
for Selected Nonresidential Floorspace (F)

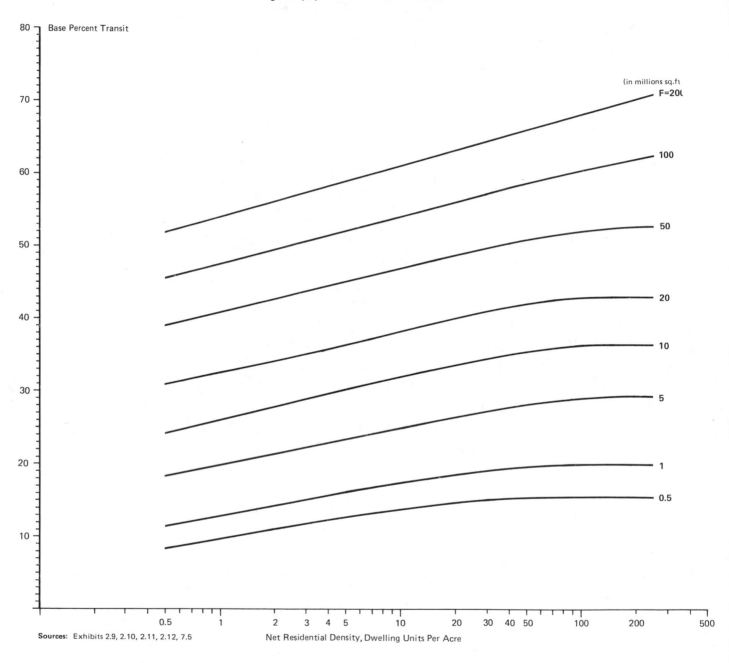

Sources: Exhibits 2.9, 2.10, 2.11, 2.12, 7.5

Net Residential Density, Dwelling Units Per Acre

EXHIBIT 7.16

Percent Transit Use for Work Trips
vs. Net Residential Density, Three
Transit Territories to Spread Clusters
for Selected Nonresidential Floorspace (F)

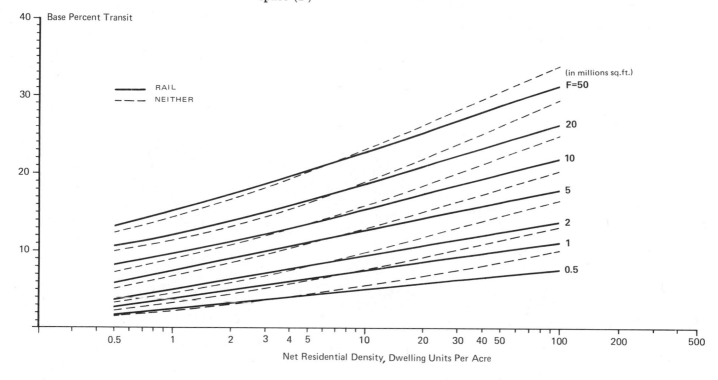

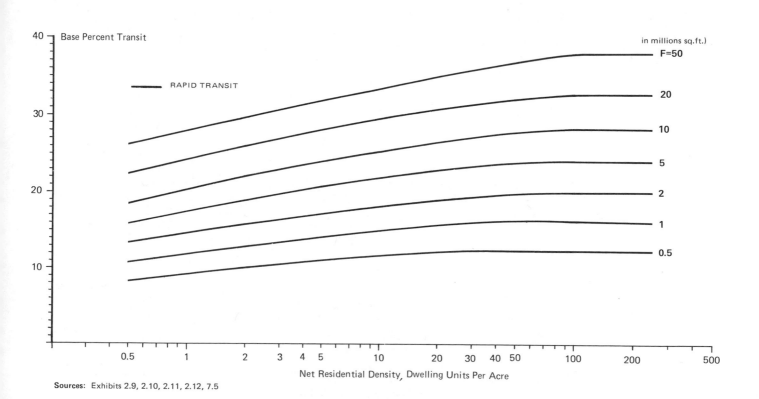

Sources: Exhibits 2.9, 2.10, 2.11, 2.12, 7.5

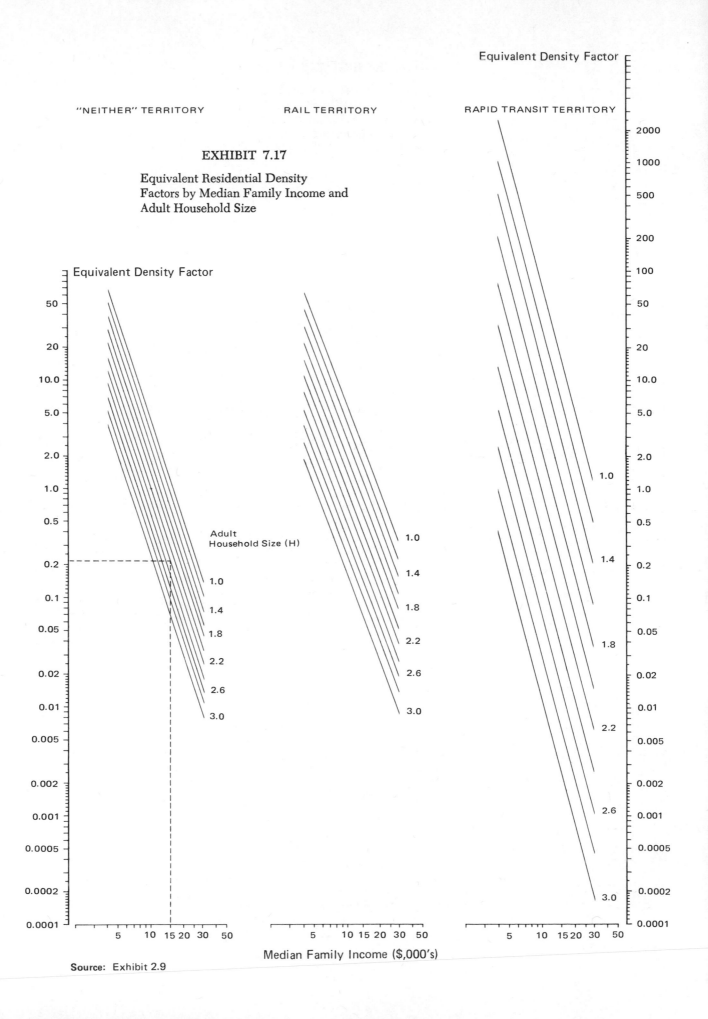

EXHIBIT 7.17

Equivalent Residential Density
Factors by Median Family Income and
Adult Household Size

"NEITHER" TERRITORY RAIL TERRITORY RAPID TRANSIT TERRITORY

Equivalent Density Factor

Median Family Income ($,000's)

Source: Exhibit 2.9

EXHIBIT 7.18

Percent Transit Increments for Transit
Service vs. Net Residential Density
for Downtown NRCs

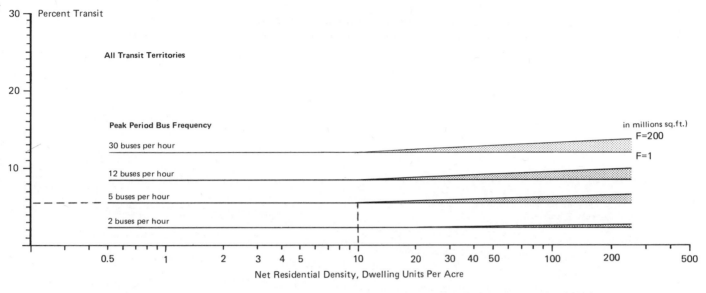

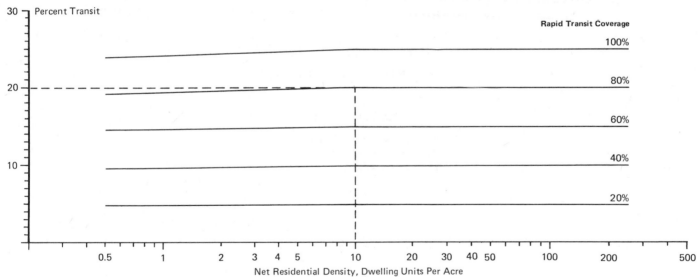

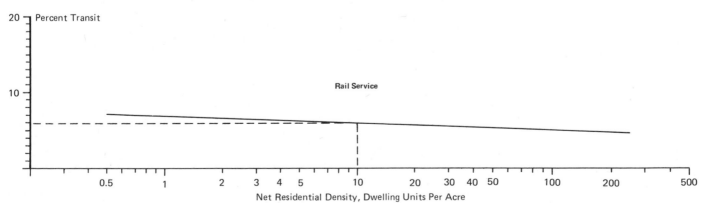

Sources: Exhibits 2.9, 2.10, 2.11, 2.12, 7.5

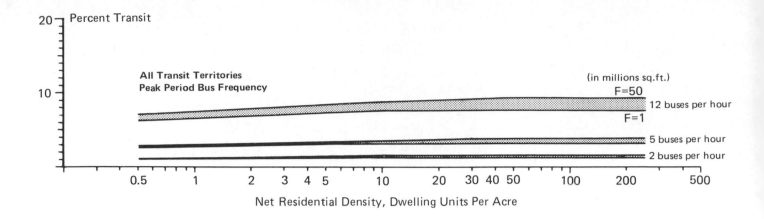

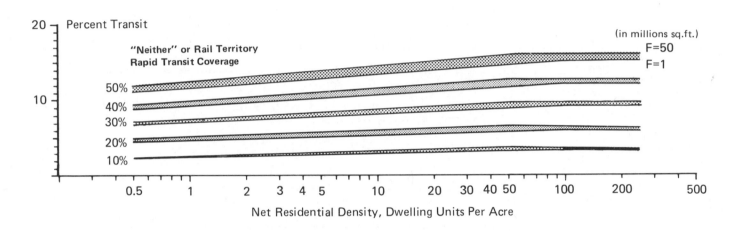

EXHIBIT 7.19

Percent Transit Increments for
Transit Service vs. Net Residential
Density for Spread Clusters

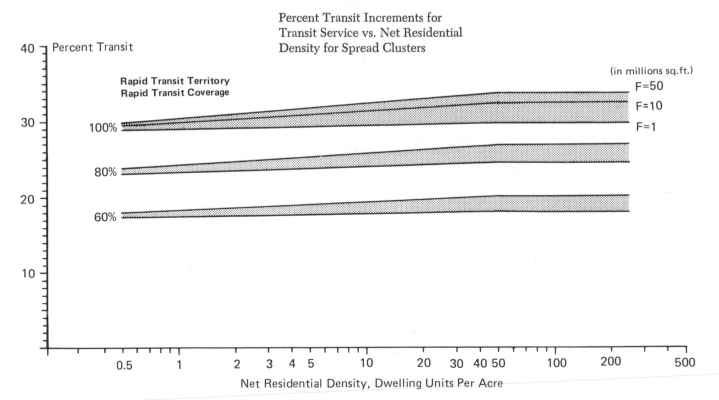

Sources: Exhibits 2.9, 2.10, 2.11, 2.12, 7.5

For the example we have been carrying forward throughout this section we will assume that neither rapid transit coverage nor rail service exist. Thus, the value of 142 total work trips is factored by 26.0% to yield 37 public transit work trips.

With the base percent public transit use determination of Exhibits 7.14 through 7.16 it was convenient to use the device of the equivalent residential density factors of Exhibit 7.17 if median family income and adult household size were not $10,000 and 2.0 respectively. However, when estimating the increments added by transit service as shown in Exhibits 7.18 and 7.19, such an adjustment can often be omitted if desired, particularly where the curves are nearly horizontal, since then the increments to be added will hardly vary with net residential density.

One further point: the original modal choice relationships for work trips were determined using net nonresidential floorspace density and then converted to nonresidential floorspace using Exhibit 7.5. Thus, if the user knows the net floorspace density of the NRC in question, he can use it directly by converting his net nonresidential floorspace density to nonresidential floorspace using Exhibit 7.5 and enter the Exhibits in this section with his "equivalent" nonresidential floorspace value.

Estimating the Percent of Non-Work Trips Using Public Transit. To estimate the percent of non-work trips between a residential area and an NRC that will be made by public transit, the user must possess the following data:
- The net residential density expressed in dwelling units per acre of the residential area
- Nonresidential floorspace of the NRC in millions of square feet
- Gross nonresidential floorspace density of the NRC measured in nonresidential floorspace per gross square mile
- Classification of the residential area by transit service territory as described earlier
- Classification of the NRC as either a downtown or spread cluster (either mixed or retail)
- The median family income of the residential area in 1969 dollars
- The average number of "adults" per household, i.e., persons 16 years or older per household.

Having assembled the data, the next step is to estimate the automobile ownership categories among the trip-makers in the residential-nonresidential stream. The reader is referred to pages 37 to 41 for the detailed description of the automobile ownership relationships.

The nomographs of Exhibits 7.20 through 7.22, one for each transit service territory, are graphically displayed solutions to the equations of Exhibit 2.9. To solve, first select the appropriate nomograph. Then draw a line connecting the value of the residential area's adult household size on the left-hand scale, H, to the median family income on the right-hand scale, I. Draw another line where the first line intersects the pivot line and connect it with the value of the net residential density scale, D. Read the solution, automobiles per household, where the second line intersects the A/HH scale. This procedure is shown in Exhibit 7.20, the "neither" territory for H = 2.0, I = 10, and D = 10, yielding 1.07 automobiles per household. Of course, if the average number of automobiles per household is already known from other sources, such as the U.S. Census, then this step can be bypassed.

The next step is to adjust the average automobiles per household of the residential area to reflect the average automobiles per household of the trip makers in the origin-destination (O-D) stream. This is done by applying the destination adjustment factor for non-work trips shown in Exhibit 7.23 for the appropriate net residential density and nonresidential floorspace. The rationale for this is explained on pages 41 to 43. For example, if dwelling units per acre equals 10 and the nonresidential floorspace of a downtown NRC equals 10, then the destination adjustment factor is 1.03, as shown by the dashed lines in Exhibit 7.23. Thus,

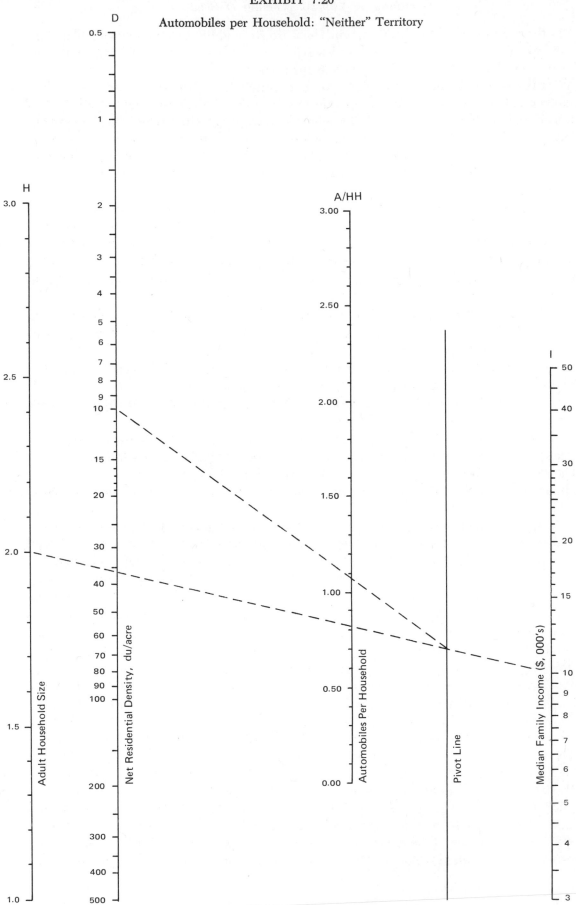

EXHIBIT 7.20

Automobiles per Household: "Neither" Territory

D

H

A/HH

I

Adult Household Size

Net Residential Density, du/acre

Automobiles Per Household

Pivot Line

Median Family Income ($, 000's)

EXHIBIT 7.21

Automobiles per Household: Rail Territory

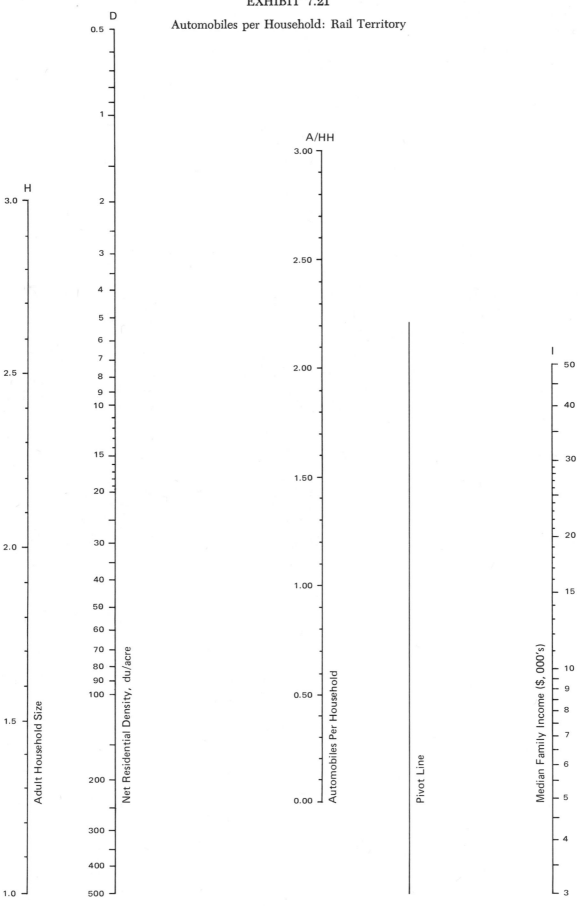

EXHIBIT 7.22

Automobiles per Household: Rapid
Transit Territory

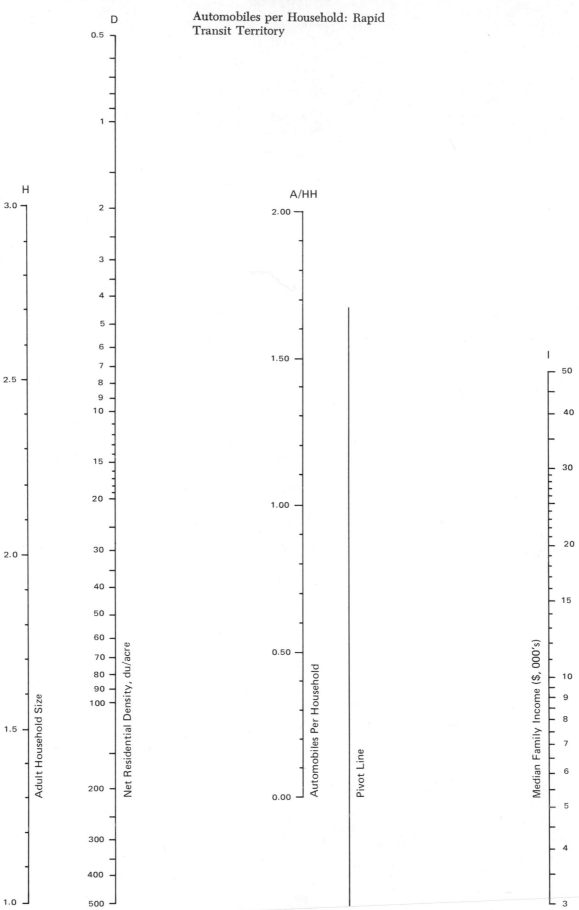

D

0.5

1

H

3.0 — 2

3

4

5

6

7

2.5 — 8

9

10

15

20

30

2.0 — 40

50

60

70

80

90

100

Net Residential Density, du/acre

Adult Household Size

1.5 — 200

300

400

1.0 — 500

A/HH

2.00

1.50

1.00

0.50

0.00

Automobiles Per Household

Pivot Line

I

50

40

30

20

15

10

9

8

7

6

5

4

3

Median Family Income ($, 000's)

Source: Exhibit 2.9

EXHIBIT 7.23

Destination Adjustment Factor vs. Net Residential Density by Non-residential Floorspace (F)

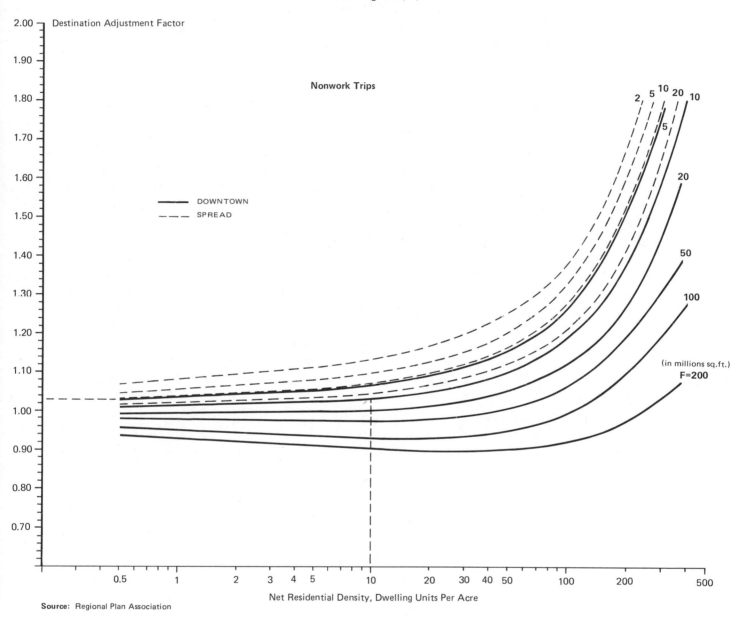

Source: Regional Plan Association

the average automobiles per household found above of 1.07 would convert to $1.07 \times 1.03 =$ 1.10 average automobiles per household of the trip makers travelling from the residential area ($H = 2.0$, $I - 10$, $D = 10$, "neither" territory) to the downtown NRC of 10 million square feet of nonresidential floorspace.

Next, the average automobiles per household in the O-D stream are split among zero, one, and two-or-more-auto households in the manner described earlier in Exhibit 2.11. For example, the average automobiles per household in the O-D stream determined above converts to 18.8% zero-auto households, 55.7% one-auto households and 25.5% two-or-more-auto households, using either the curves of Exhibit 2.11 or the equations given in that Exhibit. This last step is necessary because the modal choice relationships for non-work trips are expressed separately for each of the three auto ownership household groups as detailed on pages 51 to 55 and cannot be easily combined as were the work trips modal choice relationships. In the work trip relationships they were embedded in Exhibits 7.14 through 7.19.

With the automobile ownership splits known, it is possible to apply them to the non-work trips shown in the example given earlier in this Appendix. The 241 non-work trips thus consist of 45 trips made by households owning no autos, 134 trips made by households of one auto, and 62 trips made by households owning two or more autos.

The trip volumes made by public transit from among these three groups are estimated using the equations of Exhibit 2.18. Note that these equations use gross nonresidential floorspace density for the NRC variable and net residential density measured in population per square mile in residential use as the residential variable. Following through on our example, if we assume that the 10 million square feet of nonresidential floorspace are found in a one-square-mile area and thus are equal to a gross floorspace density of 10 million square feet per square mile, and the net residential density equals 10 dwelling units per acre, then the percent public transit use for the three auto ownership groups is 69%, 14%, and 4%. These are found by either using the equations in Exhibit 2.17 directly or estimating the values from the curves in Exhibit 2.18. If a spread cluster NRC is involved the curves of Exhibit 2.19 would be used.

If the equations are used, then net residential density must be expressed in terms of population per net residential square mile, which can be determined by using Exhibit 7.1. Applying the respective percents in our example to the previously determined trip volumes of 45, 134, and 62 gives 31, 19, and 2 non-work public transit trips for the respective auto ownership groups or a total of 52 public transit non-work trips. Earlier, 37 public transit work trips were estimated, giving a total public transit trip density for this example of 89 public transit trips. Since the gross area in our example is 1.0 square mile, the public transit trip density equals 89 trips per square mile. This is the demand density figure that must be used when evaluating the costs of supplying the transit service to meet that demand. If more than one non-residential concentration is in the corridor in question, it may be necessary to repeat this procedure and accumulate the demand densities to each NRC from a residential area.

For the assumptions underlying the procedures outlined here, and for their limitations, the reader is referred to Chapter 2.

NOTES

Chapter 1

1. For a definition of the various elasticity measures and a discussion of some of the conceptual problems, see: Carmen Difiglio, "Transit Fare and Ridership: a Review," *Technical Notes* (Washington, D.C.: Highway Users Federation, December 1974); also Michael A. Kemp, "Some Evidence of Transit Demand Elasticities," *Transportation* No. 2 (Amsterdam: Elsevier Scientific Publishing Company, 1973).

2. An expansion of the study period to cover the years 1947-1975 (including the 1975 fare increase to 50¢) and a more refined estimate of year-to-year employment changes yield the following subway ridership elasticities: with respect to fare in constant dollars, −0.117; with respect to Manhattan CBD employment, +0.754; with respect to auto registrations in New York City, −0.253; with respect to subway vehicle miles of service, +0.135. The R^2 is somewhat improved over the one shown in Exhibit 1.1, from 0.71 to 0.79. A separate calculation for subway peak hour ridership suggests that peak period elasticities may be higher, contrary to traditional assumptions. For details see: "An Examination of Future Power Requirements for Metropolitan Transportation Authority Facilities," prepared by Regional Plan Association for the Power Authority of the State of New York, *RPA Bulletin 126* (May 1977).

3. John F. Curtin, "Effect of Fares on Transit Riding," *Highway Research Record 213* (Washington, D.C., 1968).

4. John W. Bates, "Effect of Fare Reduction on Transit Ridership in the Atlanta Region: Summary of Transit Passenger Data," *Transpor-*
tation Research Record 499 (Washington, D.C., 1974), p.5.

5. James I. Scheiner, "The Patronage Effects of Free Fare Transit," *Traffic Quarterly* (January 1975), p.27.

6. Thomas E. Lisco, "The Value of Commuters' Travel Time" (Ph.D. diss., University of Chicago, 1967); also Traffic Research Corporation, *A Model for Estimating Travel Mode Usage in Washington, D.C.* (Washington, D.C., July 1962); and Arthur B. Sosslau and Arthur J. Balek, "Evaluation of a New Modal Split Procedure," *Highway Research Record 88* (1965).

7. For a review of time value studies, which includes extensive bibliographical notes, see Transportation Research Board *Behavioral Demand Modeling and the Valuation of Travel Time*, Special Report 149 (Washington, D.C., 1974). For the value of time in walking, see also Boris S. Pushkarev and Jeffrey M. Zupan, *Urban Space for Pedestrians* (Cambridge, Mass.: MIT Press, 1975), pp.67-69.

8. Edmund J. Cantilli, *Programming Environmental Improvements in Public Transportation* (Lexington, Mass.: Lexington Books, 1974).

9. Ruth Plawner and Monica von Halle, "Benefit Analysis of the Bryant Park Underpass" (New York University Graduate School of Public Administration, unpublished paper, June 1976).

10. Polytechnic Institute of New York, *Survey of Ridership of Express Buses.* Summary Report (Prepared for the New York City Transportation Administration, May 1974). Weighted averages calculated from tables on pp.37, 40, 42, 47, 50, 51.

11. Jeffrey M. Zupan, "Mode Choice: Impli-

cations for Planning," *Highway Research Record 251* (1968). Calculated by applying the rail service coefficient of 17.884 in equation on p.15 to 131 interzonal volumes with direct rail service.

12. Eugene J. Lessieu, "A Computer Aided Traffic Forecasting Technique—the Trans-Hudson Model" (Paper presented at Spring Joint Computer Conference, Atlantic City, 1971). Calculated by applying the 17.5 percent reduction on auto travel in equation on p.69 to the travel volumes on p.75, with spot verification with original data.

13. Data from American Public Transit Association, *Transit Fact Book*, 1970-71 edition Table 15, 1972-73 edition Table 5.

14. Chicago Transit Authority, *Skokie Swift Mass Transportation Project Final Report* (Chicago: May 1968), p.54, quoting Thomas E. Lisco, "Value of Commuters' Travel Time."

15. James T. McQueen et al., *The Shirley Highway Express Bus on Freeway Demonstration Project—Second Year Results*, prepared for Urban Mass Transportation Administration (Washington, D.C., November 1973).

16. California Department of Transportation, *San Bernardino Freeway Busway Patronage Report* (May 28, 1975).

17. Tri-State Regional Planning Commission, *Interstate 495 Exclusive Bus Lane, Final Report* (New York, July 1972), pp.18,19.

18. For an expansion of this argument, see: U.S. Congress, Office of Technology Assessment, *Energy, the Economy, and Mass Transit: Summary Report*, prepared at the request of the Senate Committee on Appropriations, Transportation Subcommittee, by Skidmore, Owings and Merrill and System Design Concepts Inc. (Washington, D.C., June 1975), pp.7ff.

19. The data in Exhibit 1.4 are derived from Wilbur Smith and Associates, *Patterns of Car Ownership, Trip Generation and Trip Sharing in Urbanized Areas* (New Haven, Conn.: 1968), pp.23-24 and relevant tables in Appendix A. They were used for creating a somewhat different modal split procedure in F. Houston Wynn, "*Shortcut Modal Split Formula*," Wilbur Smith and Associates (Presented at the 48th Annual Meeting, Highway Research Board, January 1969). For a chart showing diversion of auto owners to transit depending on travel time

differences, see also *Penn-Jersey Transportation Study* Vol. 1 (Philadelphia, Pa., 1964), p.83.

Chapter 2

1. Wilbur Smith and Associates, *Patterns of Car Ownership, Trip Generation and Trip Sharing in Urbanized Areas*, prepared for the U.S. Department of Transportation, Bureau of Public Roads (New Haven, Conn., June 1968).

2. For further detail on the choice of mode by income, see Regional Plan Association, *Transportation and Economic Opportunity*, a report to the Transportation Administration of the City of New York (New York, January 1973), pp.132-149.

3. Tri-State Regional Planning Commission, *Transit Supporting Densities*, Interim Technical Report 4195-4451 (New York, July 1970), p.34.

4. *Chicago Area Transportation Study*. Final Report (Chicago, December 1959), Volume 1, pp.108-112.

5. Wilbur Smith and Associates, *Transportation and Parking for Tomorrow's Cities* (New Haven, Conn., 1966), pp.74-77.

6. Boris S. Pushkarev and Jeffrey M. Zupan, *Urban Space for Pedestrians* (Cambridge, Mass.: MIT Press, 1975), table 4.7, p.130.

Chapter 3

1. Ronald Kirby et al., *Para-Transit; Neglected Options for Urban Mobility* (Washington, D.C.: The Urban Institute, 1974), pp.166-186.

2. Paul A. Anderson, "Comparison of Personalized Rapid Transit and Conventional Systems in a People-Mover Application," *The Honeywell Computer Journal*, Vol. 7, #4 (1973).

3. This is a minimum cross-section prefabricated steel guideway patented by Lawrence K. Edwards in June, 1975, under the name Project 21. The triangular beam, whose edges consist of rails for vehicles moving in two directions and incorporate ingenious switches, is about 5 feet in cross-section. In an underground application, the clear area of the needed tunnel is roughly 215 sq. ft. compared to about 400 sq. ft. for conventional subways. See *Lea Transit Compendium*, Vol. 1, No. 3 (Huntsville, Ala.,

1974), p.12; also L. K. Edwards and L. H. Donnell, "Project 21 Rapid Transit System, Synthesis of the System and Validation of the Guideway," *American Society of Mechanical Engineers Publication 74-RT-6* (1974).

4. National data calculated from American Public Transit Association, *Transit Fact Book* (Washington, D.C., March 1976); for New York Region see: "Financing Public Transportation," *Regional Plan News #98* (New York, March 1976).

5. Michael G. Ferreri, "Development of a Transit Cost Allocation Formula," *Highway Research Record 285* (Washington, D.C., 1969), p.9; see also James H. Miller and John C. Rea, "Comparison of Cost Models for Urban Transit," *Highway Research Record 435* (Washington, D.C., 1972), p.18.

6. For a similar approach, see also Douglass B. Lee, *Costs of Urban and Suburban Passenger Transportation Modes* (University of Iowa, April 1975), p.32.

7. U.S. Department of Transportation, Institute for Defense Analyses, *Economic Characteristics of the Urban Public Transportation Industry* (February 1972), pp.6-68, 6-74.

8. Price, Waterhouse & Company, *New York City Fleet Taxicab Industry Financial Survey*. Report to the Metropolitan Taxicab Board of Trade (New York, November 1970). Also: Frank Davis, *Economic Characteristics of Privately Owned Shared-Ride Taxi Systems* (U.S. Department of Transportation, October 1974).

9. Institute for Defense Analyses, *Economic Characteristics of the Urban Public Transportation Industry* (U.S. Department of Transportation, February 1972), pp.4-75.

10. Thomas B. Deen, Walter M. Kulash, and Stephen E. Baker, *Critical Decisions in the Rapid Transit Planning Process*, Alan M. Voorhees & Associates (McLean, Va., January 1975).

11. De Leuw, Cather & Co. *Report on a Comprehensive Transportation Plan for the Seattle Metropolitan Area* (Seattle, October 1967), p.85.

12. Peter Breysse and Richard Hibbard, *Feasibility of Bus Operation in Tunnels* (Seattle: De Leuw, Cather & Co., 1969).

13. Boris S. Pushkarev, "The Future of Subways," *New York Affairs*, Vol. 1, No. 2 (1973).

14. Roger Bezdek and Bruce Hannon, "Energy, Manpower and the Highway Trust Fund," *Science 185* (August 23, 1974); the 60,000 Btu per 1974 dollar can be calculated from this source; reasons for using the 77,000 Btu per dollar figure, which is derived from note 18 below, are given in: Charles A. Lave, "Rail Rapid Transit: the Modern Way to Waste Energy," paper submitted to the Transportation Research Board, January 1977.

15. Herbert Levinson et al., *Bus Use of Highways*, National Cooperative Highway Research Program Report No. 143 (Washington, D.C., 1973), p.6.

16. From the passenger viewpoint, the borderline between headway and schedule frequency has been found to be about 12 minutes. When service is more frequent, passengers tend to arrive at stations at random, expecting a vehicle to arrive any time, whereas at lesser frequencies their arrival is bunched for each anticipated scheduled run. See P. A. Seddon and M. P. Day, "Bus Passenger Waiting Times in Greater Manchester," *Traffic Engineering and Control* (January 1974).

17. Eric Hirst, *Direct and Indirect Energy Requirements for Automobiles*, Oak Ridge National Laboratory (February 1974).

18. T. J. Healy and D. T. Dick, *Total Energy Requirements of the BART System* (Santa Clara University, July 1, 1974).

Chapter 4

1. Richard C. Feder, "The Effect of Bus Stop Spacing and Location on Travel Time" (M.S. thesis, Carnegie Mellon University, Pittsburgh, May 1973).

2. Greg Thompson, *Successful Rail Transit Evolves from Multi-Destination Bus Systems* (San Diego County Department of Transportation, April 1975).

3. Tri-State Regional Planning Commission, *ITR 4204-5211, Walk Time From Vehicle to Destination* (July 1970); also *ITR 4270-2108, 5203 1970 Suburban Commuter Parking and Inter-Modal Transfer Study* (April 1972).

4. Boris S. Pushkarev and Jeffrey M. Zupan, *Urban Space for Pedestrians* (Cambridge, Mass.: MIT Press, 1975), pp.50-54; also Port Authority of New York and New Jersey, Cen-

tral Research and Statistics Division, "Summary Profiles of Railroad and PATH Passengers" (September, 1975).

5. Barbara Gray, *"How People Get to the Subway at Parsons Boulevard and Hillside Avenue During the Middle of the Day"* (New York University, Graduate School of Public Administration, unpublished paper, January 1976).

6. Regional Plan Association, *Transportation and Economic Opportunity* (New York, 1973), p.182.

7. Stephen G. Petersen, *Walking Distances to Bus Stops in the Residential Areas of Washington, D.C.* (Washington, D.C.: Alan M. Voorhees & Assoc., 1968).

8. F. Bandi et al., *Length of Walking Distances and Distances Between Stops: Their Influence on the Attractiveness of Public Transport* (Brussels: International Union of Public Transport, 1974).

9. Ford Motor Co., Transportation Research and Planning Office, *Ann Arbor Dial-a-Ride Project Final Report* (Ypsilanti, Mich., April 1973), pp.79-82.

Chapter 5

1. Kenneth W. Heathington et al., "Demand-Responsive Transportation Systems in the Private Sector," *Transportation Research Record 522* (Washington, D.C., 1974), p.53.

2. Ronald F. Kirby et al., *Para-Transit* (Washington, D.C.: The Urban Institute, 1974), p.77.

3. Marcel J. Zobrak, *The Haddonfield Dial-a-Ride Experiment; Interim Results.* International Conference on Transportation Research (Bruges, Belgium, June 1973), p.11. For theoretical discussions of the various trade-offs involved in dial-a-bus system design, see also: *Demand-Responsive Transportation Systems,* Highway Research Board Special Report 136 (Washington, D.C., 1973); *Demand-Responsive Transportation,* Transportation Research Board Special Report 147 (Washington, D.C., 1974), see esp. pp.32-69; Steven R. Lerman and Nigel H. M. Wilson, "Analytic Equilibrium Model for Dial-a-Ride Design," *Transportation Research Record 522* (Washington, D.C., 1974); Bert Arrillaga and George E. Mouchahoir, *Demand-Responsive Transportation System Planning*

Guidelines, The Mitre Corporation (McLean, Va., April 1974).

4. R. L. Gustafson, H. N. Curd, and T. F. Golob, *Measurement of User Preferences for a Demand Responsive Transportation System,* General Motors Research Laboratories (Warren, Mich., 1970).

5. Bert Arrillaga, *Socioeconomic and Traveling Characteristics of Dial-a-Ride Users.* The Mitre Corporation (McLean, Va., June 1974); also R. Augustine et al., *Ann Arbor Dial-a-Ride Pilot Project Final Report* (Ford Motor Company Transportation Research and Planning Office, April 1973); Douglas Medville and Bert Arrillaga, *The Haddonfield Dial-a-Ride Demonstration; Demographic System and User Characteristics,* The Mitre Corporation (McLean, Va., November 1973).

6. George E. Mouchahoir, *Summary Evaluation of the Haddonfield Dial-a-Ride Demonstration,* The Mitre Corporation (McLean, Va., May 1975), p.18.

7. "'Dial-a-Ride' Buses Prove Too Successful to Succeed," *The New York Times,* May 13, 1975.

8. Douglas Medville, *A Conceptual Overview of Demand Responsive Transportation Systems,* The Mitre Corporation (McLean, Va., February 1973), p.24.

9. As in the Southern California Rapid Transit District; see *City and Suburban Travel,* Issue 161 (1975), p.12.

10. *The Region's Unique Rapid Transit System in Newark.* Tri-State Regional Planning Commission Technical Bulletin (March 1968).

11. Some items to be consulted for further reference: "Light Rail Transit," *Lea Transit Compendium,* Vol. 1, No. 5 (Huntsville, Ala., 1974), Boeing Vertol Company, *Light Rail Vehicle* (Philadelphia, Pa., June 1975); Toronto Transit Commission, *Intermediate Rapid Transit Study, Submission to Ministry of Transportation and Communications Ontario on Lightweight Duorail System* (January 1973); Stewart F. Taylor, *Urban Transportation—Another Alternative; a World-Wide Survey of Light Rail Technology,* The Heritage Foundation (Washington, D.C.); *Light Rail Transit: State of the Art Review,* DeLeuw, Cather & Company, Spring 1976; *This is Light Rail,* prepared for the National Conference on Light

Rail Transit (Philadelphia, Pa., June 23-25, 1975), Transportation Research Board, Washington, D.C.; also *Light Rail Transit*, Special Report 161, Transportation Research Board, Washington, D.C. (papers presented at the above conference).

12. U.S. Congress, Office of Technology Assessment, *Automated Guideway Transit; an Assessment of PRT and Other New Systems* (Washington, D.C.: U.S. Government Printing Office, June 1975), p.52.

13. Ibid., p.54.

14. "Light Guideway Transit," *Lea Transit Compendium*, Vol. 1, No. 3 (Huntsville, Ala., 1974).

15. Frank E. Lopresti, "First U.S. Center City People Mover Debuts in Morgantown, W. Va.," *Civil Engineering* (November 1972), pp.57-62.

16. "Personal Rapid Transit—Promise and Performance," *Institute for Rapid Transit Annual Conference Digest*, Special Issue Annual Conference 1973, pp.36-39. Thomas B. Deen and David J. Hensing, *Economic, Social and Environmental Implications of Areawide Personal Rapid Transit*, ASCE National Transportation Engineering Meeting (July 1972, Milwaukee, Wis.). For an anthology mostly by PRT proponents, see J. E. Anderson et al., eds., *Personal Rapid Transit; A Selection of Papers* (Institute of Technology, Univ. of Minnesota, April 1972).

Chapter 6

1. Herbert S. Levinson and William F. Hoey, "Optimizing Bus Use of Urban Highways," *Transportation Engineering Journal ASCE*, Vol. 100, No. TE2 (May 1974), pp.443-459; see especially Table 1 and Table 2; note CBD rather than downtown definition of floorspace in Table 2.

2. Boris S. Pushkarev and Jeffrey M. Zupan, *Urban Space for Pedestrians* (Cambridge, Mass.: MIT Press, 1975), p.183.

3. Regional Plan Association, "Financing Public Transportation," *Regional Plan News #98* (March 1976).

4. U.S. Congress, Office of Technology Assessment, *Energy, the Economy, and Mass Transit: Summary Report*, prepared at the request of the Senate Committee on Appropriations, Transportation Subcommittee, by Skidmore, Owings and Merrill and Systems Design Concepts, Inc. (Washington, D.C., June 1975), p.68.

5. John Pastier, "Redoing L.A. Via Rapid Transit," *Los Angeles Times*, August 25, 1975.

INDEX

Acceleration, 107
Access: time elasticity, 16; characteristics by mode, 101–103; value, 109–110; distances, 110–113
Air conditioning, 18
Air quality standards, 21
Airtrans, 84, 85, 87 (*see also* Dallas–Ft. Worth)
Amenity, 17–18, 19 (*see also* Comfort)
Amtrak, 76
Ann Arbor, Michigan, 135
Atlanta, 14, 16
Attractiveness: of rail service, 18, 19, 26, 51
Automatic Guideway Transit (*see* Light guideway transit)
Automation, 82, 84, 85, 92, 177
Automobile: dependence on, 1; effects of fuel shortage, 2, 8–9; effects of World War II on, 2, 8–9; impact on settlement, 4–5; cost per vehicle mile, 76
Automobile occupancy, 8–9, 12, 76 (*see also* Vehicle occupancy)
Automobile ownership: influencing factors, 38; households owning zero, one, or two or more autos, 43–44; influence on mode choice, 45–55; mentioned, 173
Automobile use: restraints, 1–2, 177; in CBDs, 37, 38

Baltimore, 22–23
BART: reasons for ridership gains, 19–20; diversion of auto travel, 21; mentioned, 29, 85, 98, 107, 110, 182
Batavia, New York, 135–136
Bay Ridges, Ontario, 135
Benefit-cost analysis, 97–98, 182
Boston, 14, 15, 16, 17, 22–23, 30, 31, 157, 159

Bridgeport, Connecticut, 142, 175
Bryant Park underpass, 17
Built-up land density, 201–202
Bus: double-decked, 67; operating costs, 76, 79–81; performance measures in New York Region by system, 77; productivity, 79; as feeder mode, 110 (*see also* Local bus, Express bus)
Busways (*see* El Monte busway, Exclusive bus lanes)

Capacity of modes, 101–103
Capacity-unit: 79, 87
Capacity-unit-miles, 87–91 (*see also* seat-miles)
Capital costs, 92, 99–100, 182–185
Capital investment, 96, 181–183
Car pools, 51, 64
Census Bureau, 43
Central Business Districts, 26, 37, 38, 206, 208–209
Chicago, 29, 35, 189
Comfort, 15–17, 19, 97–98 (*see also* Amenity)
Commuter rail: influence on automobile ownership, 39–41; characteristics, 73–75, 101–104; operating costs, 76, 80, 81, 168, 171; performance measures in New York Region by system, 77; productivity, 79; feasibility, 168, 171, 189, 190; applicability, 190–192
Connectivity, 110
Corridor volumes, 158–159
Costs: per passenger, 79, 89; per vehicle mile by transit system, 79, 85–87; per vehicle hour by selected systems, 85–87; rolling stock, 91–96, 181; guideway, 96–101, 181–182 (*see also* Capital costs, Energy costs, Labor costs, Oper-

ating costs, Parking costs, Wages)
Coverage, 43–51, 139

Dallas–Ft. Worth, Texas, 5, 84, 162–164 (*see also* Airtrans)
Deficits, 76 (*see also* Subsidy)
Demand density (*see* Trip end density)
Demand elasticity (*see* Elasticity)
Density: impediments to high, 2; historical, 4–6; urbanized areas, 24; residential, 30, 122 (*see also* Built-up land density, Developed land density, Dwelling unit density, Gross density, Nonresidential floorspace density, Residential density)
Density gradients, 145, 157
Developed land density, 201–202
Dial-a-bus: characteristics, 65, 101–104; operating costs, 79, 87; productivity, 79; feasibility, 133–137, 184–185; many-to-many, 134–137; many-to-one, 134–137; route direction, 135; fare elasticity, 135–136; waiting times, 135; capacity units, applicability, 190, 192
Distance: influence on trip-making, 57–63
Diverted travel, 19, 57
Downtowns: size, 26, 57, 203–207; to support local bus, 143–148; to support express bus, 148–155; to support light rail transit, 155–162; to support light guideway transit, 164–165; to support rapid transit, 165–168; for transit feasibility, 182–184, 187–191 (*see also* Nonresidential floorspace density, Nonresidential concentrations)

239